Politics and Government

A Brief Introduction
THIRD EDITION

Lawrence S. Graham
University of Texas at Austin

Richard P. Farkas
DePaul University

Robert C. Grady
Eastern Michigan University

Jorgen Rasmussen
Iowa State University

Taketsugu Tsurutani
Washington State University at Vancouver

Chatham House Publishers, Inc.
Chatham, New Jersey

POLITICS AND GOVERNMENT
A Brief Introduction
THIRD EDITION

Chatham House Publishers, Inc.
Post Office Box One
Chatham, New Jersey 07928

Publisher: Edward Artinian
Cover design: Lawrence Ratzkin
Composition: Bang, Motley, Olufsen
Printing and Binding: R.R. Donnelley & Sons, Company

LIBRARY OF CONGRESS CATALOGING-IN-PUBLICATION DATA

Politics and Government : a brief introduction / Lawrence S. Graham
...[et al.]. — 3rd ed.
    p.   cm.
    Includes bibliographical references and index.
    ISBN 1-56643-008-9
    1. Comparative government.   I. Graham, Lawrence S.
JF51.P627   1994
320.3—dc20   94-6041
                                       CIP

Manufactured in the United States of America
10 9 8 7 6 5 4 3 2 1

Contents

Preface

This brief book is different, and we hope that it will open new vistas to students who are beginning to learn about government and politics in countries other than their own. Ultimately, they will be the ones to judge if we have succeeded. Before they begin the study of the various political systems, however, they should read the few introductory pages that follow, which are designed as a type of compass to point the way we propose to go, the objectives we hope to reach, and some of the problems or difficulties we have encountered as comparativists dealing with a changing world.

Robert C. Grady prepared chapters 1 and 2 on the U.S. political system, as the primary example of presidential systems. Jorgen Rasmussen substantially rewrote chapters 3 and 4 on European parliamentary systems (the work of Alex Dragnich in the first edition). Taketsugu Tsurutani revised his chapter 5 on the Japanese political system. Richard P. Farkas prepared chapters 6 and 7 on communist and postcommunist systems in East Europe (a major rewriting and reconceptualization of Dragnich's original material, reflecting the changes in the former Soviet Union and Eastern Europe since 1989). Lawrence Graham revised the introduction, chapter 8 on the developing countries (prepared by John T. Dorsey, Jr., in the first edition and reworked by Jorgen Rasmussen in the second edition), as well as his chapter 9 on Mexico.

Introduction

The aim of this book is to provide useful and substantive knowledge about the political world to students who know very little about it or how to proceed learning about it. It is not a first course in professional training for prospective academic political scientists but an "eye-opening" work for all students, whatever their disciplinary specializations or career plans. It is, in short, a book about government and politics in several selected countries having different political systems, plus chapters concerned largely with the problems of establishing viable political systems in the former communist countries of East Europe and in the less well-developed countries. Also, rather than introduce the study of comparative politics as the analysis of all other political systems except that of the United States, we begin with the U.S. case and from that basis proceed to other countries through comparison and contrast.

The number of political entities, variously called countries, nations, or states, existing today approximates 150. They vary considerably in geographic size, population, natural resources, and technological and economic development. They are held together by a number of factors, among them race, language, attachment (a sense of belonging) to a particular piece of territory, and some common stock of shared beliefs (ideology)—all of which contribute to the people's rendering habitual obedience to a common political authority.

There are some notable exceptions to what has just been said, particularly in the break-up of the Soviet Union and Yugoslavia into a series of highly diverse successor states, as well as in the fragility of some of the lesser developed nations. In these cases major changes in political demarcation are under way because significant segments of the population fail to render habitual obedience to a central government simply because they do not recognize a common authority. Such situations are not new; history abounds with examples. The best known to American students are the Revolution of 1776 and the American Civil War. Divisive situations exist to a degree in a number of well-established nations—for example, Northern Ireland in the United Kingdom, Quebec in Canada, and the Flemish in Belgium. Consequently, some of our generalizations in the preceding paragraph are just that—generalizations—to which there are exceptions. And political scientists are far from agreement as to the mix of ingredients necessary for a binding political cement.

Nevertheless, the modern nation-state, which really came into being only in the seventeenth century, is still the political unit that commands most people's highest allegiance. In the era of the nation-state, people have been willing to fight and die for it; no city, province, or other geographic unit has commanded a comparative allegiance. On first inspection, it might well appear that the observations do not apply to those exceptions just referred to, where local or regional loyalties (for whatever reason) are in effect unrealized aspirations to nationhood. Yet, if we look more closely at the current conflict in a number of the successor states to the former Soviet Union—for example, Armenia, Georgia, Azerbaijan—or at the former Yugoslavia or Czechoslovakia, we find that we are dealing with national communities whose self-determination has long been repressed and who see in the fluidity of current events the opportunity to form their own nation-states, no matter how small they might be.

Political scientists are interested in the form of government a given country has. In the process, they ask at least three broad questions: What are the purposes of government (the ends of politics)? What do governments do (the functions of politics)? Who exercises political power (the processes of politics)? Each of the systems discussed in this book, by its very nature, tends to answer the first question. Generally speaking, democratic systems view the end of politics to be the provision, protection, or preservation of an atmosphere or social climate in which individuals may freely seek to realize their personal or collective aspirations. In contrast, many authoritarian regimes, notably the communist ones in power before 1989, have viewed the purposes of government to be the realization of certain goals that their leaders envisage as necessary and correct. Most of the discussions in the chapters that follow deal with the last two questions, particularly the final one. These questions are related and difficult to disentangle, but they do lead to the concept of political systems, the comparative analysis of which is the oldest and most honorable tradition in political science, going back to Aristotle more than two thousand years ago.

Political systems have come into being and have evolved as a result of a complex combination of circumstances—basic beliefs and attitudes concerning human beings and their Creator, the influence of natural resources and other historical conditions or accidents, as well as the political ingenuity of those who have risen to positions of leadership. While we cannot ignore the question of how political systems came to be what they are, the emphasis in this book is on seeking to understand how they function today.

Political systems are somewhat like living organisms in that they change over time. More accurately, political systems are what political actors (government leaders and those who choose to influence them) make them, but political actors cannot always do as they wish. In large measure they are constrained and conditioned by the acts of those who preceded them and the traditions and usages passed on by previous generations generally. Hence changes in political systems are, in large part at least, controlled and guided by forces beyond the sole powers of any set of generational political actors.

In a sense, it can be said that every political system changes or evolves (unless it is destroyed) according to shifting interactions between the forces of tradition and the imperatives of the changing environment, and between the creative-innovative impulse of political forces (leaders and parties) and cultural inertia (i.e., society's resistance to change).

One could argue that each political system is a creature of unpredictable combinations of circumstances, in some cases fortuitous and in others not or less so, such as the influence of tradition, the cultural predilection of the majority in a given society, the perception of urgency and the capacity of the people to respond, the ideology and the skill of the political elite, as well as the material endowment and the technological development of the society. To a degree, the uniqueness of the combination in a crucial moment in the development of a given nation-state renders its system distinct in the nature of political authority, in the quality of popular support, in the extent of its institutional integrity, in the manner of its functioning, and in the range and kinds of tangible and intangible benefits it confers on the people.

One interesting consequence is that combinations of circumstances have produced some political systems that are similar to and some that are different from one another. This can be seen in the way the following chapters line up. Our discussion of politics and government in institutionalized systems—the United States, Great Britain, France, Germany, Japan, and Mexico—all follow substantially the some format, in the subtitles and categories of analysis utilized. In contrast, when we enter that portion of the political world in which major transitions and upheavals are under way, we abandon these categories and reframe the three basic questions identified earlier to focus on the value systems shared by political actors and their publics, the political machinery developed through which leaders seek to articulate and implement their goals, and the leadership that takes control of the apparatus of government and attempts to rule by utilizing these structures to make conscious policy choices.

In comparing and contrasting political systems, it is important to remember that in most states political boundaries are rarely congruent with cultural, technological, or economic bases of cohesion. National boundaries have often resulted from military conquest, without much consideration for ethnic, economic, or communal factors. Moreover, structures of political authority are likely to be based on a combination of force and fear, habit and convention, identification and consent. Additionally, functional arrangements for securing governmental services vary among developed as well as between more and less modernized countries. Finally, differences between political systems are real, as one could observe if he or she were to live for a time in a religious theocracy and then move to a military oligarchy, or to live first in a constitutional republic and then move to an institutionalized authoritarian regime, of the left or right. At the same time, in a certain sense all political systems perform similar functions: *protection* from the forces of lawlessness; *economic services* such as a stable currency system, postal services, and sanitation disposal; and *institutions* for resolving disputes.

In the selection of political systems to write about we have been somewhat arbitrary, but our choices have not been random. In the first four chapters we focus on the leading examples of Western democracy. These are all societies with relatively homogeneous political cultures (attitudes toward and values concerning politics, political leaders, and governmental processes) but somewhat differing systems of democratic government. In each there has been an acceptance of their respective political systems for a relatively long period of time. The first, the United States, is described as a presidential system based on the concept of separation of powers. The other three are all parliamentary systems; however, they differ considerably in terms of the homogeneity of their political cultures. When contrasted with the politics of the successor states to the former Soviet Union or of many developing countries, they appear to share in common relatively homogeneous political cultures in terms of commitment to their democratic regimes, as opposed to the alternatives. But this does not mean an absence of internal differentiation. For example, scholars confining their attention to Western political systems often contrast what they call the "homogeneous" political cultures of the United States and Great Britain with the "fragmented political cultures" of France and Germany. In so doing, they are calling attention to the fact that for relatively long periods of time, sharp disagreements as to the acceptance of their respective political systems—especially before World War II—contributed to a lack of stability. At the same, as a close reading of the chapters on the United States shows, one can also question the extent to which the image of the United States as having a homogenous political culture really fits the 1990s.

In chapter 5 we examine the political system of Japan, a non-Western developed nation embarked on a new experiment in democracy. Like Germany, since World War II it has replaced sharp differences over the desirability of democratic government with a strong commitment to political democracy. Japan is the only advanced industrial democracy in a largely undemocratic non-Western world. In chapters 6 and 7 we deal with the East European states, first under communism and then in their transition away from communist rule toward a very different kind of politics and economics. In chapter 8 we consider, in broad outline, the political systems of the developing world, a large number of which gained independence only after World War II, although some are relatively old states. Unlike most developing countries, Mexico exemplifies political stability. Although it has essentially a one-party system, it possesses quasi-democratic attributes and quasi-authoritarian ones. As a neighbor of the United States, Mexico in the main sees its future as closely related to that of the United States. The large number of developing or modernizing societies, the similarity of their problems, and the probable impact of what happens in them on the more advanced societies—all are singular reasons for treating them in this book. By dealing with these societies, moreover, we are able to give to our introduction to politics and government a much broader perspective than would otherwise be the case.

We believe that our choice of political systems is at once fairly broad and representative. It constitutes a good beginning for anyone seeking a general introduction to comparative politics, as well as for anyone interested in an introductory approach to politics or the study of political science generally. Because several chapters treat more than one political system, whereas others concentrate solely on one country, we believe that the result is more genuinely comparative presentation.

In each of the chapters, or pairs of chapters, dealing with institutionalized political systems, we discuss constitutions, their history and evolution, and the substance of their provisions, as well as present practice. Also, we examine the social forces that are contending for influence if not predominance. We identify major interest groups, their aims, their organizations, and how they seek to attain their goals. Next we consider political party systems, the nature and number of parties, how they are organized, how they seek support, and how they accept responsibility for governing. Finally, we deal with the governmental institutions, their nature, powers or functions, and their relations to one another and to the public. In the end, we make some observations on the systems in action, their performance in the task of governing as well as their difficulties and failings and their future promise.

Each chapter, or pair of chapters, is followed by a list of selected works as suggestions for additional reading. We have attempted to choose substantive books, as well as to pick those that concern themselves with various aspects of a political system. At the same time, we have endeavored to include some that are reasonably up-to-date and thus reflect contemporary developments.

1. The U.S. Political System: The Dynamics of a Presidential System

The United States is the world's oldest constitutional democracy. The Constitution provides a separation of powers among legislative, executive, and judicial institutions at the national level. It provides federalism for the allocation of powers among the national government and the states—the latter being equivalent to the regional jurisdictions or provinces of other nations. Both principles—separation of powers and federalism—are rooted in eighteenth-century balance-of-power theories that power could be exercised with restraint when distributed among institutions that have overlapping functions and responsibilities. According to the *The Federalist Papers,* each branch would have a "partial agency" in the other. A modern description is presidential scholar Richard Neustadt's "separated institutions sharing power." The president has significant legislative powers and the ability to be engaged in the legislative process, and the Congress can intervene in executive functions, review executive policy implementation, and withhold approval of executive branch appointments. Such shared and overlapping activities can provide both the means and the incentives for balancing power.

Over long periods of time, this system can become "imbalanced." Today, the U.S. system is popularly known as presidential government, suggesting that the president is the central figure and the presidency the dominant institution in the national government. Two hundred years ago, such a statement would have been unthinkable or dangerous to the generation that created the Constitution. Writing in *The Federalist Papers,* James Madison argued, both as a matter of fact and as a preferred principle, that, in a republic, the legislative branch necessarily prevails. One hundred years ago, the idea of presidential government seemed contrary to experience, although

I

desirable. Political scientist Woodrow Wilson titled his doctoral dissertation *Congressional Government* (1888), arguing (and lamenting) that Congress was at the center of the American system. Later, as President Wilson, he and subsequent strong presidents of the twentieth century played major roles in changing the power relationship between the two branches.

In a system of presidential government, the president serves both as head of state—representing the nation to the world, carrying out national functions and duties—and head of government—chief executive, administrator, legislator, and so on in performing governing functions. Congress no longer predominates. The U.S. system differs from, say, the British system, where the monarch is the head of state and the prime minister the head of government, or from the French system, which incorporates elements both of the U.S. system, with its president, and of the British system, with its prime minister. Unlike parliamentary government, or cabinet government (such as the British system), the power of the president does not derive from maintaining a legislative majority, and powers of the presidency are not functions of congressional decisions. Moreover, the separation-of-powers system invites inefficiency and seeming indecision in government by encouraging conflict, rather than cooperation, between president and Congress.

The Constitution

Constitutions allocate powers, define spheres of governmental activity, and provide a framework for political processes. Some constitutions have been created through deliberative acts—a constitutional convention or plebiscite, for instance; others have evolved over time—Britain's "unwritten" constitution, for instance. However established, constitutions limit government both by prohibiting actions that would curtail basic freedoms and by requiring that power be exercised justly and fairly. In other words, they contain both substantive and procedural safeguards. Constitutions may be detailed, legalistic codes or relatively brief statements of basic principles. Finally, formal constitutions usually are buttressed by less formal elements: basic laws, judicial interpretations and rulings, precedents established by governments, customs and traditions.

The U.S. Constitution was created through conscious, deliberative action: framed at the Philadelphia convention of 1787 and ratified by conventions in the states. It has been amended and buttressed through formal and informal means. The Constitution was formed from a combination of historical studies and political principles; experiments in self-government; and pragmatic compromises reflecting different political, economic, and social interests and the necessity to bring the deliberations of the convention to a conclusion. The study of history produced examples of republics that governed small, sparsely populated territories, many of which had been destroyed by factional infighting or demagoguery. There were numerous other examples of governments that controlled large, contiguous territories—the Roman and Ottoman empires, for example—but these were empires, ruled, at best, by benign monarchs or oligarchs. The convention delegates were faced with crafting a constitution for which there was no precedent: a government capable of providing defense and preserving law and order for an expansive, contiguous territory while maintaining republican liberty.

The writings of political thinkers reinforced the delegates' commitments to republican principles and provided insights for overcoming the dilemma of creating republican government in a large territory. Locke's notions of property rights and limited government and Montesquieu's prescriptions for balancing power within government and over large territories were prominent influences. Also important were Harrington's and Machiavelli's theories about properly balanced classes, each holding a "stake" in the political system, and the latter's and ancient Roman writers' ideas about civic responsibilities and patriotism. Adapting these ideas to the territory of the former thirteen colonies, the convention delegates proposed a constitution in which the various societal interests would check and balance one another through their representatives within the government and throughout the territory. The advancement of self-interest and commerce would affirm citizens' stakes in the political system and promote civic responsibility and patriotism, or so the delegates hoped.

The colonists' experiments in self-government, which occurred under varying degrees of autonomy from British power, helped shape the framing of the new constitution in several ways. For decades prior to the Revolutionary War, seeds for independence were sown as several of the colonies developed into independent trading entities and as royal governors were largely ignored by locally elected or appointed assemblies. When the Crown proceeded to collect revenues to prosecute the Seven Years War (1756–63; French and Indian War in the colonies), however, colonial resentment and then outright opposition developed. From the Sugar Act of 1764 through the First Continental Congress in 1774, colonists appealed to Parliament to have a say in policy, as did other British subjects: "No taxation without representation" was a cry for political equity and reform, not for revolution. British policy proved unremitting, however, and radicals, whose influence had been growing, became the leading voices for independence. Fighting began in 1775, and when the Declaration of Independence was made in 1776, the former colonies became independent states and began replacing colonial charters with constitutions. Many of these constitutions severely restricted governmental powers, grounded their authority on popular or legislative sovereignty, and contained bills of rights.

The first U.S. constitution was, of course, the Articles of Confederation. Written and proposed to the states in 1776, it was not finally ratified until 1781. Structured as a confederation, the national government was weaker than the state governments under their new constitutions. The Articles provided for a congress and an executive committee, but no strong executive and no judiciary. Members of the congress were appointed (and recalled) by their state governments. States had equal voting power in the congress (regardless of their population or financial contribution to the government). Constitutional amendments required unanimity among the states. The congress could not pass laws applying directly to individual citizens, and it could not compel states to maintain agreements with other states or with the congress. Finally, it lacked powers to tax and to regulate domestic and foreign commerce.

Such restrictions on the government invariably meant that the society would be plunged into economic and political chaos, and as this occurred, disenchantment with the Articles grew. Nevertheless, the Articles cannot be counted a total failure. Establishing a weak government was understandable from the perspective of colonists who were in the midst of throwing off the yoke of despotism, as they frequently depicted British rule. And the political and economic failures of the Articles provided a valuable learning opportunity to culminate the experiments in self-government; they convinced political leaders that a stronger government was necessary.

Nationalist agitation emerged in 1783; many of its advocates were instrumental in calling for the Annapolis and Philadelphia conventions. Meeting in Annapolis in 1786, representatives from five states petitioned the congress to convene delegates from all states in a convention "for the sole and express purpose of revising the Articles of Confederation." If the Articles had been revised or amended, the U.S. system might have evolved into a parliamentary form of government. There was an executive committee under the Articles, and a plural executive selected by the legislature could have laid the foundation for the development of cabinet-led parliamentary government.

As the fifty-five delegates (out of seventy-four appointed) convened in Philadelphia in May 1787, James Madison and others had laid the groundwork for jettisoning the Articles in favor of a new constitution. They prepared the Virginia Plan, which, when presented at the outset of the convention, effectively set the agenda to support the nationalists and their advocacy for a new constitution. At the beginning of the convention, the leading delegates recognized that "a national government ought to be established consisting of a supreme legislative, executive, and judiciary." The result of the convention's deliberations produced a constitution grounded on six basic principles (brought up to date in a few instances).

First, limited government, or constitutionalism. Government is created to preserve and enhance basic rights and liberties; it must, therefore, be limited in order not to violate these rights and liberties. This means that government must act under the rule of law, not the rule of personal interest or individual will. Such procedural requirements as due process, public disclosure and decision making, and equal protection of the laws are paramount in order to ensure that lawful, orderly decisions are made, not those based on whim, caprice, or other motives.

Second, republican government. Ultimately, sovereignty resides with the people, but they do not exercise it; sovereignty is exercised through elected representatives. Madison argued that popular representation was the "pivot" of the Constitution, that is, the point on which the constitutional edifice turned.

Third, federalism. Federalism divides sovereignty among two levels of government—national and state. Neither level acting alone can change the Constitution. Federalism initially implied "dual sovereignty" (sometimes called dual federalism). Constitutional supremacy, the fifth principle (see below), is a basis for resolving conflicts between the federal units. In practical terms, first, the Civil War and, second, a revolution in judicial thinking were necessary to resolve basic conflicts. Technically, the term "federal government" refers to the whole system of federalism, national and state governments inclusively. In common usage, however, "federal government" and such terms as "federal courts" and "federal administrators" are used to refer to the central or national government. Our usage hereafter reflects common usage.

Fourth, separation of powers (and an operational corollary, checks and balances). Separation of powers is a functional division of power among executive, legislative, and judicial branches of the national government. It is operational thanks to the corollary principle of checks and balances—a principle that also pervades national and state relations under federalism. Congress is "checked" by the existence of two houses, by presidential veto, and by judicial review. The president is checked by Senate approval of treaties and certain appointments, by congressional policymaking and appropriation of revenues (or refusal to appropriate) for programs, and by judicial review. The judiciary is checked by presidential appointment of judges, by the power of Congress to impeach and try judges, determine federal court jurisdiction, and fund the courts. Theoretically, the result is a "balance" of contending claims to power, without one branch gaining excessive power.

Fifth, constitutional supremacy. The principle of constitutional supremacy provides a basis for resolving disputes of a federal nature or among the separated branches of government. If the lack of final authority in the Articles of Confederation was an extreme reaction to British rule, this principle is the constitutional convention's reaction to the Articles. (Even the New Jersey Plan recognized the need for it.) Significant constitutional and governmental powers that were necessary but ineffectual under the Articles are sanctioned by this principle—the power to regulate commerce, to tax, to coin money and provide for a common currency, and so on.

Sixth, the independent judiciary, which has the power of judicial review. An independent judiciary is a corollary of constitutionalism or the rule of law. How independent the judiciary actually is, is controversial, because political considerations always influence judicial appointments. But judicial behavior—judging—is not subject to interference by the other branches of government. Judicial review is also a corollary of constitutional supremacy. It was not spelled out in the Constitution, however, and had to be established by judicial precedent in *Marbury* v. *Madison*.

The basic principles of the Constitution reflect the accrual of historical experience, theories and ideals of republican thinkers, and American experiments in self-government. Collectively, these informed and sustained the normative principles of basic rights and liberties maintained through limited government, popular representation, the rule of law, and the principle of balance, as in the checks and balances of the separation of powers and the balancing of state and national interests in federalism. How these were developed and incorporated in the Constitution, and many of the operational principles that make the Constitution workable, were produced by pragmatic compromises. The convention delegates represented different political, economic, and social interests, and these were key elements in creating those elements of the Constitution that are products of compromise. Likewise, certain constitutional provisions reflect simply the necessity felt by delegates to bring their deliberations to a conclusion.

The compromise considered most important was the Connecticut, or Great, Compromise, which reconciled the Virginia and New Jersey plans. The first had favored large states by basing a state's congressional representation on population. The second, proposed as an alternative to the Virginia

Plan, lessened the impact of large states by giving each state equal representation, as under the Articles of Confederation, which the plan merely revised. The Great Compromise broke the deadlock by proposing a bicameral (two-chamber) legislature with a lower house, the House of Representatives, based on population and an upper house, the Senate, giving each state two votes or senators. While the large states held the upper hand in a purely numerical sense (which also tended to correlate with the economic well-being of states), several small states made clear that ratification would not be unanimous without compromise, and the larger states accepted the compromise as one price of union.

Another major compromise, which actually was reached before the Great Compromise, is known as the Three-Fifths Compromise. The populations of Maryland, Virginia, the Carolinas, and Georgia averaged 30 percent slaves; 90 percent of the slaves in America lived in these states. These states wanted to count slaves in the census enumeration that would be the basis for representation in the House of Representatives (and for the state's electoral votes). But these states did not want slaves counted for purposes of apportioning direct taxes. The conflict was regional and economic, not one based merely on the power of population size, as in the other disputes between large and small states. It turned on the difference between paid and slave labor as the basis for a state's economy and thus the extent to which property (in the form of slavery) should be represented yet not taxed. The compromise was that three-fifths of a state's slave population would count for purposes of representation and apportioning direct taxes. Related to this, the Constitution's power to regulate commerce, a corrective to the deficiency of the Articles, was general and broad except that exports (the heart of the agricultural South's economy) could not be taxed and the importation of slaves could not be limited for twenty years (before 1808). Again, the compromise and related constitutional provisions were considered necessary conditions for ratification.

Provisions for ratifying the Constitution and amending it reflected a combination of popular sovereignty and state sovereignty. Ratification would be by representatives of the people in their states at specially elected conventions, not by the state legislatures (many of which had an interest in retaining the Articles). Ratification was no easy task. New York barely ratified after Alexander Hamilton, John Jay, and Madison collaborated on a series of promotional essays in newspapers. Later known as *The Federalist Papers,* they are now widely regarded as some of the best statements of constitutional intent and constitutional interpretation. Earlier, Massachusetts ratified the Constitution only after promises were extracted from Federalists (the promoters of the new Constitution) to create a constitutional bill of rights through the amendment process.

The amendment process begins when an amendment is proposed either by two-thirds votes of both houses of Congress or by a convention called by Congress (the latter has never been used). Amendments are ratified on a state-by-state basis: by legislatures or by specially elected conventions in three-fourths of the states (the latter has been used once, to repeal the Prohibition amendment, at a time when elected conventions more adequately than state legislatures represented state urban populations). The amendment process is but one way, and the slowest, for the Constitution to change. Almost 9750 amendments have been introduced in Congress, but only 29 have been proposed by Congress and only 27 have been ratified. If the first ten amendments—the Bill of Rights—are considered to be part of the original Constitution, the remaining seventeen average less than one every dozen years.

Judicial interpretations, precedents, and traditions also effectively amend the Constitution. For example, the Supreme Court's power to overturn acts of Congress or of state governments required judicial precedents —first *Marbury* v. *Madison,* then *McCulloch* v. *Maryland.* The president's power to dismiss executive branch officers is not found in the Constitution, but the requirement that his appointments receive the "advice and consent" of the Senate is there, and it implies senatorial concurrence with dismissals. Nevertheless, presidents early on established the precedent to dismiss on their executive authority alone. The important roles political parties play in elections and representation, the organizational structures in Congress that control the activities of Congress and the scope of its decision making (the committee system, for example), the expectation that elected representatives live in the district they represent—all of these are examples of customs and traditions that have changed the Constitution without formal amendment.

The Bill of Rights illustrates how constitutional principles can be amended formally and through judicial interpretation and precedents. The Bill of Rights was proposed during the first Congress and promptly ratified by state legislatures. It is a body of civil liberties placing limits on government and permitting, thereby, individual freedom in the areas designated (speech, religion, protections for the criminally accused, and so on). Originally limiting the federal government, Bill of Rights protections were slowly "nationalized" in the twentieth century and applied to the states also through judicial interpretation that "incorporated" them into the Fourteenth Amendment. In a related vein, the original Constitution does not directly protect civil rights; these are introduced into the Constitution through the Thirteenth, Fourteenth, and Fifteenth amendments; however, it took a mass movement—the civil rights movement—and significant change on the Supreme Court before civil rights were widely acknowledged and protected by the state governments. Further civil rights and "human rights" guarantees have been effected in the twentieth century by broad presidential interpretation of the power to maintain peace in the states (in the late nineteenth century, such power was used to curtail civil rights in labor relations) and by presidential executive orders.

The U.S. Constitution is sometimes referred to as a "living document" because it has proved to be adaptable to meet changing circumstances. The preceding examples of constitutional changes that did not occur through formal amendment underscore this point. Likewise, changed relationships between the federal government and the states (to be discussed later) and the transformation of the separation of powers from congressional dominance to presidential dominance (as noted at the beginning) exemplify the adaptable nature of the Constitution.

Social Forces

The United States began as a nation of immigrants and it continues as one. From an initial population of less than 4 million shortly after the Constitution was ratified, the nation grew to approximately 250 million people at the time of the 1990 census. Significant waves of immigration have occurred periodically in the nation's history: The 1840s and 1850s brought numerous Irish and German Catholics; the 1870s, Chinese; the 1890s through early 1900s, diverse ethnic nationalities and religious groups from southern and eastern Europe; recent decades, Latino and Asian nationalities. By the late 1960s, the annual immigration of the latter groups exceeded immigration of groups with European origins for the first time in U.S. history, and by the end of the 1980s, their annual immigration rates exceeded those with European origins by over five times.

Each wave of immigration has brought increased cultural, religious, and ethnic and racial diversity and new language barriers to overcome. Each wave has been met with attempts to slow down or curtail "alien" influences by groups whose forebears immigrated to the United States. Recent efforts to limit immigration have included preference for persons with advanced education and job skills. Immigrants find conflicting responses to their presence: Movements to require English as the official language in some states are balanced by bilingual education programs in other states. Further, the federal government has tightened requirements for political asylum (created only as recently as 1980), excluding such potential émigrés as El Salvadorans, Guatemalans, and Haitians on grounds that they seek to immigrate for economic, not political, reasons.

With the exception of Native Americans, the U.S. population reflects its immigrant origins. The populace is a complicated mixture of nationalities, races, and religions that maintain in varying degrees the cultural and social traditions of their ancestries. Earlier in this century it was fashionable to refer to America as a "melting pot." This is no longer fashionable or accurate. The U.S. population is rather like a "tossed salad." There is growing ethnic and cultural awareness and an emphasis on cultural diversity and multiculturalism in local communities and educational institutions. Some observers worry that such emphasis may undo the American culture and produce a "balkanization" of the nation. Others believe that such emphasis is necessary to reaffirm the values of freedom and opportunity that were available to white immigrants but that have been historically limited for immigrants and Americans of color.

RACE

The most significant areas of tension and conflict over diversity are in race and ethnic relations. The respected social observer Studs Terkel calls race the American obsession. While the term "race" may include such minorities as Native Americans and people of Asian and Middle East origin, in the United States it is used most frequently in relation to African Americans. Unlike many other groups, the original African American immigrants did not come to the United States freely but as slaves, and slavery was perpetuated for three of the past four and one half centuries. After the Civil War, de facto slavery persisted in many parts of the southern states. One result was northward migration. In 1910, 90 percent of 10 million African Americans lived in the southern states; by the 1990 census, approximately one-half of almost 30 million lived outside the South.

In the 1950s and 1960s, most efforts to improve race relations centered on the civil rights movement and hopes for political justice and economic opportunity. Advocates of improved race relations believed their goals would be realized through social integration. Even as the civil rights movement succeeded, however, its leaders encountered opposition from Black Power and separatist movements. The latter were strengthened by mounting evidence that black urban America was largely left out of the social and economic pie that other Americans shared. In the 1960s, a major assessment of urban violence concluded that it would not be alleviated until the United States faced up to its economic inequities and lack of opportunities for minorities. But increased welfare programs and efforts to engage in affirmative action in placing minorities (and women) in jobs and educational opportunities faced a backlash in the late 1970s and 1980s.

In general, rates of improvement in social and economic status by racial and ethnic minorities in the 1970s did not end but stagnated in the 1980s. As of the 1990 census, the poverty and unemployment rates for 30 million African Americans, 22 million Latinos, and 2 million Native Americans exceeded the rates for other racial and ethnic groups. In 1992 Los Angeles erupted in riot after a jury acquitted white police officers of brutality charges incurred after they had severely beaten and permanently injured a black suspect while making his arrest. Observers of race relations noted that urban America was little changed since the assessment of urban violence in the 1960s.

URBANIZATION AND REGIONAL CHANGE

The U.S. population generally has shifted from rural areas in the nineteenth century to urban and suburban areas in the late twentieth century. In 1950, slightly over 55 percent of the population lived in urban and suburban areas; slightly under 44 percent in rural areas. At the time of the 1990 census, these had changed to approximately 77 percent urban and suburban and 23 percent rural. And between 1950 and 1990, the real growth of urban and suburban America occurred in the suburbs. The population of cities declined slightly from 33 to 31 percent, while population in the suburbs increased from 23 to 46 percent. This dramatic increase in suburban populations, the lack of growth but not of change in urban populations (which have undergone a transformation of ethnic and economic makeup), and the decrease in rural population helps explain much about modern American government that is often misunderstood. Population shifts change the kinds and amount of demands on governments for services. Urban areas once grew at the expense of rural areas, with the promise of employment, better schools and public services, and the like; now suburbia grows at the expense of central urban areas, with the promise of better schools and services, lower taxes, and less racial heterogeneity.

Demographic changes have had far-reaching consequences. Contemporary urban America has vast reaches of suburban and sub-suburban developments moving away from crumbling central cities. Some cities have done well; others not well. Likewise, a discernible shift took place in the 1970s and 1980s with significant employment opportunities being relocated from the old industrial, or "rustbelt," states to the "sunbelt" states. By the late 1980s, many of the former industrial states had opened up new economic opportunities, though in the process union membership declined and income disparities increased, with many of the new jobs not paying as highly as earlier jobs had. And the population noticeably aged, and continues to do so, as the "baby boomers" approach retirement in the early twenty-first century.

Many demographic changes occur with impetus from public policy, or they produce significant public policy implications. For example, the shift from urban to suburban lifestyles, the increasing degradation of the environment from automobile emissions, erosion, and ground and surface water contamination, and the economic decline of older urban areas are linked to conscious policy choices in earlier decades. The Interstate Highway Trust Fund, instituted in 1956 to promote commerce and provide civil defense and military routes in national emergencies, generated major conduits for suburban sprawl, commuter traffic, and the like. The trust fund virtually redesigned America from a rural and central-city nation, with viable urban mass transit and long-distance freight transit on railroads, to a suburban nation, dependent on automobile commuting to distant workplaces and freight transit on trucks. It reflected the interests and forces of growth in the post–World War II era that were creating significant changes in the demographic landscape of the United States. As reliance on automobile commuting increased and road construction facilitated the growth of suburbs, the job base (which became centralized as the nineteenth- and early twentieth-century population shifted from rural areas to the cities) became more decentralized, and central cities lost businesses and tax revenues. Gradually, employment commuting shifted from suburb-to-city routes to suburb-to-suburb routes, further speeding the economic deterioration of central cities.

Within the states, state and local tax policies and restrictions on urban governments' annexation powers limited the fiscal ability and growth of older urban areas and encouraged the growth of new communities. With cheaper land and lower taxes, new communities had competitive advantages over older communities. Required to provide more infrastructure and services, but facing reduced property values and revenue sources, urban areas have further declined. Lower-income Americans find themselves in underserviced central areas with fewer employment opportunities, unable to afford to move to more affluent suburban areas and regional job centers, and frequently blocked entry when they can afford to do so by real estate redlining. The changes created de facto segregated housing, schools, and recreation areas and other municipal services as lower-income people were left behind in declining neighborhoods when more affluent, and mainly white, residents moved farther from the central city.

CLASS, STATUS, CASTE

A traditional distinction between American and European and Latin American societies is supposedly the absence in the United States of a rigid class system. Some observers trace this, and a weak or nonexistent leftist or socialist tradition, to the absence of feudalism in America's history. Certainly no class of landed gentry has flourished in the United States since the fall of the southern plantation system, nor has there been a closed aristocracy of public servants, clergy, or military as in other nations. Moreover, the ethnic and racial diversity created out of waves of immigrants has served to create tensions and conflicts among people of similar economic class, weakening the development of unions and class solidarity. Consequently, an objective analysis of class in the United States must always be circumscribed by people's subjective perceptions of their status.

Nevertheless, in some ways American society is stratified, and repeated studies of its communities have revealed a kind of class system based on wealth and income levels: People with comparable incomes, occupations, and social positions tend to associate with one another, to live in neighborhoods distinguished by similar property values, hence by wealth and status, and to share similar political and social outlooks. Also, upper-income groups in affluent suburbs now tend to perpetuate themselves over generations. Although there are no class-based major political parties, there is a clear class differential in voting turnout, with those most likely to benefit from government programs voting at the lowest rates of the population (excepting younger voters). For example, in the 1992 presidential election, people with family incomes under $15,000 constituted 25 percent of the population but only 14 percent of the voting public; those with family incomes between $15,000 and $50,000 constituted 51 percent of the population and 54 percent of the voting public; those with incomes of $50,000 and above constituted 24 percent of the population and 33 percent of the voting public. The class differential is not as pronounced as in European societies, where some parties are organized around economic classes and some election outcomes reflect class votes, but it is perhaps more striking because the United States is a self-styled "classless" society.

Possibly the concept of class is inappropriate to a study of U.S. society. Instead, "status" may better explain how people perceive themselves and others. For example, in Europe, corporate executives receive lower salaries and bonuses than their American counterparts, and their corporate boards commonly have union representation, which is exceedingly rare in the United States. In the United States alone, the salary ratio of corporation chief executive officers to workers skyrocketed from an already high 35 to 1 in 1980 to 135 to 1 in 1990. Nevertheless, American society seems to accept the privileged status of business leaders more easily than do other societies. Some Americans may acknowledge that the privileged status of some groups confirms the existence of class stratification—or at least status stratification—in their society. But few will admit to the existence of a caste system—that is, a system of class stratification based on birth and from which there is no escape. Yet the position of certain minority groups—central-city African Americans and Latinos in particular—have characteristics of a caste system. Social scientists now study regularly the urban "underclass." The political scientist Andrew Hacker observes that many white Americans assume, often unconsciously, African Americans are a "subordinate caste," which helps them (lower- and middle-income whites in particular) rationalize limitations on their own upward social and economic mobility.

POLITICAL CULTURE AND THE AMERICAN DREAM

One of the enduring myths of American political culture is that anyone can succeed with initiative and hard work. The "American dream" holds that each generation can improve over the status of the preceding one as a result of such effort. For most Americans, improved economic and social status does depend on getting an education and exerting initiative and hard work. But for most Americans also, the American dream myth has been sustained through significant doses of public policy and economic subsidization by governments. Publicly financed education, government-backed mortgage insurance, government-stabilized interest rates, and government-provided college educations and housing subsidies for World War II and Korean war veterans helped underwrite the expansion of the middle class. And as discussed earlier, the Interstate Highway Trust Fund helped redesign America from a rural and urban nation with local employment to a suburban sprawl nation with commuting problems, increased needs for two-income households to pay for suburban homes and second automobiles, and heightened pressures for child care and for public schools that provide before- and after-school activities.

Public education has been a traditional venue for cultural and ethnic integration and for class mobility; the American dream aspiration has been socialized through it and sought with it. That continues; approximately 40 percent of college students are from families with incomes below $35,000, and many of these are the "first generation" college students of their families. Whether the United States can sustain rising expectations to fulfill the American dream is another matter.

At the start of the 1970s, the United States had the highest gross domestic product (GDP) per capita of any nation in the world. Over the next ten years, GDP per capita declined, and the United States was no longer number one, ranking tenth or lower among major industrial nations. Further, the ability to increase manufacturing productivity and thereby produce jobs received a negative impact with the expansion of the federal debt between the start of the 1970s and the 1990s. In the 1970s, federal debt held by investors was between 20 and 30 percent of GDP; by the start of the 1990s, it was approximately 50 percent. In the same period, national government interest payments on the federal debt expanded from between 6 and 8 percent to 12 percent. With the exception of a brief period between 1981 and 1986 (when federal tax law gave unusual preference to property investment), investment in government debt instruments became a better option than private-sector investment, which could promote economic development. Median income—a more tangible measure for Americans—also stagnated, and this continued into the early 1980s. Tax cuts and government expenditure programs (the major ones in defense procurement) in the 1980s boosted GDP per capita.

When the distribution of national income is divided into quintiles from highest to lowest, it is clear that income inequalities became more disparate in the 1980s: The top one-fifth of the population increased its share of national income from approximately 40 percent in 1970 to approximately 47 percent in 1990; the middle one-fifth decreased its share from approximately 18 percent to approximately 16 percent, as did the lowest two-fifths combined. Further, poverty levels in the United States, at the start of the 1990s, remain among the highest of the industrialized nations. Poverty rates among African American and Latino citizens (respectively, 33 and 28 percent) are higher than among other groups (11 percent for the white population), and this reinforces tensions and conflicts among race and ethnic groups. (In absolute terms, the majority of the poor are white: 21 million compared with 10 million African Americans and 5 million Latinos.) These tensions are exacerbated by the residential disparities between largely white suburbs and largely minority urban centers, which are accompanied by limited opportunities for urban citizens, limited resources for urban governments, and greater affluence and resources for nonminority suburban residents.

As employment opportunities increasingly arise in information processing and services and as they decline in manufacturing, policymakers, media opinion leaders, and educators are more actively analyzing such alternatives as a national industrial or economic policy. Other forms of policy and organizational change dominate the agenda of the 1990s: in education (twelve-month education is offered in some states), health care (managed private competition or a government-provided system is debated), environmental quality, waste disposal and recycling (transforming a "throwaway" culture into a recycling one and developing means to create, not displace, jobs while enhancing the environment). As America's society continues to grapple with economic and environmental change, its political choices and its changing social forces exist interdependently.

CULTURE WARS: MORALITY, INTENSITY, AND POLITICS

Tensions and conflicts emerge in other ways, many within the public schools and colleges. Should public schools, as part of the elementary curriculum, teach birth control and the causes and preventives for AIDS and explain homosexual and lesbian lifestyles? Should public schools and colleges move from a curricular canon dominated by "dead white males" to one emphasizing minorities and women and reexamining, for example, the relationship between slavery and the emergence of classical civilization? At times American society seems to be engaged in "culture wars" or a "clash of cultures," to use phrases popular in the early 1990s. Life in contemporary society involves conflicts over these and other values as ethnic, religious, gender, and "lifestyle" groups promote their interests. Liberals and egalitarians seek to rectify grievances perpetuated by misguided adherence to the past. Conservatives and religious fundamentalists seek to overcome injustices newly created by a misguided disregard for the past. The United States is not balkanized, but cultural, moral, religious, and lifestyle value clashes take on a vehemence and intensity unmatched in more traditional interest-group and political party conflicts.

Interest Groups

In a constitutional democracy, citizens have a variety of ways to influence government. They may personally contact their elected representatives or government bureaucracies. They may write letters to newspapers or purchase advertisements in the media to influence the public and government officials. They may litigate, that is, file suit in an effort to force government action. They may even take to the streets to protest government actions. All these activities can be done by isolated individuals, but each requires resources, communication and organization skills, and the like that are distributed unequally among members of society. Therefore, most attempts to influence government are more effective when done as part of group or through collective action, since more resources are available and more leverage can be exerted with accumulated resources and strength in numbers.

To undertake collective action individuals must join interest groups or work with political parties in election campaigns. Interest groups are organizations that engage in activity relative to government decisions; that is, they try to influence government officials (by lobbying and other forms of pressure) for some kind of policy action, favor, or redress of grievances. Political parties, in contrast, nominate their own candidates for office and run their election campaigns in an attempt not simply to influence government but to control it. In this section we discuss interest groups; in the next, political parties and elections.

Some further distinctions between interest groups and political parties are useful. Interest groups tend to be organized around a relatively narrow range of issues or policy concerns; political parties, around a broad array of issues or policy concerns. Interest groups tend to be exclusionary, restricting membership and representing social or private-sector (or functional) concerns. Political parties tend to be inclusionary, sometimes representing interest-group concerns but also seeking broad-based membership or support and representing coalitions that necessarily compromise narrower group concerns. Interest groups provide functional representation or linkage between social organizations and government; political parties provide popular representation or linkage between citizens and government.

These distinctions beg certain questions. Are "movements" distinct from interest groups and parties? Can governmental bodies—an agency or bureaucracy, or an interconnected web of agencies, congressional committees, and groups—be considered interest groups, or must the concept be limited to the private sector? Movements probably deserve separate treatment, but because they share certain characteristics with interest groups that lack substantial resources and influence, they are included in the discussion here. Government-based interest groups are more straightforward; when they attempt to promote policies to serve their own organizational goals (let alone goals of private-sector interest groups), they are, or are equivalent to, interest groups.

INTEREST-GROUP FORMATION: OBJECTIVES AND INCENTIVES

In general, interest groups originate not spontaneously but through the efforts of "entrepreneurs," who mobilize support with a variety of incentives or benefits that outweigh the costs of organizing or joining a group. Material or tangible benefits are more commonly associated with such economic interests as businesses, agriculture, labor unions, banking, and the like. In some instances, membership may be compulsory (a union shop workplace, for example) or necessary (membership in a trade or professional association to be licensed or maintain practicing credentials). In others, membership may be voluntary, and the group must devise ways of extracting support (chiefly financial) from nonmembers, or it must limit its objectives and activities. Group benefits often extend to nonmembers—for example, individual firms that get tax breaks negotiated by business associations; workers who receive employment safeguards negotiated by unions in an open shop. Since these "free riders" benefit from group action without contributing to it, organizations need to find ways to compel contributions or membership to prevent reluctant members from dropping out and getting a free ride.

Other benefits are purposive, or "cause" oriented. Public interest and citizens' groups often appeal to ideological values and commitments in promoting environmental quality, justice, and so forth. Here membership incentives correspond to group benefits and objectives. Finally, there may be "solidarity" benefits in belonging to a group or organization. Solidarity can mobilize local citizens' groups, tied together by a cause—a threatened factory shutdown, for example—and unite groups of people who are "outsiders" to the political process or are oppressed by the process—for example, a homeless action committee that links homeless people and activists in protest but seldom with tangible results (acquiring homes).

While interest groups may face the problem of the free rider—how to get beneficiaries of group action to pay for the benefits—society faces an obverse sort of problem. In promoting their interests or seeking benefits, interest groups generally want to "externalize" their costs (for example, shift the costs of pollution from the manufacturing process to society) or to have the costs widely distributed to the general taxpayer (for example, river and harbor improvements benefit localities and tax loopholes benefit designated classes, and costs for these are absorbed by the larger society). For the better part of the nineteenth century, government promotional policies for agriculture, railroads, exporters and industry provided precisely such benefits at the general public's expense, although the "public interest" justification was (and is still) economic development, jobs, and opportunities of the American dream. As government regulatory policies increased in number and scope from the late nineteenth century through the New Deal (when general regulatory powers became judicially sanctioned) to the present, and likewise as redistributive policies increased after World War II, traditional economic interest groups had to learn to protect themselves, and interest groups that benefited from regulations and the redistribution of resources learned to promote them. In short, as government has become more regulatory and redistributive in its activities, interest groups have expanded in number and in the scope of their activities. (We discuss this further in the Policymaking and Implementation section in chapter 2.)

KINDS OF INTEREST GROUPS
There is little consensus about how interest groups should be classified. Some scholars distinguish between voluntary and involuntary associations, others between membership and institutional groups, others between economic and noneconomic interests, and so on.

Most interest groups have economic interests to promote, and they organize themselves around specific material and tangible objectives. These include businesses and trade associations (including banking), labor unions, agricultural associations, and professional associations. Consulting firms, public relations firms, "think tanks," and the fabled Washington law firms are interest groups that serve other interest groups. These are associated principally with economic interests, and, like those interests, material or tangible reward or gain is the glue that holds them together, but, for a fee, they also can work for other kinds of interests.

Groups and individuals with noneconomic interests tend to organize around intangible objectives, and they are held together or motivated by purposive, sometimes moralistic, objectives and a sense of group solidarity. These often include "public interest" groups and "cause" and "single issue" groups. Such groups have become increasingly active, in part because more government hearings are open and televised, and recorded votes are taken, enabling group leaders to monitor legislation and bureaucratic behavior and to create targets for intense activity. The base of support is fluid, even unknown, for some of these groups. Computer-based telephone and address banks enable them to contact targeted supporters or likely supporters with fund-raising solicitations. Some scholars estimate that two-thirds of the money raised must be used to cover overhead. Such a poor cost-to-benefit ratio suggests the groups are less effective than they claim. The claims for influence made by group leaders, particularly those of cause and single-issue groups, may be exaggerated, but they gain currency and reinforcement through the media, which the leaders take advantage of when they stage media events to gain publicity (see below).

Typical noneconomic public interest and cause groups include the National Association for the Advancement of Colored People (NAACP), the Urban League, the National Organization for Women, Common Cause, the state-based Public Interest Research Groups, and the Sierra Club. To the extent that the leadership of these organizations benefits from their activities, it is incidental to their causes of, for example, promoting civil rights denied African American citizens and women, reducing deaths from automobile accidents, or decreasing environmental pollution. Critics of such groups claim that they are "special" interests, just as businesses and unions are, because minorities, women, and upper-middle-class environmentalists benefit from their activities. True, but the benefits are not limited to group members or those for whom the group advocates. Benefits are available to all members of society; that differentiates "public interest" groups from traditional economic interest groups.

The National Right to Life Committee, Operation Rescue, and the National Abortion Rights Action League are examples of single-issue groups. A sense of morality and even a moral crusade frequently animate such groups. It is often difficult to differentiate single-issue groups from movements. Movements are nascent interest groups. Their objectives may be economic or noneconomic, but as movements, their adherents are generally motivated by purposive and solidarity values. Most interest groups involved with abortion issues began as movements. The women's movement and the civil rights movement originated with grassroots activists as well as organized interest groups, and other interest groups were spawned by these movements.

Many of the newer single-issue groups are associated with conservative fundamentalist religious movements. They take stands on such things as abortion, homosexuality, secular humanism, and family values as earlier religious groups attempted to make central political issues out of prayer in school (1960s) and teaching creationism (1980s). The Moral Majority attempted to influence the 1980 elections, and in 1988, the Reverend Pat Robertson, a television evangelist of the Christian Broadcasting Network and its 700 Club, made a brief bid for the Republican presidential nomination. Neither could claim success. An aspect of their failures is that campaigning for election required them to broaden their appeal beyond their narrow religious agendas and that proved implausible to many voters.

The preceding generalizations about economic and noneconomic interest groups should not be treated as iron laws; there are exceptions and overlapping cases. The National Rifle Association provides many tangible benefits to members (shopping discounts, firearms training), but it increasingly has taken on characteristics of single-issue groups in unbending opposition to gun control. Veterans groups (the American Legion and Veterans of Foreign Wars), senior citizen organizations (American Association of Retired Persons), and civil rights organizations (NAACP, Urban League) tend to have solidarity and cause motivations and incentives for action. Nevertheless, they also promote the economic well-being of their members, the veterans and seniors associations especially, and their membership rosters tend to be more stable than the more ephemeral single-issue groups.

Governmental departments and bureaucracies function as interest groups. "Iron triangles" or "subgovernments" are combinations of bureaucracies and congressional committees functioning as interest groups in conjunction with nongovernmental interest groups. For example, for years the tobacco lobby was an iron triangle composed of House and Senate agriculture committees, the Department of Agriculture, and tobacco farmers and cigarette manufacturers. It sustained tobacco subsidies and weakened attempts to regulate cigarette advertising in the face of mounting criticism of smoking. Likewise, the military-industrial complex, of which President Eisenhower warned in his farewell address, refers to an iron triangle or subgovernment composed of House and Senate Armed Services committees, the Department of Defense and the respective military services, and such key defense industries as Lockheed, General Dynamics, Rockwell International, Tenneco, General Electric, and McDonnell-Douglass, which benefit from weapons specification bidding and procurement.

Intergovernmental organizations serve as lobbying and influence umbrella organizations for state and local governments and their elected and appointed public officials. For example, the National League of Cities, U.S. Conference of Mayors, and International City Management Association represent urban political and governmental interests in Washington, frequently lobbying for infrastructure and environmental funding from the federal government. Some states grant governing authority to regional government associations—municipal planning organizations and councils of government; some states do not. Congress, however, has delegated authority to them to implement elements of the Clean Air Act Amendments (1990) and the Intermodal Surface Transportation Efficiency Act (1991), just as Congress delegates authority at the national level to administrative agencies to make policy in conjunction with interest groups.

INTEREST-GROUP TACTICS AND SIGNIFICANCE

In promoting their interests, interest groups provide venues for individuals to participate in politics, they represent people who may feel unrepresented by their elected representatives, and they help shape political agendas and policies. The means or methods of promotion tend to vary with the kind of interest group and the incentives used to maintain membership.

Education and public relations can be targeted at the general public, particular constituents of public officials, and government officials. The general public may be targeted to maintain or develop a favorable climate of opinion for the interest group's goals or a favorable image of the group. Television spot commercials that portray caring teachers or health-care professionals aim to reinforce public support for those professions. When an education or public relations campaign is directed at constituents of public officials, such grassroots lobbying is usually designed to mobilize people (whom politicians recognize as voters and taxpayers) to pressure their representatives through telephone calls, letters, contacts with local politicians, and so on. Interest groups may provide phone numbers and messages to call in or formats for letters. Public relations campaigns directed at public officials are often designed to educate them concerning their constituents' views, that is, to convince them that there is public support for the interest group's position. (Expert testimony is another form of information for public officials discussed later.)

Interest groups, obviously, can engage in partisan politics. They can promise to deliver or threaten to withhold votes, for example. Labor unions have long used the promise of grassroots support during campaigns, as well as a strong union membership turnout on election day, to help politicians (usually liberal Democrats) who would promote union positions. More recently, conservative groups have published voting records of liberal members of Congress and urged their supporters, frequently single-issue oriented in their voting, to work and vote against liberal incumbents. Partisan activity includes all forms of election campaign help—canvassing and making door-to-door contacts, providing office space, equipment, phone banks, fund-raising assistance, and public appearance venues—in short, virtually anything a campaign needs.

With passage of the Federal Election Campaign Act (FECA) in 1971, Congress opened the door to a new campaign activity by interest groups. Loopholes in the act, coupled with the Supreme Court's striking down a provision that limited campaign spending by candidates (*Buckley* v. *Valeo*, 1976), provided incentives to funnel campaign contributions through political action committees (PACs). PACs existed before the passage of FECA; most were labor union committees. But with FECA, PACs became the "new" or preferred form of campaign organization for interest groups, particularly for corporations (corporate PACs are now the dominant form). The number of PACs increased beyond any reasonable expectations. In 1974, before the first elections conducted under FECA rules, there were approximately 600 PACs; by 1980, there were 2500, and by 1990, 4200. (PACs are discussed in the Political Parties and Elections section, which follows.)

Lobbying is the traditional form of influence for interest groups. The term derives from the nineteenth-century practice of meeting legislators in the lobby of the capitol building to press claims on them. Today it includes virtually any contact between interest-group representatives (and their surrogates) and public officials—legislators, members of the executive branch, bureaucrats. Group representatives may include members of the group (corporate or union officials), paid lobbyists (lawyers, consultants, public relations firms, and former members of Congress and the executive branch), volunteers (for many of the grassroots, loosely organized groups), and constituents persuaded by the group to intercede with their representative or other public official. Lobbying encompasses activities from face-to-face contact in the public official's office or at social events, through testifying at committee hearings, conducting research and writing speeches for members of Congress and White House staff, funding interns, and reporting on agency activity, to mobilizing grassroots lobbying and other constituency pressures and organizing coalitions of constituent groups and interest groups that share similar positions. The intent of lobbying generally is not to convert opposition members of Congress and, it is hoped, not to alienate allies with excessive pressure, but to reinforce commitments and draw greater attention to a policy. For elected officials, direct lobbying may be connected to partisan assistance in reelection campaigns; that is, future assistance is taken for granted when officials support the interest-group position.

Access is both a means, like lobbying, for exerting influence and a resource. An interest group with access does not need to exert the usual pressures associated with lobbying because the lobbyist already has the sympathetic ear of the public official. This resource of ready access is predicated on significant past political support, expertise and knowledge central to the public official's role, an identity of interests with the official's constituents, or all of these. In other words, access is for "insiders," those interest-group members who are part of the decision-making process. With access, an interest group may not simply influence the appointment process or writing of administrative regulations; it may be part of the process, having its representatives appointed to executive departments or congressional staffs where they can be directly involved in framing regulations. The iron triangle or subgovernment, discussed previously, provides one of the most effective, and notorious, forms of access when a congressional committee is in a position to protect and sustain relationships among agencies and interest groups through funding, favorable policies and regulations, and the like.

Direct litigation by interest groups occurs when they file suit to test laws, as the NAACP did during the civil rights movement and as industrial groups and environmentalists have done to test or expand protections of environmental regulations. An interest group may also file an *amicus curiae* brief in a suit. Technically such a brief provides additional information to the court. In practice, interest groups may file such briefs to bring media attention to the litigant, to develop a legal argument the litigant's attorney may not recommend, and to provide additional information to the attorney in instances where the litigant lacks financial resources. Generally, litigation is a tactic that emerges when an interest group lacks resources to exert influence in the legislative or administrative process or when an influential interest fails at those levels and the policy threatens its tangible interests.

Protest and direct action are the means available to "outsiders," to those who lack direct political and lobbying influence or resources, to those who are excluded from legislative and executive-administrative processes for political reasons (that is, because decision makers reject their standing), and to those who lack resources for litigation. It is possible to generalize that interests operating more or less within established conventions and values of the political culture tend to use more conventional means of promoting their interests—education, public relations, going public and going partisan, lobbying, access, and the like—whereas those operating outside societal conventions or on the fringes of political consensus must resort to more intense, direct measures. Further, groups within the mainstream generally can afford traditional tactics; those outside generally do not have the financial resources to purchase public relations, governmental contacts, and so on. Nevertheless, as interest groups have learned the value of the "media event"—of staging an event, rally, or protest to garner television coverage—increasingly mainstream groups rely on pseudo protest and pseudo direct-action techniques as a means of obtaining cheap publicity and disseminating their views.

In conclusion, interest-group activities are inevitable, and their tactics are effective in influencing government. As the role of government has expanded and more groups with broader scope for their activities have emerged, interest groups remain exclusionary, not inclusionary, however. They are more likely to reflect interests of the upper economic strata and politically well placed than the lower economic groups and politically weak. People with resources—wealth, education, organizational skills—are more likely to join and lead interest groups than are people lacking such resources. In principle, the inequalities and differences among citizens can be equalized or canceled out in the voting booth, since elections are inclusive.

Political Parties and Elections

Elections permit citizens not only to influence government but to control it, at least indirectly. Elections do not take place in a vacuum, however. Candidates must be selected and organized in "slates" with programs of action ("platforms"). Political parties fulfill these roles. When a party or a coalition of parties wins control of government through constitutionally sanctioned elections and attempts to bring the various offices and processes of government under its control, it assumes general responsibility for the conduct of public affairs and attempts to govern based on proposals in the campaign platform. Citizens can hold the governing party accountable for performance or nonperformance at the next election.

The French political scientist Maurice Duverger made a useful distinction between "mass" and "cadre" parties when explaining European party organization earlier in this century. Mass parties are typified by socialist and labor parties (before the postindustrial decline of labor movements). They have formal membership, frequently overlapping that of unions, and mechanisms for enforcing party discipline over both the party's elected officials and the mass membership. They are organized from the top down and centrally directed by powerful national party machines. Cadre parties are typified by moderate to conservative, middle-class parties (British Conservatives, German Christian Democrats). They do not have membership recruitment conduits in industry or society, and they therefore rely more on volunteers to coordinate, rather than control, party activities.

Organizationally, U.S. political parties are similar to cadre parties. There are few formal members (approximately 2 percent of the eligible electorate, according to some estimates). Most party supporters are considered to be loyalists or "party identifiers" (identifiers may range from persons with strong psychological and emotional ties to a party to persons with weak affinities for a party). The parties are loosely organized from the bottom up, or grassroots, and follow the structure and logic of federalism. State and local party organizations are the key building blocks. The national parties are actually coalitions or confederations of state parties. The national parties have national committees, which are the year-round governing organizations except in presidential election years when their national conventions temporarily become the parties' final authority. National committees generally lack the means to enforce discipline over their elected officials or their supporters, however. (The chief exception occurs when the convention enforces committee rules, usually with the threat of invalidating a state delegation's credentials.) For the most part, the relationship between national party organizations and state and local parties is one of cooperation, with cooperation at its highest during presidential election campaigns and considerably lower at other times.

It should come as no surprise that U.S. political parties are relatively weak and coalitional in nature. The size and diversity of the nation compounded by its federal structure of national and state and local intergovernmental relations almost guarantees that national parties can be organized only as cadre parties. This tendency is reinforced by a Constitution that does not formally recognize political parties, and by a history in which the Founders and early presidents were leery of political parties and in which many party and electoral reforms have had a distinct antiparty flavor. It should not be surprising either that each state regulates parties in its own way, and that U.S. parties are more heavily regulated than parties in other democratic nations. (Only five states do not regulate the internal organization and rules of the state parties.) U.S. parties are therefore not "responsible" or strong parties, but they are capable mechanisms for "interest aggregation," for combining diverse interests before the election. Voters do have a sense of what the government will look like if their preferred party wins. In multiparty systems, smaller, more disciplined parties are often responsible, but they accomplish interest aggregation poorly if at all. Coalitions within government frequently must be formed after the election results are in (Israel and Italy being prototype cases); ironically, voters who support strong, responsible parties may find their partisan commitments compromised after the election as the actual governing coalition is formed.

THE TWO-PARTY SYSTEM: ORIGINS AND CHARACTERISTICS

Since near the end of the presidency of George Washington, the United States has had some sort of two-party competition for offices in the federal government. Although the campaign to ratify the Constitution was waged by groups that could have evolved into political parties (for example, the Federalists and the Antifederalists), only remnants of the Federalists became organized as a political party in Washington's administration; in fact, some of the leading ratification Federalists became leaders of the first opposition party. Alexander Hamilton and John Adams retained the Federalist label in promoting commercial and economic development and organizing a coalition of partisans with business, industrial, and financial interests in New England and the Middle Atlantic states. Thomas Jefferson, Washington's secretary of state, and James Madison, member of the House of Representatives from Virginia, led an emerging opposition coalition of planters, small farmers, debtors and artisans. Known first as Jeffersonian Republicans when Jefferson won the presidency over Adams in 1800, the party evolved into the Democratic Republicans and finally the Democratic party, which today claims to be the world's oldest party in a democratic government.

From the end of the Jefferson administration through the election of 1824, the semblance of two-party competition disappeared, and in a period of "good feelings" the party caucuses in the Congress controlled nominations for the presidency. In 1824, a four-way race resulted in the House of Representatives selecting the president (John Quincy Adams) under constitutional provisions invoked when no candidate receives a majority of electoral votes. Andrew Jackson, who was the leading candidate in the popular vote, pushed his faction of the Democratic Republican party to organize a national nominating convention for the election of 1828. There Jackson was nominated for president, and the modern Democratic party was born. Remnants of the Federalists joined anti-Jackson National Republicans, and by 1834 a new opposition party, the Whig party, provided a degree of two-party competition. In the next two decades, Democrats and Whigs divided over the issue of slavery, sectional conflicts, and the power of the federal union. In 1854, the Republican party was formed largely in opposition to slavery, and the Whigs died after failing to field a presidential candidate in 1856.

After the Civil War, through the end of the nineteenth century, the two parties alternated in control of Congress, and the Republicans most frequently controlled the presidency. From the latter part of the nineteenth century until the 1930s, the Republican party coalition of northern industrial and financial groups and midwestern farmers dominated national politics, while the Democrats labored under the onus of being the party of rebellion. With the end of radical reconstruction in the former Confederacy, the Democratic party dominated the southern states. Its elected officials reintroduced de facto slavery through laws regulating landownership and tenancy after 1876, and they supported various forms of de jure segregation, particularly after the *Plessy* v. *Ferguson* decision of 1896. The economic distress of farmers and laborers in the 1920s and 1930s led more members of these groups into the Democratic coalition and provided the basis for an era of Democratic party dominance of national politics beginning with the election of 1932, in the midst of the Great Depression. Democrats have held a majority of seats in Congress since then, with the exception of the early 1950s and early 1980s, when Republicans controlled the Senate. Since the consecutive terms of Presidents Franklin Roosevelt and Harry Truman, however, Democrats have won the presidency only in 1960, 1964, 1976, and 1992.

Although the parties have clearly differed on policy matters at particular periods in history, their differences have changed and evolved through the years. In some instances, complete reversals have taken place: Once Democrats were more likely than Republicans to be internationalist in foreign relations (prone to use military intervention, for example) and defenders of states' rights against federal incursions in the states' domains; since the 1960s, the parties have done a virtual flip-flop on such issues. In contrast, in the same period Democrats have generally remained more favorable to government regulation of business, social legislation, and redistributive policies than Republicans. In comparative terms, today the Republican party can be construed as a right-of-center party, the Democratic party a centrist party; each party, the Republicans in particular, is hospitable to various elements of the ideological right, but neither party seems hospitable to elements of the ideological left. Democratic and Republican activists tend to be more clearly divided along ideological lines than the parties' respective followers, or identifiers, who tend to overlap in the middle of the ideological spectrum. Consequently, there is a tendency in national elections for the two parties to converge toward the ideological middle of the road.

Competition for the ideological middle in national elections is reflected in the stances the parties take in presidential-congressional relations. The demarcation line between the Democratic and Republican parties is often blurred, and the parties are divided into various wings or factions, such as liberal and conservative Democrats and moderate and conservative Republicans. The vaunted tax plan of President Reagan—the Economic Recovery and Tax Act of 1981—passed with strong Democratic support, not in spite of Democratic opposition. Nonetheless, when roll-call votes are taken in Congress, the members' party affiliations are the best predictors of their votes, and in the 1980s there seemed to be greater party discipline and more rigid differentiation between the parties in Congress, probably the result of the majority party being the opposition party to the presidential party.

Occasionally, the system of two-party competition (or one-party dominance in a two-party system) has been interrupted by third or minor parties. This is in sharp contrast to the multiparty nature of many other Western and industrialized democracies. The Republican party originated as a third party, and its becoming one of the major parties was accompanied by the demise of another, the Whigs (although the Whig party was not really a dominant force before the Republican party emerged). Minor third parties have surfaced, frequently as parties for protest votes, but the major parties have proved adept at co-opting them by taking over vote-getting planks of third parties when it has become apparent that the smaller parties were making inroads into one of the major party's sources of support. Populist, Greenback, and Progressive parties of the late nineteenth and early twentieth centuries, and the American Independent party of the 1960s and tax revolt movements of the 1970s had impacts on the major parties, either finding certain of their major campaign issues taken over by the Democrats or Republicans or finding the parties shifting subtly to the left (in the cases of the earlier third parties) or to the right (in more recent instances). In 1992, Ross Perot ran as an independent and garnered more popular votes than any third-party candidate before or since Theodore Roosevelt bolted the Republican party and ran under the Bull Moose banner in 1912. Unlike other third-party candidates, Perot was not propelled into the leadership of a mass movement that had organized under a party banner; like Theodore Roosevelt, he originated his own campaign, and he created his "party"—United We Stand, America—in his image. Shortly after the election, Perot attempted to reformulate or repackage his campaign organization into an interest group. It is not clear if the Perot factor will emerge as a viable third party or as an interest group or if it will simply fade away.

FACTORS SUSTAINING A TWO-PARTY SYSTEM

Why has a two-party system been the norm, and why have third parties been short-term influences but hardly ever significant factors in election outcomes or in winning elective offices in the United States? Various factors have been cited by scholars and pundits alike to explain the persistence of the two-party system, and we now review the major ones.

First, there are historical and cultural explanations for the persistence of a two-party system. The oldest explanation is that after a party formed in opposition to the governing clique in the Washington and Adams administrations, state and local slates for office began to be organized around the national parties to take advantage of the appeal of the national ticket, and loyalties to first the Jeffersonian (later Democratic) party and later the Whig and Republican parties deepened. When partisan loyalties and identification become ingrained among the electorate, a party defeated nationally still can remain viable at state and local levels in our federal system. Further, the American public tends to be moderate and to prefer moderate or middle-of-the-road parties and candidates. Therefore there is little interest in radical or nonmoderate party alternatives, and no room in the middle for a third party (the fate of the Whig party is frequently cited to illustrate how a major party that loses touch with the electorate can be displaced by another moderate party, the Republican party, not a party with a radical agenda).

Second, there are institutional explanations. Most elections at every level in the United States are plurality-win elections in single-member districts. In other words, a candidate who gets the most votes (not necessarily a majority) wins the office. This winner-take-all electoral process tends to discourage third and other parties from entering the election campaign, and, when they do attempt to do so, it tends to discourage voters from voting for them because they doubt the third party has much chance of victory. Hence, the reasoning goes, a vote for a third-party candidate is a "wasted vote" because it was not cast for one of the two candidates who have any real chance of winning. At the presidential level, this sort of explanation is reinforced by the Electoral College. Each state is a type of single-member district, since the presidential candidate who gets the most votes in a given state receives all the state's electoral votes. Further, given the Electoral College bias toward states with large numbers of electoral votes (all of which can be won by getting just one more popular vote than the opponent), the two major parties pour enormous resources into such states—resources third-party candidates do not have because potential contributors calculate their odds are significantly lower than Democrats' or Republicans' for winning a given state. Finally, although the United States does not have institutional incentives for congressional and presidential parties to work together as legislators and cabinet must in parliamentary systems, the institutional separation of president from Congress means there is little likelihood that a third party could form a swing voting bloc or force the necessity for a governing coalition, as one may do in a parliamentary system.

Third, there are political explanations for the persistence of a two-party system. Most state legislatures have imposed restrictive requirements for ballot access by minor parties. This collusion between Democrats and Republicans is reflected also in decennial efforts to redistrict following the census. Each party attempts to draw district lines to favor itself, but neither intends to open up the electoral process to third and minor parties. The preceding institutional explanations of single-member districts with plurality win provisions are explained also on political grounds, since neither major party has any incentive to weaken itself. For example, there are no good political reasons for the major parties to promote multimember or at-large districts with majority-win provisions, since these can provide third parties the basis for some electoral success and give them leverage to swing the vote in a close election. This would force one of the two major parties to negotiate with the third party and perhaps promote some of its policy options. Typically, some explanation other than a political one is used publicly to justify these sorts of restrictions on third parties. The usual explanation is that such requirements prevent frivolous candidacies from cluttering the ballot and confusing voters or that plurality-win elections simplify choices and expedite the outcome. This explanation is no doubt correct, but so too is the political explanation for ballot access and voting procedure restrictions on third parties. Democratic and Republican legislators do not like to encourage competition. (More blatantly political are the efforts by Congress to legislate campaign finance reform, which are discussed later in this section.)

CAMPAIGN AND ELECTION RULES AND PROCESSES

Elections have expanded citizen involvement in politics as compared with earlier eras when democratic government was nonexistent or the exception in the world. Elections today can further expand citizen participation; however, the United States seems less successful at this than other democratic nations, which have higher voting rates. Rules governing elections establish the acceptable conditions for participation (who is allowed to vote and under what conditions) and how votes are counted (equal weighting of each vote—"one person, one vote"—or some other method; majority- or plurality-win or some form of proportional method for distributing offices).

Today in the United States, virtually anyone eighteen years old or older who has resided in a community for thirty days can vote. Yet compared with other democracies, average national voting participation hovers in the 50–60 percent range, and it is much lower in nonpresidential national election years and in state and local elections. Restrictions on voting are negligible, but attempts to reduce them further often have difficulty passing, since proponents and opponents alike see a political angle in reforms. For example, "motor voter"—automatic voter registration when one renews one's driver's license—was vetoed by President Bush; increasing the number of registered voters is often thought to benefit Democrats more than Republicans. (Congress passed and President Clinton signed into law a motor-voter bill in early 1993.) Whereas earlier in the nation's history there were property qualifications, then taxpaying qualifications, these were all but eliminated by the time of the Civil War. The Fifteenth Amendment gave African American citizens the right to vote, although southern states established numerous legal and informal restrictions on voting. For example, poll taxes, literacy tests, and white primaries were used to exclude people from voting, and racial gerrymanders and at-large electoral districts were used to dilute black voting strength. Little by little these were overturned, either by Supreme Court decisions invalidating state legislation or by congressional enactment (chiefly the Voting Rights Act of 1965 and subsequent amendments to it). Women did not have the right to vote nationwide until the Twentieth Amendment was ratified in 1920; prior to that, women could vote in only twelve states after 1869. (Women voted in several colonies before the American Revolution; thereafter, the states began to ban women voting; the last was New Jersey in 1807!)

In the late nineteenth and early twentieth centuries, a series of reforms of electoral and governmental processes were introduced successfully. (Governmental reforms are discussed in the section on bureaucracy.) State electoral reforms were designed to expand direct popular participation in party candidate selection, in the recall of public officials before the conclusion of their terms of office, and in placing policy initiatives on the ballot for public vote. Such procedures as direct primary elections to replace party caucuses, ballots listing candidates by office to facilitate ticket-splitting among candidates, and the initiative and referendum are now institutions in many states. The reformers' efforts also had the effect of weakening the roles of parties. Some reformers were antiparty and wanted to increase direct democracy by the people and decrease influence of representatives and partisans believed to have unsavory, self-interested motivations for entering politics. Others were not antiparty but merely middle- and upper-class citizens who wanted to increase influence of the "better people"—people who happened to have education, income, and community status, like so many rising middle-class reformers! Their purpose, in the words of Woodrow Wilson before he became president, was to "restore, not to destroy, representative government." In the late 1970s, a citizens' "tax revolt" that started in California inspired renewed use of initiatives, referendums, and recall elections nationwide, including advisory state referendums on national issues and legislative referendums ranging from auto safety and environmental policies to term limits for state and congressional representatives.

At the national government level, the most important recent reforms have affected the selection of the political parties' presidential candidates and congressional elections. First, reforms of political party rules, which govern the selection of delegates to the national convention and the conduct of presidential primary elections, have been created by the parties themselves. Second, changes in rules governing the financing of campaigns have been created by Congress.

First, the political parties' rules for selecting their presidential candidates have far-reaching consequences. In the beginning, nominations for most offices in the United States were made by party caucuses or conventions. Increasingly the nomination process has been undertaken through direct primary elections. The four-year national party convention remains the theoretical governing body for both the Democratic and the Republican parties, but most delegates are chosen through state primary elections, wherein the delegates are also pledged or committed to cast their first convention votes for a particular presidential candidate. Through the 1960s, the party conventions did in fact make decisions about who the parties' presidential candidates would be. In the aftermath of the 1968 Democratic party convention, the Democrats initiated a series of reforms, some of which the Republicans adopted. Since then, the conventions have basically ratified the results of presidential primaries held in a majority of the states.

Reformers had two objectives: to expand public participation, mainly mass identifiers, in the process of nominating the party's presidential candidate; and to expand representation of key groups within the party, chiefly minorities and women (and early on, youth) so that the nomination process and convention would more adequately reflect the demographics of the party identifiers and the general electorate. The first objective was sought by expanding the number of presidential primary elections. (Democrats initiated this change, and Republicans followed when state legislatures mandated primaries to meet the Democratic party's guidelines.) This has indeed increased total participation (although the rate of voter turnout is very low): Before 1968, about 10 percent of the eligible electorate participated in primaries; now more than 20 percent participate. It also produced unexpected and counterproductive results, which are discussed below. The second objective—to increase the representative characteristics of the convention delegates—has resulted in significantly increased participation by minorities and women in the Democratic party and by women in the Republican party, and the parties' enforcement mechanisms have served as something of a model for voluntary compliance in affirmative action for minorities and women.

Unexpectedly, and counterproductively in the view of many party stalwarts, the parties began to lose control over the nomination process itself as a result of the reforms. The staggered calendar of state presidential primaries produces an overly long campaign schedule for both parties. Some candidacies have been declared and campaign work has begun two years before the election. To be successful requires early support from campaign contributors, the development of an organization of personal loyalists, and success in early primaries so that media will respond positively to the candidate and additional campaign contributors will join the candidate's cause. This has enabled candidates, who may not appeal to a broad national electorate, to gain control over large blocs of delegate votes, and it gives the victorious candidate's personal loyalists and contributors disproportionate influence relative to other party loyalists in the general election campaign. After the nomination, the party's anointed candidate hopes the other primary opponents will unite in support and that their various individual campaign organizations can be blended and work with state party organizations in order to field a successful general election campaign effort.

The Democrats began to retract some of their reforms after the 1980 convention. Party leaders wanted to assure that more professional politicians and elected national officials would participate as voting delegates at the conventions. They also wanted to give candidates of national stature better odds of winning the nomination and reduce chances of nominating a candidate who might lack broad national appeal. From the 1972 through 1980 conventions, many senators and members of the House had been excluded because they did not run as delegates and win seats in state primaries; beginning with the 1984 convention, additional voting delegate slots were set aside for these "superdelegates." Similarly, beginning with the 1984 presidential primaries, blocs of state primaries were consolidated on the same date in an effort to give both nationally known candidates and significant regions a greater say in the outcome of the nomination process. Nevertheless, these "counterreforms" did not preclude seemingly weaker candidates from winning the party's nomination and the presidential election. In 1991, many of the best-known Democrats declined to seek their party's nomination, apparently convinced that President Bush's popularity was insurmountable. The nomination battle was fought by a handful of lesser-known candidates including, of course, Arkansas Governor Bill Clinton, who proceeded to defeat Bush in the general election.

Second, campaign finance reforms created by Congress have affected both presidential and congressional election campaigns. Passage of the Federal Election Campaign Act (FECA) in 1971 represented the first major campaign finance reform effort since 1925. The act and its subsequent amendments (1974, 1976, and 1979) provide matching funds for presidential candidates with cost-of-living provisions that apply in succeeding election years. For example, beginning with a $20 million base year of 1974, each party's candidate qualified for $21.8 million of FECA matching funds for the general election campaign in 1976, and by 1992 that amount had grown to $55.2 million. (In addition, FECA permits "soft money" contributions—money raised by parties for such activities as voter registration and get-out-the-vote drives—and contributions to cover certain legal fees. In 1992 these totaled roughly $45 million for Clinton and $28 million for Bush.)

FECA clearly is biased against third parties, or in favor of the two major parties. Candidates of the two major parties are fully funded (and may benefit from soft money and other contributions noted above); third-party candidates may be only partially funded. This has had the effect of introducing self-financing and of reinforcing personal campaign organizations that are not beholden to the parties in the presidential nomination process. In the first instance, billionaire Ross Perot could afford to bypass the funding restriction on third parties; he funded his own campaign (of $69 million in contributions, $65 million was self-financed). Also, Congress has exempted itself from public funding for congressional campaigns, and the FECA's so-called restrictions on special-interest campaign contributions actually helped usher in the era of political action committee (PAC) influence in elections. Major interest groups, particularly labor unions, had used PACs for years before FECA was passed, but FECA provided incentives for other organizations, particularly corporations and cause groups, to use PACs as a way of channeling campaign support and bypassing the ostensible intent of FECA to limit the influence of special-interest money in politics. Most evidence indicates that PACs favor incumbents over challengers and occasional third-party candidates, thereby adding to incumbents' advantages. For example, in the 1992 House election, PACs contributed 9.5 times more money to incumbents than to challengers, making average contributions of $261,976 and $27,621, respectively. (In terms of overall expenditures, House incumbents outspent their challengers by an average of $582,330 to $154,607.)

VOTER CHOICE AND CAMPAIGNING

In campaigning for office, candidates and their organizations are concerned with three principal factors that influence voters' decisions: party identification, the effect of the perceived character of the candidates (or the images they project), and issues or policy positions of candidates as they relate to policy preferences of voters.

Partisan identification is the most significant long-term influence on voting decisions. In a typical presidential election year, for example, about 40 percent of the voters commit themselves to their party's candidate even before one is nominated at the party convention. Candidates and their campaign organizations "shore up" their base of support and then develop strategies to identify voters who are "leaning" in their direction and attempt to mobilize them to vote. The successful presidential candidate will be supported by most voters who identify with the party, by most independent voters, and by a significant percentage of voters who identify with the other party but who may ticket-split in the election (vote for a presidential candidate of one party but for candidates for other offices from the other party). The 1992 presidential election year was not typical, however. George Bush attempted to shore up the Republican base and failed. Bill Clinton sought to bring into the fold Reagan Democrats (Democratic identifiers who had split tickets and voted for Republican presidents previously) on the theory that first shoring up the base would produce failure as previous Democratic presidential candidates had failed. The third-party candidacy of Ross Perot hurt Bush more than Clinton by attracting greater proportions of Republican than Democratic identifiers. Perot also eroded independent voter support for Bush; for the first time since 1964, the Democratic candidate received a higher percentage of independent voters than the Republican.

The importance of partisan identification has declined in part because the Democratic party's original basis for voters developing loyalty to and identification with the party—the New Deal coalition—has weakened. But its importance has waned also because political campaigns have become "candidate centered" and personalized, and such campaigns preempt programmatic campaigning and discount the role of parties. Moreover, the core of party-based campaigns and the vehicles for sustaining partisan loyalties among key activists—efforts of large numbers of volunteers—have given way to campaigns based on new technologies (polling, computer-generated phoning and mailing lists) that require enormous sums of money rather than volunteer "foot soldiers." Individuals with personal fortunes and with followings of personal loyalists are better positioned to organize campaigns and become successful nominees of parties than are candidates who represent mass-based classes (industrial workers, for example) or groups of partisans.

Also, studies indicate that issue voting has increased since the 1950s, but voters' evaluations of candidates' issue positions are often intertwined with their perceptions of the candidates' character or image. The image or perceived character of a candidate is especially important when voters lack information about the candidate's past behavior and policy stands. For example, Ronald Reagan's 1980 candidacy depended on providing voters with a more favorable prospective image to contrast with Jimmy Carter, whom many voters judged harshly based on a retrospective analysis of his administration's policies and of his image as a less than capable executive. Relatively few voters choose candidates principally according to their positions on issues; frequently issue positions are viewed through the lenses of image or character: whether the candidate is sufficiently "tough" to make hard choices. In the 1992 election, certain character and issue themes (marital fidelity and the absence of a military record) seemed to interrelate in a curious way that first hurt Bill Clinton's chances and then reinforced his image as someone who could withstand adversity and make reasoned judgments. And the issues believed tapped by candidate Ross Perot seemed, in the end, to be responses to the image he paid so much to project to the public. His "infomercials" (televised commercials in which he presented campaign information) may have tapped voters' interest in issues, but they were packaged with a particular design and enveloped in a presentation of seeming candor or "folksiness" that were defining aspects of the candidate's image. In short, issue voting, or the apparent demand of voters for issue-oriented campaigning, has increased, but the new campaign techniques and increased personalizing of campaigning have made it more difficult for voters to undertake reliable issue analysis. Further, the increased salience of both issues and imagery seems to correlate with a decline in the breadth and depth of partisan identification as a factor determining voting decisions.

TICKET SPLITTING, DIVIDED GOVERNMENT, AND ELECTORAL COLLEGE REFORM

Since the 1980 election, and arguably since the 1950s, voters have shown a propensity to choose "divided" government, that is, a national government in which the two elective branches are controlled by different parties (typically, the presidency by Republicans and Congress by Democrats). Do voters prefer or rationally choose divided government? Since the late 1960s, voters have demonstrated a tendency to vote a split ticket, switching parties in choosing candidates for different offices. At the national level, such ticket splitting seems to come at the expense of Democratic candidates for president, since ticket splitters who vote for Republican presidential candidates tend to vote for Democrats not only for Congress but for other offices as well. In other words, voters who vote chiefly for Democrats on the ballot, split and vote Republican for president more frequently than the obverse. Increased ticket splitting does not necessarily support the proposition that voters are more issue oriented in their voting or that they are more knowledgeable and independent. In voting for Congress, there is a noticeable incumbency effect that gives an edge to incumbents (mostly Democrats) over challengers; for example, incumbents receive far more PAC money than challengers.

Divided government also may be an artifact of the Electoral College. The Electoral College method of electing the president separately from the party's congressional candidates reinforces institutional disincentives for cooperation among executive and legislative branches, which parliamentary systems encourage. Many proponents of reforming the Electoral College believe an electoral process that more adequately reflects popular majorities will reduce institutional incentives for "deadlock" or "gridlock." The 1992 presidential election would have tested some of the reform panaceas. In the three-way race in which Perot received more popular votes than any third-party candidate except Theodore Roosevelt, he nonetheless received no electoral votes. Clinton held a popular vote plurality (43.0 percent to Bush's 37.4 percent and Perot's 18.9 percent) and a decisive electoral vote majority (370, or 69 percent).

Had the Electoral College been replaced before 1992 with a national popular vote system, Clinton's popular vote plurality and thus his governing mandate would be diminished; under the current system, popular pluralities fade in significance when compared with the magnitude of such electoral vote majorities as Clinton received. Reformers recognize this problem and include provisions for a runoff election if a popular majority is not attained. But a runoff election might also erode the authority of the presidency. For instance, voter turnout in runoff elections is frequently lower than in general elections (though there has never been such an event nationally), and the runoff winner could achieve a lower vote total than he or she received in the general election. Also, a national popular vote with runoff provisions may elicit charges of political chicanery, deal making, and the like. It is likely that a third party would try to leverage its position vis-à-vis one of the major parties in exchange for postelection considerations, perhaps withdrawing its candidate shortly before the general election in anticipation of special considerations or instructing its voters to vote for one of the other candidates in a runoff election.

Such speculation, of course, is used to derail Electoral College reform efforts. One current effort, the Electoral Fairness Project, attempts to minimize such charges. It allocates the electoral vote to the House of Representatives districts in a state instead of allocating it to the state as a whole, but it does not reallocate electoral vote totals differently than provided in the Constitution (that is, each state's electoral vote is equal to its combined House and Senate delegation). From the standpoint of responsible, disciplined parties and the goal of avoiding divided government, the project has merit because it increases incentives for presidential candidates to campaign with their party's congressional slates. There would still be a campaign bias toward large or "key" electoral vote states, but by more closely aligning presidential and congressional campaigns, the reformers hope for greater cooperation among president and Congress after elections. Since each state may devise its own electoral vote allocation method, no formal constitutional amendment is required to adopt the Electoral Fairness Project formula. The plan has been discussed since the 1950s, and two states have adopted it (Maine and Nebraska). In the future, other states may adopt it also, and the role of parties will continue to evolve through this informal form of constitutional amendment.

2. The U.S. Political System: Governmental Institutions

The Presidency

Formal powers of the presidency are provided in Article II of the Constitution, which begins by vesting the government's "executive power" in the president and concludes an enumeration of powers and duties with the charge to "take care that the laws be faithfully executed." (The method for selecting the president, discussed subsequently, is also provided.) The constitutionally designated presidential powers are broad, including not merely appointive and administrative powers but also diplomatic, military, judicial, and legislative powers. The president appoints certain executive branch officials and federal judges with the "advice and consent" of the Senate and may require the advice of executive branch officials. Foreign ambassadors present their portfolios to the president, who appoints U.S. ambassadors (again with the Senate's advice and consent) and makes treaties, subject to Senate approval. The president is commander-in-chief of the armed forces and may use this power (through interpretation of Article IV and statutory powers) to protect states from invasion and (at least pro forma, at their request) from "domestic violence." The president is empowered to grant reprieves and pardons for federal offenses (excluding impeachment). The president also has certain legislative responsibilities to provide Congress with information about the state of the union, to recommend to Congress bills for passage, to veto bills (granted in Article I), and to convene and adjourn Congress under certain circumstances. These legislative powers coupled with the power to make judicial appointments, to bring suits before federal courts, and to enforce judicial decisions are the institutional means that enable presidents to share powers with or have "partial agency" in the other branches of government.

SOURCES OF PRESIDENTIAL GOVERNMENT

Aside from the aforementioned powers and duties, the Constitution leaves it to presidents, to Congress, or to the courts to determine the scope of the president's "executive power." The Constitution's lack of specificity contrasts with its clarity in granting to Congress the specific legislative powers that are named "herein" (notwithstanding the implied powers clause). For example, the Constitution is silent about the removal of executive branch appointees. Presidential precedents sanctioned by federal court decisions have established the president's control over the removal power (with the exception of judges or such quasi-judicial appointees as independent regulatory agency officials). Nor is it obvious what the Constitution requires for laws to be "faithfully executed." Some presidents have vigorously enforced laws; others have made merely "good faith" efforts; still others have balked at enforcing certain laws on grounds they violate the spirit of the Constitution or for politically expedient reasons.

In his classic study of the presidency, Richard Neustadt argued that presidential power depends on the ability to persuade. Power is not command; it is the ability to bargain and to convince others that what the president wants is in their interests also. The ability to persuade is a function of one's ambition, skill, tenacity, and so forth and of how well one can develop and capitalize on one's prestige and reputation. From this perspective, formal, constitutional powers are resources that must be marshaled effectively to exert power. The successful exercise of power therefore depends on the personal characteristics of presidents as well as the circumstances in which they find themselves. Constitutional vagueness provides presidents—if they are capable—with the leeway to claim and justify inherent powers and prerogatives. They have done this by exerting power and establishing precedents, sometimes aided by the absence of a congressional challenge or by supportive or acquiescent judicial rulings.

Most nineteenth-century presidents were inclined to defer to Congress (or lacked the resources to do otherwise), whereas most twentieth-century presidents have been "chief legislators" in expanding the presidency at the expense of Congress. Several early presidents, however, did not defer to Congress but took actions that provided a basis for an expanded presidency. For example, George Washington asserted presidential control over the Cabinet, responsibility for suppressing domestic disorder (in the Whiskey Rebellion), a monopoly on communications with foreign governments, and presidential direction of foreign policy in his proclamation of neutrality in a war between the British and French. Washington's precedents implied the notions of inherent powers and prerogatives that subsequent presidents overtly proclaimed. Thomas Jefferson took the unprecedented initiative (contrary to his prepresidential claims on limiting the executive) of presenting Congress with a fait accompli in the Louisiana Purchase instead of first seeking its policy guidance or assent. Andrew Jackson vigorously enforced the laws of the land and did not hesitate to use the veto as a political tool to force policy changes on Congress (rather than justify his vetoes on constitutional grounds). Abraham Lincoln blockaded ports, summoned state militias, issued the Emancipation Proclamation, and suspended habeas corpus without congressional policy direction or assent. He is said to have believed there were two options: to save the Constitution or the union, and he invoked presidential prerogative in proclaiming the emergency powers that suspended parts of the former to preserve the latter. As the first twentieth-century president, Theodore Roosevelt popularized the idea, implicit in the actions of these earlier presidents, that the president should act as a "steward" for the country, taking the initiative in using powers and setting policy when Congress could not or would not do so.

Thus contemporary presidents have at their disposal an array of extraconstitutional powers established and refined by their nineteenth- and early twentieth-century predecessors. Certain extraconstitutional powers are so frequently used that they are taken for granted, as if they originated with the Constitution. These include executive agreements in lieu of treaties (and in lieu of senatorial consent), executive orders in lieu of asking Congress for legislation, claims to executive privilege in the face of congressional oversight and investigations (all introduced within the first three presidential administrations), and the impoundment of funds, that is, refusal to spend monies appropriated by Congress for specific programs. Further, particularly since the 1930s, Congress has delegated authority to the president and the executive branch bureaucracy (as well as independent regulatory agencies) to formulate and implement domestic policy. Early in the Franklin D. Roosevelt administration, the Supreme Court invalidated regulatory programs and, in the case of the National Industrial Recovery Act, congressional delegations of authority that it deemed to be overly broad and lacking clear guidelines for the executive branch to follow. The Court never effectively sustained this ruling, however, adhering instead to an 1825 ruling that permits Congress to establish broad guidelines and to allow executive branch and independent regulatory agencies to "fill in the details," that is, to make policy.

Likewise, Congress has delegated virtually all foreign and military policy responsibility to the president. Not that Congress had much control in this area in the first place. The intent of the constitutional convention may have been for Congress to restrain the "dog of war," as citizen Thomas Jefferson observed in 1789; but from 1801, when President Thomas Jefferson sent naval and marine personnel to fight a "defensive" war in Tripoli, to 1901, presidents used armed forces abroad without a declaration of war by Congress on forty-eight different occasions. Further, in the nineteenth century, the ratio of executive agreements to Senate-approved treaties was about even. Between the turn of the century and 1932, it was approximately two to one, and from then through 1944, three to one. Since 1945, the ratio has ranged from ten to one to twenty to one or more. Higher ratios of executive agreements to treaties generally occur when government is divided between, say, Republican presidents and Democratic Congresses, but the point should not be missed that the ratio has increased dramatically during the eras of U.S. world power and then superpower status, when Congress has been more acquiescent to the president. With or without congressional acquiescence, presidents have reinforced their roles over foreign and military policy, in some cases expanding constitutional interpretation and usage. President Harry Truman, in sacking General Douglas MacArthur for exceeding his authority in the Korean war, demonstrated formal presidential and civilian control over the military. The domestic uses of the military were also reaffirmed by Presidents Eisenhower, Kennedy, and Johnson, who left little doubt that presidents can deploy troops to enforce civil rights policy and attempt to quell "domestic violence" in the states.

CRISIS LEADERSHIP AND THE PERSONALIZED PRESIDENCY

With the conclusion of World War I, and especially after World War II and the advent of the Cold War and the Vietnam quagmire, the superpower status of the United States propelled it on a course of "crisis management" or "crisis leadership" for foreign and military policy. Modern presidential government is the focal point for crisis management, and its role has been reaffirmed with the end of the Cold War, the decline of Soviet hegemony in Eastern Europe, the Middle East, and north Asia, and the increase of intense ethnic and nationalist conflicts.

Nevertheless, there are limits to crisis leadership. These are evident in the circumstances surrounding President Nixon's resignation in the aftermath of the Watergate fiasco and in the precipitous drop in public opinion support for President Reagan after the Iran-*contra* revelations. Their apparent abuses of presidential power stemmed in part from preoccupation with crisis at the expense of accountability. And future presidents may learn that crisis leadership is insufficient for long-term political success. President Carter was virtually hostage to managing the Iran hostage crisis during his quest for a second term, and his successors claimed they would never be en-trapped in that way. Yet President Bush's enormously high public support during and immediately after Operation Desert Storm in 1991 dwindled and could not be restored in the face of domestic problems in his 1992 reelection bid. Moreover, crisis management is not simply a matter of presidential leadership. One of the lessons of the Vietnam war appears to be that presi-dents cannot simply order military action without assurance to the armed forces—that is, without exerting the power of persuasion over the mili-tary—that resources and support are sufficient for an expeditious and suc-cessful operation. During the administration of President Bush, the invasion of Panama and Operation Desert Storm against the Iraqi regime were under-taken with inordinate logistics preparation and presidential assurances to back the military effort fully.

The Constitution's Article II and subsequent amendments provide for two four-year terms of office for a president, with election through a college of electors. The provisions of this Electoral College effectively require a state-by-state campaign in which candidates seek to gain all of a state's elec-toral votes (equal to the number of House representatives plus the two sena-tors) by winning pluralities of popular votes in a sufficient number of states. Notwithstanding the state-based election of the president (similar in many ways to the election of members of the Senate), with the growth of presiden-tial government, the presidency has come to be viewed as the only nationally elected office. Twentieth-century presidents have expanded their constituen-cies to include the entire nation.

Further, changes in political party nomination procedures, and changes in campaign finance rules, at least for two decades between the late 1960s and the early 1990s, have brought presidential candidates in closer contact with voters by weakening the candidates' relationships with the political parties, as we indicated in chapter 1. Presidential candidates seeking their party's nomination have been able to bypass the established party leadership and identify with the public as outsiders or agents of change. The McGovern candidacy (1972) and the successful Carter (1976) and Reagan (1980) candidacies capitalized on the candidates' appearance of personal contact with the public and distance from established party and government elites. Campaign finance reforms have helped reduce the rate of increase of presidential campaign costs and have benefited the two major parties' candi-dates at the expense of alternate or minor parties. But these reforms also have provided the venues for PACs to erode further the role of the congres-sional political parties in influencing elections and enforcing party discipline over PAC-financed incumbents. And weakened congressional parties have contributed to the independence of presidents from partisan constraints and helped presidents increase their ties with the electorate.

Moreover, the presidency has become "personalized." First, mass media communications enable presidents to address the public directly. President Franklin Roosevelt brought his voice to the homes of Americans via radio, and President John Kennedy was able to initiate the modern use of television by using his interpersonal skills more effectively than his immediate predecessors. President Ronald Reagan was so well practiced in the use of television communications he was dubbed the "Great Communicator" as well as the "Teflon president" for his ability to deflect criticisms and responsibility in his appeals to the public. Also, presidents have learned to adjust their messages based on conducting scientific public opinion polls to identify and address people's hopes and fears. With the 1992 election and subsequent continuation of his campaigning style in office, President Bill Clinton has demonstrated that the modern president can engage in personal dialogue with "average" representatives of the public, thus giving other citizens a vicarious sense of conversing with the president.

THE INSTITUTIONAL PRESIDENCY

With the growth of presidential government, the persons elected to the office have come increasingly to rely on an expanded institutional presidency—a bureaucracy that presidents staff partly by using their patronage powers to bring in their loyalists and aides, but also one that has many career personnel who serve as part of the permanent institutional presidency. The extent of the institutional presidency would have been unimaginable two hundred years ago, or even sixty years ago.

By the 1990s, the White House Office (WHO, or the White House Staff), those persons performing the necessary day-to-day tasks of the personal president, had grown to almost 700 personnel from about 150 during the Franklin Roosevelt administration (45 full-time employees and 112 assigned from other agencies). Presidents Reagan and Bush, who had promised to reduce the size of the federal government bureaucracy, increased their own. In fact, during these administrations the number of full-time employees of the WHO increased dramatically over that of the Carter administration (which had reduced staff below Nixon and Ford administration levels). Meanwhile, the number of WHO staff temporarily assigned from outside agencies remained stable. (In fairness to Presidents Reagan and Bush, they simply followed a pattern of other Republican presidents, in increasing WHO staff when facing Democratically-controlled Congresses.) Like other recent presidential candidates, during the 1992 campaign Bill

Clinton promised to reduce the White House and Executive Office staffs, specifying a 25 percent reduction. Attainment of that target remains debatable because the effective size of the president's staff is affected by the use of personnel on loan from agencies.

The Executive Office of the President (EOP), created by Congress in 1939, is the formal management institution for the executive branch. The EOP is truly the embodiment of the institutional presidency. The EOP employs approximately two thousand people, if those assigned from non-EOP agencies are included. Among the agencies within the EOP are the Office of Management and Budget (OMB), the National Security Council (NSC), the Office of Science and Technology Policy, the Office of Special Representative for Trade Negotiations, the Council of Economic Advisers, and others. Presidents use these agencies in different ways. For example, President Reagan downplayed the Council of Economic Advisers while President Bush restored it to a prominent role. Two of these EOP offices have tended to be predominant: OMB and NSC. Under the Clinton administration, economic, trade, and environmental policy areas appear to be the growth areas for the EOP and for the Cabinet.

The Office of Management and Budget was created in 1970 in a reorganization in which it replaced the Bureau of the Budget. Congress had established the Bureau of the Budget in 1921, in recognizing an executive-centered budget process. OMB essentially is an extension of the bureau, and it has not disappointed advocates of executive-directed budgeting. OMB has been overtly in the service of the president and his administration, however, whereas the Bureau of the Budget was known for technical expertise and neutrality, serving the presidency rather than presidents. OMB is not only the central control agency determining the budgetary needs of all government agencies, but it is the president's policy clearinghouse for administrative agency proposals, which are to be submitted to Congress for budgetary appropriations, since agency budgets must receive "legislative clearance" by OMB.

The National Security Council was created in 1947 to help the president coordinate military and diplomatic policy. The NSC is composed of the president, vice-president, secretaries of Defense, State, and Treasury, the attorney general, and others invited, such as the president's national security adviser and the director of the Central Intelligence Agency. The NSC is a Cold War institution dedicated to systematic planning and preparation. It served initially to develop and implement the Containment Doctrine (a policy designed to limit the spread of communism) and the requirements for military actions and war. The NSC had the capacity not only to coordinate military and foreign policy but to coordinate these with domestic resource mobilization capabilities and policies. President Eisenhower used the NSC extensively, as did President Nixon, where it served as the advisory board for the national security adviser, Henry Kissinger. The NSC's value as a co-ordinating mechanism has been criticized. With the Nixon administration and the Reagan administration, the NSC gained increased operational responsibilities, but exposure of the Iran-*contra* scandal in the second Reagan administration weakened these roles. The Bush administration, seeking to avoid problems of an operational NSC, attempted to restore its advisory and coordinating role. For military policy, President Bush also relied directly on the Joint Chiefs of Staff and its chair, General Colin Powell. (President Clinton's troubles with the military early in his administration reflect in part the renewed importance military leaders felt they had received during the Bush administration and their concerns that it might wane under the Clinton administration.)

Just as presidents use their EOP agencies in different ways, so too they give more or less emphasis to their Cabinets. President Bush attempted to develop a strong, policymaking Cabinet, whereas his predecessor, President Reagan, did not. Some presidents place strong leaders and loyalists in the leadership positions of Cabinet departments (as secretaries and undersecretaries). Others parcel out Cabinet positions as a form of patronage, rewarding political allies and leaders of their party's coalitions. Most presidents develop their Cabinets with a combination of these approaches, placing potentially strong leaders and loyalists in departments that the president anticipates will be central to the administration's "mandate" and policy objectives and making patronage appointments to the leadership of departments expected to have less visibility. President Clinton, for example, signaled the importance of economic and budget policy with his appointment of Senator Lloyd Bentsen to head Treasury, Representative Leon Panetta to head OMB, and Harvard professor Robert Reich, a personal loyalist and prominent advocate of industrial policy, to head Labor. (Vice-president Albert Gore is also playing a lead role in the latter area.) Cabinet department status itself also symbolizes an area of importance in policymaking. Thus the Office of Veterans Affairs was elevated to Cabinet status in the Reagan administration, and President Clinton has promised to give a similar promotion to the Environmental Protection Agency. President Carter created a Department of Education in a reorganization and redesignation of the Department of Health and Human Services (formerly Health, Education, and Welfare), and President Reagan promised to dismantle it; he did not, and therein lies an indication of the importance of Cabinet status.

The U.S. Cabinet is unlike cabinets in parliamentary systems, however. Cabinets in parliamentary systems consist of the policymaking ministries that, with the prime minister, formulate government policy and collectively assume responsibility for the prime minister's policies. In the U.S. separation-of-powers system, with its contemporary tilt in the direction of presidential government, real policymaking often occurs within the EOP or with hybridized decision and policymaking venues consisting of presidential advisers, EOP offices and staff, and Cabinet departments. For example, most presidents use the OMB to coordinate and control Cabinet department (and other agency) policy and budget requests. And the NSC was created in partial recognition of the fact that Cabinet departments do not make coordinated government policy but tend to protect their own agendas and budgets—or turfs. Secretaries of departments (and their undersecretaries) cannot always control their permanent department staffs, which often have long-established policy mandates. When presidents rely on Cabinet officers and their assistants, it is individually, as advisers, confidants, and friends, not collectively. Congressional committees often have greater control and influence over Cabinet departments than do the secretaries. The committee members frequently use department staff to provide constituency and clientele services, and the departments are among the chief mechanisms for distributing pork-barrel legislation benefits. President Reagan's promise to dismantle the Department of Education could not be kept because, in part, the department (first funded in 1979) already had established strong clientele connections in Congress and among education interests and lobbyists. Likewise, President Clinton's promise to elevate the Environmental Protection Agency to Cabinet status no doubt reflects his desire to have its policy objectives and funding more permanently institutionalized within Congress (as well as his response to key election support from the environmental community).

PRESIDENTIAL-CONGRESSIONAL RELATIONS

Congress has attempted to regain some control over the presidency by revamping the budget process and creating its own Congressional Budget Office as a counterweight to the OMB, in its Budget and Impoundment Control Act (1974), and by requiring across-the-board budget cuts if spending ceilings are exceeded, in the so-called Gramm-Rudman-Hollings Act (1985), to name two examples. These acts provide Congress with reactive mechanisms, however, not constructive ones for confronting the president, and both actually have enhanced the power of the OMB. (Moreover, in the latter act, Congress avoided addressing constituent sources of expanding budgets by exempting key entitlement programs from mandatory reductions.)

A more consistent attempt by Congress to restrain the presidency has been made through the legislative veto. Like the efforts just cited, however, the legislative veto is an indirect way of acting; it is a way of stipulating, in statutes, that the executive branch can act in the future to accomplish some objective (specified in the statute) unless Congress disapproves or vetoes the action. The legislative veto came into use because Congress had mixed results in exercising power indirectly in two other ways: through the delegation of its legislative authority to the executive branch (discussed earlier in this section), and through the use of investigative oversight to constrain executive branch use of delegated authority. The legislative veto was ruled unconstitutional by the Supreme Court in 1983 (*INS* v. *Chadha*). The Court held that Congress must act through the "presentment" clause of the Constitution; that is, to stop an act of the executive branch, both houses must pass a bill and present it to the president for signature or veto. Congress had regularly invoked legislative vetoes since the 1930s, and at the time the Court ruled, there were more than two hundred legislative veto provisions in law.

Since the ruling, Congress has persisted in evading the Court's intent, using joint resolutions and joint legislative vetoes in efforts to limit the executive branch. (The Court technically invalidated one-house legislative vetoes.) But the effectiveness of Congress in these efforts ultimately turns on whether the standing president wants to play the game. Before and since the Supreme Court's ruling, there have been significant instances where presidents have simply ignored Congress. The so-called War Powers Resolution of 1973 is perhaps the outstanding example. The heart of the resolution is a legislative veto (to force the withdrawal of troops from abroad), but its stipulation hinged on acknowledging the president's power to commit military forces in the first place, and, with two or three exceptions, presidents have ignored a notification requirement in the resolution.

Congress

Compared with other parliamentary bodies, Congress is a formidable institution. Most parliaments serve as representative assemblies for the public or other constituents. Through extended debate, they offer advice and consent to the executive. (The term parliament derives from the French *parler:* to talk). But they do not actually make policy, or legislate, except in limited ways. In the British House of Commons, 97 percent of the government's bills are passed; members of the Commons have a twelve-day span in which they can introduce minor bills, and fewer to make motions and amend major bills. The French parliament is in session for less than half the year, and the constitution prohibits the National Assembly (lower house) from legislating on certain matters (for example, regulatory policy), while the prime minister and Cabinet can legislate by decree. In short, most parliaments are representative and decision legitimating, but not legislative, assemblies; they ratify bills sponsored by ministerial departments and the Cabinet (and support executive decrees), or they reject them (as in a vote of no-confidence).

The U.S. Congress, however, is a legislative body as well as a representative one. In keeping with the Constitution's separation of powers, which operates through checks and balances, Congress is extremely jealous of its legislative prerogatives vis-à-vis the president. This remains the case today, although, compared with the Congress Woodrow Wilson observed in the 1880s, Congresses have delegated to the executive branch many of their legislative responsibilities. Congress seldom pays the political price for its actions that parliamentary representatives in other nations must pay when they assume collective or party responsibility for accepting or rejecting the government's policies. It is no minor matter to bring about the collapse of a government and new elections in which parliamentary representatives may be voted out of office. Congressional majorities are seldom implicated in presidential transitions, partly because weak congressional parties absolve members from collective responsibility.

LEGISLATIVE POWERS

The statutory or legislative powers of Congress are both expressly delegated in Article I of the Constitution and implied there and through precedent and judicial decisions. The principal delegated powers concern revenues, expenditures, commerce, and defense (only two and one-half of the eighteen paragraphs in Article I deal with other subjects: naturalization, establishment of lower courts, and governance of the capital district). For a bill (a draft of proposed legislation) to become law, it must be passed by each house of Congress and approved by the president. If the House and Senate versions of a bill differ, they must be reconciled. To do this, a conference committee is convened. (A conference committee is usually composed of members from the standing committees of each house where the bill was originally proposed. The committee system is discussed below.) The conference committee reports its reconciliation, or compromise bill, to each house for floor approval. The bill then goes to the president, who can approve or veto it. A vetoed bill can be overridden and become law if two-thirds of each house vote to override. Most vetoes are sustained.

The Constitution also expressly grants certain constituent powers relating to the proposal of amendments and to Congress's internal rules and the eligibility of its members; presidential electoral powers to determine election dates and for the House of Representatives to act if the Electoral College vote fails to produce a president; enabling powers concerning the implementation of constitutional amendments (and specified therein); and, in the case of the Senate, the power to give advice and consent for certain executive appointments and treaties (including formal approval of treaties). In other respects, bicameralism, or the two-chamber Congress, works on a more or less coequal basis.

Implied powers of Congress derive from a variety of sources. Precedents and tradition have secured a wide array of powers. For example, top-level executive appointments require senatorial approval, and legislative investigations and oversight are implied for Congress to determine if the laws are "faithfully executed" by the president, particularly where Congress delegates its decision-making authority to the executive branch. These and judicial decisions have further extended congressional powers. For example, the power to regulate commerce "among" the states has ranged from a literal interpretation that *inter*state commerce is only that which is conducted between states to a broad twentieth-century interpretation that includes *intra*state, that is, within state, commerce. Also, the idea of what constitutes "commerce" has changed from goods in transit to production components and labor-management relationships. The most explicit source of congressional implied powers is, of course, the necessary and proper clause in Article I of the Constitution (also called the implied powers, or elastic clause), which Congress and the courts have interpreted to give wide latitude to an array of express powers—and some that were not expressly delegated in the first place. This last source of congressional power has affected, most notably, the constitutional provision for federalism and the regulatory powers of the national government, as is discussed later.

REPRESENTATION

The authority underlying the legislative powers of Congress derives from the principles of representative government. Representation is the core of republican government, according to James Madison's analysis in *The Federalist Papers,* and it is clearly central to the norms and ideals underlying the Declaration of Independence and the early rallying cry before the revolution: "No taxation without representation." Article I of the Constitution and the Fourteenth and Seventeenth amendments prescribe the selection process for representatives and senators, but the Constitution is silent on the issues of how the members of Congress are to carry out their powers of representation.

Whom do members of Congress represent, and how? The two issues are interrelated. To represent is to stand for or act on behalf of constituents and their interests. Members of Congress may identify with the voters of their geographic districts or with more specific groups within the districts: the voters who count in reelection campaigns, loyalists, advisers, friends. A constituency can also be defined as an inclusive interest for the district, or even the nation, or as a "special" interest, one that may happen to be the predominant one in the electoral district. Members of Congress represent the diverse constituents that make up their electorates while exercising their lawmaking responsibilities, while overseeing the executive branch, and, of course, while providing services to these constituents and educating them about public affairs.

Before the 1960s, state legislatures did not always reapportion House districts after the decennial census, and malapportionment (the overrepresentation of some electors and underrepresentation of others) was common. In 1964, the Supreme Court ruled that the principle of "one person, one vote" must be followed, and state legislatures have since been required to make electoral districts as equal in population as practicable. The Senate is excluded from this requirement, since the Constitution expressly designates senators as representatives of their corporate states, but most senators consider themselves to be representatives of the people of their states, not representatives of states as corporate bodies. (The Supreme Court has also applied the one-person, one-vote principle to state and local legislative bodies, including the upper chambers, or senates, of state legislatures, even where state constitutions attempt to formulate a "federal" model combining population and geography for their upper houses.)

When redrawing electoral districts, state legislatures meet the letter of the "one person, one vote" requirement, but not always its spirit. House districts (and state and local legislative districts) are frequently gerrymandered, that is, their boundaries are manipulated to give an advantage to some groups or partisans and a disadvantage to others. The Supreme Court ruled, in 1960 (*Gomillion* v. *Lightfoot*), that a racial gerrymander is unconstitutional because it denies one the equal protection of the laws by attempting to weaken or exclude voters from political representation based on race, and Congress, in the Voting Rights Act of 1965, reinforced the Court ruling. The Court, however, has qualified the extent to which a political gerrymander—one designed to give advantage to one political party and disadvantage to another—may be unconstitutional. As long as such a politically inspired gerrymander, taken "as a whole," does not frustrate the "will of the majority" or deny political minorities a "fair chance to influence the political process," it passes constitutional scrutiny (*Davis* v. *Bandemer,* 1986). Thus with each decennial census, state and local legislative bodies redraw electoral district boundaries in such ways as to maintain equal populations and not (overtly) discriminate based on race, but also to give advantage to the majority political parties within the legislatures.

How members of Congress represent their constituents also varies, partly as a function of whom they think they represent, partly as a function of self-identified roles or styles, and chiefly as circumstances shape their alternatives. In principle, a member of Congress can choose a role or style of representation from among two models: the representative as instructed agent or the representative as trustee. (Edmund Burke, the eighteenth-century British writer and member of Parliament, defended the latter when he observed that a representative owes constituents "his judgment" and fails them if judgment is sacrificed to slavishly following constituents' opinions.) In practice, the representative's role is less a matter of choice than a matter of circumstances and the context in which the member operates. The bicameral distinction between House and Senate is one such factor: When the Constitution was framed, *The Federalist Papers* authors expected the House of Representatives to be the more radical or liberal of the two houses because it was to be directly elected by the people, who may not restrain themselves and may support, for example, policies to redistribute wealth, whereas senators would be selected by state legislatures and would be more apt to deliberate as trustees in representing the corporate interests of the states. (This is not unlike the contemporary practice of Germany, where members of the Bundesrat, or upper house, are selected by the executive branches of the states, or *länder.*) The expectations of *The Federalist Papers* have not been realized. After passage of the Seventeenth Amendment to the Constitution in 1913, senators have been elected by the voters of the states, in statewide electoral districts. They more easily identify with the voters than with the state as a corporate body, but in doing so, they have tended to be less provincial than their House counterparts, although this is a function also of other aspects of bicameralism.

Two-year terms tend to keep House members more closely attuned to events within their districts and provide incentive for them to represent and benefit dominant interests in the district, whereas six-year terms of senators give them more autonomy to act, or claim to act, as trustees by representing interests with statewide or even national organizations. To act as an agent reinforces the idea that the representative is attuned to constituents' interests, whereas to act as trustee suggests one is not beholden to special interests but acts on behalf of the public interest. Some members appear to play either role as circumstances and personal orientation dictate. Particularly in the House, members develop their own "home styles" according to the needs and interests that prevail in their districts. Also, the likelihood of regular electoral challenge keeps some more attuned to constituent needs as their agents, whereas relatively safe seats permit others greater freedom to act as trustees. Over the past two decades, the number of marginal or competitive congressional seats has declined. This should give members of Congress, collectively, greater job security and therefore greater autonomy to play the role of trustees, but, individually, they tend to constituent concerns as though constantly "running scared" of facing a costly campaign against a challenger in the next election.

THE ORGANIZATION OF CONGRESS

Congress is organized around political parties and the committee system. An increasingly important component of organization is the staff system for committees and individual members of Congress. Also, there are a number of informal caucuses—the Democratic Study Group, the Black Caucus, the Woman's Caucus, and other caucuses and alliances organized around regional or economic interests. Finally, the norm of seniority still has a role, in weakened form.

The presiding officer of the House of Representatives is the Speaker of the House. The Speaker is the acknowledged leader of the majority party, nominated by it and formally elected by the full House. The presiding officer of the Senate is the vice-president, who has no real institutional role, but who can cast the tie-breaking vote on floor votes. Thus the vice-president rarely attends (presiding on projected close votes in which the president has a stake and a tie-breaking vote may be needed), and the president pro tempore, a senior member of the majority party, presides.

At the beginning of each congressional session, in each house the parties meet as caucuses and elect floor leaders: majority and minority leaders and whips. (The Senate majority leader is the party-leader counterpart to the Speaker of the House.) When the congressional parties take positions on key legislation (frequently with or against the president), the floor leaders attempt to mobilize their respective partisans to support the leadership's position. The single best predictor of a vote by a member of Congress is the member's party affiliation, but compared with other parliamentary systems, collective party responsibility, or discipline, is low. It is also low in historical terms. Party voting increased in the 1980s, compared with the two preceding decades, but remains in decline compared with the late nineteenth and early twentieth centuries (in the era of congressional, not presidential, government). Generally, party leaders can succeed in getting partisan support on floor votes when the leadership is committed and active and the issues are procedural and have low visibility. But when substantive issues are at stake, when they have great visibility, and when there is mobilized constituency or interest-group pressure, party responsibility weakens and party voting declines. Party leaders have few tangible incentives with which to ensure collective party discipline or responsibility.

The committee system does most of the substantive work of Congress. The House has 22 standing (that is, permanent) committees, which in turn have 138 subcommittees; the Senate, 16 standing committees and 86 subcommittees. On average, House members have two committee and four subcommittee assignments; senators, three and seven, respectively. Membership on congressional committees is roughly in proportion to party membership in each house. The party leadership makes committee assignments based on seniority, membership preference, and the like, with the final assignment ratified by the party caucus. Both senators and representatives seek particular committee assignments to further their reelection chances, to make good public policy, and to exert power in Congress—and in roughly that order of preference. Some House committees—Appropriations, Budget, Rules, and Ways and Means—exercise significant power within the chamber, and senior members from safe seats tend to gravitate to them. Other committees in the House and Senate deal with broad policy matters and with constituency services and benefits, the latter significant for reelection.

Committee leadership is based chiefly on seniority, a long-standing tradition in both the House and the Senate. Seniority was introduced in the House early in the twentieth century as a more or less neutral rule for making committee assignments and selecting chairs (previously the Speaker had made such decisions), since only time in rank, not political favoritism, is the criterion of decision. By the 1960s, it was apparent that the rule was not so neutral, since it favored congressional leaders from relatively safe seats —that is, conservative, usually older, Democratic members from the South. Formally, seniority as a rule for rank in committees ended in 1975; informally, it remains the basis for assignments and rank, although occasionally the party caucuses reassign committee personnel and leaders (House Democrats removed nine committee or subcommittee chairs from 1975 to 1990).

For the most part, standing committees are functional units that correspond to executive branch bureaucracies and clientele interests, and they serve as "little legislatures." When bills are introduced in their respective chambers, they are assigned to standing committees, usually based on the type of bill and function of the committee. Most bills do not survive committee scrutiny; typically, about 90 to 95 percent of the more than 8000 bills introduced annually die in committee, and about 175 may be passed into law. Important bills are generally divided and assigned to the committee's subcommittees, where hearings are held and testimony is taken (from experts and lobbyists) and the bill sections are "marked up" (revised and rewritten). The bill or its sections are reported back to the full committee, which can also hold hearings, accept the subcommittee recommendation, reject it, or table the bill. Most bills reported out of committee for floor action are passed by the full chambers. When a committee reports a bill to the floor, its leadership has usually determined that the bill has a reasonable chance of passage. Between committee and floor, the committee sponsors and likely floor managers of significant bills try to have them considered by their political party's leadership (the steering and policy committees) for support. In the House, major bills (routine, noncontroversial ones excepted) go before the Rules Committee where special floor debate, amendment, and voting rules are considered. (The House Rules Committee is the closest approximation to a sponsoring British Cabinet ministry, inasmuch as this committee determines whether amendments can be allowed from the floor.) In the Senate, a "unanimous consent" agreement is necessary to limit debate. If this cannot be achieved, a form of unlimited debate, known as a filibuster, can occur. Members opposed to a bill use it as a delaying tactic to extract concessions from the bill's sponsors. Filibuster can be curtailed with a "cloture" vote (requiring three-fifths of the members).

Throughout this process, members of Congress rely on staff support. Committees of both houses average over fifty staff assistants (since 1980, House and Senate committee staffs grew by approximately 50 and 25 percent, respectively). House and Senate members also have staff assigned to their offices (additional aspects of their roles are discussed later). Staffers research issues, generate reports, organize and help run hearings, serve as liaison with constituents, interest groups, and executive branch committees, and so on. Staff support gives the committees and members greater independence from the executive branch, which otherwise could control information, and more ability to place issues on the national agenda independently of the president or the political parties.

THE INSTITUTIONALIZATION OF CONGRESS

The public generally does not hold Congress in high regard for its legislative activities. Regularly published polls register greater public disfavor with Congress than with virtually any other public or corporate institution. Recent public criticism has been directed at Congress's perquisites ("perks"), the compromising effects of PAC contributions (epitomized by the "Keating Five" in the Senate), a so-called banking scandal in the House, and the exemptions Congress gives itself from adherence to norms and laws of decency (for example, sexual harassment allegations raised in Senate Judiciary Committee hearings for the Supreme Court nomination of Clarence Thomas and similar allegations against Senator Robert Packwood have brought the Senate "old boy" system under hostile scrutiny). In reaction to these and other problems associated with Congress, term-limitation referendums were placed on state ballots in the 1990 and 1992 elections. In 1990, one state ballot proposal limiting congressional terms was approved (two others limiting state legislative terms were approved); in 1992, fourteen of fourteen state ballot proposals limiting congressional terms were approved. (Those same states returned to Congress 93 percent of the incumbents standing for reelection!)

Notwithstanding the public's disdain for Congress as an institution, individual members of Congress seem to be held in high regard by their most important public—their voters. House incumbents regularly win reelection at a 90 percent or better success rate, and Senate incumbents win reelection 75 to 80 percent of the time. (Since 1950, there have been only three elections in which less than 90 percent of House incumbents were victorious. In the same period, victories by Senate incumbents fell below 70 percent in only five elections.) The margin of victory for incumbents declined in 1990, however, and many pundits had expected the 1992 election to be an exception to the incumbency success norm, but it was not. Only 7 percent of the incumbents lost general election races (a 93 percent incumbency success rate); another 4 percent lost primary races, and 12 percent resigned rather than stand for reelection. A few retirements and defeats were affected by the House banking scandal. And some of the retirees took advantage of the last opportunity to convert excess campaign contributions to personal holdings on retirement—a campaign finance loophole that further eroded congressional credibility.

This phenomenon of public disfavor with the institution juxtaposed to voter support for incumbents is not lost on members of Congress. Most of their activities consist of representing the interests of their elective and interest-group constituents, which, of course, serve to reinforce ties between the incumbents and these constituents. Members of Congress attempt to reinforce these ties by promoting pork-barrel legislation (legislation that only incidentally serves a national or collective interest but principally serves constituents' economic interests). They reinforce them also when they act specifically on behalf of constituents by performing constituent services, meeting with constituent groups in "public education" or information venues, and undertaking casework and intervention with administrative agencies on behalf of constituents. The cumulative benefits of these activities produce an incumbency effect that is more significant than the redistricting advantages of gerrymandering in explaining the high rate of reelection success by incumbents.

Further, members of Congress enhance their constituency representation abilities by maintaining certain perks that clearly give advantages to incumbents. The franking privilege allows members of Congress to mail news items, opinion surveys, and the like (4 million items daily). The purpose of the surveys is chiefly to remind voters of the representative's activities, not to solicit voters' views to inform the representative. Congressional travel budgets coupled with schedules that provide light legislative agendas on Mondays and Fridays permit members to travel to their home districts and meet with constituents. Aside from the legislative support noted previously, funding for expanded congressional staffs enables House members in particular to assign personnel to handle constituency service and representation activities. Approximately one-third of a senator's staff personnel, and 40 percent of a representative's, work outside Washington in the member's home district to enhance his or her capacity to represent and serve constituents. (Since 1980, Senate members' staffs, averaging thirty personnel, but ranging from fifteen to seventy depending on the size of the state, remained constant; House members' staffs, now averaging fifteen personnel, grew by about 21 percent.)

Finally, visible and successful incumbents breed increased financial support for their campaigns. Political action committees are a major source of the money spent in congressional election campaigns, and PACs clearly prefer incumbents to challengers, as we saw in chapter 1. Although Congress failed to consider serious campaign finance reform for itself in the 1970s and 1980s, with the advent of the Clinton administration it began work on reform that could affect congressional elections.

Incumbency advantages—pork, popularity, perks, and PACs—are not necessarily the causal factors in explaining incumbency successes in reelections. Incumbents probably won their first elections because they campaigned successfully as the more credible candidates, and in subsequent elections, opposition parties often have difficulty finding credible challengers. Also, it is likely that incumbents in general do good jobs as representatives. Although most members of Congress do not take systematic, scientific polls, where polling data exists, it seems that voting records of congressional representatives are consistent with district and national opinions approximately two-thirds of the time. Representing constituents and interest groups is also more politically advantageous than undertaking the responsibilities (and risks) of legislating and governing. The former permits members of Congress to ask constituents what they want and how the members can help them. The latter requires members of Congress to take votes on matters that regulate and coerce, that say, in effect, "do this, don't do that" rather than pose the representational question, "what can I do for you today?" Consequently, it is understandable that Congress finds delegation of its authority to executive branch administrative bodies more politically palatable than exercising collective responsibility through its legislative enactments.

Nevertheless, the public's generally negative evaluation of Congress the institution persists largely as a result of the legislative failings of Congress or its failure to exercise collective responsibility. Perhaps the twentieth-century Congress has reached this state of affairs because of factors over which it no longer can have any real control. Congress's inability to develop and maintain collective responsibility (as opposed to individual members' representing their constituents) has been reinforced by the decline of political parties and party discipline in the Congress and elsewhere—a phenomenon traceable to turn-of-the-century progressive reforms, which emphasize individual candidate behavior rather than party discipline, and which entered Congress when the power of the Speaker of the House was weakened and replaced with the nonpartisan seniority rule. Also, the emergence of the United States as one of the world's superpowers necessarily gave the president increased responsibilities as well as public visibility. Finally, the complexities of legislation in the era of the modern, positive state make it virtually impossible for Congress to develop statutes with clear, unambiguous intent and specific means to implement the objectives, but instead encourage its habit of delegating legislative responsibilities to the executive branch. Once formed, the habit is hard to break.

Policymaking and Implementation: The Administrative State

Max Weber, the famous German sociologist, identified several characteristics of bureaucracy that can be summarized under the headings functional specialization (or division of labor), chain of command (hierarchy of authority), and generalizable rules based on clear standards to minimize individual discretion. As many critics and pundits note, the word bureaucracy derives from the French *bureau,* or woolen desk cover, and the Greek *kratios,* for rule by, to produce "rule by desk tops"—which underscores the idea of the faceless, humorless, and impersonal bureaucrat.

ORIGINS OF THE ADMINISTRATIVE STATE

In the United States today, bureaucracy exists at the intersection of the legislative and executive branches. Bureaucracies make and implement public policy, sometimes in conjunction with the other branches, sometimes autonomously. The rise of the administrative state has coincided with the emergence of presidential government. In terms of its functions, however, it is more accurate to refer to bureaucracy as a fourth branch of government than to locate it within the executive branch. The emergence of this fourth branch began late in the nineteenth century.

First, the roles of the professional civil service and public administration received increased attention with Progressive era reforms that attempted to reduce both political influence over staffing and congressional influence over the implementation functions of the executive branch. The Civil Service or Pendleton Act of 1883, passed in part in response to the assassination of President Garfield by a disgruntled office seeker (who was not "patronized" by the president), established the Civil Service Commission and began the process of replacing political patronage with merit-system qualifications for staffing middle and lower levels of the federal bureaucracy. Further, political reformers, such as Woodrow Wilson, who had criticized government by congressional committee, supported attempts to increase the roles of trained experts and of modern business management techniques. Advocates of public administration combined Weber's insights with those of the management specialist Frederick W. Taylor to promote the role of the expert over the generalist, the administrator over the politician.

Second, policy formulation and implementation became increasingly complex, not only in the areas of foreign and military policy, but also in domestic policy areas. Regulation of business and labor practices, market fluctuations, and public health and consumer safety increased in several waves. By the end of the nineteenth century, small business and agricultural entrepreneurs and free-market economics were being displaced by large corporations and corporate dominated markets that affected the entire society. Nineteenth-century populist movements and early twentieth-century muckraking journalism helped inspire legislation to regulate trusts and monopolies, utilities, foodstuffs and medications, and with the collapse of the economy in the Great Depression, the national government began systematically to regulate the economy and underwrite social security during the New Deal. These programs and additional consumer and environmental protection regulations were greatly expanded in President Lyndon Johnson's Great Society and in the 1970s. And from the late 1970s onward, there have been increased efforts to reallocate public standards to the market, or to "deregulate." With each new phase of regulations and protections, new bureaucracies have been created, or new missions assigned to existing departments. As the role of the positive, interventionist administrative state has grown, Congress has deferred to the executive branch departments and agencies for the formulation of policies and programs, retaining its power as a representative body to check executive actions.

Third, with the growth of the administrative state has come the growth of entitlements and public expectations. A useful tool for economic regulation is fiscal policy: Government expenditures and purchases of goods and services can stimulate the economy; reductions of these can slow it down. Likewise, income tax reductions can be stimulative; tax increases can slow down an inflationary economy. Once initiated as programs with targeted beneficiaries, however, expenditures are difficult to retract; beneficiaries expect these as entitlements. And tax cuts that may require deficit spending are popular, but citizens generally oppose tax increases to erase deficits, to stabilize an inflationary economy, or to pay for the programs they want. Moreover, regulatory programs that promote economic growth or that protect industries and sectors of the economy frequently develop clientele that, understandably, lobby Congress and the president to sustain or even increase the program and its budget. The objectives of interest groups and government programs thus frequently become indistinguishable.

Had Progressive era reformers, who wanted to reduce the influence of politics and special interests in the formation and implementation of the public interest, anticipated that their goals would require the installation, development, and growth of the modern bureaucracy, one wonders if they would have been so optimistic. Ronald Reagan's quip that "government is like a big baby—an alimentary canal with a big appetite at one end and no responsibility at the other"—evokes a bureaucratic image. And when Americans complain of big government, most have bureaucracy in mind (even mislabeling Congress a bureaucracy—which aspects of it are—by confusing unresponsiveness and bureaucracy). Most bureaucrats, of course, are not administrators or clerks but trained legal, scientific, or technical experts, and most do not see themselves as wastefully consuming taxpayers' dollars but believe their missions are in the public interest.

BUREAUCRATIC STRUCTURE AND FUNCTIONS

The executive branch of the national government in 1991 employed about 3.1 million civilian and slightly fewer than 2 million uniformed military personnel. Approximately 98 percent of the national government's civilian workforce—the "federal service"—is employed in the executive branch. The legislative branch employs 37,500 personnel (1.3 percent); the judiciary, 21,500 (.7 percent). Although the federal service continues to grow in absolute terms, in relative terms the rate of growth lags behind both private-sector employment and state and local government employment, where so many federal functions are implemented and where, since the late 1970s, state and local governments perform former federal services. To put this in perspective, there are approximately 4.2 million state and 10.2 million local government employees.

It is a common mistake to think most federal employees in the executive branch are directly subordinate to the president in a hierarchical structure. Most federal service employees are covered by some form of civil service merit system. The Civil Service Commission was replaced in 1978 with three boards to administer testing, recruitment, and labor relations. One of these, the Office of Personnel Management, administers the civil service system for most departments, although such specialized ones as the Public Health Service, National Aeronautics and Space Administration, and others have their own civil service rules and procedures. Certain upper-level policymaking positions are covered by the Senior Executive Service, also established in 1978, to foster a senior civil service somewhat similar to the British model, although tenure is subject to political and policy changes that occur with changes in presidential administrations. Finally, there are the top political appointments—department heads and undersecretaries and assistant secretaries. Thus only a very small fraction of executive branch employees can be hired and terminated by the president—some of the Senior Executives and, of course, the top political appointees. Presidential patronage does not loom large as a source of control over the federal service bureaucracy.

The simplest way to think of the federal bureaucracy is in terms of formal structure (division of labor and hierarchy of authority) and the legal standing of the various bureaus. There are the Cabinet departments at the top of the hierarchy, followed by various executive branch commissions and agencies (for examples, Environmental Protection Agency, National Aeronautics and Space Administration), and government corporations (Tennessee Valley Authority, Pension Benefit Guaranty Corporation). Independent regulatory commissions and agencies do not fit within the hierarchy of authority (Federal Trade Commission, Consumer Product Safety Commission). The job tenure and reporting activities of regulatory commissioners are independent of the president, although initial appointments are made by presidents with Senate concurrence. Finally, executive branch agencies can bid work to "contract bureaucracies" (for example, the Department of Defense solicits bids from contractors to design, develop, and produce weapons systems) or assign federal functions to "third-party governments" (for example, the Department of Housing and Urban Development contracts with local authorities and nonprofit agencies to provide subsidized housing for low-income persons).

The most accurate way to think of the federal bureaucracy, however, is to look beyond formal organization and examine the functions that departments, agencies, and commissions perform. These functions vary with the type of bureaucracy, its mission, and the interests affected by its activities (these interests can include the congressional oversight committees and counterpart agencies or personnel elsewhere in the executive branch).

Some bureaucracies provide public goods or services whose benefits are available to the general citizenry and whose costs are borne (usually) by the general citizenry. Chief among these are the departments of Defense, State, Justice, and Treasury. The implementation of their principal objectives does not, in and of itself, differentially affect citizens, although aspects of their activities may overlap with other bureaucratic functions, noted below, as they promote or regulate particular interests or redistribute benefits from one group to another.

Other bureaucracies promote particular interests with benefits that are not available to the general citizenry. Promotional activities include providing services or fostering the well-being of interest groups or sectors of the economy. Promotional bureaucracies are chiefly Cabinet departments and various executive agencies and government corporations created to "foster, promote, and develop" (in the words creating the original Department of Commerce and Labor) domestic economic and social programs. Frequently, program administrators develop clientele relationships with their constituent groups and with congressional oversight subcommittees in mutually supportive relationships. These provide functional representation in decision making for interests that otherwise may not be represented in legislative floor debate or within the presidency.

A common thread for promotional activities is that the benefits accrue to a narrow segment of society, typically interest groups and businesses, while the costs are borne by a broader segment, typically consumers, who pay higher prices, or taxpayers in general. Promotional activities are not always publicized as such. They can be subtle and couched in language promoting the public interest, as when they are provided through regulatory commissions. All regulations are not necessarily perceived negatively by the regulated; some are requested and supported by them. For example, the old Interstate Commerce Commission was created (in 1887) partly because farmers wanted the benefits of regulated railroad rates. In short order, the

ICC was protecting railroads from competition, and this function was transferred to the trucking industry as it emerged as an alternative to railroad shipping. Similarly, the old Civil Aeronautics Board set rates and routes for airlines. When the Carter administration proposed to deregulate the functions of the ICC and the CAB, the strongest opponents were truckers and airlines (the commissions were terminated in 1990 and 1984, respectively). And the Federal Communications Commission exists to limit access to the airwaves, thus limiting competition.

The more conventional view of regulatory functions and policies is that they benefit relatively broad segments of the population while imposing costs on relatively narrow segments. To regulate, regulatory commissions and agencies engage in adjudication and rule making. Adjudication is a case-by-case approach to gain compliance with some legislative or administrative rule. Rule making permits the commission or agency to legislate for a particular sector of the economy or for a particular classification of business. Also, regulatory agencies gain compliance with regulations through consent decrees, in which the subject of regulation agrees to meet certain agency requirements (usually in exchange for a lesser restriction than adjudication may produce). For example, the Consumer Product Safety Commission enforces consumer protection and public safety regulations and the Environmental Protection Agency enforces environmental and public health standards, at cost to the offending interests. Because the costs of compliance are usually borne by businesses (and some labor unions indirectly), such regulations as these are often criticized as being antibusiness and adding to the costs of business.

Finally, bureaucracies can engage in redistributive activities. For example, both the Treasury Department and the Federal Reserve Board engage in regulatory activities that are also redistributive. Both fiscal policy (Treasury) and monetary policy (the Fed) shift income from some groups to others in ways that can either be progressive or regressive but that are hardly ever neutral.

BUREAUCRACY AND DEMOCRACY?

Implementation of public policy is no simple government activity. It is not merely a matter of ensuring that the laws are "faithfully executed." (To implement policy generally means to carry out, execute, enforce.) What if the law is vague? Or requires the implementing agency to write rules for compliance or enforcement? Or even make the policy? To what extent is enforcement to be implemented? To the strict letter of the law or policy? To a reasonable extent with the administrator's discretion to be exercised on a case-by-case basis?

Bureaucracies frequently receive vague or unclear missions or objectives when Congress passes their enabling or authorizing legislation. In some instances, the legislative charge to the agency amounts to a statement of goodwill. For example, what does it mean for the Federal Trade Commission to follow the "rule of reason" or for the Interstate Commerce Commission to set "reasonable rates" or for the National Labor Relations Board to enforce "fair standards" in labor negotiations—and all these agencies to act "in the public interest"? When the mandate or mission is vague, conflicting or unclear policies, rules, and regulations are predictable. The exercise of administrative discretion inevitably follows, whether in rule making or in enforcing existing rules. This in turn lends support to critics of bureaucracy who claim it is out of control, although such claims often are made by those who oppose an agency's mission. President Reagan's Grace Commission was established to find waste in government, and, by its own standards, it found much, though few cost-saving measures were implemented. President Bush's Competitiveness Council was established to review the cost effectiveness of business regulations—usually consumer or environmental protection regulations that required businesses to absorb the costs of protection rather than externalize them. And President Clinton's "Reinventing Government" task force (National Performance Review), chaired by Vice-President Gore, proposes improved service delivery with greater efficiency.

Occasionally, there is criticism that regulatory agencies become "captured" by the firms or sectors they are supposed to regulate; that is, that regulatory objectives are subordinated to special-interest objectives. In such instances, the mission of providing benefits for a broad segment of society may remain, but the bureaucracy's principal mission becomes one of providing benefits for an interest group or sector of the economy. This can occur when the bureaucracy's mission is vague or incorporates conflicting priorities in the first place. For example, the Atomic Energy Commission was charged to promote the development and use of nuclear energy in generating electricity (part of the Eisenhower administration's "atoms for peace" campaign) and to regulate nuclear energy. The AEC subordinated the latter objective to the former, became a government booster of nuclear energy, and was "captured" by the utilities, nuclear equipment producers, and construction companies that were developing nuclear energy plants. Other agencies that resist capture may be undercut when they encounter conflicting political priorities. A good illustration is the saga of the Federal Trade Commission in its attempts to regulate tobacco companies. Until the mid-1960s, the FTC regulated tobacco companies on a case-by-case basis, seeking limits to advertising claims before administrative law tribunals. Then it attempted to establish rules to regulate the cigarette industry. The FTC's rule-making capacity was short lived, as the tobacco iron triangle mobilized congressional support to restrict the FTC. Congress again restricted the FTC when, in the late 1970s and early 1980s, it attempted to expand its consumer protection activities under a Carter administration appointed chair, and business interests mobilized congressional support to restrict rule making and enforcement actions that appeared to be antibusiness.

Since the advent of the Carter administration, every presidency has signaled its intent to get bureaucracy under control through cost containment, administrative reform, rational budgeting (the adjective does not necessarily create an oxymoron), strict application of benefit-cost analysis to regulations, reduction of duplication and red tape, deregulation and privatization, and so on. The bureaucracy is a favorite target of politicians and the public. When the public is polled and its scorn for bureaucracy is elicited, however, the pollsters also find public support for the programs the bureaucracy provides. And when presidents and other politicians propose to cut bureaucratic waste and unnecessary, costly regulations, they are selective about their targets. There has been a tendency, for example, for recent Republican presidential administrations to target agencies whose regulations impose costs on business activities but not agencies whose regulations protect or promote business activities (the Reagan era Grace Commission, and the Bush Competitiveness Council). The last two Democratic administrations (Carter, Clinton) have attempted the opposite. Yet when presidents and Congresses agree, even agencies that promote and subsidize businesses can go the way of the dinosaur (the CAB under airline deregulation). Underlying the particular political agendas of elected officials is the broader problem of how to reconcile bureaucracy with democracy.

The great reliance on bureaucracy in a democracy underscores the problem of the relationship between expertise and accountability, or better, the *conflict* between expertise and accountability. Is it possible to keep the politics out of policy (for example, to have experts overrule pork-barrel projects), or is it desirable to keep democratic accountability out of policy? And if democratic accountability means doing what satisfies the test of the next reelection cycle, short-term planning and superficial but newsworthy events may supersede the judgment of those who look beyond the election cycle and may not be responsive to the public's longer-term needs. A bureaucracy's commitment to a long-range mission may be more "representative" of the public and may better serve the public interest than the actions of elected officials. Attempts to delay use of the automobile airbag speak volumes about the shortsightedness of politicians and the common sense of bureaucratic safety experts. On the other hand, promotion of electricity generated by nuclear energy with behemoth facilities and faith in future technology to handle wastes speak volumes about bureaucratic tunnel vision and capture by special interests, and volumes about the common sense of citizen movements and elected officials. At this level, at least, it is possible to recognize a need for balance between expertise and politics.

The Judiciary

The U.S. judiciary is more visible, has greater prestige, and wields more power with respect to the interpretation, application, and legality of public policy than its counterparts in most of the modern nations of the world. (One measure of its visibility and prestige is that, on a per capita basis, the United States has three times the number of attorneys as Britain, and twenty times that of Japan.) Unlike the European tradition of the code-law system, which almost equates judging with technical administration of the law, the United States judicial system, like the British, is rooted in the common-law tradition, which relies on judicial interpretation and precedent. But the U.S. judiciary differs from the British in the ability of the former to nullify legislation, something the latter cannot do in the absence of a written constitution that is paramount to Parliament. This is known as the power of judicial review. The Supreme Court can exercise it to determine if state or national laws are constitutional, and it can void those laws, that is, declare them unconstitutional. The U.S. judiciary has taken upon itself the responsibility charged it by Chief Justice John Marshall when, in *Marbury v. Madison* (1803), the Court established the principle of judicial review: "It is emphatically the province and duty of the judicial department to say what the law is."

ORGANIZATION AND FUNCTIONS

The Constitution's provision for the "judicial Power," in Article III, is that it "shall be vested in one supreme Court, and in such inferior Courts as the Congress may from time to time ordain and establish." Like its stipulation of the executive power, discussed earlier, the Constitution is vague about what the judicial power involves. Presumably it means judging, but judging what with respect to what? Article III spells out certain types of jurisdiction, including all cases in law and equity arising under the Constitution and laws of the United States, and cases affecting public officials and the United States, the states, and citizens of states. It grants the Supreme Court original jurisdiction (that is, trial jurisdiction) in cases involving ambassadors and other public officials and those in which a state is a party; the Court has appellate jurisdiction in all other types of cases enumerated in Article III and "with such Exceptions, and under such Regulations as Congress shall make."

Judges everywhere settle disputes and apply the law. Dispute resolution by courts is based on law and fact. Disputes may involve civil law issues between individuals or between individuals and government about such matters as equity, enforcement of contracts, negligence (tort law); or disputes may involve criminal law issues in instances when government charges individuals with violating the law. ("Individuals" include groups and such organizations as corporations and unions.) The U.S. judicial system is an adversary system; that is, an individual or government must claim harm or injury for court action to be undertaken. U.S. courts also can change or modify public policy, and they can establish policy, which in effect means that the courts can make law. Both occur through the adversary system of dispute resolution; the judiciary does not provide "advisory" opinions or issue rulings about hypothetical or possible future situations.

Authority for judicial decisions derives from four sources: case law, statutory authority, administrative law, and the Constitution. Case law is judge-made law—for example, the common law in state jurisdictions, equity rulings, and judicial precedent. For the most part, case law is developed through application of the common-law precept of *stare decisis* (essentially, adherence to judicial precedent), although some courts and judges are criticized for legislating independently of established precedent or statutes. Statutory law is law made by legislatures. In the United States, with the emergence of a national economy and regulation of firms that operated in several states at once in the late nineteenth century, state legislatures began to codify common law (that is, transform it into statutory law), and the process continues. (There is no common law at the federal level.) As with the common-law tradition, judges rely on judicial precedents in interpreting and applying statutory law. Administrative law is similar to statutory law and has the same binding effect, but it is made by independent regulatory commissions and administrative law tribunals (delegated the authority to do so by Congress). These agencies can establish administrative law by either promulgating rules and regulations or adjudicating disputes about rules, and usually the court of original jurisdiction is an administrative tribunal. Constitutional law is based on the language and structure of the Constitution and its amendments, and on court interpretations of the Constitution and constitutional law. Theoretically, the Constitution is written by "the people," that is, it is the juridical embodiment of popular sovereignty; in practical terms, constitutional law is derived from judicial decisions, since ultimately the constitutional standing of administrative and statutory law depends on judicial interpretation.

The United States has a dual court system. This is a product of the constitutional provision for federalism and of the first judicial enabling legislation passed by Congress. The federal structure of government means that there is a national or federal court system, which deals with national law, and state court systems, which deal with state laws. In such a dual court system, state judiciaries are autonomous. Citizens have more contact with state courts (where about 95 million cases are filed each year) than with federal courts (where 300,000 cases are filed annually). In certain types of cases, however, state courts may be asked to rule on federal laws, and federal courts on state laws (as in fact happens today). How are such potential conflicts resolved? The Constitution itself is not clear. An implication of the Constitution's Article VI, which says the Constitution and its national laws "shall be the supreme Law of the Land" and "the Judges in every State shall be bound thereby," is that the decisions of state judiciaries can be reviewed by the Supreme Court.

FEDERAL COURT JURISDICTION

The first Congress established inferior courts and fleshed out the constitutional guidelines. In the Judiciary Act of 1789, it established three appeals courts and a district court in each state, and it delineated certain jurisdictional guidelines for the federal courts. Congress also expanded the scope of the Supreme Court's original jurisdiction in the thirteenth section of the act. And it laid the basis for the Supreme Court to exert binding appellate jurisdiction over the states. The twenty-fifth section of the Judiciary Act gave the Supreme Court appellate jurisdiction whenever a state court of last resort ruled against the constitutionality of a U.S. treaty or law, ruled in favor of a state act that a litigant challenged as being unconstitutional, or ruled against a litigant's claim for a constitutionally or federally sanctioned right or privilege. In other words, a state judicial assertion contrary to the Constitution could be appealed to the Supreme Court. Over the next three decades, Supreme Court rulings asserted the priority of the Constitution's supremacy clause. *McCulloch* v. *Maryland* (1819) proved to be the landmark case that affirmed both constitutional supremacy and the Court's authority to enforce it through its appellate jurisdiction over state acts. The *McCulloch* ruling applied the principle of judicial review—the determination if a law or governmental action is constitutional—to state acts. In fact, both the powers of statutory interpretation (judicial alteration, clarification, or modification of public policy) and of judicial review can be at issue in the federal judiciary's appellate jurisdiction over state courts and state actions. These are discussed below, after first considering the procedures and criteria used in judicial decision making.

The Supreme Court today exercises appellate jurisdiction over certain types of cases from state courts of last resort (usually named state supreme courts) and U.S. courts of appeal. For the U.S. or federal court system, there are eleven regional appellate courts plus one for the District of Columbia, which hears most appeals from the quasi-judicial hearings of regulatory agencies, and one for the "Federal Circuit," which hears principally cases involving patents, tariffs, and claims against the government. The twelve regional courts are appellate for the ninety state and District of Columbia district courts and five territorial district courts. (Congress increased district court judgeships from 400 to 649 judges between 1978 and 1990, largely in an attempt to increase efficiency in the administration of justice.) In a typical year, approximately 300,000 cases are filed in district courts and before administrative tribunals; 40,000 are filed for appellate review, with about 5000 of these being accepted for review by the courts of appeal. About 5000 cases are filed with the Supreme Court from both state supreme courts and federal appellate courts. Technically, these requests come to the Supreme Court as "writs" of *certiorari,* appeal, and *habeas corpus. Certiorari* is the most common route for obtaining Supreme Court review; it is discretionary and based on the agreement of four justices to review the case. Appeals are rare, involve direct state-federal conflicts, and are often "remanded" (referred) to a lower court for disposition. A writ of *habeas corpus* is available for convicted prisoners under state jurisdiction, and is rarest. The technical distinctions are important for lawyers and legal scholars; for students of government, the important distinctions involve criteria the Court uses to decide whether to hear a case and on what terms.

In a typical year, the Supreme Court will hear approximately 150 cases. The Court attempts to review cases that appear to be vehicles to confirm clearly, change, or establish judicial policy or law. It literally undertakes the administration of justice, since it must maintain its annual docket at a manageable level. If the Court is too free in granting review, its load becomes unmanageable; if too restrictive, significant constitutional issues may be decided by lower courts. (Since 1989, the Court has reduced its docket by nearly one-third.) Over the years, the Court has developed criteria it employs to screen cases, which lower courts employ also, and the Court appears to be responsive to certain external, not overtly "political" influences.

The courts require that the case be a real case or controversy. The case must be "ripe," that is, all other remedies must have been exhausted; the issue raised must be concrete, not abstract or hypothetical, and it must not be "moot," that is, the issue should not already have been resolved in another way. Litigants must have "standing" and the Court must have jurisdiction. For example, since 1948, the Supreme Court has refused to enforce racially restrictive covenants. The Court reasoned that the Fourteenth Amendment prohibits an agency of government from denying equal protection of the laws; therefore, courts lack jurisdiction over racially restrictive covenants, and one seeking their enforcement has no standing to sue (*Shelley* v. *Kraemer*). (Congress eventually responded to the Court's obvious message. The 1968 Civil Rights Act outlawed restrictive covenants.) The landmark case for judicial review, *Marbury* v. *Madison,* was resolved because the Court claimed it lacked jurisdiction.

Further, a case must be "justiciable," that is, a legal issue appropriate for a judiciary to decide; it cannot be a "political question," that is, a matter of policy appropriate for the "political" branches or state governments. Until the 1960s, electoral district reapportionment cases were claimed to be political and reserved to state legislatures under the Tenth Amendment (following the 1946 *Colegrove* v. *Green*). Then the Court discovered the relevance for representation of the equal protection clause of the Fourteenth Amendment, and such cases became justiciable (*Baker* v. *Carr,* 1962), with the Court subsequently requiring "one person, one vote" for both congressional and state legislative districts (*Wesberry* v. *Sanders,* 1964; *Reynolds* v. *Sims,* 1963). (The reapportionment cases illustrate also that state-federal conflicts should involve a "substantial" federal question.) Also, the Court is disinclined to review questions of war, claiming they are political and to be resolved between the president and Congress, as it did when the constitutionality of the draft and of the invasion of Cambodia were challenged during the undeclared war in Vietnam (*Massachusetts* v. *Laird,* 1970; *Holtzman* v. *Schlesinger,* 1973). On the other hand, not all separation-of-powers questions are avoided by designating them political. In 1974, the Court ruled that the president cannot claim an absolute right of executive privilege rooted in inherent powers, although there is a limited or conditional one (*United States* v. *Nixon*). (The Court ruled after President Nixon had resigned. It is interesting to speculate how it might have ruled had the issue arisen before the enervating effects of the Watergate scandal.) And in 1983, the Court declared unconstitutional the congressional legislative veto (*INS* v. *Chadha*).

The Supreme Court also appears to consider the likelihood of a case being so controversial that its ruling may be difficult to enforce. Unlike congressional control over monies and presidential control over enforcement agencies, Supreme Court justices have no tangible enforcement resources. They must rely on public acceptance, and on the willingness of the other federal branches and of state policymakers to support their rulings. They appear to consider the extent to which lower courts, especially state lower courts, have the ability to enforce decisions. Interest groups, which are not parties to suits but which have symbolic or other interests in their outcomes, recognize the Court's concern with public acceptability. Consequently, they may attempt to aid litigants and, in effect, to help the Court consider other consequences than those articulated in the litigants' respective briefs, by filing *amicus curiae* briefs. Such "friend of the court" briefs are designed to be informative briefs to aid the court's deliberations, although the friend of the court has no tangible interest in the case.

Finally, the Court also may be influenced by the role of the U.S. solicitor general—the chief practicing lawyer in the Justice Department. The solicitor general represents the government before the Supreme Court and screens cases to determine the government's position, whether to appeal for review by the Supreme Court, and the strategy in the government's brief and oral argument. Approximately one-half of the cases on the Court's docket are under the supervision of the solicitor general. In effect, the solicitor general provides a powerful "cue" to the Court as to the thinking of the executive branch and the enthusiasm it has for a particular outcome. Moreover, the solicitor general can enter a case with an *amicus curiae* brief. This also is a cue to the Court as to the executive branch position on the issue. For example, in an important affirmative action case that originated as a challenge to the constitutionality of affirmative action programs, President Carter's solicitor general filed an *amicus curiae* brief supporting the policy's constitutionality. The Court ruling turned on the statutory applicability of the program in the plaintiff's case, not on broad constitutional grounds (*Regents of the University of California v. Bakke,* 1978).

THE JUDICIARY'S ROLE IN ALTERING, MODIFYING, OR CREATING PUBLIC POLICY

As indicated previously, the common-law tradition of judicial interpretation and precedent virtually invites a policymaking role for judges. This role is enhanced with a Constitution that is the "supreme law of the land" and with a Court that thinks it is the final arbiter of constitutional matters—and that others think is the final arbiter. Judicial review means that the judiciary can modify existing public policy or establish new policy by declaring unconstitutional existing law or policy; in other words, it can make law. If the

Supreme Court can review acts of Congress, the president, and the states as to their constitutionality, then certainly it can engage also in statutory interpretation. Statutory interpretation means that the judiciary can alter or modify existing public policy by ruling about the meaning, scope, and applicability of existing policy and statutes without overturning them.

Although the Constitution is silent about judicial review and vague about the judicial power, there is ample evidence that the courts were expected to exercise judicial review. The notions of Sir Edward Coke, the seventeenth-century jurist, that the common law and Magna Carta embodied natural law and could be used to control acts of Parliament, remained fashionable in the colonies, though discounted in England. Alexander Hamilton enunciated a provisional doctrine of judicial review in *The Federalist Papers*. And the Supreme Court itself ruled, in 1796 (*Hylton* v. *United States*), that it had the authority to declare unconstitutional an act of Congress (although it found constitutional the one being litigated). In 1803, the Court established its authority, in *Marbury* v. *Madison,* when it invalidated section 13 of the Judiciary Act of 1789. Subsequently, as we have seen, it extended this authority to acts of state governments.

The exercise of judicial review has gone through three discernible periods in U.S. political history. First, for about the Court's first seventy-five years, or until the Civil War, it acted chiefly in the areas of governmental structure and the scope of governmental power. The Court, under Chief Justice John Marshall, confirmed principles of national supremacy, and then, under Chief Justice Roger B. Taney, adopted "dual federalism" (and reinvigorated states' rights). In both instances, the Court's rulings on commercial regulation and the scope of federalism served to promote economic growth. Second, from after the Civil War through approximately the middle of the New Deal, the scope of governmental power remained critical, but the Court became increasingly activist on behalf of business interests, finding an unexpected "substantive" due process or contract right in the Fourteenth Amendment, which it used to invalidate federal and state legislation regulating business. Third, since World War II, the Supreme Court has exercised judicial review chiefly in the areas of civil liberties and civil rights, with a discernible "presumption of constitutionality" being extended to congressional enactments concerning economic regulation.

The Court under Chief Justice Earl Warren, in the 1950s and 1960s, was highly active in areas of civil rights and liberties. Subsequently, reshaped by the appointments of conservative presidents, the Supreme Court has been claimed to be more attentive to literal legal interpretation than to expansive rulings by "activist" justices. And as the Court has retreated from some of the precedents established under the Warren Court, a movement known as the "new judicial federalism" has emerged wherein some state supreme courts have developed protections for rights (and created some new rights) under the frameworks of state constitutions. For example, where the U.S. Supreme Court has avoided the issue of educational resources in dealing with discriminatory public education (e.g., *San Antonio v. Rodriguez,* 1973), the Kentucky supreme court, in 1988, invalidated the property tax system of funding public schools because it failed the right-to-equal-education standard of the state constitution.

The political, policy-modifying, and policymaking roles of the judiciary are unavoidable. To a very real extent, the increasing scope of judicial responsibilities parallels the expansion of the administrative state in the policymaking and implementation nexus of Congress, president, and bureaucracy. While judicial review may not be as extensive as it could be, statutory interpretation is increasingly important. When agencies promulgate policies and regulations under the auspices of vague or general guidelines from Congress, litigation is not likely to challenge their constitutionality; the Court now takes for granted the constitutionality of Congress's power to delegate authority. Litigation instead is likely to challenge the applicability and scope of the agencies' rules and regulations, and to question if they follow the "intent" of Congress, evidence for which is found in the "legislative histories" of congressional debate. (Congressional debate is recorded. When resultant legislation is not exceedingly clear, regulatory agencies and courts have recourse to this record, which constitutes the legislative history.) Under these circumstances, federal courts are even more likely to be accused of legislating than in the past when, for example, the Warren Court elicited criticism of "judicial activism" and calls for "judicial self-restraint" and for the appointment of "strict constructionist" judges and justices who would adhere to the "original intent" of the Constitution's founders.

A discussion of the judiciary's role in making or changing public policy and law invariably requires consideration of the politics of court appointments. In the United States, federal court appointments have always been overtly political, with the president offering nominations to the Senate for its advice and consent, and each branch calculating the probabilities that the nominee will sustain or oppose their policy preferences. State court appointments, in contrast, vary with respect to the type of political decision making and degree of political influence that judicial selection involves. For twenty-three states, electoral politics determines judicial selection (with ten states using partisan and thirteen using nonpartisan elections). Only eleven states approach the U.S. model with either gubernatorial appointment (with some version of legislative approval) or legislative election. And sixteen states appoint judges through a form of merit plan. Likewise, other nations approach judicial appointments differently. For example, Germany screens potential judicial appointees through the Ministry of Justice, and the making of appointments is alternated between the two legislative branches.

In judicial appointments for the U.S. court system, the president plays the central role, and, notwithstanding high-flown rhetoric, he nominates candidates chiefly on the basis of political considerations. Even Chief Justice Marshall, sanctified by judicial historians as the "great" chief justice for his role in consolidating federal power, national unity, and the constitutionality of contract law and property rights, had marginal judicial qualifications. Although he had developed a reputation as a practicing attorney and advocate of the Constitution during ratification, his principal qualifications were his service as a loyal Federalist party activist and administrative appointee of President Adams, who nominated him to the Court. In recent years, there has been much criticism that presidents have used "litmus tests" for nominees to the federal courts, screening them based on whether they are pro-choice or pro-life, devoted to original intent, and so on.

The charge is not new; President Grant had to be assured that his appointees were prepared to reverse an earlier Court decision invalidating the Legal Tender Acts. And to pass presidential muster is not to be assured that there will be no senatorial litmus tests of political considerations. The Senate Judiciary Committee has been known to give overbearing "advice" and to refuse "consent," assuring that the president's nominee exits voluntarily or is defeated on the Senate floor (in recent decades, this has occurred once with President Johnson and twice with Presidents Nixon and Reagan). Presidents in all periods of our history have paid attention not only to the party affiliation of their prospective nominees but also to their political, economic, and social philosophies and views. Judges are inescapably political actors. They are appointed with partisan and policy considerations in mind, and they come to the bench with developed political, economic, social, and religious values. They are not necessarily ideologues in the fanatical or unbending sense, but they tend to have well-developed ideologies in the sense of a philosophy of social and political life and an understanding of the consequences of public policy and judicial decisions.

The System at Work

At times, the U.S. system seems to be an eighteenth-century anachronism, one given to "deadlock" between the executive and legislative branches, rather than capable of governing both democratically and effectively. These misgivings frequently are reinforced by an uncritical view of parliamentary democracies with their presumably strong, disciplined political parties. The apparent deadlock brought about by the separation of powers and compounded by weak political parties is further intensified when voters choose "divided" government, that is, choose to have one branch controlled by one party and the other branch controlled by the other party. In President Reagan's second term and President Bush's sole term, deadlock compounded by such partisan divisions was characterized as "gridlock."

A campaign theme of Democratic and Republican presidential candidates in 1992 was to end gridlock by unifying the branches under one party (the candidate's party preferred!). Divided government formally ended with the election of President Clinton, a Democrat, and the return of a Democratically controlled Congress. Gridlock perhaps ended, but checks and balances did not disappear. The legislative fortunes of President Clinton and the congressional Democrats ebbs and flows throughout his tenure in office. Early in his term, the House of Representatives overwhelmingly approved the president's economic stimulus and deficit-reduction proposals. The votes were almost purely party line votes—that is, 98 and 100 percent of the Republicans voted against the respective proposals and 91 and 96 percent of the Democrats voted for them. In the Senate, the proposals were promptly confronted by a Republican filibuster. The economic stimulus package was defeated and deficit-reduction proposals changed by a coalition of Republican and conservative Democratic senators. In both houses, party discipline among Democrats has increased compared with their behavior during the years of divided government, but not to the extent to ensure safe passage for all the president's proposals. The end of divided government gives the majority party greater incentives to maintain party discipline on key votes, but it does not necessarily lead to strengthened political parties that can impose majority rule on behalf of a president. Other, longer-term factors influence the relationships among president and Congress, as well as their relationships with the bureaucracy and the judiciary.

Consider the following example. In 1988, the secretary of Health and Human Services (HHS) in the Reagan administration interpreted family planning guidelines in Title X of the 1970 Public Health Service Act to disallow funding for postconception planning, specifically, for abortion counseling. The secretary was sued by Dr. Irving Rust and others, who asserted the HHS regulations were not authorized by Title X. The Supreme Court, in *Rust* v. *Sullivan* (1991), upheld the position of the executive branch, citing the "broad language" of Title X and its failure to define "family planning."

Members of Congress and abortion rights activists criticized the ruling. But in reality, none of the three branches is faultless, and the example illustrates the difficulty of achieving clear-cut standards in a separation-of-powers system. HHS acted as an agent of the president's political agenda; it appeared to go beyond the intent of the 1970 act, for which the ensuing eighteen years provided precedent. The Supreme Court legislated the content of Title X by finding on behalf of the president rather than overturning the broad legislative rules and forcing Congress to write legislation that would be constitutional. Congress, at least some members of Congress, understood the legislative intent of the 1970 act, but did not make it sufficiently clear and precise as to avoid the politically inspired interpretation by the executive branch. After the 1992 election, the Clinton administration rescinded the HHS policy with an executive order. Publicly funded abortion counseling remains subject to prevailing political and electoral winds, instead of being clearly established in explicit statutory law, and that result is not unusual with the separation of powers.

The U.S. political system—both the separation of powers and federalism—is a system that responds to but also creates conflicting political priorities. When conflicting political priorities exist, different units and levels of government assume conflicting or overlapping responsibilities. Conflicting responsibilities are evident when the Corps of Engineers proposes (or is asked to propose) a flood-control dam and confronts the Endangered Species Act and the Environmental Protection Agency. Overlapping and conflicting responsibilities occur when the Public Health Service, Consumer Product Safety Commission, and Federal Trade Commission, all at one time or another, have been involved in regulating or limiting tobacco smoking, while the Department of Agriculture has subsidized tobacco production. The Department of Health and Human Services food stamp program subsidizes low-income people, and Department of Agriculture price-support programs subsidize farmers and increase food costs. In the Department of Defense, the Army has an air force, and, of course, so does the Air Force.

Separation of powers and federalism were designed to limit power. In the late twentieth century, they clearly limit the systematic and consistent use of power. But it seems also, after two hundred years of trial and error, that the "living Constitution" has evolved into an instrument that permits power to grow—not unchecked, certainly, but seemingly haphazardly. As we examine other developed and evolving political systems, the comparative perspective will enable us better to evaluate the adequacy of the U.S. system.

SUGGESTIONS FOR ADDITIONAL READING

General

GREENBERG, EDWARD S., and BENJAMIN I. PAGE. *The Struggle for Democracy.* New York: HarperCollins, 1993.

LIPSITZ, LEWIS, and DAVID M. SPEAK. *American Democracy.* 3d ed. New York: St. Martin's Press, 1993.

LOWI, THEODORE J., and BENJAMIN GINSBERG. *American Government: Freedom and Power.* 2d ed. New York: Norton, 1992.

The Constitution

HAMILTON, ALEXANDER, JAMES MADISON, and JOHN JAY. *The Federalist Papers.* Any edition.

ROBINSON, DONALD L. *Government for the Third American Century.* Boulder, Colo.: Westview Press, 1989.

WOOD, GORDON S. *The Creation of the American Republic, 1776–1787.* New York: Norton, 1972.

Social Forces

HACKER, ANDREW. *Two Nations: Black and White, Separate, Hostile, Unequal.* New York: Scribner's, 1991; Ballantine Books, 1992.

HERMAN, EDWARD S. *Corporate Control, Corporate Power.* New York: Cambridge University Press, 1981.

JENCKS, CHRISTOPHER. *Rethinking Social Policy: Race, Poverty, and the Underclass.* Cambridge, Mass.: Harvard University Press, 1992.

MCCLOSKY, HERBERT, and JOHN ZALLER. *The American Ethos.* Cambridge, Mass.: Harvard University Press, 1981.

SCHLESINGER, ARTHUR M., JR. *The Disuniting of America: Reflections on a Multicultural Society.* New York: Norton, 1991.

TERKEL, STUDS. *Race: How Blacks and Whites Think and Feel About the American Obsession.* New York: New Press, 1992.

Interest Groups

BERRY, JEFFREY M. *The Interest Group Society.* Glenview, Ill.: Scott, Foresman/Little, Brown, 1989.

CIGLER, ALLAN J., and BURDETT A. LOOMIS, eds. *Interest Group Politics.* 3d ed. Washington, D.C.: CQ Press, 1991.

PARENTI, MICHAEL. *Democracy for the Few.* 5th ed. New York: St. Martin's Press, 1988.

SCHLOZMAN, KAY LEHMAN, and JOHN T. TIERNEY. *Organized Interests and American Democracy.* New York: Harper & Row, 1986.

Political Parties and Elections
DUVERGER, MAURICE. *Political Parties.* New York: John Wiley, 1955.
EPSTEIN, LEON D. *Political Parties in the American Mold.* Madison: University of Wisconsin Press, 1986.
MAISEL, L. SANDY. *Parties and Elections in America.* 2d ed. New York: McGraw-Hill, 1993.
POMPER, GERALD M., et al. *The Election of 1992.* Chatham, N.J.: Chatham House, 1993.
SABATO, LARRY. *The Party's Just Begun.* Glenview, Ill.: Scott, Foresman, 1988.
WAYNE, STEPHEN J. *The Road to the White House 1992.* New York: St. Martin's Press, 1992.

The Presidency
EDWARDS, GEORGE C. III. *The Public Presidency: The Pursuit of Popular Support.* New York: St. Martin's Press, 1983.
LOWI, THEODORE J. *The Personal President: Power Invested, Promise Unfulfilled.* Ithaca, N.Y.: Cornell University Press, 1985.
NELSON, MICHAEL, ed. *The Presidency and the Political System.* 3d ed. Washington, D.C.: CQ Press, 1990.
NEUSTADT, RICHARD E. *Presidential Power: The Politics of Leadership from Roosevelt to Reagan.* Rev. ed. New York: Free Press, 1990.

Congress
FENNO, RICHARD F. *Home Style: House Members in Their Districts.* Boston: Little, Brown, 1978.
FIORINA, MORRIS P. *Congress: Keystone of the Washington Establishment.* 2d ed. New Haven: Yale University Press, 1989.
_____. *Divided Government.* New York: Macmillan, 1992.
JACOBSON, GARY C. *The Politics of Congressional Elections.* 3d ed. New York: HarperCollins, 1992.
VOGLER, DAVID J. *The Politics of Congress.* 6th ed. Dubuque, Iowa: Brown & Benchmark, 1993.

Policymaking and Implementation: The Administrative State
ANDERSON, JAMES. *Public Policymaking.* New York: Holt, Rinehart and Winston, 1979.

FESLER, JAMES W., and DONALD F. KETTL. *The Politics of the Administrative Process*. Chatham, N.J.: Chatham House, 1991.

KINGDON, JOHN W. *Agendas, Alternatives, and Public Policies*. Boston: Little, Brown, 1984.

RIPLEY, RANDALL B., and GRACE A. FRANKLIN. *Congress, the Bureaucracy, and Public Policy*. 3d ed. Homewood, Ill.: Dorsey Press, 1984.

SKOWRONEK, STEPHEN. *Building a New American State: The Expansion of National Administrative Capacities, 1877–1920*. New York: Cambridge University Press, 1982.

The Judiciary

ABRAHAM, HENRY J. *The Judiciary*. 7th ed. Boston: Allyn and Bacon, 1991.

BAUM, LAWRENCE. *The Supreme Court*. 4th ed. Washington, D.C.: CQ Press, 1992.

McCLOSKEY, ROBERT G. *The American Supreme Court*. Chicago: University of Chicago Press, 1960.

O'BRIEN, DAVID M. *Supreme Court Watch — 1992*. New York: Norton, 1992.

3. European Parliamentary Systems: Britain, France, and Germany

Since Britons and Americans speak the same language (although someone once said they were two people *separated* by a common language), one might have expected Britain to have been included in the previous chapter. But given the number of fundamental differences—no separation of powers, no federal system, no written constitution, no two-party system—Britain is better considered along with France and Germany.

Many Britons would object to such a grouping. They, especially the political elite, value the so-called Anglo-American Special Relationship. Certainly, Britons never have been regarded as Good Europeans—zealous advocates of European unity. Britain was late to join the European Community and remains one of the member countries least committed to tighter economic integration and highly skeptical, if not outright hostile, to common European defense and foreign policy making.

Nonetheless, Britain's future does lie with Europe, and it shares the parliamentary, fusion-of-powers system of government with the continental powers. Still, the British judicial system and electoral system closely resemble those of the United States and contrast with French and German practices. Thus Britain serves as a transitional link between the American and the continental systems.

The Constitutions

The American Constitution is relatively short and general, even vague. This gives it a great deal of flexibility, which is one of the reasons it has endured for two centuries with few formal amendments. The British constitution carries these features to the ultimate extreme because Britain lacks a written

80

constitution. No single framework document setting forth the powers and procedures of the primary governmental organs has even been drafted, let alone adopted or ratified.

The main elements that serve Britain as a constitution are not unfamiliar to Americans. Conventions of the constitution resemble what in the United States is called custom and usage—traditional practices that people feel bound to observe. Although no written constitution or even a law so provides, a prime minister who loses a vote of confidence in the House of Commons must either resign or call an election because this is the convention. Judicial decisions on fundamental issues also are considered to form part of the British unwritten constitution. An American parallel would be the famous Supreme Court case of *Marbury* v. *Madison*. The power of the Supreme Court to declare laws unconstitutional is founded on this decision, not on any grant of power in the U.S. Constitution. The third element of Britain's constitution is acts of Parliament that deal with the powers and procedures of the main organs of government. The Parliament Acts of 1911 and 1949, which curtailed the powers of the House of Lords, are examples.

Although American analogies can be found for each of these three elements, Britain's constitutional situation differs in two fundamental ways. The third element means that Parliament can amend the unwritten constitution whenever it wishes to do so through normal legislative procedures. No special majorities, such as are needed in the United States, are required. Furthermore, no additional action must be taken to ratify Parliament's action. The second contrast is even more striking. Whatever Parliament does is automatically valid; no court can declare any law unconstitutional. This is known as parliamentary supremacy, quite a difference from American practice, which permits the Supreme Court to void acts of Congress.

As a result, Britain lacks a judicially enforceable bill of rights to protect citizens from legislative invasion of basic freedoms. Although freedom of speech flourishes as much in Britain as in the United States, Parliament could curtail this and other liberties. In recent years a number of people in Britain have grown concerned about this potential threat to basic freedoms. Establishing a bill of rights, if not an entire written constitution, has been widely discussed. A basic problem, however, has been how to "entrench" a bill of rights. If, as current constitutional practice provides, Parliament is supreme, then how could a bill of rights be protected from curtailment at will by Parliament? Would submitting a bill of rights to the citizens for ratification, something that never has been done in Britain and has no basis in current constitutional practice, be sufficient to guard its provisions from legislative amendment? Thus, despite a lively current debate, Britain is unlikely to adopt a written constitution in the near future and will continue to follow practices at fundamental variance to those of the United States.

Britain also differs from the United States in being a monarchy. Initially the monarch's power was virtually unrestrained. Gradually, the legislature limited it by refusing to approve taxes until the monarch agreed to redress grievances presented in various petitions. During the seventeenth century the legislature and the monarch struggled for dominance. Civil war broke out, the king was executed, and a republic was proclaimed. When this proved unsuccessful, the monarchy was restored. Continuing conflict culminated in the Glorious (because bloodless) Revolution of 1688. William of Orange and his wife, Mary, the daughter of the deposed king, accepted the legislature's invitation to rule the country. The price was acknowledging that Parliament's will would prevail in any clash on fundamental matters. Thus in the past three centuries no monarch has challenged the supremacy of Parliament.

As a result, the power and, to a considerable extent, the influence of the monarch has declined steadily. In practice, the monarch cannot veto legislation but must sign automatically whatever has been passed by the legislature. Although all acts of government are performed in Her Majesty's name, the decision-making power is exercised by politicians. The leaders of the executive are appointed by the monarch, but she has virtually no discretion in doing so. General elections determine which party will be in power and its leaders must be appointed to run the government. Thus Britain's monarch is a symbol, a figurehead; the contrast with the republican United States is not as great as appearances might suggest.

France presents the other side of the constitutional coin to Britain. Over the past two centuries it has had about a dozen and a half constitutions. (During the same time the United States has had only one constitution, which it has amended only twenty-six times or sixteen if you consider the first ten amendments to be part of the original document.) Despite this extensive experience in drawing up fundamental framework documents, France has had great difficulty in drafting one that could long survive the conflicts generated by the country's political cleavages. France's experience tends to support the point made earlier that general, rather than detailed, constitutions tend to provide the flexibility and adaptability required for longevity. The French constitution that survived the longest, about two-thirds of a century, was the one that was shortest and least detailed.

Since the end of World War II, France has had two constitutions. The current one is thirty-five years old, which makes it the second-longest-lived constitution that the country has had. Few would have predicted such a future for this document when it went into effect in 1958. It was not the product of a series of compromises such as produced the U.S. Constitution. Instead, it was drawn up to satisfy the desires of a single individual, Charles de Gaulle, who had returned to power in what was virtually a coup. Even if those opposed to him were too weak to resist during his period in office, most assumed that once he departed, fundamental changes—perhaps even another constitution—would be made. As he himself once said, *"Après moi, le déluge"* (after me, chaos).

Surprisingly, that did not occur. De Gaulle's initial successors shared many of his views and would not be expected to have sought constitutional change. Eventually, however, his long-time rival, François Mitterrand, the leader of the Socialists, came to power. Despite having opposed de Gaulle's constitution from the beginning, Mitterrand left his rival's system intact. Although minor changes, such as reducing the length of the presidential term, currently are being discussed in France, any change will not be fundamental. France certainly is not on the verge of adopting a new constitution, and the current system may well double its life to become the country's most enduring constitution.

The French system is known as the Fifth Republic, a label that in itself suggests the many changes in constitution over the last two centuries. What this system has managed to do is to strike a workable balance between the competing French practices of "assembly government" and the "administrative tradition." Assembly government resembles British parliamentary supremacy. In both cases, the final word is to lie with the legislature. In practice, the two systems have differed. In Britain the executive, in the form of the Cabinet, has come to dominate and direct the legislature largely because of strict party unity and the existence of only two major parties. This does not occur under French assembly government because a fractionalized party system and low party discipline prevented most Cabinets from obtaining a reliable legislative majority. Thus in France the legislature dominated both in theory and in fact.

Under both the Third and Fourth republics, a period of nearly a century, France practiced assembly government. The typical result was stalemate government, with a weak executive unable to deal effectively with the country's problems. This outcome deeply embarrassed, indeed, affronted Charles de Gaulle, France's World War II leader in exile. He wanted a strong executive that could restore to France the glory it had known as a major international power centuries earlier. He was determined when he returned to power in 1958 to establish a new constitution that would break with the tradition of assembly government.

Fortunately for his objectives, France possessed an alternative constitutional tradition on which he could base his reforms. The administrative tradition was just the reverse of assembly government; under it the executive was dominant and the legislature played little more than a consultative role. This tradition was best embodied in the rule of Napoleon Bonaparte, but other French regimes—both before and after the French Revolution—also are examples of such a system. When de Gaulle's constitution first went into effect, most observers regarded it as a swing of the pendulum from assembly government to the administrative tradition, an oscillation that had characterized nearly two centuries of French politics. While de Gaulle held office, that view probably was accurate. What has become increasingly clear during the rule of his three successors, however, is that the Fifth Republic, for the first time in French history, has managed to balance the two traditions. By not swinging too far in either direction, the current constitution has won the support, or at least the acceptance, of the great bulk of the French people.

The constitution of the Fifth Republic is a hybrid; the system cannot be classified with either the American presidential system or the British parliamentary one, but partakes of elements of both. France has a president, who serves as head of state, and a prime minister, whose role is head of government. In contrast to the Third and Fourth republics, the president is more than a figurehead (unlike the British monarch) and possesses significant powers, especially during emergencies. As was true in the Third and Fourth republics, the Cabinet is responsible (can be voted out of office) to the legislature but has broader powers to control the legislature than had been the case. Moreover, the powers of the legislature now are specifically enumerated and thereby limited, in contrast to the parliamentary supremacy prevailing in the two previous republics. Finally, a limited form of judicial review (the power of courts to void acts of the legislature) is established as a further reversal of assembly government. Thus the provisions of the current French constitution are not unprecedented either in French tradition or in that of other countries. The specific mix of the various elements, however, is quite distinctive and has given France greater constitutional stability and governmental effectiveness than it has enjoyed for generations.

The French constitution can be amended by a majority vote in each of the houses of the legislature, after which the change must be ratified either by a three-fifths majority vote in a specially called joint meeting of the two houses or by popular referendum, if the president of the republic prefers the latter procedure. In 1962 President de Gaulle circumvented these explicit procedures by submitting a proposal for direct election of the president to a referendum without either house of the legislature, to say nothing of a joint session, having approved it. When the referendum approved this change, the proposal was deemed part of the constitution. Thus, contradictory though it may sound, the French constitution was amended unconstitutionally. That is to say that although a written constitution may appear to offer more protection than a British-style unwritten one, it is not an ultimate safeguard.

Since Germany was not unified as a single country until the latter part of the nineteenth century, it has had only somewhat more than a century of constitutional practice. During that time it has experienced about as much constitutional change as has France during those years. The current German constitution, however, is a decade older than the French one.

As a result of a series of wars, Prussia managed to combine most German-speaking political entities into an empire in 1871. While some aspects of the empire's political system were democratic, others were autocratic. The lower house of the legislature was popularly elected but was not permitted to exercise much real power. It could not remove the head of the executive, the chancellor, from office, since that official was responsible only to the emperor and served at his pleasure. Freedom of religion, freedom of speech, and freedom of political association all were violated at various times.

Germany's loss of World War I brought an end to this system. The collapse of Germany's military efforts and uprisings on the home front forced the emperor to abdicate and flee the country. A republic was declared and in a few months a new constitution was adopted. At the time this document was regarded as one of the most advanced democratic systems in the world. The chancellor was made responsible to the powerful lower house of the legislature, which was popularly elected. The electoral system ensured that even the smallest fraction of electoral opinion obtained a share of the seats in the legislature proportional to its share of the popular vote. Direct popular participation in decisionmaking was provided for through such procedures as referendums.

Despite such apparently attractive features, the Weimar Republic (so-called because that is the town in which the new constitution was drafted) never won widespread popular support. The electoral system fractionalized party strengths in the legislature. Cabinets were unable, just as in France under the Third Republic, to construct a viable legislative majority. As a result, the executive could not cope with the country's severe problems as one chancellor followed another in disconcerting rapidity. And severe the problems certainly were. Not only were many Germans alienated from their government by the loss of territory and the reparation payments that the World War I victors had imposed on the country, but unemployment and inflation seemed to be destroying the basic fabric of society. Inflation reached such astronomical levels that workers had to collect their wages in carts or wheelbarrows. And they were the lucky ones because they still had jobs.

As conditions worsened, the support for radical parties increased. Together, the Communist party and Adolf Hitler's National Socialist German Workers (Nazi) party polled half the vote in 1932. Since these extremes of the political spectrum detested each other, no majority Cabinet was possible. Early the following year the president invited Hitler, as the leader of the largest party, to serve as chancellor and try to govern the country. Hitler quickly made himself the dictator of a one-party state. Political opponents of the Nazis were imprisoned or assassinated; civil liberties were abolished. Various legislative acts transferred all significant powers, including the power to amend the constitution, to Hitler and his henchmen. In effect, a Nazi constitution for a Third Reich replaced the Weimar constitution. Domestic atrocities soon were followed by international crimes as Nazi Germany embarked on a war of conquest to seize "living space" from its "inferior" Slavic neighbors and to incorporate all German-speaking people into a single nation.

Once again military defeat brought Germany a new constitutional system. Only this time the victors decided to play a fuller role in the drafting process. Although the Germans were permitted to draw up the constitution, the victors gave them guidelines for their work and retained the right of approval. Thus the result was an amalgam of German, British, French, and American constitutional traditions.

Similar to American practice and German, but not British and French, tradition, the new constitution created a federal system. Power was divided between the national government and the states, an arrangement that neither level can alter unilaterally. In keeping with European, but not American, tradition, a parliamentary, not a presidential, system was established. The chancellor is responsible to the lower house of the legislature. The office of president also was created, but the role of this official is much more limited than that of the U.S. president and corresponds to French practice in the Third and Fourth republics (the Fifth French Republic still was in the future when the German constitution was drafted). Guarantees of such basic rights as freedom of speech, press, and assembly were included. And, another American import and a complete break with German tradition, a constitutional court was established with powers to declare unconstitutional any law or governmental action violating basic liberties.

A two-thirds vote of both the upper and the lower houses of the legislature is required to amend the constitution. No ratification of this action is required. Some provisions are stated to be unamendable. These include the federal system, sections providing for the basic democratic structure of government, and sections protecting fundamental liberties.

All this is only part of the story. The victorious Allies soon fell out after World War II; the West moved in one direction and the communist Soviet Union in another as a Cold War between the two sides developed. The constitutional system just described is what was set up in what came to be called West Germany, areas that had been Occupation zones for the United States, Britain, and France. In the Soviet zone, a communist system was created, which came to be called East Germany.

The Germans hoped that this division of their country would not become permanent. Therefore, what has been discussed here as the German constitution was not actually called that. It was known instead as the Basic Law. It was supposed to remain in effect only until such time as Germany could be reunited and a true constitution for the entire country could be established. Increasingly over the next forty years the hope of reunification seemed no more than an illusion. The West German Basic Law was in all but name the country's constitution.

Then in 1990 the international situation was transformed and Germany entered a new era. The Soviet Union under Mikhail Gorbachev decided to wind down the Cold War. No longer would the Soviet Union provide the military support that had propped up satellite regimes in Eastern Europe. The East German regime collapsed with amazing speed and virtually no bloodshed. West and East Germany came together in a single country. Contrary to original intentions, however, no new constitution was drawn up. The West Germans decided that their Basic Law had proved too satisfactory to be replaced; convening a constitutional convention to start drafting a new document from scratch was too risky. Since West Germany had much the stronger economic system and since the governmental structure of East Germany was crumbling, the simplest procedure was for the West, in effect, to absorb the East. The necessary changes, such as the number of representatives in the legislature for the East German states, were made in the Basic Law, and it was retained as the framework document for the united country.

Germany's constitutional success is remarkable. As we have seen, both Britain and France had evolved democratic traditions over the years, although these were more firmly rooted in Britain and less subject to challenge by alternative traditions. In Germany, however, except for the Weimar constitution—which never established its legitimacy—there had been no democratic constitutional tradition at all on which to build after World War II. Nonetheless, somewhat as occurred in France under the Fifth Republic, a balanced mix of traditions (in the German case *both* domestic and foreign) has been devised to create a constitutional structure that has proven its worth. Now all three leading European powers can be said to possess viable democratic constitutional traditions, a statement that a generation ago would have seemed highly dubious.

Social Forces

In every country certain segments of society because of their strategic location, control of resources, or size are able to control the government or, at least, greatly influence its actions. During the medieval period, although the particular individuals of power and prominence might change rapidly, the significant segments of society and the relations between them remained frozen from one century to the next. Modern societies, however, are characterized by rapidly changing social forces.

Leading determinants of long-term social change are scientific and technological advances. These greatly affect a country's economy and thus the relations between social forces. They also significantly alter the values and beliefs of people, thereby altering social relations. Scientific and technological change tends to be gradual, to accumulate over a considerable period of time. Many years go by before its influence is felt or, at least, detected.

The greatest producer of short-term social change is war. Not only do wars accelerate technological change, but they tend to disrupt and dislocate the existing order of society. Once the war is over, a society may seek to return to "normalcy," as an American president expressed the effort after World War I, but things are never the same again. For example, although Britain was moving early in the twentieth century toward enfranchising women, the changes that World War I produced in Britain virtually forced extending the right to vote to them shortly before the end of that war.

The key question is whether a country's political system is sufficiently flexible to adapt to social change by accommodating the desires of rising social forces and incorporating them into the governmental structure. Rising groups that remain shut out from power present a continuing threat of social disruption, if not revolution. Britain, perhaps because of its adaptable, unwritten constitution, has been more successful than either France or Germany in responding to social change. A discussion of social class in these three countries helps to illustrate this point.

Rhetoric notwithstanding, all Americans are not equal. Discrimination by race, gender, or ethnicity is common. Even within particular groups, differences in wealth and occupation produce a good deal of contrast in social status. Nonetheless, compared to most countries, the United States *is* a relatively equal society—much more so than the three major European powers. In Britain, France, and Germany society is much more hierarchically structured. Levels of social status are much more clearly distinct, and mobility from one level to another—even from one generation to the next—is uncommon.

As a result, various social groups tend to develop contrasting lifestyles. Family and gender relationships, recreational activities, type and amount of education, patterns of speech and dress, and even eating arrangements vary by social class. The ways of those outside one's own social community seem strange and contribute to feelings of suspicion. An us-versus-them mentality tends to develop. Since social mobility is limited, most people do not think of getting ahead through individual effort. Improving one's circumstances can be achieved only by advancing the interests of the group.

European politics, therefore, differs fundamentally from American in being class based. Furthermore, the interests of the classes are perceived as opposed to each other. That is, politics is regarded as a zero-sum game—my gain can occur only at your loss. Such a conception of politics usually has been absent in the United States; the chief exception would be the strongly opposed sectional interests whose mutually exclusive goals resulted in the American Civil War.

The situation has been exacerbated in France and Germany by the addition of ideological concerns. British politics, like American, rarely has involved much ideological conflict. British philosophy has had little interest in abstract concepts and has focused more on empirical entities. This preference among intellectuals and academics has permeated British society and has created a widely shared culture emphasizing a practical, pragmatic approach to social problems, rather than broad, all-encompassing social reform. Piecemeal, evolutionary change has been the British way.

In France and Germany, grand theory has seemed more attractive, more intellectually satisfying than British "muddling through." Grand theory offers an integrated critique of all aspects of society, an explanation of why life is as it is. Developed as a political ideology, it also provides a prescription for change. Since the ideology, by definition, is logically integrated, implementing parts of the prescription bit by bit over time makes no sense. The entire remedy should be administered all at once. Thus those in power are regarded by those who are out as exploitative enemies, while those in power consider the outs to be implacable opponents whose success could only transform society to the ins' detriment.

A classic example of ideology on the left of the political spectrum is Marxism, which enjoyed a great deal of popular support in France and Germany in the late nineteenth and much of the twentieth centuries. On the right of the spectrum, although not as elaborately developed as an integrated intellectual critique of society, was fascism, vying with Marxism for adherents in France and Germany. Neither of these two social movements made much headway in Britain. Thus, again, Britain provides a transitional link between American and continental European politics. British politics, although not entirely unaffected by ideological concerns, has been largely spared the ideological clash that has bedeviled efforts to deal with social problems in France and Germany. Thus political conflict in Britain has resembled that in the United States more than that on the Continent. Yet Britain, like the continental powers, has had class-based politics, which has been largely absent from the American scene.

One of the principal perpetuators of class differences in Britain has been the education system. This has reinforced differences between classes in appearance, manners, and, especially, speech patterns and accent. Significant government financial support for primary schools was not provided until after 1870 and for secondary schools not until after the turn of the century. In the meantime, a number of private schools (called "public" schools in Britain because they were not run as commercial enterprises intended to make a profit) had developed. Indeed, some of the most prestigious public schools have existed for five or six centuries! Although the quality of public schools varies, many of them provide the best education available in Britain. Public school education costs a great deal of money, which further reinforces the idea that those who have enjoyed it are a social elite. Those belonging to this select group are virtually certain to attain positions of power and prominence regardless of whether they also obtain a university degree. Furthermore, those who attended a particular public school, no matter how many years apart, feel a special bond, and therefore the education system tends to produce a network of personal connections among the political elite.

Although the public school system continues to be socially divisive, it has instilled in its products a sense of pragmatism and fair play. It has contributed to the realism and adaptability of Britain's governing elite. In the eighteenth century landed property owners dominated British politics. Then, as Britain became the pioneer of the Industrial Revolution, it experienced rapid social change. The power elite responded with what proved to be a century-long process of electoral reform, of extending the right to vote: the industrial middle class in 1832, industrial workers in 1867, and agricultural laborers in 1884. Gradually, rising social forces were granted a voice in decision making. By the close of the nineteenth century this process enabled industrial workers to launch a viable political party to advocate their interests. By the middle of the twentieth century this party not only had advanced from minor to major party status but had obtained a commanding majority in the legislature.

The British political system was able to accommodate profound social change without violence because of the enlightened self-interest of the propertied class. While not willing to relinquish power without a struggle, it recognized that the political battle had to be waged in accord with agreed-upon rules. It was able to offer incremental changes in political structures and procedures that were acceptable to rising groups. Having discovered that they were not beating their heads against a stone wall, these groups decided that gradual reform was in their interest as well. If one were patient, the costs and risks of violence and revolution could be avoided.

Such a strategy in France and Germany seemed much less sensible. In the latter part of the nineteenth century the right to vote was more extensive in both France and Germany than it was in Britain. But, as already explained in the discussion of German constitutional traditions, this right conferred little power. The role of the German legislature in policymaking was quite curtailed, its power much less than that of the British Parliament. Furthermore, government repression of working-class parties and trade unions was common. Rising social groups in Germany might well conclude that only through revolution could they wield power. And since they were shut out of significant decision making, they had no opportunity to test their ideology against reality to ascertain whether it was of any use.

Education also has been a factor in class divisions in Germany. The country long has had an excellent vocational training program apprenticing young people for skilled trades. The aim is to generate the skilled workers needed for an expanding economy, however, not to produce knowledgeable citizens. Furthermore, those who receive an elite education have little of the British public school ethos of paternalism and fair play inculcated.

In France the Industrial Revolution had less impact than elsewhere in northern Europe. The traditional social formations (the peasants, small shopkeepers, landed aristocrats, family business operators, and unskilled workers) retained their power and status much longer than in Britain or Germany. France urbanized more slowly than either of the other two. To a considerable extent, even today the small town remains more typical of French life than is the sophistication of Paris. The small artisan and the family farmer retain an influence far exceeding their numbers because they seem to embody what is deemed best in French life.

New social forces generated by advancing industrialization (a managerial class, skilled workers, technicians, engineers) eventually managed to obtain a share in power. The problem was that the means by which they did so usually were more revolutionary than evolutionary. In contrast to Britain, those in power usually were willing to concede nothing to their opponents. When they were displaced, they were offered, not surprisingly, few sops by the victors. Therefore the old order remained unreconciled to the new and simply bided its time until it could manage to regain power by any means that might be effective.

The establishment of the Third Republic in 1875 might appear to have been based on widespread basic consensus, since the system endured until ended by military defeat in 1940. That was not the case. The forces of democratic reform managed to triumph and impose their system simply because the conservative old guard—the aristocracy, clergy, military officers, and portions of the peasantry and traditional middle class—were divided among themselves. These social groups never conceded legitimacy to the Third Republic but continued to clamor for a less democratic, more executive-dominated system that would rescue the church from the anticlerical hostility of the government. Although the Vichy regime of World War II was largely a puppet government of the Germans, it fulfilled in many ways what the opponents of the Third Republic had sought for decades.

Given such long-standing challenges to the basic nature of the political system, the social forces that had come to power under the Third Republic could regard politics only as a clash of fundamentally opposed views. Their victory seemed tenuous, and any concessions to opponents seemed highly risky. Thus politics was an ideologically charged, class-based struggle. France, as well as Germany, had failed to achieve the British accomplishment of incorporating all significant social groups within the existing political system so that politics could be merely an argument about details rather than a clash over fundamentals.

In addition to class, another major social force in European politics has been the church. The English Civil War in the mid-seventeenth century was in large part over whether the country would be Catholic or Protestant. The French Revolution toward the close of the eighteenth century was as much a repudiation of the Catholic church as it was of the monarchy. Even at the end of the twentieth century, both Britain and Germany, to the amazement of Americans, have official, established churches: the Anglican church in Britain and the Lutheran church in Germany. This does not mean that religious freedom (including the right to have no beliefs) is absent from these countries (although Catholics were persecuted for a time in Germany toward the close of the nineteenth century). But it does mean, for example, that in Germany people are taxed, in effect, to support the established church, while in Britain basic church policies, such as the decision to ordain women as priests, must be approved by the national legislature.

Somewhat surprisingly, since the overwhelming majority of the people are at least nominally Catholic, France does *not* have an established church. Nonetheless, church-state relations in France, especially in the matter of support for and control of church-operated schools, remain a perpetual issue. Several twentieth-century French political parties, at various points on the political spectrum, have been strongly committed to defending the role of the church in French society and implementing its values in public policy. The church remains a major social force in France.

Although the Lutheran church is established in Germany, it has not spawned a political party. During the Weimar period, Germany had a major Catholic party. Since World War II, the leading party in Germany has been a Christian Democratic one. Despite its label, the religious element of its policies is quite diluted and, significantly, it combines *both* Catholics and Protestants. In contrast to past German history, the Catholic church no longer had to feel like an embattled minority because the West German population was about equally divided between the two branches of Christianity. The merger of East and West Germany should not alter the situation, even though historically Protestantism has been by far the dominant faith in the eastern parts of the historical Germany.

Religion has ceased to be a major factor in German politics. Only occasionally does it impinge on politics. In the 1970s, for example, the Catholic church formally instructed its priests to warn their parishioners on Sunday morning not to vote for the Socialists in the upcoming election. At the close of the 1980s the role of various Protestant groups in providing the final shove that brought down the East German regime is worth noting.

As for Britain, the Anglican church now wields little power or influence. Religion matters little in English life, although that is less true in Scotland and, in particular, in Wales. Only in Northern Ireland are people such fervent believers that they still think, as did most people several centuries ago, that killing people of other faiths is acceptable. The Protestant majority and the Catholic minority are engaged in an endless guerrilla war over whether Northern Ireland should remain part of the British political system or be incorporated into the Republic of Ireland, with which it shares the island. Because of geographic propinquity, this religious conflict spills over into politics around Liverpool in England. With this exception, religious groups are not significant social forces in Britain.

Race and ethnicity long have been sources for major social forces in the

United States. Historically, this has not been the case in the three major European powers because their populations have been much less diverse than that of the United States. Currently, however, race and ethnicity, if not social forces, certainly are political issues in all three countries. Following World War II, Britain experienced a good deal of immigration from its former colonial possessions. Blacks came from Africa and the West Indies and Pakistanis and Indians (both of whom the British consider to be nonwhite) from the Indian subcontinent. Although nonwhites account for only about 5 percent of the British population, they tend to be highly visible. Many work for the London transportation system, while others operate restaurants and convenience stores. Their non-British customs—neighbors complain, for example, about the smell of curry—have made them a source of conflict and an object of discrimination. Although not as horrendous as events that have occurred in such American cities as Los Angeles and Detroit, destructive racial disturbances have occurred in British cities.

Britain has sought to control immigration with laws than often seem racist, while attempting to protect minorities already living in the country with antidiscrimination legislation. Because the British have preferred mediation to litigation, most of these laws have been rather ineffective. Furthermore, because racial diversity is relatively new in Britain, most people have yet to be sensitized. Words that would create a scandal if used in the United States still can be heard in conversations in Britain. Race and ethnicity are rising social forces to which Britain has not yet adapted.

France's ethnicity problem, like Britain's, goes back to its imperial past. Much of North Africa was French territory. Algeria, although now independent, was a special case. Despite its location across the Mediterranean Sea, it was constitutionally part of the French governmental system, just as Alaska and Hawaii are incorporated in the American system despite not being contiguous to the continental United States. As a result of this past close association and geographic location, many people from North Africa have settled in France, especially in the southern part. Virtually all of these people have an Islamic background. Customs and appearance seem to set them apart from society, and many French workers feel threatened by competition for jobs and housing. Others claim to fear the permeation of the school system by foreign values and language. These "out" groups make up nearly twice as large a proportion of French society as do nonwhites in Britain. Ethnicity is a significant source of tension and conflict in French society.

West Germany recovered very quickly from the destruction of World War II and soon had a booming economy. So rapidly was it expanding that not enough Germans were available to fill all the jobs, especially the menial ones. So the Germans recruited what they called "guest workers." These workers came from less prosperous countries—Italy, Greece, Yugoslavia, Turkey—where what could be earned was below even the lowest German wages. They account for about the same proportion of Germany's population, not quite a tenth, as do foreign national and ethnic groups in France. As the label implies, the Germans intended for these foreigners to be a re-volving-door workforce. Any given worker would stay for a few years and then return home to be replaced by a new worker from a similar country. Some of the guests, however, began to take up permanent residence.

In some instances—Italians, for example—this caused no great prob-lems. But when appearance, religion, and customs greatly differed—Turks and some of the Yugoslavs, for example—a distinct group that was a likely target for discrimination existed. The ending of the Cold War with its result-ant turmoil in Eastern Europe exacerbated the situation. Germany had a very liberal asylum law, which made it possible for those who were not be-ing politically persecuted by their home government, but simply were seek-ing better-paying work, to gain entry. Nearly two hundred thousand sought asylum in Germany in 1990; the next year, the figure surpassed a quarter of a million; the following year, it was more than a third of a million.

Perhaps a prosperous Germany could have absorbed this influx without incident. Shortly after World War II, West Germany had managed to absorb an incredible number of refugees fleeing from communist tyranny. In 1961 nearly a quarter of the country's population was exiles and refugees. In what must rank as one of history's greatest acts of social generosity, West Ger-many enacted the Equalization of Burdens Law, which provided that anyone owning property in 1948 was required to pay one-half of its value in install-ments over a twenty-year period to help those who had nothing. The funds generated were used to provide housing, welfare assistance, and compensa-tion for lost possessions to those dispossessed by war and communism.

At the start of the 1990s, however, the great costs of trying to revive the moribund economy of what had been East Germany adversely affected the economy of the newly united Germany. Economic growth virtually ceased. With 40 percent of the workforce in what had been East Germany unemployed, Germany did not want an influx of people seeking jobs and was unwilling to pay the costs of resettling them and supporting them if they did not find employment.

Although the great bulk of the influx at the start of the 1990s were Yugoslavs and Romanians, the largest group of guest workers in Germany remained the Turks, about a quarter of all such people in the country. Furthermore, their distinctiveness made them easy targets. So they, in particular, suffered as neo-Nazi and antisocial "skinhead" youths rioted, attacking guest workers and burning their homes and the living quarters of asylum seekers. Given Germany's Nazi past, ethnicity will remain a major social force or issue.

For much of American history, regionalism would have to be considered in any discussion of social forces. Given the geographical size of the country, uniformity from border to border hardly could be expected. Regional strains eventually grew so great as to cause a civil war. Since Britain, France, and Germany all are much smaller than the United States, the more limited, but not inconsequential, impact of region is not surprising.

Regionalism has given French politics a certain stability underlying what appears to be constant flux. Studies have shown that certain areas vote the same way decade after decade no matter what constitutional changes have occurred. What has disguised this stability is change in the party system. Certain areas of France always vote left, for example, but at one point in time the most "advanced" or progressive party on offer was the Radical Socialists, later it was the Socialists, and still later the Communists. Thus apparently shifting behavior actually was evidence of a stable outlook.

Insofar as regionalism is a source of social strain, it is largely a matter of Paris against the provinces, as suggested by the comments earlier concerning social class in France. Indeed, the chief reason why five years passed after the fall of the Second Empire before the Third Republic was formally launched with only a few brief framework laws to serve as a constitution was the conflict between the progressive forces of Paris and the conservative groups of the rest of the country.

As could be expected in a country unified relatively late, Germany has exhibited regional differences. Stereotypical has been the contrast between the no-nonsense north German and the jovial Bavarian of the south. Southern Germans also have tended to be more Catholic and conservative. Such differences pale into insignificance, however, compared with the current divisions between the former East and West Germanies. While the latter was experiencing four decades of democracy, the former was living under communism. Not only do the West Germans know about self-government, but they have the entrepreneurial experience needed to run a productive economy. Unfortunately, the West Germans are inclined to regard East German lack of experience and initiative as evidence of laziness, while the East Germans feel that West German instruction consists more of arrogant orders than helpful cooperation. Treated by the West Germans as inferiors, many East Germans are inclined to take out their hurt feelings on asylum seekers from other countries. Germany has been unified only constitutionally; a real union has yet to be built. Until it is, east-west divisions will produce major social forces in the country.

The religious conflict in Northern Ireland is not the only case of important regional contrasts in Britain. As the country's official name, the United Kingdom of Great Britain and Northern Ireland, suggests, the country is composed of four nations. In addition to the Irish in Northern Ireland and the English themselves, the Scots and the Welsh are distinct nations. For most of the twentieth century, the status of Scotland and Wales was not a political issue. During the last two decades, however, nationalist movements have flourished in both nations. Although they sometimes have found it politically expedient to tone down their policies, basically both movements seek independence from Britain. In Scotland nationalism has been fueled by North Sea oil. The Scottish National party has proclaimed that "it's Scotland's oil," knowing that if that point were conceded, Scotland would be economically viable as an independent country.

In 1979 the people of Wales and Scotland were given an opportunity to vote for a greater share of self-government. The Welsh soundly rejected any change in the existing arrangement within Britain. A majority of Scots favored more self-government, but low participation in the referendum kept the vote from reaching the level required for any change. Thus the fundamental structure of the United Kingdom was unaltered; nonetheless, nationalism remains an active movement in both Scotland and Wales. Regionalism is among the important social forces in Britain.

In summary, class is a significant social force in all three countries, as is race/ethnicity. Region is important in Britain and Germany, but less so in France. Religion, the church, continues to matter a great deal in France, while only occasionally having much impact in Britain and Germany. To some extent social forces are expressed through interest groups and parties. But not all important forces are channeled through these structures. Furthermore, groups and parties serve as vehicles for segments of society that would not be regarded as social forces. Therefore we need to discuss, in turn, groups and parties.

Interest Groups

Because the power of any single individual is limited, people join together to try to influence public policy. Some groups are organized to advocate a particular position on one or two issues. These groups seek to win over public opinion to their way of thinking and to convince public officials to run the government in accord with their views. Other groups combine people drawn from a particular segment of society and are dedicated to protecting the interests of that segment. They also seek to win the support of the public and the acceptance of officials. Although the range of concerns varies from one group to another, few offer a broad, integrated program of policies addressing the full range of public issues of the day. And none seeks to staff the government by offering candidates at elections; interest groups attempt to influence, not provide, public officials.

Interest-group activity frequently is referred to as "lobbying." This derives from the practice of interest-group personnel seeking to buttonhole legislators as they exited from the legislative chamber into the surrounding halls of the building. Unfortunately, this term suggests that interest groups target only legislators for their efforts. The narrow connotation of the term helps explain why for many years interest-group activity was thought to be less important in Britain than in the United States. British interest groups devote much less effort to influencing members of Parliament (MPs) than American groups do to members of Congress. This is quite sensible because in the British House of Commons legislative committees cannot kill or mutilate a bill. Furthermore, MPs are told by their parties how to vote; interest groups cannot persuade them to alter their votes.

Nonetheless, MPs do have their uses for interest groups. A group may wish to be certain that some MP will voice its views during a debate on an issue of importance to it. And MPs are more likely than the common citizen to get a considered response when they approach the bureaucracy for information or assistance. Therefore many trade unions in Britain "sponsor" MPs. Typically, this means that a union will pay an MP's constituency party for some or all of the expense of running the election campaign. The union may also provide money for secretarial or research assistance during the course of the year. Somewhat similarly, some interest groups may feel that their standing with the public can be improved by having the name of a member of Parliament on their letterhead. The MP may not be expected to provide any extensive service in exchange for some financial support.

The really significant group activity, however, and the reason why the term lobbying as usually understood is so especially inappropriate in the British context, lies in contacts between groups and the bureaucracy. The administrative agencies of the government frequently consult many of the most prominent and long-established groups. Most departments have advisory committees representing various relevant interests. Ideas for new legislation will be run by the appropriate interest groups to ascertain their reaction to possible changes in the law.

Relations in the area of delegated or administrative legislation are of even greater importance. In modern, complex society many of the acts passed by the legislature simply set goals and provide some guidelines for attaining them. The task of working out specific regulations to achieve the desired ends is left to civil servants. Many of the actual rules that govern life in Britain are statutory instruments, regulations drawn up by civil servants on the basis of a general grant of authority by Parliament. The bureaucracy consults quite closely with interest groups as it formulates these administrative regulations. Whereas a draft of a proposed law normally would not be shown to a group before its introduction in Parliament, draft regulations are submitted to interest groups as a matter of course, giving them considerable opportunity to persuade the bureaucracy to modify the draft along lines more acceptable to the group. The bureaucrats are willing to grant groups this important influence because a group's goodwill often is valuable to the government. Applying a host of regulations to some activity goes much more smoothly if the relevant group is cooperative, rather than hostile. Furthermore, successful regulation requires extensive knowledge about the relevant activity. Groups have expertise and information that are not readily available to the government. Thus British interest groups and the government practice a close symbiosis. These activities may not be as visible as lobbying is in the United States, but a strong case can be made that the British arrangement provides groups with at least as much influence on public policy.

To some extent, interest-group activity in France has tended to resemble American practice more than British. This was especially true during the Third and Fourth republics. Not only was the party system fractionalized along a broad political spectrum, but several parties lacked the strongly disciplined party-line voting common in Britain. That is, members of the French legislature tended to vote as do members of the American, shifting alliances from one issue to the next and voting solidly with the other members of their party only occasionally. Such a legislature obviously provides fertile ground for lobbyists to till.

When this opportunity coincided with a sacred element of French culture—wine—how could the alcohol lobby lose? Beet growers, grape cultivators, and distillers enjoyed great success in maintaining state purchase of alcohol at premium prices during the Fourth Republic. About 4 million people in France were estimated to derive profit in some way from the manufacture, sale, or transportation of alcohol. One of the prime ministers during the Fourth Republic became concerned about alcoholism in France and tried to launch a campaign for the French to drink more milk and to stop consuming wine with every meal as though it were water. His efforts were not notably successful.

Once one departs from the legislative arena, the similarity between French and American interest-group activity largely vanishes. France has a tradition of direct—that is, not through formal channels—action to influence government. Strikes for political purposes, refusal to pay taxes, fiddling the books to reduce taxes, while not unheard of in the United States, are not a way of life as they virtually are in France. Beyond that, peasant blockading of roads with tractors, food, or farm animals, seizure of public buildings, and sabotage hardly are typical interest-group tactics in the United States.

Depending on how broadly one defines the term interest group, one could argue that interest groups caused the collapse of one French regime and, in another instance, drove a president from office. Some analyses of interest groups identify institutional groups, a label for agencies of government that act beyond their primary purpose in an effort to influence public policy in other areas. The French military long operated as an institutional interest group, having considerable influence on policy concerning Algeria. As conflict over Algeria came to dominate French politics in the late 1950s, the military became the decisive factor. The threat that the paratroopers stationed in Algeria were about to invade the mainland and seize the government caused the collapse of the Fourth Republic and the return to power of Charles de Gaulle.

A decade later, another type of group was instrumental in toppling de Gaulle from the presidency. Students were no more than an amorphous interest group, what might be labeled an anomic or alienated group. They did represent the interests, however vaguely articulated, of a particular segment of society. Their demonstrations and riotous confrontations with the police in the spring of 1968 threw the government into panic. Although de Gaulle eventually managed to exert control, his rule had been undermined. A year later, he left office.

Thus group activity in France exhibits a wide range of tactics and encompasses various types of groups. In some instances American parallels are easy to find, but in others the contrasts with both British and American practice are considerable.

Although Germany also has the kind of voluntary associations that characterize democratic societies, a distinctive feature of its interest-group system is that some organizations are established by law and membership in them is obligatory for relevant segments of society. Among such groups are business, farmer, and worker organizations. For example, a handicraft worker must join a handicraft council, a manufacturing business an industrial council, and in some German states all farmers are required to belong to the state agricultural council. Such councils act not only as interest groups to promote the concerns of their members but also perform such regulatory functions as setting standards for output, controlling entry to the activity through licensing, and training apprentices.

As for the more familiar voluntary type of groups, the discussion of activities in France and Britain made clear that groups focus their efforts where the power is. Because the power structure varies from one country to another, the details of interest-group action will exhibit some common themes, but also a number of contrasts. As in many other countries, German interest groups seek to influence the outcome of elections by providing financial support and campaign assistance to parties. In the 1950s business groups formed associations to channel money to nonsocialist parties. Eventually, such arrangements were ruled illegal by the Federal Constitutional Court and business interests had to devise other means of supporting parties favorable to their concerns. Some of these subterfuges were of dubious legality and led to long-running embarrassing prosecutions involving high-level government officials.

Besides being active in election campaigns and supportive of parties, German interest groups maintain close relations with officials in the executive branches of both state and national governments. At times, for example, the ministry of agriculture has seemed to be a permanent possession of the Free Democrats, a leading German third party. Whichever particular Free Democrat headed the ministry at any given time labored diligently to advance the concerns of the German Farmers' Union and other agricultural groups. As in Britain, departmental advisory bodies populated by interest groups are common in Germany, as is consulting interest groups before issuing administrative regulations.

Lobbying of the legislative type, however, is more prevalent in Germany than in Britain. The German legislature is not dominated by only two parties, so interest groups have some scope for trying to construct temporary majorities favoring their objectives, despite rather strong party discipline. This is especially true for legislative committees, which do the bulk of the work in determining public policy. The role of the German committees is much closer to American practice than is the British and offers the same opportunities for interest-group activity as in the United States.

In any industrial democracy an organized interest of major significance is the trade unions. Union density, the proportion of the workforce belonging to unions, varies considerably, however, from one country to another. In Britain nearly two-fifths of the workers are unionized, and in Germany about a third are. This is far higher than in the United States, where only about a sixth are union members. Europe is not consistently more unionized than the United States, however, since in France union density is only about an eighth.

During the 1970s many Britons became concerned that their country's unions had become too powerful. They seemed to be able to dictate policy to the government or, at the least, to be able to veto any action they disliked. Their ability to thwart the government's efforts to control wages and prices exacerbated Britain's declining economic fortunes. Rising unemployment during much of the 1980s weakened the power of British unions. After Prime Minister Margaret Thatcher won a major confrontation with the miners' union, she followed up with various laws curtailing union power. As a result of these developments, union density, which had been well over half in Britain when she took office, had declined to two-fifths when she gave up power, and few thought any longer that the unions were too strong. Nonetheless, the formal organizational linkage between the unions and the Labour party gives this interest group an influence it lacks in most countries.

In Germany, in contrast, the unions officially are nonpartisan. This arrangement is a break with the traditional practice prior to World War II. The existence of a contrary tradition, however, along with a similarity of policy views, has made it difficult for the Trade Union Federation to remain politically neutral. Many of the federation's officers also are leaders in the Social Democratic party (SPD), and its staff "unofficially" assists SPD candidates in election campaigns.

German unions have been quite successful in promoting "co-determination" to give workers a voice in the management of the enterprises for which they work. German law requires that a certain number of seats on the governing boards of companies of a specified size are to be filled by trade union representatives.

The political influence of French unions is limited not only by the much lower level of unionization there compared with Germany or Britain but also by fractionalized organization. Some French unions are communist dominated. Workers opposed to such a political orientation broke away to found two chief competing union organizations, one favorable to the Socialists and the other to the Christian Democrats. Thus the relatively low union strength is further diluted by the inability to speak with a single voice. Yet the political, as distinct from the economic, strike is much more common in France than in Germany or Britain. As a result, union efforts to influence government often are more visible in France than in the other two nations and have the capacity to cause the average person a good deal more inconvenience. Whether such actions have much effect on the French government, however, is highly questionable.

In fact, French unions have much less impact on the government than do the much smaller agricultural interests. In the past twenty years the number of people working in agriculture has been halved in France, declining to only 6 percent of the workforce. Nonetheless, that proportion is higher than in Germany and about three times as great as in Britain. Although agriculture generates only about 4 percent of France's wealth, some estimates suggest that about a fifth of the population makes a living directly or indirectly from farming. Furthermore, farmers as a group and the bucolic way of life have considerably more public sympathy in France than in Britain or Germany. Unification has complicated the German situation. Farms in the former West Germany tended to be relatively small and inefficient. They required a good deal of government support to remain viable. Farms in the former East Germany, the traditional agricultural heartland of nineteenth-century Germany, were quite large and potentially could be highly efficient. The problem is to convert them from the inefficiencies of communist collectivized farming.

Thus, before the unification of the two Germanies, the West German government was responsive to the German Farmers' Union's desire for high subsidies and agricultural tariffs. As a result, Germany was reluctant to support reform of the European Community's protectionist Common Agricultural Policy (CAP). Pressures for change in CAP reached a climax early in the 1990s during worldwide negotiations for trade liberalization under the General Agreement on Tariffs and Trade (GATT). Although the bulk of the reforms concerned industrial products, the United States would not accept the package unless the protection European agricultural output enjoyed from efficient American competition was reduced. The reactions of agricultural interests in the three main European countries to the deal eventually agreed on illustrates national contrasts in group tactics and influence.

The National Farmers' Union in Britain warned against sacrificing the interests of British farmers, but issued no threats. The German Farmers' Union had been rather more vocal about protecting CAP from fundamental reform, but it was relatively restrained in its response to the outcome of the GATT negotiations. The French reaction differed fundamentally, as the farmers' organization, the FNSEA, went ballistic. Tractors surrounded town halls and, in one case, a Coca-Cola bottling plant. Tires and American flags were burned in front of various McDonald's. Farm leaders cited these events as just the beginning of extensive demonstrations that easily could become violent if their interests were not protected. Some farmers went so far as to attack and deface the home of the former minister of agriculture and called for his trial for having betrayed the interests of French farmers earlier in the year. All of this generated a major debate in the French legislature, in which each party competed to see which could be most supportive of the farmers. As for other groups, even industrial interests were reluctant to oppose the farmers, despite the fact that were France to veto the deal, the country's manufacturers would lose a great deal of money that freer trade in their products would have earned. It does not seem to be stereotyping to say that it was all very French. Each country has its own political style and this can be seen as easily in the functioning of the interest-group system as in the operation of government.

Political Parties and Elections

Parties are the other side of the coin to interest groups. They seek to gain control of the government and place their adherents into office. Parties offer the electorate a set of candidates willing to cooperate to implement an integrated program of policies sufficiently comprehensive to address the principal public issues of the day. Although this description of party function applies across many national boundaries, British, German, and most French parties differ from American ones in important respects. The contrasts between European and American parties have been summed up in the labels "mass parties" and "cadre parties." A mass party is a highly organized structure based on a nationwide formal membership. A cadre party is a loose network of candidate-organized electoral machines relying on volunteers.

Simply calling oneself a supporter is not sufficient to become a member of a European mass party; instead, one must regularly pay dues to be allowed to participate in party activities. Furthermore, many parties require those who wish to join to declare their acceptance of basic party doctrines. A corollary of this provision is a party's power to eject from membership anyone who refuses to abide by party rules of procedure or who persistently dissents from party policy.

As this suggests, European parties are more centralized, indeed, hierarchically organized, than American parties. To a considerable extent party organization in the United States runs from the grassroots up to the national level, while in Europe the structure is reversed. National party headquarters in Europe actually possess power over the party's branches at the constituency level. Outside of France, American-type parties—a rather loose association at the national level of a number of local personal machines created by politicians to perpetuate themselves in office—are un-known. European politicians do have personal followings, but party organization in their electoral districts existed before they were elected and will continue to function after they depart. Furthermore, in Europe parties have formal procedures for making policy and for articulating their views on current issues, and all branches at the constituency level are required to advocate these stands.

Although, as already discussed, various segments of society seek to advance their concerns through interest groups, whose functions can be distinguished from those of parties, parties can be regarded as an amalgam of various social forces and interests. A country with the geographical variation and the ethnic and religious diversity of the United States can operate a two-party system only with loosely organized parties of the cadre type. Seeking to require all Democrats throughout the country, for example, to adhere to the same policies would only fragment such national organization as does exist into a variety of splinter parties. Each major American party, therefore, is a coalition of diverse groups. Indeed, the trick of winning a presidential election is to piece together a majority coalition that can withstand the tensions of a lengthy campaign.

On the European continent, although less so in Britain, parties are not such broad coalitions and may well represent a fairly narrow segment of society. As a result, Europe has had multiparty systems. This in turn means that coalition building occurs at a different time and place than in the United States. In the United States coalitions are built *before* an election *within* parties. In Europe coalitions are formed *after* an election *between* parties in the legislature. In either case, negotiating skills, tolerance, and a willingness to compromise are essential for success. In this sense democratic politics is fundamentally the same in all these countries.

In Britain

Some histories trace British parties back a couple of centuries. True, various factional groups did exist in the British legislature at that time. These, however, can be considered no more than cadre parties, if that. They had virtually no national organization outside the legislature. And since the electorate was so small—rarely more than a couple of hundred in any constituency—organization at the constituency level hardly qualified even as an electoral machine.

As the right to vote was expanded gradually in the nineteenth century, party organization became necessary to mobilize the growing electorate. By the last quarter of the century, two national organizations, the Conservatives and the Liberals, competed for votes. Early in the twentieth century, personal rivalries and policy differences split the Liberal party. These divisions and the party's lack of a core clientele in the social structure reduced it to third-party status before World War II. Meantime, beginning at the turn of the century, a new party financed by the trade unions and based on the support of working-class voters begin to rise to prominence. At the end of World War II, this Labour party won a landslide victory. Thus, in half a century, the British party system had evolved from a two-party system that pitted Conservatives against Liberals to a two-party system in which Conservatives were opposed by Labour, with the Liberals an irrelevancy—at least as far as strength in the legislature was concerned.

The British party system seemed to have solidified in this form, but events of the last decade have caused speculation over whether a basic transformation might occur. The Labour party, which traditionally had pursued moderate policies, swung so far to the left that several of its prominent members broke away to form a new Social Democratic Party (SDP). To avoid mutual destruction, the SDP and the Liberals formed the Alliance to fight elections in concert. Although the Alliance obtained more than a fifth of the vote in elections during the 1980s, the British electoral system denied it any appreciable strength in the legislature. Eventually the two parties attempted to merge. A rump of the SDP opposed this step and remained separate for a few years before going out of existence. The merged party, called the Liberal Democrats, has so far been unable to regain the electoral support that the Alliance had obtained. Nonetheless, the continuing weakness of the Labour party, its inability to drive the Conservatives from power, continues to fuel speculation about a change in the British party system.

The party that has best weathered more than a century of social and political change, the Conservatives, initially established a social base among the landed interests. As merchants and manufacturers obtained the right to vote in the nineteenth century, some of them supported the Conservatives. The party also was able to obtain support from middle-class professionals. All of these, however, could not have provided sufficient votes for the Conservatives to win elections in the twentieth century. Essential to the party's electoral success has been the support of many working-class voters. The ability of the Conservatives to win the bulk of white-collar workers is, perhaps, not too surprising. What is remarkable is the party's strength among skilled manual workers; at times during the 1980s, the Conservatives won more votes from this social group than did the Labour party.

In the 1950s and 1960s voting behavior in Britain was influenced primarily by social class. Although neither class was monolithic in its partisan preferences, the middle class tended to vote Conservative and the working class Labour. Then, in the closing decades of the twentieth century, party loyalty declined. The electorate had become better educated and was tending to rely more on relatively objective television than on the partisan print media for its news. The ineffectiveness of parties in the 1970s, their inability to deal with Britain's economic problems, disillusioned many people and weakened the electorate's ties with parties.

Even when voters' partisan preferences did not change, their reasons for supporting a particular party often did alter. Voter decision making has become more a reasoned choice based on a person's basic values and assessment of parties' past performance and alternative programs for the future. Demographic factors still are important in voting behavior, but social class per se has declined in significance. Now such characteristics as the type of house (government owned or private) in which one lives and whether one's source of income is the government or private enterprise—factors that do not correlate perfectly with social class—have become important.

Despite these changes, both the Conservative and Labour parties retain a core clientele. This gives them a considerable advantage over the Liberal Democrats. The proportion voting for the Lib Dems does vary somewhat from one social class to another. The party comes much closer, however, than do either of the major parties to obtaining the same share of support across the board. Furthermore, commitment to the party is quite tenuous. The Lib Dems both gain and lose a lot of voters in each election; few vote for them election after election, as many do for the Conservatives and Labour. All that the Lib Dems can hope is that the declining importance of social class in voting behavior has made the electorate more open to persuasion; if the party can get its policies across, maybe it can expand its share of the votes.

Unfortunately for the Lib Dems, more votes may do little to enhance the party's power. Britain uses the same electoral system as does the United States, the single-member, simple-plurality system. The candidate obtaining the largest number of votes, no matter what the share, is elected. When two parties receive virtually all the votes, as do the Democrats and the Republicans in the United States, this electoral system produces few strange results. Should a third party win a substantial number of votes throughout the country, however, as has occurred in Britain in recent years, it is greatly disadvantaged. For example, in 1983 the share of the vote won by the Alliance was only two percentage points less than that received by Labour, yet Labour won nearly ten times as many seats in the legislature. In the 1992 election, although nearly a fifth of the voters supported the Lib Dems, the party received fewer than two dozen seats in the legislature, only about 3 percent of the total membership.

The impact of the electoral system is not the only significant difference between British and American elections. In the United States primary elections provide voters an opportunity to determine who will be the candidates in the general election. Britain does not hold primary elections; candidates are selected by the party organization in each constituency. One must be at least a formal party member and, usually, has to be one of the party's officers to have a voice in candidate selection.

To get on the ballot a candidate must submit a deposit (around $750 at the beginning of 1994), which will be returned only if he or she receives at least 5 percent of the vote. Many minor parties are unable to do this well. All of the Greens' candidates, more than three hundred, lost their deposits in the 1992 election. Even a third party like the Lib Dems, which does not lose many deposits, is disadvantaged by having close to half a million dollars tied up in deposits and therefore not available to buy campaign materials.

At the national level British parties can spend whatever they wish on election campaigns. Since the formal campaign is only about a month long, however, total spending is much lower than in the United States. At the constituency level, candidates are limited in the amount they can spend. The total varies according to the size of the electorate, but rarely is it more than $10,000—virtually nothing by American standards. Neither parties nor candidates can buy radio or television time. A limited amount of time is provided free of charge. This goes primarily to the major parties; Labour and the Conservatives typically receive five programs of ten minutes each. Other parties are given much less; the Greens had only one five-minute program during the 1992 election campaign.

Scheduling of elections is highly flexible in Britain. No regular interval between elections is required. Elections can be no more than five years apart but may occur any time sooner. The prime minister, in consultation with party colleagues, decides when to call an election. Obviously, he or she tries to pick a time when his or her party is most popular. The prime minister, especially a Conservative one, is the key figure in his or her party's campaign. The counterpart in the other major party is the Leader of the Opposition, who will become prime minister if his or her party wins the election.

Both major parties in Britain are much more highly organized and centrally directed than are American parties. National party headquarters is to a considerable extent the personal political machine of the Conservative Leader. He or she appoints the key staff and has the final word for policy and party finance. Although the Conservative Leader is quite powerful, he or she certainly is not invulnerable. Once each year, any prominent Conservative legislator who wishes to do so, can challenge the party Leader. Margaret Thatcher was voted out as Leader, and therefore as prime minister, by her fellow Conservative legislators in November 1990. The Labour party is less willing to allow its Leader to exercise extensive power. For example, national headquarters is under the direction of the party's National Executive Committee (NEC), not the Leader. The Labour Leader used to be chosen by the party's MPs. Now, representatives of trade unions and constituency Labour parties cast most of the votes. The procedure for electing the Leader was one of three major conflicts between the right and left wings of the party during the 1980s. A second issue concerned the drafting of the party's manifesto (election platform). The left wing wanted this done solely by the NEC, hoping that this would prevent electoral considerations from moderating party policy. After much struggle, the existing system of joint drafting by the NEC and the legislative leaders was confirmed.

The third battle was over candidate selection. Since many constituencies in Britain are "safe," won by the same party election after election, and since there are no primary elections, being chosen as a candidate often has been tantamount to tenure—one could serve in the legislature for life with virtually no accountability to anyone in the constituency. The British system was democratically indefensible. Those in the Labour party who wanted a change, however, were not just engaged in an intellectual debate about abstract principles. This was a power struggle, and the reformers were trying to ensure that Labour legislators would be forced to support left-wing policies. Now every Labour constituency party must discuss following every general election whether it wishes its incumbent to be the party's candidate in the next election.

In the autumn of 1993 Labour switched to a one-member, one-vote (OMOV) procedure for selecting candidates for the legislature. Although this new arrangement permitting every party *member* to participate is more democratic, it falls far short of American practice of allowing all registered *citizens* to make the choice in a primary election. Yet another example of the greater than expected contrast between British and American electoral practices is the absence of any requirement, legal or informal, that MPs live in the constituencies they represent. Localism (*pace* Speaker "Tip" O'Neill) matters little in British politics.

IN FRANCE

Although they can trace their ancestry back many years earlier, most French parties in their current formation date only from the founding of the Fifth

Republic in 1958. Nonetheless, they still embody to a considerable extent the traditional divisions of French politics. The left in France long has portrayed itself not only as the most progressive on social and economic policy but as the only true democrats. Support for the republics, from the first one late in the eighteenth century through the fourth one after World War II, has been concentrated on the left of the political spectrum. Fervent republicans were committed to universal manhood suffrage (France did not extend the right to vote to women until after World War II), a strong legislature combined with a weak executive, and hostility to the Catholic church. During those times when France was not a republic, such as the Second Empire, the right was politically dominant. Then the executive overshadowed the legislature, the church had a greater say in public life—especially in education —and military officers were part of the social and political elite.

For about a century following the French Revolution, politics remained a highly polarized conflict between the left and the right. As the Third Republic, launched in 1875, moved into the twentieth century, the political struggle moderated a bit. The rise of new parties on the left pushed former "radical" groups toward the center of the spectrum. Whereas the new parties were mass-membership parties, the old parties were of the cadre type, ill-defined legislative groupings willing to participate in an ever-changing sequence of coalitions. So amorphous was the center of the French political spectrum that it became known as the "swamp."

Nonetheless, whenever events or policy proposals forced attention to focus on the role of the church in French society or the basic nature of legislative-executive relations, French politics became quite ideologically charged. The republic was deemed to be threatened and political activists rushed— usually figuratively, but occasionally literally—to man the barricades. The return to power of Charles de Gaulle in 1958 under threat of a military coup seemed, as Yogi Berra is supposed once to have said, "Déjà vu all over again." What was unusual, as we later see in examining French governmental institutions, is that for the first time a strong executive and power for the right coincided with the republican form of government. As the Fifth Republic has developed over more than three decades, much of the traditional left-right polarization has become irrelevant. The French party system, however, remains more fractionalized than either the British or American system and extends farther toward the extremes than does either of them. A brief survey of the main political forces from left to right will illustrate these characteristics.

Communists (PCF). An exception to the relatively recent founding of

French parties, the PCF was formed in 1920 because of a split in the Socialist party over whether to join the international association created by the then new Soviet Union. Following World War II, the PCF for a time became the most popular party in France, able to poll more than a quarter of the vote. In recent years, however, the party's fortunes have waned and its support has fallen to about a tenth of the voters.

In addition to a substantial portion of the working class, especially unskilled manual workers, many French intellectuals voted for the PCF for some time following World War II. People who had rejected the faith of the church as superstition often found that their lives lacked meaning. The pseudo-scientific trappings of Marxist ideology provided a set of values that transformed history and current affairs from merely random events into purposeful evolution. Furthermore, the Communists' emphasis on correcting injustice and eradicating poverty in French society, along with their plans for an extensive government role in running the economy, seemed admirable and logically conceived.

Economic prosperity helped reduce the PCF's attractiveness, but what really undermined its popularity was its position on international affairs. A French socialist politician once said of the PCF that it was not so much left as east, referring to its slavish commitment to the Soviet Union. The PCF was willing to support enthusiastically almost anything—the invasion of Afghanistan, for example—that the Soviet Union did. Initially after World War II the Soviets were regarded as freedom fighters who had helped to liberate Europe from the Nazis. At that time, admiration for the Soviet Union could easily be an electoral asset. But as the Soviet Union's repressive and imperialistic nature became increasingly manifest during the Cold War, the PCF's knee-jerk endorsement of its actions became an electoral liability.

Communist parties elsewhere in Europe—Italy is a prime example —were much more willing to criticize the Soviet Union and, in contrast to the PCF, were able to enhance their image. In short, the PCF was the most Stalinist—rigidly authoritarian and doctrinaire—of any European communist party. This orientation carried over into the party's internal organization. The so-called democratic centralism meant that once the party's leaders had proclaimed a policy, all members were required to advocate it down to the last detail.

For a time early in the 1970s, the PCF moderated a bit and agreed to a common program with the Socialists. This later fell apart because of disagreements over France's nuclear weapons and the extent to which government should acquire private enterprises. At the start of the 1980s, when the Socialists came to power, they gave the PCF a few seats in the Cabinet. Policy differences proved too great, however, for even this form of cooperation to last more than a few years.

Since both the Communists and the Socialists are on the left of the political spectrum, they still vote together at times in the legislature. Occasionally in the early 1990s the Socialist government was able to avoid defeats in the legislature only because of support from Communist representatives. Nonetheless, formal cooperation between the two parties is unlikely. And should electoral trends continue, the PCF soon will reach the level of irrelevance to French politics.

Socialists (PS). Various socialist parties have existed in France since the latter part of the nineteenth century. For all practical purposes, however, the current party dates from the early 1970s when François Mitterrand (president of France since 1981) reorganized and revitalized an almost moribund organization. His chief accomplishment was to make the party sufficiently attractive that it surpassed the Communists in popular support. Once the electorate saw that it did not have to vote Communist to support a reformist party, the decline of the PCF accelerated. The PS surged in 1981 to what in a multiparty system was a landslide victory—well over a third of the popular vote and a majority of the seats in the legislature. The party's electoral support remained at about that level for the rest of the 1980s, although its legislative strength declined. Nonetheless, it remained the largest party and controlled the government for all but two years of the decade.

French political culture is such that many Socialists enjoy using revolutionary jargon that would shock most people in the Democratic party in the United States. Whatever the Marxist tinge of the party's rhetoric, however, the PS clearly is a moderate reform party. When in 1981 the party returned to power following a long period in opposition, it expanded the scope of government ownership of business and provided new benefits to workers; these hardly were radical policies. Furthermore, when many of their economic policies did not seem to be working, the Socialists implemented an austerity program about as stringent as a right-wing government would have introduced.

By the 1990s, France, largely under Socialist direction, had achieved a rate of economic growth higher than that of either Germany or Britain and a rate of inflation substantially less than either of the other two countries. Despite these major achievements, the Socialists' popularity declined. In part this was because unemployment was two-thirds higher than it had been a decade before. The percentage of the workforce unemployed in France was twice as great as in Germany. Furthermore, the Socialists seemed beset by scandals. Charges were made that prominent Socialists had peddled influence to raise party funds. A well-known terrorist entered the country for medical treatment and managed to depart without being apprehended. And the government failed to test adequately and safeguard the blood supply, so that many people were infected with AIDS. Thus the competence, if not the policies, of the party was being called into question.

As a result, the PS was crushed in the 1993 legislative elections. Subsequent factional fighting and bitter recrimination over the electoral defeat have weakened the party further. Whether the party that dominated French politics during the 1980s can manage to survive to the end of the 1990s is doubtful.

Union for French Democracy (UDF). Although not a party, the UDF is a major political formation. The organization loosely combines, largely for electoral purposes, various center and right parties. The largest of these is the Republican party (PR). Although an outgrowth of a Fourth Republic party of another name, the PR itself was organized early in the Fifth Republic primarily as the vehicle of Valéry Giscard d'Estaing. Subsequently, from 1974 to 1981, Giscard served a term as president of France. The PR has combined modest social reform—liberalizing divorce and abortion laws —with economic conservatism.

Next in size within the UDF is the Center of Social Democrats (CDS). This is France's Christian democratic party, although anticlericalism is sufficiently strong in the country that the party does not dare to use that label. A forerunner of the CDS was briefly France's largest party during the Fourth Republic. The CDS is more liberal on economic issues than on social ones, since its reformist views are tempered on the latter by the influence of the church. While the PR has favored European integration, the CDS' support for the European Community has been even more fervent.

Another element in the UDF is the Radicals. France's major party during the Third Republic, the Radicals once were quite progressive. Despite their successes, the Radicals remained a cadre, rather than a mass membership, party. Currently, not only have they declined to only a handful of supporters, but they also have moved to the right of the center on the political spectrum.

The UDF usually cooperates during elections with the RPR (to be discussed next). In 1988 the two political forces joined forces to offer candidates under the label of the Union of the Rally and the Center (URC). This formation received as much popular support and legislative strength as did the PS. Since the URC was merely an umbrella group, however, and was weakened by policy differences and personal rivalries, it lacked the influence of the PS.

Again in 1993 the UDF and the RPR ran a joint campaign, this time known as the Union for France (UPF). The disrepute in which the public held the PS helped the UPF to a landslide victory. It won more than three-quarters of the seats in the legislature. Even though differences between the UDF and the RPR, along with factional tensions within both organizations, attenuate this victory, the center and the right clearly are in command of the French legislature.

Rally for the Republic (RPR). For a time during the Fourth Republic, a party existed to advance the plans for constitutional reform of Charles de Gaulle, France's great military hero of World War II. Despite some successes, this party ultimately failed. Therefore, when de Gaulle did return to power to create the Fifth Republic, a new party had to be organized from scratch. Although this party took positions on a variety of issues, its primary purpose was to advocate whatever de Gaulle wanted. Thus it was even more of a personal political vehicle than was either the PS or the PR. The surprise proved to be that after de Gaulle withdrew from politics and died a few years later, the party continued to exist. This was largely because the movement was taken over and reorganized in its present form by another prominent politician, Jacques Chirac. Chirac has been mayor of Paris for many years and twice has served as prime minister of France.

Gaullists (those who supported de Gaulle) have tended to be cautious on social reform but somewhat more liberal on economic matters. Social services and some economic reform were seen as means of winning support from workers, who otherwise would have been likely to vote Communist. Thus such measures would help unite the country across class divisions. If this brief summary seems to suggest that Gaullists had a good deal in common with supporters of the CDS, that is true. Where the two parted company was over Europe. Charles de Gaulle was a fervent nationalist. For him, the European Community could serve only to facilitate its members' cooperation; he would not tolerate a tightly integrated organization that in any way might limit French sovereignty.

Chirac has not taken so nationalistic a stand. In 1992, when France held a referendum on the Maastricht Treaty, an agreement intended to add monetary union and some measure of political integration to the European Community's single economic market, he announced that he favored voting yes. Nonetheless, a majority of the supporters of the RPR voted no.

The 1993 legislative elections made the RPR France's largest party as it won two-fifths of the seats. This success has produced an unexpected problem for the RPR. As the largest party it provided the new prime minister, Edouard Balladur. Balladur has become so popular that he poses a threat to the ambitions of RPR leader Chirac to run for president in 1995. Furthermore, Giscard of the PR wants to be president once again. While these three leaders are happy to cooperate to dispose of the Socialists, their jockeying for position in the presidential race means that neither the RPR, nor the right in general, is as strong and united as its legislative strength might suggest.

National Front (FN). This party is so far to the right as to be considered neofascist. Its principal policy is bigoted denunciation of North African Arabs in France. Although this is presented at times as a legitimate concern about competition for scarce jobs when unemployment is high, the underlying motivation is xenophobia and racism. The party is led by Jean-Marie le Pen, a disreputable rabble-rouser. Like the Communists, the National Front has been obtaining the support of about a tenth of the electorate.

Turning from parties to electoral procedures, France has altered the relevant laws almost every time it has held an election. The country has shifted back and forth between proportional representation (PR) and the double-ballot system. Under PR, the country is divided up into many multimember constituencies. In each constituency the seats are allocated among the parties roughly in proportion to the share of the vote each receives. Thus, in an eight-member district, a party with a quarter of the vote could expect to win two representatives. France used one form or another of PR all during the Fourth Republic; in the Fifth Republic (that is, since 1958) it has employed this electoral system only in 1986.

With that one exception the electoral system in the Fifth Republic has been similar to what was in effect for the Third Republic—the double-ballot system. As is the case for Anglo-American practice, each constituency returns only one representative. In contrast, however, under the double-ballot system a candidate must receive more than half the vote to be elected. In a country with a multiparty system this usually does not happen. Therefore, a week later, another election is held in all the constituencies where no one was elected on the first try. In the interval between elections, parties negotiate deals, withdrawing their candidate and throwing their votes to another party in one constituency in exchange for that party reciprocating elsewhere. On the second ballot the candidate with the most votes wins regardless of whether that is a majority of the vote. The double-ballot system does not produce proportional results any more than does the single-member, simple-plurality system used by Britain and the United States. For example, in 1981 the PS received less than half the vote, 38 percent, but won well over half, 57 percent, of the seats in the legislature.

The election procedures described apply only to the lower house of the legislature. The upper house of the French legislature is elected indirectly. Electoral colleges composed primarily of local governmental officials are created throughout the country. The number of legislators elected by each college varies according to the population of the area. The larger districts use PR, while the smaller employ the double-ballot system. In contrast to the United States, an electoral college is not involved in electing the French president. The electorate votes directly for the office using the double-ballot system. The primary differences from lower-house legislative elections are that the interval between the two elections (assuming no one wins on the first ballot) is two weeks, and only the top two candidates on the first ballot are permitted to run in the second election. The latter regulation ensures that the person elected president will have received a majority of the votes cast.

Since French parties can cooperate on an ad hoc basis from one constituency to another for legislative elections, they have little incentive to submerge their differences to organize broad-based parties like those in the United States. Thus the party system remains fractionalized. If one discounts the extreme parties at each fringe of the spectrum (although they account for a fifth of the vote between them), France has three main forces: the Socialists, the UDF, and the Gaullists. But inasmuch as the UDF is a combination of parties, this suggests greater focus than the party system actually exhibits. Whether the British party system differs fundamentally from the American may be debatable; however, the French system clearly is in another category.

IN GERMANY

Although Germany remained democratic under the Weimar Republic in the 1920s and early 1930s, its party system was even more fractionalized than France's has been. When democracy was restored in West Germany after World War II, this pattern was expected to be resumed. Rapidly, however, political forces began to consolidate so that for most of the postwar period German politics have been dominated by only three fairly well-defined political groupings. The unification of the former West Germany with the former East has not reversed this development.

Christian Democrats (CDU and CSU). Following World War II, Christian democratic parties were founded in many European countries. Most of these parties were Catholic oriented, but differed from their late nineteenth- and early twentieth-century forerunners in being rather liberal, especially in economic affairs. They embodied a Catholic reform tradition that usually had been overshadowed by much more conservative, even reactionary, factions within the church, a tradition that ultimately would flourish in the Third World as liberation theology.

Although the German version was part of this development, it differed in one significant regard. In Germany Christians, whether Catholic or Protestant, were so appalled by the crimes of the Nazi regime that they decided to join forces in a political movement sufficiently strong to prevent any such horrors from being repeated. Thus Christian democracy in Germany was not a sectarian movement; the resultant party drew Protestant and Catholic support relatively equally. Furthermore, in part through Christian trade unions, the party was able to add considerable working-class support to backing from business and farmers.

The result was a party rather like American ones—effective in winning elections precisely because it stressed general principles and orientations, instead of offering a detailed, well-integrated program, to say nothing of a full-blown ideology. Insofar as the party's policies had a lodestar, it was firm commitment to the United States as the only means of ensuring that West Germany would not fall prey to the Soviet Union. While such a stance would have been sufficient to win the support of many Germans, what really solidified the party's dominance was its success in rebuilding Germany from the rubble of World War II and establishing a prosperous economy.

Strictly speaking, as the initials at the head of this section indicate, Christian democracy in Germany is not a single party. The Christian Democratic Union (CDU) was organized throughout Germany with the exception of Bavaria, the country's largest state, which is located in the south. In Bavaria, and only there, the Christian Social Union (CSU) operated. Despite what the name might seem to suggest, the CSU is more conservative than the CDU, clearly to the right on the political spectrum rather than around the center. Furthermore, regardless of the many links between the CSU and the CDU, they remain separate parties with their own organizations and officers both in the country and in the national legislature. Since they do not compete during elections and do share the Christian democratic tradition, however, they often are discussed as a single political force. Once communism collapsed in East Germany, West German parties were able to operate across the former Iron Curtain. The CDU, as the party that had pressed for rapid unification, initially was quite popular in the former East Germany and had little difficulty in expanding its organization. The CSU did not attempt to enlarge on its Bavarian base.

The Christian Democrats were out of office for a period of more than a decade primarily during the 1970s. For the rest of the time since 1949, when Germany was reborn, they have controlled the government. The CDU and the CSU together receive more than two-fifths of the popular vote, and in the 1990 election won nearly half the seats in the legislature.

Socialists (SPD). Germany's other major party is its oldest. Founded in the latter part of the nineteenth century, the SPD adhered to Marxist ideology for many years. By the twentieth century, the SPD clearly was willing to operate within the political system; it was Germany's leading party for much of the Weimar Republic. Nonetheless, some elements of the old ideology lingered on after World War II and anti-American neutralism had some support. The SPD transformed itself in 1959 by adopting the Godesberg Program. In a break with traditional party policy, the SPD rejected pacifism and anticlericalism and endorsed a mixed economy with a substantial free-enterprise sector.

The SPD first obtained a share of power in the Grand Coalition with the Christian Democrats toward the close of the 1960s. When the Christian Democrats were put out of power during the 1970s, the SPD became the dominant party controlling the government. During this time the party demonstrated that the Godesberg Program had not been just an electoral ploy. The economy was not transformed to embody an elaborate socialist command system, and Germany remained a reliable member of the Western alliance. Clearly, the SPD was a moderate left reform party, its socialism more in name than in practice.

Although the SPD's popularity declined somewhat early in the 1980s, what put the party out of power was not so much voter discontent as it was the withdrawal of support by its coalition partner the FDP (discussed next). During the 1980s the party's support continued to erode. By 1990 it had only a third of the popular vote, some ten percentage points less than it had received in 1980. All that the party could hope was that the economic difficulties arising from the unification of the former East and West Germanies would make the Christian Democrats so unpopular that many voters would swing back to the SPD.

Free Democrats (FDP). The FDP embodies the liberal tradition, that is, nonsocialist reform. Key elements in this tradition have been a stress on individual liberties and anticlericalism. In the nineteenth century liberalism meant laissez-faire government economic policies, while in the twentieth century the term came to mean an economically activist government. Both orientations can be found in the FDP. The party bears some similarity to the British Liberal Democrats. And as is true in the British case, FDP policies and the mix of interests active in the party vary a good bit from one part of Germany to another. Middle-class professionals are a major source of support for the FDP, which also wins the backing of some farmers and those small business people who feel that the Christian Democrats are too oriented toward big corporations.

The FDP usually polls about a tenth of the vote, that is, less than half the usual support for the Liberals in Britain. Because of the German electoral system (discussed below), however, the FDP enjoys much greater influence. Looking at the entire postwar period since 1949, the FDP has been in office more years than either of Germany's major parties. Only for three years, at the close of the 1960s, was the party not included in the governing coalition. Neither of the major parties has had sufficient strength to govern the country without FDP support. The FDP's position at the center of the political spectrum has enabled it at times to support the Christian Democrats and on other occasions to assist the SPD. Thus although it clearly is a third party in the German system, labeling it a minor party understates its significance.

Other Parties. During the mid-1980s the Greens had nearly as much strength in the legislature as did the FDP. In addition to taking the environmentalist stands that one would expect of a party with such a name, the Greens also advocated policies that put them to the left of the SPD. Not only were the Greens against nuclear power for peaceful purposes, they also opposed siting U.S. nuclear weapons in Germany under NATO arrangements. Quasi-Marxist, anticapitalist views were common among the Greens. The party also took an antiestablishment tack that enjoyed puncturing stereotypical German pompousness. In the first election after the unification of the two Germanies, support for the Greens collapsed, and the party won only a handful of seats in the legislature.

Although West Germany outlawed one communist party, it did not bother to take legal action against another one organized subsequently. Since this party had virtually no support, it could be ignored. As communism collapsed in East Germany, part of the former ruling party reorganized itself in hopes of retaining at least some support. Claiming to be Democratic Socialists (PDS), this party contested the first election after unification. Although it managed to win a few seats in the legislature, it received only a couple of percentage points of the vote. It will be fortunate to retain even this support in the future.

West Germany also outlawed one neo-Nazi party but did not bother with various successors because of their minuscule popular support. At the start of the 1990s, however, neo-Nazi violence directed against foreigners increased considerably. To demonstrate its condemnation of such behavior, the government again outlawed several groups of this type. Some people were more concerned over apparently growing support for a party called the Republicans. Very conservative and clearly hostile to foreigners, the Republicans were not explicitly anti-Semitic and did not advocate violence. Perhaps the Republicans could be called the acceptable face of extremism. This was precisely the danger. If one did not have to apologize for supporting them, they were likely to poll a greater share of the vote. No realistic estimate suggested that the Republicans could win as large a share as did the National Front in France. Remembrance of past atrocities, however, made the German developments alarming to many people who were little bothered by what was going on in France.

The Germans have tried, by means of a hybrid electoral system, to protect their government from again falling prey to extremists. The American single-member, simple-plurality system could have had this effect. Since the Germans anticipated that they would have a multiparty system as in the past, however, the American system was inappropriate. The discussion earlier of British electoral procedures indicated the peculiar results this system produces when a country diverges even somewhat from a two-party system. Adopting pure PR, however, would permit extremist parties to be represented in the legislature. So the Germans combined the two systems in a complicated arrangement intended to prevent any extremist minor parties that might arise from putting down the roots that would enable them to grow into a threat to democracy.

Germany is divided into 331 single-member constituencies. In each constituency the candidate winning the most votes, regardless of what percentage that might be, is elected—just as happens in American and British elections. These representatives, however, account for only about half the membership of the legislature. Every German voter is permitted a second vote, which is cast for one or another of the lists of candidates that parties offer. Each German state is a multimember constituency for a PR component of the election. Parties are permitted to add candidates from their state party lists to those already elected in the single-member constituencies. These additional representatives are allocated in such a fashion that each party's share of seats in the legislature will correspond closely to its share of the total popular vote.

The PR component is prevented from fractionalizing the party system and opening the door to representation of extremists by a threshold requirement. In order to participate in the proportional allocation of seats, a party either must win three of the single-member, simple-plurality seats or obtain a minimum of 5 percent of the total national vote. Even a well-established third party like the FDP lacks sufficient support to win even one of the constituency seats. Thus the threshold becomes, in effect, a 5 percent barrier. This has proved sufficient in Germany to keep extremist groups out of the legislature. At times, extremist parties have seemed to be growing, especially in certain states, but when a national election has occurred, they have been unable to surmount the barrier. And lacking a national base, they have soon dwindled into insignificance. Of course, no one can guarantee that the electoral system will continue to be so effective. Perhaps the Republicans will manage to surpass the threshold in 1994. Nonetheless, those concerned about neo-Nazi sentiment in Germany should recognize that the current system, unlike its Weimar predecessor, does possess some effective institutional defenses against extremists.

4. The Political Systems of Britain, France, and Germany: Governmental Institutions

In the United States, power is fractionalized. At the national level, power is *separated* among the three branches of government: legislative, executive, and judicial. The United States has an independent chief executive. Furthermore, power is *divided* between the national government and state governments. The national government possesses only those powers delegated to it by the Constitution; other powers are reserved for exercise by the states.

In Europe, power is more concentrated. Germany, like the United States, has a federal system dividing power between the national and state governments. In France and Britain, however, subnational governmental structures are simply the creatures of the national government. Regional and local governments carry out only those tasks granted to them by the national government and continue to exist only by sufferance of the national government. Furthermore, at the national level both Britain and Germany practice *fusion* of powers. The parliamentary system of each country merges the legislative and executive branches so that the chief executive needs the support of the legislature to survive in office. France, as well, has a parliamentary system, but in addition possesses a second chief executive independent of the legislature. French government partakes of elements of both fusion and separation of powers.

Thus each of these three European countries has its own distinctive arrangement of governmental institutions. The German allocation of powers resembles the American in one way, the French in another, and the British in neither. What is common among the three is less diluted power than in the United States, less concern to devise an elaborate system of checks and balances. Nonetheless, in the case of the executive branch the Europeans have divided the various roles played by the American president.

Executive Officials

The American president is both head of state and head of government. The former role is a ceremonial or symbolic one. The president represents the country on formal state occasions; his signature may be required on certain documents to indicate that they are legal. The head of government role confers decision-making powers. In this capacity the president directs the actual operation of the government. In part because of a monarchical tradition, which the United States lacks, European countries divide these two roles between separate officers.

Britain, in contrast to France and Germany, retains a monarch as head of state. Although the pomp associated with the monarch's activities suggests great power, that no longer is true. Queen Elizabeth opens the legislature each year, for example, with a speech comparable to the American president's State of the Union Address. She has not, however, had any voice in its contents; she merely reads what the politicians have written for her. Centuries ago, all governmental power inhered in the person of the monarch simply by virtue of being monarch. Neither the legislature nor the people had conferred power; some monarchs claimed to possess it by divine right. Furthermore, few constraints existed on the exercise of this power. Over the centuries the powers of the monarch as a person were transferred to the Crown as an abstraction. Many activities—such as appointing officials, concluding international treaties, convening the legislature—are given legal form by being done in the name of the Crown. These actions are taken, however, not at the monarch's discretion but because politicians have decided to do so. Thus the monarch functions primarily as a unifying national symbol, perhaps the equivalent of a living flag.

Germany has not had a monarch since the end of World War I. Under the current system the head of state is a president elected indirectly (by a gathering of national legislators and delegates from the state legislatures) for a five-year term. Despite being an elected politician rather than hereditary royalty, the president's powers and duties are comparable to those of the British monarch. Once in office, the president is expected, whatever the previous links, to be nonpartisan in order to serve as the national figurehead of all Germans. Since the role is ceremonial, the president possesses little discretionary power. With rare exceptions, formal actions require a countersignature by a relevant member of the government.

France has not had a monarch since 1870, so, like Germany, it has a politician as head of state. There the similarity ends, however, because the French president is an extremely powerful, independent chief executive. As explained already in the discussion of French elections, the president is chosen directly by the voters. He or she serves a seven-year term and is no more subject to the legislature than is the American president. Although the French president is the head of state, the role goes well beyond the ceremonial figurehead functions performed by the British monarch and the German president.

The French constitution imposes on the president duties of the most fundamental importance. The president is to "see that the constitution is respected. He shall ensure, by his arbitration, the regular functioning of the governmental authorities, as well as the continuance of the State. He shall be the guarantor of national independence, of the integrity of the territory." To fulfill these obligations the president needs considerable discretion. The proposed actions of other members of the executive are not automatically endorsed by the French head of state and, conversely, the president frequently can act without the approval of other executive leaders.

The president designates the head of government (an important power in a system of fractionalized, less than tightly organized parties), appoints department heads (has joint decision power, not just formal ratification of someone else's choice), and can require the legislature to reconsider a bill it has passed. This latter power is not quite the same as a veto because no extraordinary majority is required for an override. All that the legislature needs to do is to pass the bill a second time. Nevertheless, in a legislature where no party has a majority of the seats, as is typically the case in France, getting enough support to repass a bill can be as difficult as overriding the veto of an American president. The president can dissolve the legislature at any time (although no more frequently than once a year) and can call for new elections. Although the head of government must be "consulted" before the president acts, he or she does not need to approve. The head of government is supposed to be removable from office only by the vote of the legislature. Nonetheless, several heads of government have resigned during the Fifth Republic simply because the president told them to do so.

The president's greatest potential strength is the emergency power granted in Article 16. When the nation is threatened or the functioning of its institutions is interrupted, the president is instructed to "take the measures required by these circumstances." All that needs to be done before invoking this power is to "consult" with the head of government, the heads of both houses of the legislature, and the Constitutional Council. While the emergency powers are in effect, the president is free to act, constrained only by the limit that the legislature must be permitted to meet. Only once during the Fifth Republic, and that just for a few months, has a president resorted to Article 16. The emergency, an attempted military coup in Algeria, was handled without an abuse of power. Nonetheless, an unscrupulous president could become a virtual dictator through this power.

The president can call a referendum on various proposals by the government or the legislature. Again, in contrast to heads of state in other countries, this action is not just a formality; the president could decide not to call for a popular vote, regardless of what other political leaders desired. Furthermore, de Gaulle, when he was president, frequently called referendums on his own initiative, although the constitution does not grant the head of state that power.

The style of French presidents has varied from de Gaulle's aloofness to Giscard's monarchical pomposity to Mitterrand's Machiavellian inscrutability. Before coming to office, Mitterrand had argued that the president's powers should be reduced. But even he, like all his predecessors, made clear that he intended to be the dominant power in French government. The other main executive, the head of government, would serve only as the implementer of the president's program.

Despite the contrasts in the arrangements for head of state, the three countries have made fundamentally similar provisions for head of government. In each case the head of government presides over a collective executive composed of the political heads of the various departments—Defense, Agriculture, and the like. This Cabinet must retain the support of the legislature to remain in office. Thus the executive and legislative powers are fused to form a parliamentary system.

In Britain the prime minister and the Cabinet can be removed from office by losing a vote of confidence or by a motion of censure in the House of Commons, regardless whether a majority of all the legislators vote against them. This rarely happens; only once since World War II, for example, has the Commons voted no-confidence in the executive. Although Britain has a fusion-of-powers system, in practice it is the people through elections, rather than the legislature through motions of confidence, that determines who will be head of government.

On the Continent, Cabinets have been much less stable. A typical head of government has served only for several months before being replaced, as a result of shifting coalitions in the legislature, by another politician. To avoid such executive instability and obtain some continuity in public policy, both France in the Fifth Republic and Germany have established procedures more complex than those in Britain for removing the head of government from office.

A motion of censure cannot be considered in the National Assembly, the lower house of the French legislature (the upper house lacks the power to remove the executive from office), unless supported by at least 10 percent of its members. Furthermore, should the motion not pass, then those who put it on the agenda may not initiate another motion of censure for the rest of that session of the legislature. To pass and, thereby, remove the prime minister from office, the motion must receive the votes of more than half the members of the National Assembly. Thus the prime minister could be out-voted but remain in office because absences and abstentions kept the votes against him or her under 50 percent. Further strengthening the executive is a procedure permitting the prime minister and the Cabinet to declare that passage of a particular bill is a matter of confidence. When this is done, the bill is considered to have passed unless the legislature carries a motion of censure against the executive. Thus bills that more legislators opposed than supported can become law because those voting against them were fewer than half the house.

The German head of government is known as the chancellor. The legislature can remove the chancellor from office only by a "constructive vote of no confidence." Merely losing a vote in the legislature does not require the chancellor to resign. The Bundestag, the lower house of the legislature (again, the upper house lacks this power), must choose a new chancellor supported by more than half of all its members. This provision is aimed at avoiding negative majorities of left- and right-wing extremists, who could agree only on what they opposed and not on what policies they wanted.

All the members of the British Cabinet serve simultaneously in the legislature, another instance of fusion of the legislative and executive branches. The Cabinet governs Britain, deciding what the main themes of public policy will be and coordinating the implementation. Most of its work is done through a variety of committees. As a result, under normal circumstances the full Cabinet meets only once a week for a session of about two hours. Once the Cabinet decides on a policy, everyone in the executive branch must advocate it. Anyone who argued against it must now switch positions or resign from the executive. This procedure of "collective responsibility" is one of the conventions of the British constitution.

The prime minister, the Leader of the majority party in the House of Commons, presides over the Cabinet. He or she appoints (technically recommends to the monarch) the Cabinet and the rest of the executive leaders. These appointments do not require any legislative confirmation, and the prime minister can remove the appointees from office and replace them with others at will. Thus, although the prime minister long was described as being only first among equals, he or she clearly is the most powerful member of the executive. Although the prime minister does not dominate the Cabinet to the extent that the president does in the United States, he or she has the final word in determining government policy and actions.

Since Germany has a written constitution, the roles of the head of government and the Cabinet are set forth more explicitly than in Britain. The constitution authorizes the chancellor to determine the general lines of policy and makes that official alone responsible to the legislature. The absence of British collective responsibility clearly makes the other members of the German executive subordinate to the head of government. Nevertheless, since the German Cabinet typically is composed of people from two or three parties, the executive does not speak with one voice as regularly as in Britain. Fusion of powers in Germany, as in Britain, means that members of the executive simultaneously serve in the legislature, although exceptions occasionally occur. The special position of the chancellor notwithstanding, the roles of the German and British Cabinets are fundamentally similar. Each runs the country and is the main source for new legislation.

The distinctive position of the president in France makes the country's other executive arrangements diverge somewhat from those of Britain and Germany. According to the constitution, the prime minister and the Cabinet have power to "determine and conduct the policy of the nation." It also declares that the "Prime Minister directs the action of the Government," is responsible for national defense, assures the execution of the laws, and exercises the executive decree powers. As already explained, however, every French president has made clear that he was in charge and insofar as prime ministers have been allowed to utilize these powers (in some instances the president has done so himself), it has been at the president's direction.

Relations between the head of state and the head of government become complicated, however, when they come from different parties, as was the case from 1986 to 1988 and again beginning in 1993. In both instances the president (Mitterrand) was a Socialist (PS), but the prime ministers (Chirac in the 1980s and Balladur in the 1990s) were Gaullist (RPR). This partisan contrast, which the French call "co-habitation," occurred because the center and right-wing parties managed to win a majority of seats in the 1986 and 1993 legislative elections. (The PS won the intervening 1988 election.) During co-habitation, the president has been less dominant than usual. Sometimes the president has gotten his way on executive appointments and policy issues, while other times the prime minister has prevailed.

Relations between Mitterrand and Chirac were quite strained, raising the question whether co-habitation was a dysfunctional arrangement. Mitterrand has gotten on much better with Balladur, both because the latter is more diplomatic than was Chirac and because Mitterrand has become more retiring as he nears the end of his political career.

Whatever these complications within the executive, relations with the legislature resemble those in Britain and Germany. True, France does depart from typical parliamentary practice in one way: When legislators are appointed to the Cabinet, they must give up their seats; they cannot serve in both an executive and a legislative capacity as in Britain and Germany. Thus fusion of powers is somewhat attenuated. Despite the executive leaders being more separate in France, they, as in Britain and Germany, are the source of the legislative program. The legislature is more a reactor than an initiator. Areas where the French executive has been weak in the past have been significantly reversed in the Fifth Republic. The Cabinet's bills have priority on the legislature's agenda. On financial matters the legislature no longer can use delay as a tactic for forcing concessions from the executive. If the legislature has not passed the budget seventy days after presentation, the Cabinet can enact it by decree. Although such changes for the Fifth Republic were major reforms, they did no more than give the French executive the type of power long enjoyed by the British Cabinet.

The Legislatures

All three countries have bicameral (two-house) legislatures, as does the United States. In each the lower house is composed of popularly elected representatives. Although all three countries, even united Germany, have much smaller populations than does the United States, each has about half again as many members in the lower house of its legislature as does the U.S. House of Representatives.

The upper houses not only differ from one another but also from the American arrangement. Before the ratification in 1913 of the Seventeenth Amendment to the U.S. Constitution, the legislature of each state chose that state's senators. Somewhat similarly, the French Senate is elected indirectly by colleges composed primarily of local and regional officeholders. Senators serve for nine years, with a third of their terms expiring every three years. In Germany the executive branch of each state selects its state's members in the Bundesrat (three to six, depending on a state's population). These members have no set term and are replaced whenever their state executive branch so desires. The Bundesrat represents the state governments, not the people of each state, as is the American practice in the twentieth century. All of a state's delegates in the Bundesrat vote as a bloc according to instructions given them by their state's executive.

Most curious of all from an American perspective is the British House of Lords. The Senate and the Bundesrat may not represent the people directly, but at least they do represent something; the House of Lords does not represent anything. The bulk of its membership is hereditary; a man inherits a title when his father dies (virtually no peerages descend through the female line) and thereby becomes a member of the House of Lords. Because Britain has an established state church, the Lords also includes a few dozen bishops and archbishops. And because the Lords is Britain's highest court, a dozen eminent jurists are appointed as Law Lords. For about the past thirty years, the Lords has included a fourth type of member: life peers. These are people whose distinguished careers—usually, but not always, in politics—are recognized by granting them titles (formally by the monarch, but in reality on the decision of the prime minister). In contrast to the hereditary title, this peerage lapses on the death of its holder and does not pass on to his or her children. Note that despite the variety of members, none of the Lords is elected.

Centuries ago, when the British Parliament began to develop, the House of Lords was the more powerful house. Gradually, the House of Commons gained significance and, in the twentieth century, two laws were passed that clearly relegated the Lords to a limited role, its main power one of delay. On financial legislation the Lords can hold up passage for only a month; then the will of the Commons prevails. For other legislation, opposition by the Lords prevents passage. When the two houses disagree, the bill simply shuttles back and forth until one or the other refuses to offer any more concessions. No joint committee, such as is used in the U.S. Congress to seek a compromise, is convoked. Should a bill that the Lords has blocked be passed again by the Commons the following year, however, it becomes law regardless of the dissent of the Lords. The Lords often holds informative debates and is useful in discussing parts of bills for which the Commons lacked time for careful consideration. Thus the Lords is helpful and, at times, perhaps influential; but it is not a powerful legislative chamber.

Whether the lower house prevails in France is a bit more complicated. As in Britain, the standard procedure calls for approval by both houses of the legislature. When the two disagree on a bill in France, the prime minister *may* convene a joint conference committee to work out a compromise text. If this compromise is acceptable to the prime minister, he or she asks both houses to approve it. Should the two houses still not agree, the prime minister *may* ask the lower house, the National Assembly, to "rule definitively," that is, cast the deciding vote. Thus the prime minister decides whether the Senate is able to exercise a veto. If he or she does not act, Senate opposition kills the bill. Should he or she give the decision power to the National Assembly, however, the Senate's opposition is futile. The Senate checks the National Assembly only when the prime minister wants it to do so. Normally the prime minister will be supported by a majority of the National Assembly's members and therefore probably will not need any check on its actions. Yet the way in which the Senate's seats are apportioned and the indirect election procedure employed make it more conservative than the National Assembly. A center or right-wing executive might be happy to have a potential ally in the upper house to keep a more liberal lower house in line.

Germany's upper house is the most powerful of the three. Only Germany is a federal system; Britain and France are unitary systems. Therefore, only in Germany is having a house in the national legislature to defend states' rights important. All the executive's proposals for new legislation must go first to the Bundesrat for comment before being introduced into the lower house. Legislation that significantly affects the states can be enacted only with the Bundesrat's approval; in such cases the two chambers have equal power. Where the interests of the states are not at stake, the Bundesrat has only a qualified veto. The Bundestag, the lower house, can enact such a bill, despite Bundesrat opposition, by passing it a second time. Should the upper house have voted against by two-thirds or more, however, the lower house needs a two-thirds vote to override. When the two houses disagree, a mediation committee composed of members of each house attempts to work out a compromise. Insofar as one house or the other can be said to "win" in this process, most observers conclude that more often than not, it is the Bundesrat.

Although bills may originate in either house of the British legislature, most are introduced in the House of Commons. The great bulk are proposed by the executive, since it controls the major share of legislative time. Individual members of Parliament (MPs) are permitted so little time for their legislative pet projects that they literally hold a lottery to determine which of them can use what is available. In contrast to the United States, bills go to committee for consideration of details only after passage on second reading. Whereas congressional committees have to weed out bills to permit only a manageable few to get back to the floor for further consideration, a Commons committee works on improving the specific provisions of a single bill, which it is expected to report back promptly. Although called "standing" committees, these are not permanent, subject-matter committees, like those in the U.S. Congress. Commons committees are designated only by the letters of the alphabet, are appointed only when a bill has passed second reading and is ready to go to committee, and cease to exist as soon as the bill is reported back to the Commons. Thus these Commons committees do not hold hearings on a topic of legislative concern and cannot function as a check on the executive through investigations or oversight.

Nevertheless, the Commons has some devices for calling the executive to account that the U.S. Congress lacks. Monday through Thursday, at the start of the legislative day, MPs have an hour in which to direct questions to members of the executive about the substance and administration of public policy. To some extent this procedure requires those who are running the country to respond to criticism. Another procedure facilitates a full-scale debate on matters of controversy. Opposition parties in the Commons can set the agenda for twenty meetings each year. Obviously, they will focus the debate on those aspects of government policy and performance that are most vulnerable to complaint. Such debates influence the vote of few MPs but are important in informing the public about the parties' contrasting policy programs. A variety of adjournment debates, some on broad issues and others on specific details, also require those in power to account for their actions. The British executive controls the legislature and almost always gets its legislative proposals enacted. The House of Commons is more than a rubber stamp, however, because it can call the executive to account. If the prime minister and the Cabinet fail to respond convincingly to the concerns expressed in the Commons, they are likely to find that public opinion has swung against them at the next election.

In contrast to the British executive's dominance of the legislature during the twentieth century, in France the legislature has prevailed. That is, until the start of the Fifth Republic in 1958. Many legislative procedures were altered then to shift the balance of power. Parliament is limited to two sessions a year, each of them three months or less. The prime minister may convene a special session. Although the constitution provides that a majority of the National Assembly also can call for one, President de Gaulle refused to comply with the legislators' desire for such a session in 1960.

The French legislature, like the British, had been free to legislate on whatever it regarded as important. Now its power is restricted to those matters specifically listed in the constitution. On other topics, the executive possesses the power of decree. The Cabinet draws up the National Assembly's agenda, thus ensuring priority for the executive's legislative program. This program is protected from the committees by a requirement that the legislature must debate a bill in the form submitted by the executive, not as amended by a committee. Thus opponents of the executive have the problem of trying to piece together enough votes to amend the bill, rather than the executive's having to hunt for votes to reverse the committee's mutilation of its proposal.

In terms of power over the content of public policy, the French legislature is not appreciably weaker than the British Parliament. The question is whether it lacks the ability of the House of Commons to call the executive to account. For example, question time in France is limited to a single session each week. Nor are there the same opportunities for the opposition parties to set a portion of the agenda or criticize the executive in adjournment debates.

The Bundestag falls between the National Assembly and the Commons. The German legislature is not as completely dominated by the executive as is the French, but it fails to make as effective use as does the British Parliament of its procedures for calling the executive to account. Legislators can question members of the executive at the start of each sitting of the Bundestag, but since only two or three meetings are held each week, questions are less frequent than in Britain. Furthermore, questions cannot be directed to the chancellor, despite his being the central formulator of government policy. A "topical hour" procedure requires the executive to make a policy statement that then can be discussed by legislators. Despite these and other such procedures, Bundestag sittings are rather lifeless, with little give-and-take between the executive and the legislature. In part this reflects the tradition established by the practices of the first chancellor. Konrad Adenauer was rather autocratic and disinclined to cooperate with the legislature. He frequently would not divulge information that the legislature sought and instructed his executive colleagues to do the same.

Even more important in stultifying floor debates in the Bundestag is German political culture. German culture tends to be more legalistic than British culture. The legislative process is not regarded as a search for accommodation among competing interests but as a technical procedure in which legal experts devise the "right" wording for statutes. Clearly, partisan debate is irrelevant to an activity perceived as an intellectual exercise. Party-line voting is no more stringent in the Bundestag than in the Commons, which is to say that debates influence no fewer votes in Germany than in Britain. But, in contrast to Britons, Germans tend not to see legislative debate as educating the public on current affairs and requiring the executive to justify its actions. Little seems at stake in the Bundestag's sittings, and debate becomes largely formalistic.

Nonetheless, the Bundestag plays a more important role in shaping German public policy than does the National Assembly in formulating

French policy. Precisely because of the German conception of the legislative process, the committees are quite significant. Here the detailed provisions of bills can be examined meticulously. Party rhetoric is avoided, and voting across party lines is more common than on the floor of the Bundestag. Therefore the executive is not always certain that it can control the committees and is more likely to make concessions. In short, it is in the committees that the real legislative work is done; by the time a bill returns to the floor, the key decisions have been made and the debate truly is for form's sake only.

Despite a number of significant differences among the three legislatures, all of them play a fundamentally similar role—one that differs from that of the U.S. Congress. Congress is a decision-making legislature; its actions have a major effect on the content of public policy in the United States. European legislatures are decision-legitimating legislatures. The key public policy decisions in Britain, France, and Germany are taken in the executive branch and are communicated to the legislative branch for endorsement. The essential elements of the executive's legislative program will be enacted. The fact that this program must be discussed and justified before passage is what distinguishes the process from those that prevailed in undemocratic systems like the former Soviet Union.

Policy Implementation

The task of implementing public policy in Britain is the job of approximately two dozen central government departments. Each is headed by a politician usually referred to as a minister or, more formally, a secretary of state. Most of these ministers will be members of the Cabinet and, with only rare exceptions, members of the House of Commons. Thus under the British fusion-of-powers system they have both legislative and executive duties. In addition to voting in the House of Commons and participating in its debates, they are responsible for directing the administrative activities of their departments.

They are assisted in their executive duties by two or three other politicians, who also are MPs. The great bulk of the work, however, is entrusted to permanent civil servants, that is, merit-system government employees. The politicians are replaced whenever another party wins a majority in the House of Commons and thus gains control of the government. The civil servants continue on in their posts regardless of partisan shifts. In charge of the work of all the civil servants in a department is the permanent secretary. He or she will have been involved in the department's activities for a much longer time than has the minister and therefore is likely to be much more familiar with that portion of public policy. Although the minister is in charge, the permanent secretary may well be the real decision maker.

This relation poses a potential problem for democratic government. The permanent secretary is not elected and is not accountable to the people; to permit him or her to make policy would be undemocratic. Therefore it is essential that the minister not lose control over the permanent secretary. Virtually all civil servants observe the strict partisan neutrality required of them; they carry out the instructions given them by their political masters of whatever party. The problem is that many civil servants tend too easily to see a myriad of difficulties in doing anything different from what their department has been doing. When ministers come into office with their newly elected party's policy reforms, they are likely to be to told by their permanent secretaries that these are wonderful ideas, but they won't work. Only a determined minister will insist that the civil service figure out how to make them work. Of course, should something then go wrong, the permanent secretary will point out that he or she tried to warn the minister, who would not listen.

When something goes wrong in the running of a department, the minister must shoulder the blame. To keep civil servants out of politics so that they can be politically neutral, they are insulated against public criticism of their actions in policy implementation. Not only did the minister decide on one course of action rather than another, but his or her job was to see that the civil servants properly implemented the decision. Their failure to do so is the minister's fault; he or she must account to Parliament for administrative shortcomings. Should the errors be sufficiently bad, the minister is expected to resign as political head of the department. This is the British constitutional convention of ministerial responsibility. It should not be confused with the Cabinet's collective responsibility, which deals with the substance of policy, rather than with its implementation.

The civil service plays an increasingly important role in public policy formation because of delegated legislation. The growing complexity of modern life and the expanded role of government make foreseeing all eventualities in any particular area of public concern increasingly difficult. Therefore, in most countries legislation is written in broad terms, setting forth general objectives and providing guidelines for obtaining them. The administrative agency assigned the task of implementing the legislation is entrusted with the power to make rules and regulations fleshing out the legislative outline with detailed procedures.

In Britain this delegated legislation takes the form of statutory instruments. Most of these, composing a substantial segment of all British law, are written by (unelected) civil servants. In some instances statutory instruments must be approved by Parliament before going into effect. But at other times they become binding if not vetoed by Parliament within a stated period. The House of Commons has little time to examine statutory instruments, so many become law without any legislative scrutiny. One of the useful functions of the House of Lords is to review some of the statutory instruments, thereby providing a bit more of a check on administrators' policymaking than otherwise would exist.

The content of public policy varies less geographically in Britain than it does in the United States. Not only are decisions on virtually all important policies made in London, but national officials are responsible for implementing most policies. This is because Britain is a unitary system. Subnational units of government exist only insofar as national government has created them and have only those powers national government permits them to exercise. Even their existence is subject to the national government's discretion. When the legislature in Northern Ireland proved increasingly unable to deal with religious conflict there, the national legislature in London assumed direct control in 1972 and suspended the local body—which remains the situation more than twenty years later. When in the 1950s and 1960s school integration was a major problem in the United States, Congress had no power directly to govern defiant southern states and suspend their governments. The federal system established by the U.S. Constitution forbade such action.

Local authorities, the term used for subnational government in Britain, are involved mainly with such matters as sanitation, street lighting, recreational and cultural facilities, and child welfare. These matters are not insignificant, but hardly can be considered major responsibilities. Although portions of the educational system (the hiring of teachers, for example) are under local control, the national government is becoming increasingly involved. The basic curriculum requirements are set by national government, which also prescribes a system of tests at various ages. Similarly, although some local control over the police remains, the Home Office in the central government has significant supervisory powers.

Finances also make local government a creature of central control. National legislation determines what taxes can be imposed locally. Local authorities have some discretion about the level of service they wish to provide—they can keep the parks open for more or fewer hours—and this will effect their spending and tax level. But they must employ only the taxes permitted by central government. What they are able to raise locally covers less than half their expenditures. Most funds come in the form of grants from the central government. To obtain this support local government must comply with various guidelines established in London.

Like Britain, France also is a unitary system and is even more highly centralized. France's administrative framework was created by Napoleon early in the nineteenth century. The key subnational unit is the department (about a hundred exist). Although each department has a popularly elected council, it used to wield little power. The department actually was run by the prefect, a nationally appointed civil servant. The prefect could compel local government in the area to provide specific services at the level established by the central government. If local government failed to pass the taxes needed to finance these services, the prefect could impose them. The prefect could suspend mayors of cities and towns for failure to discharge their duties. These are only a few of the powers that made the prefect a department's executive officer and established a direct line of administrative control from the central government down to the smallest unit of government. Thus both the substance and the implementation of such important policies as education and the police were under national control.

In the 1980s this system was reformed. Many of the powers formerly exercised by the prefects were shifted to local councils and their presiding officers. When a prefect objects to a local decision, he or she no longer can order a change but must refer the matter to an administrative tribunal that will examine, not the advisability, but the legality, of the action. The prefect becomes more the national government's chief field administrator with the task of coordinating administration, instead of imposing policy.

These reforms made French government less centralized. Those who regard socialists as people wishing to concentrate all power in the hands of the state will be surprised that this change was enacted when the Socialist party controlled a majority of the seats in the National Assembly. Local government, which had been little more than an organ in a national administrative network, now possesses some limited decision-making power. Nonetheless, the key policy decisions for the nation still are taken in Paris, which is to say that France now is about as centralized as is Britain.

At the national level, French administrative structure is not as hierarchical as the British. Like the United States, France lacks a civil servant comparable to the permanent secretary. Politicians heading departments bring with them a small group of assistants personally committed to them to staff the top positions in their departments. Despite the partisanship implicit in this arrangement, some of these assistants will be high-ranking civil servants. This is one of the reasons why the French civil service, although highly competent, does not have as great a reputation as does the British for strict partisan neutrality.

Whatever their partisan differences, many of the French governmental elite share a common educational experience. In 1945 France established the National School of Administration to serve as a recruitment and training channel for top civil servants. Only about 150 people are admitted each year to the two-and-a-half-year program that combines practical with academic training. Some of the graduates of the program decide to go into politics or business, rather than the civil service. Thus the school's influence extends widely throughout French society, and top politicians and administrators may be able to work more effectively together because they have learned similar methods of analyzing public problems.

In contrast to France and Britain, Germany is a federal system; subnational units of government play a larger role in the policy process. German federalism differs from American. Although the national government has a larger role in making nationwide policy than is true in the United States, the German states are more extensively involved in implementing these policies than are the American ones. The chief areas of state decision making relate to education, cultural affairs, and police. Their areas of administrative responsibility, however, are much broader.

Compared to most other countries, the German central government departments are skeletal organizations. The task of a department is to coordinate administration, which involves some planning, setting of standards, and supervision of administration. The actual implementation of national laws, however, is the responsibility of state and local civil servants. Thus uniform national requirements can be somewhat moderated in practice to take account of regional differences.

German national administrative structure is similar to the British. Each department is headed by one or two politicians. One or two state secretaries, comparable to the British permanent secretary, are in charge of supervising staff implementation of politicians' decisions. In contrast to British practice, civil servants have much greater freedom to participate in partisan politics. They may obtain a leave to serve in the Bundestag without any loss of seniority and pension rights when they return to their civil service position. While such activity makes attaining a neutral civil service more difficult, the Germans feel the cost is worth paying to obtain the legal expertise they regard as essential to the legislative process.

The Judiciary

Britain and the United States share the common-law system, in which judicial interpretation of the law and the precedents of past decisions are quite important. On the Continent, the code-law system prevails, in which highly detailed laws are enacted to minimize the need for interpretation and the significance of past judicial decisions. The role of British judges differs from that of American ones in one fundamental regard, however; in Britain, judges lack the power to void an act of Parliament by declaring it unconstitutional. In this respect, German judicial practice is much closer to American procedure than is British.

Britain has one system of courts for England and Wales and another for Scotland, which is omitted here for the sake of simplicity. The courts are organized into two hierarchies, one for civil cases (conflicts between private individuals) and one for criminal cases (offenses against public order prosecuted by the government). These two hierarchies are partially unified at the level of the Court of Appeal. As its name suggests, this court does not try any cases originally, but handles only appeals against the decisions of lower courts. Since every case, therefore, will have had an opportunity for a rehearing, the great majority of legal proceedings go no further.

Exceptional cases of extraordinary importance will be heard by the court of last resort—the House of Lords. Clearly, the entire house of hundreds of members, most of whom have no legal training, is not able to handle these appeals. The cases are heard instead by groups of usually three to seven Law Lords, legal experts appointed to the Lords for life to perform this function. Even though these judges serve as Britain's highest court, they cannot declare any act of Parliament unconstitutional. Their main task is to clarify what the law requires in those instances where various provisions are at odds. Although they are the final court, in some senses their rulings are not definitive. Should Parliament not like the holding, it can overturn it simply by passing a new law. In contrast to the United States, no elaborate procedure of constitutional amendment is required, since the Law Lords are interpreting a statute, not a written constitution.

The German constitution does provide for a Federal Constitutional Court, which can examine acts of the legislature for constitutional validity. Some of the cases heard by the Constitutional Court reach it in the familiar way of appeal against the decisions of lower courts. In addition the national executive, a state executive, or one-third of the Bundestag can request the Court to rule on the constitutionality of a law. Finally, any citizen can raise what is called a "constitutional complaint," alleging that a law violates some basic right guaranteed by the constitution. Because of the great volume of such complaints, they are weeded out by a screening committee and only a few actually are considered by the Court. The Court has dealt with a number of highly significant issues including the financing of political parties, abortion, the status of civil servants, and the outlawing of extremist parties.

The nomination of judges for the U.S. Supreme Court has caused considerable controversy in recent years, as has the practice of some judges staying on despite age and illness in hopes that a president more in tune with their values may win election and be able to appoint their replacements. In the 1960s many southern states were upset by what they regarded as Supreme Court violations of states' rights. Therefore, German practice on staffing and tenure of its Constitutional Court should be of particular interest to Americans. The central government's Ministry of Justice maintains a list of potential nominees composed of top judges and others suggested by the national executive, a state executive, or a party in the Bundestag. Vacancies on the Court are filled alternately by the Bundestag and the Bundesrat. Thus the states have a major voice in both nominating and selecting the top judges. Furthermore, the national chief executive has a much more circumscribed role in the process than is true in the United States. Finally, the appointment is for twelve years only, and judges are prohibited from succeeding themselves.

In addition to the Constitutional Court, Germany has a full range of other courts. Somewhat similarly to arrangements for administration, the three lowest levels of courts are all state ones. These courts try cases arising under either national law or state law. As a result of this arrangement, the national judiciary can be limited primarily to hearing appeals in criminal and civil cases. The national government also has established an elaborate system of special-purpose courts to deal with such matters as commercial disputes, labor relations, and tax questions. In addition, administrative courts have been created to hear complaints against bureaucrats who citizens feel have acted arbitrarily.

France also has both a regular court system to handle civil and criminal cases and an administrative court system. At the head of latter system is the Council of State, perhaps the most prestigious organ of French government. The council is famed for its integrity and independence from executive pressure. The regular courts sometimes seem rather more concerned to defend the government than to protect individuals from violations of basic rights. Justice seems more often to be done in the administrative court system. Procedures are relatively inexpensive and access is fairly easy. The administrative courts play an important role in protecting French citizens from the abuse of power by public servants.

Perhaps because they were not ruled by a dictator in the 1930s, as was Germany, the French have not gone as far in establishing a court to protect the constitution. Under the Fifth Republic a Constitutional Council was created. It can invalidate laws but only in very limited circumstances. The president, the prime minister, the presiding officer of the National Assembly or the Senate, or sixty members of either the National Assembly or the Senate may challenge the validity of a law. Individual citizens may *not* raise the question. Furthermore, the challenge must occur during the two weeks between the legislature's passage of the law and its signing into effect by the president. If no challenge is raised at this time, then the law never can be invalidated. That is, in all cases in which the law is applicable, the courts must apply it regardless whether the result seems to violate basic rights. In allowing for any challenge to a law the French have qualified legislative supremacy more than the British have, but they have not gone nearly as far as Germany and the United States have in enabling citizens to defend themselves against oppressive legislation.

The United States inherited the idea of limited, constitutional government from Britain. The ways in which Americans have implemented that idea, however, have produced a system that departs from British practice in many aspects. So far as limiting power through federalism and judicial review are concerned, the United States has more in common with Germany than with Britain. Similarities between the United States and France are relatively few. Nonetheless, the idea of separation of powers came to the American founding fathers from an eighteenth-century French political philosopher. And only France resembles the United States in having a head of state who plays much more than merely a symbolic role. Thus, despite its influence on American political values, Britain is not always the system that most closely corresponds to the United States. Americans can obtain insights relevant to the operation of their governmental system by studying German and French government, as well as British.

As for comparisons among the three European countries themselves, despite their many differences, all utilize the parliamentary system in some form, and none of them adheres to a strict two-party system. Furthermore, they are closely linked economically and politically through a formal governmental structure. Therefore, this consideration of European parliamentary democracy must conclude with a discussion of Europe's political structure.

Europe's Political System

On New Year's Day 1993 the European Community (EC) officially launched single market. Now a German could visit France and bring back all the wine and cigarettes she wanted—there were no quantitative limits and no customs duties at the border. During the next few months measures supportive of the single market and of even broader common policies were ratified.

Thus on New Year's Day 1994 the EC formally evolved into the European Union (EU).

The single market is intended to make the EU's twelve members—Germany, France, Britain, Denmark, the Netherlands, Belgium, Luxembourg, Spain, Portugal, Ireland, Italy, and Greece—an integrated trading area without any internal barriers. Goods, services, people, and capital are to move as freely across national boundaries as they do over state lines in the United States. Banks authorized to do business in Ireland, for example, can set up operations in Italy without having to meet any new requirements. Hairdressers who have met the standards for their occupation in France can move to Britain and open a shop there without any further approval. A Briton with money to invest no longer is limited to the securities available on the London market but can buy them on any of the other markets in the EU. Should, in fact, a citizen of one EU country be resident in another EU country, he or she could vote in that country's local elections.

Although the great majority of the changes that the twelve member countries needed to make to establish the single market had been implemented by the end of 1992, some actions remained to be taken. Britain, for example, still required a show of passports by visitors from other EU members. Higher education degrees were not yet recognized throughout the EU. An insurance company operating in one member country was not yet fully able to sell policies in other member countries without complying with their regulations. Nonetheless, the various national economies of the twelve members had been integrated to an extent that hardly could have been anticipated when the six founders—Germany, France, Italy, the Netherlands, Belgium, and Luxembourg—began the process in the late 1950s.

One might think that future versions of this chapter could ignore the government and politics of particular countries and concentrate only on the operation of the EU's system. This might well seem the appropriate level for study because the EU is not just a cooperative agreement for closer economic relations but a fully elaborated system of governmental organs functioning across national boundaries. Some people would argue that just as the United States and Germany have both a number of state governments and a central government, so the EU has "states"—the twelve countries that are members—and a central community government. They see the EU as a supranational organization, the beginning of a European federal system.

The EU's unicameral Parliament is composed of representatives allocated to the various countries roughly according to population. In addition to their national and local elections, EU members now hold elections to select their representatives in the European Parliament. The Court of Justice hears disputes concerning the Union's regulations and possesses the power to require a national government to change its actions or law to comply with EU policy.

The third branch of government, the executive, is more complex and less supranational than are the legislative and judicial branches. The most federal organ is the Commission. Although the Commission's seats are allocated among the various countries, their appointees are not to function as national representatives but to become Union officials. The Commission would seem to resemble a country's Cabinet, with its presiding officer, known as the president, similar to a prime minister. The existence of two other executive organs, however, complicates matters.

The Council of Ministers is more a title than a specific organ because it lacks permanent membership. The national representatives who attend its meetings vary with the subject matter. Thus, for example, sometimes the Council of Ministers is a meeting of the agriculture ministers of the member countries; at other times, it is a meeting of the economic ministers. Unlike the Commission's members, these ministers *do* voice their country's interests. The Council would be an intragovernmental, not a supranational, body were it not for the voting arrangements. Whereas originally decisions in the Council had to be by unanimous vote, increasingly action can be taken by majority vote. A country may find itself outvoted and therefore required to take action that it did not favor.

Also part of the executive is the European Council. This is a meeting, usually twice a year, of the heads of state and of government of the member countries. They discuss broad policy and objectives for the EU. This focus, along with the status of the participants, makes the European Council the most powerful part of the executive, even though it lacks the Commission's day-to-day impact on details. Every six months another country is given the responsibility of organizing and presiding over European Council meetings. Rather confusingly, given the title of the Commission's presiding officer, the head of government directing the European Council also is known as the EU's president.

Despite its importance, the European Council is not integrated into the EU's regular decision-making process. Typically this begins with a proposal from the Commission. After the European Parliament has debated this, the Council of Ministers decides whether to make any changes. The proposal then returns to the Parliament. If it approves or rejects, the matter comes back to the Council of Ministers for final action. Should the Parliament amend the proposal, then it goes to the Commission before returning to the Council of Ministers. Although national interests are well protected in the process, it clearly has elements of a supranational legislative procedure. The main problem is that the power of the European Parliament is limited, although it is the only organ directly responsible to the people. As a result, some observers have worried about the EU's "democratic deficit."

Some members of the EU have been more at ease with its supranational elements than have others. In December 1991, when the Dutch were in charge of preparations, the European Council agreed to a treaty in the town of Maastricht. This treaty was intended to facilitate the move toward a single market. The final touches were put on economic union and to this was added monetary union. The financial systems of the various members were to become more tightly linked with creation of a European central bank (rather like the American Federal Reserve System) projected and even a common currency foreseen. That is, a day would come when the British pound sterling, the French franc, the German deutsche mark, and the rest would disappear in favor of a European dollar. The Maastricht Treaty also contained provisions for greater unity on foreign and defense policy.

Despite the fundamental significance of Maastricht in shifting power away from the member countries to the Union, all seemed able to live with its changes, even if they were not enthusiastic about them. Therefore, most everyone assumed that the treaty would be ratified over the next several months without any hitch. The year 1992 proved, however, to hold a series of disasters for the EU.

In the summer the Danes, never enthusiastic about a supranational Union, voted against the treaty in a referendum. Since the treaty required approval by all the EU members to go into effect, coping with the Danish problem became a major issue for the next six months. The Danes' vote encouraged those in Britain who had opposed any further loss of sovereignty to the EU. As a result of their opposition, the process of British approval of Maastricht slowed to a snail's pace and stretched out into 1993. France, like Denmark, opted for a referendum on the treaty. Although this vote was favorable, the fact that approval was eked out with a margin of only a few percentage points further weakened enthusiasm for Maastricht. Adding to these woes was currency speculation on the British pound, which forced Britain to withdraw from the system linking the various EU currencies to one another. Since the lira had been subject to the same pressures, Italy pulled out as well. Monetary union appeared to have shifted into reverse.

Toward the close of 1992, a bit of optimism returned. The European Council meeting in Edinburgh managed to devise wording interpreting Maastricht that proved to be sufficient to persuade the Danes to vote yes in another referendum to be held in 1993. Subsidiarity was given increasing emphasis. The thinking behind this term was similar to that responsible for the Tenth Amendment to the U.S. Constitution. Decisions were to be taken by the level of government as close to the people as possible. Brussels (shorthand for the EU bureaucracy), long regarded as ever greedy for more power, was not to spew forth regulations on everything. More matters were to be left to the member countries to decide for themselves, thus allowing as much variation within the EU as possible without impeding the common policies necessary for economic integration. Such an orientation, it was hoped, would make the EU more acceptable to those who were anxious about the loss of national sovereignty and who felt that uniform regulations took insufficient account of contrasting national situations and values.

The European Council also agreed at Edinburgh to press ahead with the several applications for membership that the EU had received from other European countries. Within the next few years a half dozen—a 50 percent increase in members—could be admitted to the EU. If that occurs, then the EU's structure will be transformed. So varied and numerous will the EU be that its supranational elements will be substantially diluted. The economies may be integrated to a considerable extent, a single market quite similar to that within the boundaries of the United States will exist, but decision making will be largely cooperative through discussions among national representatives. The EU's "government" will differ only slightly from that of the United Nations, not the United States. Studying the national systems of such countries as Britain, France, and Germany will remain essential for those wanting some knowledge of European politics.

SUGGESTIONS FOR ADDITIONAL READING

On Britain

BEER, SAMUEL H. *Britain Against Itself.* New York: Norton, 1982.

DUNLEAVY, PATRICK, ANDREW GAMBLE, and GILLIAN PEELE, eds. *Developments in British Politics.* 3d rev. ed. New York: St. Martin's Press, 1990.

EWING, K.D., and C.A. GEARTY. *Freedom under Thatcher: Civil Liberties in Modern Britain.* Oxford: Clarendon Press, 1990.

JONES, BILL, and LYNTON ROBINS, eds. *Two Decades of British Politics.* Manchester, England: Manchester University Press, 1992.

KING, ANTHONY, ed. *The British Prime Minister.* 2d ed. Durham, N.C.: Duke University Press, 1985.

_____ et al. *Britain at the Polls, 1992.* Chatham, N.J.: Chatham House, 1992.

McKENZIE, R.T. *British Political Parties.* 2d ed. New York: Praeger, 1964.

MacKINTOSH, JOHN. *The British Cabinet.* 3d ed. London: Stevens, 1977.

NORTON, PHILIP, ed. *Parliament in the 1980s.* New York: Basil Blackwell, 1985.

RASMUSSEN, JORGEN. *The British Political Process: Concentrated Power vs. Accountability.* Belmont, Calif.: Wadsworth, 1993.

ROSE, RICHARD, and IAN McALLISTER. *The Loyalties of Voters: A Lifetime Learning Model.* London: Sage, 1990.

On France

ANDREWS, WILLIAM G., and STANLEY HOFFMANN, eds. *The Impact of the Fifth Republic on France.* Albany: SUNY Press, 1981.

ARDAGH, JOHN. *France Today.* London: Penguin, 1988.

ASHFORD, DOUGLAS. *British Dogmatism and French Pragmatism.* Winchester, Mass.: Allen and Unwin, 1982.

CONVERSE, PHILIP E., and ROY PIERCE. *Political Representation in France.* Cambridge, Mass.: Harvard University Press, 1986.

FREARS, JOHN. *Parties and Voters in France.* London: Hurst, 1991.

HALL, PETER, JACK HAYWARD, and HOWARD MACHIN, eds. *Developments in French Politics.* New York: St. Martin's Press, 1990.

ROSS, GEORGE, STANLEY HOFFMANN, and SYLVIA MALZACHER, eds. *The Mitterrand Experiment: Continuity and Change in Modern France.* New York: Oxford University Press, 1987.

WILSON, FRANK L. *Interest-Group Politics in France.* Cambridge, England: Cambridge University Press, 1987.

On Germany

BAKER, KENDALL L., RUSSELL J. DALTON, and KAI HILDEBRANDT. *Germany Transformed.* Cambridge, Mass.: Harvard University Press, 1981.

BLAIR, PHILIP. *Federalism and Judicial Review in West Germany.* Oxford: Clarendon Press, 1981.

CERNY, KARL, ed. *Germany at the Polls: The Bundestag Elections of the 1980s.* Durham, N.C.: Duke University Press, 1990.

CONRADT, DAVID. *Unified Germany at the Polls: Political Parties and the 1990 Federal Election.* Washington, D.C.: American Institute for Contemporary German Studies, 1990.

DALTON, RUSSELL J., ed. *The New Germany Votes: Unification and the Creation of the New German Party System.* Providence: Berg, 1993.

KOMMERS, DONALD P. *Judicial Politics in West Germany: A Study of the Federal Constitutional Court.* Beverly Hills, Calif.: Sage, 1976.

PADGETT, STEPHEN, and TONY BURKETT. *Political Parties and Elections in West Germany: The Search for a New Stability.* New York: St. Martin's Press, 1986.

SMITH, GORDON, WILLIAM PATTERSON, and PETER MERKL, eds. *Developments in West German Politics.* Durham, N.C.: Duke University Press, 1989.

WALLACH, H.G. PETER, and RONALD FRANCISCO. *United Germany: The Past, Politics, Prospects.* Westport, Conn.: Praeger, 1992.

On the European Union

NUGENT, NEILL. *The Government and Politics of the European Community.* Durham, N.C.: Duke University Press, 1989.

PINDER, JOHN. *European Community: The Building of a Union.* Oxford: Oxford University Press, 1991.

SPRINGER, BEVERLEY. *The Social Dimension of 1992: Europe Faces a New EC.* New York: Praeger, 1992.

URWIN, DEREK. *The Community of Europe: A History of European Integration since 1945.* New York: Longman, 1991.

5. The Japanese Political System

Until 1854, Japan lived in seclusion, geographically removed from the rest of the world, untouched by outside events, secure from external aggression (with the exception of attempts by Kublai Khan's Mongol Empire in the thirteenth century), and sufficient unto itself. The age of Western colonial expansion slowly but steadily crept up to its perimeters. It was none other than the United States, seeking stopovers for its merchant ships engaged in trade with China, that intimidated the theretofore impermeable island nation with its "black ships" into opening its doors to foreign traders and diplomats. Suddenly and forcefully exposed to a threatening world dominated by expansionist and superior Western states, Japan, after a brief period of vacillation and confusion, began—from scratch, so to speak—the arduous, desperate, and perilous task of transforming its moribund, deeply fractured feudal society into a powerful modern state. Today, Japan is *sui generis:* the only advanced industrial, as well as stable democratic, nation in the underdeveloped, largely undemocratic non-Western world. Small, overcrowded, and bereft of natural resources, Japan is the second-largest economic power in the world and equal to the United States on a per capita basis. Japan's post–World War II democratic political system has demonstrated remarkable stability, with its people firmly committed to its maintenance. Notwithstanding its superior accomplishment, Japan remains largely unfamiliar to Americans, except for its high-tech manufactured goods, which flood their market.

Constitutional Development

Throughout its feudal period, Japan was governed not by any constitution or series of constitutions in the modern sense of the term but largely by custom and tradition. Its first modern constitution, promulgated by Emperor Meiji in 1889, was a response to the perceived requirements of the time. First and foremost, it was the product of an acute awareness by the nation's modernizing leaders that their nation was regarded by superior Western powers as backward and inferior, a quaint Oriental society outside the mainstream of history and progress. The principal reason for this view was Japan's lack of a modern constitution—a rule of law—which most of these powers had long developed as the fundamental political feature of a modern state. The modernizing Japanese leaders therefore believed it incumbent on them to establish a constitutional polity as the essential condition for persuading the Western powers to begin dealing with their nation on an equal footing.

The Meiji Constitution was intended to meet certain other requirements that the modernizing leaders considered crucial. Among them were the consolidation of these leaders' power in the new national government, the maintenance of sociopolitical discipline during the period of rapid national development through sacrifice and perseverance, and the promotion of national unity in order to withstand the danger posed by the Western powers. These requirements, among others, dictated the establishment of an authoritarian political system. Accordingly, the Meiji Constitution was based on the doctrines of Imperial sovereignty and governmental omnipotence. Democratic rights and liberties enumerated for the "loyal subjects" were not inherent; they were "gifts" from the benevolent Imperial sovereign, to be exercised only "within the limits of the law," that is, within such limits as the Imperial government deemed appropriate. There is no independent judiciary to rule on the constitutionality of any of those limits. To the modernizing elite of the Meiji period, confronted by a task of unprecedented magnitude and urgency, the most fundamental precondition of national progress and viability was order, not liberty; and even for the most progressive among them, liberty could hope to grow only on the firm basis of order.

From an evolutionary developmental perspective, the Meiji Constitution, authoritarian as it was, should perhaps be considered appropriate to the spatial and temporal context of a nation in perilous transition from tradition to modernity. And however circumscribed those rights and liberties were, they nevertheless provided a general basis for the eventual growth of modern democratic practices and arrangements. Subsequent developments demonstrated that the constitution admitted of such evolutionary political progress. Party politics and electoral competition quickly emerged in response to the constitution's prescription for a popularly elected assembly. Moreover, even though the power of the assembly was significantly circumscribed, the Imperial Cabinet soon found itself having to deal and work with the assembly in order effectively to function as the nation's supreme governing institution. By the 1910s the practice of "party government" had become well-nigh institutionalized, and in 1925 the political franchise was extended to all male adults. In the meantime, "oligarchs" of the Meiji period had one by one passed away, leaving the nation in the hands of younger generations of leaders more attuned to party politics and popular electoral competition.

Japan's incipient democracy was dealt an unexpected and fatal blow by the Great Depression, which also contributed to the destruction of many new democracies in Europe. Widespread economic dislocations and subsequent social unrest, and prospects of political disorder, rendered the nation increasingly vulnerable to the demagoguery of antidemocratic forces that promised salvation through autocratic political order at home and imperialist expansion abroad. Consequently, the most illiberal elements of the Meiji Constitution were resurrected and distorted in practice; the nation, now led by militarists and their antidemocratic civilian allies, marched down the path of increasing domestic repression and blatant external aggression toward ultimate humiliation in 1945.

The constitution under which Japan is governed today came into being in 1947. Against the background of bitter national experiences of the 1930s and early 1940s, the new constitution was explicitly designed to institute and safeguard democracy. It is based on the doctrine of popular sovereignty, unambiguously guaranteeing civil liberties and political rights of the people, holding the government accountable to the electorate, and relegating the emperor to a ceremonial role as the symbol of national unity. The trauma of defeat caused by militarists also led the 1947 constitution to address the issue of war and peace and to renounce for the nation the right to wage war and use force for settling disputes with other nations. To ethnocentric Western democrats, it may appear surprising that such a quintessentially democratic constitution has proven so viable in an Eastern state with so recent a record of authoritarian practice and aggressive militarism. How can the "democratic transformation" of Japan be explained?

Democracy requires certain preconditions for its viability—widespread political literacy, social stability, and economic well-being or its promise. The Japanese in the late 1940s were among the best-educated people in the world, not in mere literacy, but also in some crucial political experience. They had known the authoritarianism of the modernizing Meiji oligarchs, the incipient popular democracy of the late 1910s and 1920s, and the repressive regimes of the late 1930s and early 1940s. The shattering defeat of 1945 brought all these experiences under intense collective scrutiny. The virtually unanimous conclusion of the people was that democracy provided the only path to national restoration, progress, and well-being.

Japan is an extraordinarily homogeneous nation with little or no internal social hostility, despite socioeconomic differences among various strata of people and the traditional compartmentalization of groups. And patterns of interpersonal and social relations that evolved through the nation's long history of solitary existence, as we later see, help obviate or minimize the kinds of social conflict that are common in other societies.

A third prerequisite for democracy is material well-being. It is axiomatic that democracy cannot survive in a society on the verge of starvation or without hope for a decent life for its people. In 1947 Japan was indeed at the depths of poverty and deprivation caused by war and defeat, but there was confidence among the people that they could restore their economy and promote its growth. Motivated by this confidence, they did indeed work with unflagging diligence and perseverance, and their government guided this collective national endeavor in achieving recovery and subsequent growth and expansion so rapidly that it astonished the world as an "economic miracle." The combination of popular confidence and its consistent vindication has reinforced the Japanese people's commitment to their postwar constitutional system.

Democracy in Japan shares a number of fundamental features with that in the United States and other practicing democracies. Nevertheless, no two democracies are altogether alike. Within the Western world we have seen variations in democratic practices. This is entirely natural, for the political system of any nation, however similar it may be to that of another, finds its stability in the tradition and culture of the soil in which it thrives. This indigenous culture and tradition at once add to the system's viability and make it distinctive. Japanese democracy is no exception. It is to these unique features of Japanese democracy—indeed the fabric of Japanese society—that we now turn.

Social Forces

Japan as a nation and a society evolved free from the force of events in and pressures from other parts of the world. Japan lived by itself, sufficient unto itself, adopting foreign cultural traits (mostly Chinese) only when it suited it, eclectically and selectively. This environmental autonomy and existential solitude prior to the mid-nineteenth century engendered an unusual degree of cultural homogeneity among the Japanese, a fact that exerts significant influence on the character of social relations and political interaction among groups and institutions in contemporary Japan. In discussing social forces in Japan it is more illuminating to examine certain manifest behavioral features deeply rooted in culture and history than to describe social classes, ideological currents, or group dynamics.

Interpersonal and social relations came to be controlled and regulated by historically evolved, largely unwritten rules of conduct (originating in small isolated rice-cultivating village communities). In short, there evolved an extraordinarily potent sense of community at each level and context of those relations (which cumulatively came to constitute a mutual-aid society nationwide). This communitarian character of relations tends to avoid conflict and competition and instead to stress harmony and cooperation. Individualism, as Americans understand and value it, is predicated on conflict and competition and is therefore incompatible with this character. In each context of social relations in Japan, there is a powerful inclination toward behavioral conformity and collective interest.

The central criterion of decision making in the United States is majoritarian democracy, in which decisions are made on the basis of numerical strength. It not only presupposes conflict and competition among participants in each decisional context but also views them as inherently beneficial for progress. It also signifies division between a victorious majority and a defeated minority. Since communitarian harmony is the most important collective interest in Japan, conflict and competition are eschewed in decision making. Generally speaking, substantive decision making is by consensus, not by a majority (although in a formal decisional arena, such as the legislature, a vote is taken according to written rule). Decision making by the criterion of sheer relative strength of the larger number is viewed as inherently unfair to the minority. The interest of the minority, however small, should be scrupulously respected and judiciously accommodated, for otherwise internal harmony would be eroded. Thus, while decision making in the United States boils down to choosing one option among many, in Japan it is, as one analyst put it, "the coalescence of the only possible compromise out of all."

The principal requirement of communitarian harmony in Japanese culture imposes on the leader or leadership in each group or decisional context the kind of role that is vastly different from what is expected of leadership in the American context. To begin with, there is no Japanese word for leadership. The person in a formal leadership position does not "lead" in the sense that his American counterpart does. He occupies the position, not because he is bright, experienced, decisive, innovative, or otherwise endowed with the qualities Americans usually associate with leadership, but because of his relative seniority in the group or institution concerned and, particularly important, of his outstanding paternalistic qualities, such as warmth, magnanimity, attentiveness to his subordinates' personal feelings and problems. Typically, his subordinates refer to him affectionately as "old man," "Pappy," and the like. An individual displaying an incisive mind, a forceful personality, or an aloof deportment is unlikely to become or be accepted as a leader, for the leader is not expected to overwhelm his subordinates by the superiority of his mind or position, or the decisiveness of his conduct, nor to dictate or impose his own preference on them, but rather to be the core of the human nexus that is the group, to be its father figure. In decision making his role is one of a cooperative team player, a consensus builder, a compromise promoter among differing views and preferences. Decisional brilliance and dispatch are subordinate to decisional harmony.

Given the character of leadership in Japanese culture, the impetus for decisions and the substance of them tend to flow from the bottom upward, rather than from the top downward. Brilliance and imaginativeness are qualities valued in the subordinate, not in the leader, and it is the subordinate who is expected to provide the leader with ideas and options. (Consider, for example, that it was a group of low-ranking *samurai* that promoted the modernization of the Meiji period and that it was restless junior members of the Army Officer Corps in the 1930s who precipitated the aggressive drive against the civilian government and for overseas conquest. In both cases, their superiors—leaders—followed their lead.) The subordinate members within each group or decisional context discuss options freely among themselves, cultivate support for them, and integrate and accommodate differing views and preferences so as to ensure their acceptance by the group or institution when a decision has to be made formally. There is indeed an osmotic character to Japanese decision making. The leader adopts decisions thus arrived at and represents them.

As the reader may already suspect, consensualism is not very conducive to making hard decisions, for it is inclined to avoid a problem or issue that sharply divides the group concerned as long as possible or until it becomes palpably dangerous to do so. Internal disagreement is consciously repressed, and its catalysis into decisions is occasioned by an external input to the decision process. Consequently, consensualism as the principal criterion of decision making, when applied to the level of government, may seriously handicap a nation in coping effectively with its domestic as well as external environments. For, however preservative of internal harmony and order, it could critically deprive the nation of a vital capacity for decisive, expeditious, and responsive decision making that rapidly shifting circumstances may dictate.

Community and consensus generate a powerful tendency toward conformity, for they are incompatible with idiosyncrasy and personal self-interest, which cause annoyance and conflict. And this conformity renders each group, and ultimately the nation, unique in the minds of its members. Even a casual foreign observer in Japan would notice the sartorial uniformity of various classes of workers (e.g., white shirts and somber, more often than not gray, suits and matching ties for male white-collar workers; company-specific work clothes for blue-collar laborers). There are also company badges to be worn on the coat or jacket lapel. Persons find their own value only by being members of a group, the indispensable human nexus (community), and by partaking of its interest (consensus). American workers identify themselves by the profession or occupation they are in. ("I am an accountant" or "I am a civil servant," for example.) The Japanese do so by the group they belong to. ("I am with Toyota" or "I work for the Ministry of Finance.")

At the national level, too, this is largely true, albeit perhaps less compelling than at a lower level. The Japanese unself-consciously take it for granted that they are a unique people. For example, they assume their cultural exclusivity, while Americans believe in their culture's universality. Thus the Japanese think that foreigners can never master their language nor really like such uniquely Japanese dishes as *sashimi* and *sushi,* and are astonished when they do; Americans assume that everybody should speak English and love hamburgers, and are disappointed when they do not. This notion of exclusivity renders the Japanese highly ethnocentric in their external orientation and, conversely, communitarian and conformist in their internal outlook. In their own eyes the Japanese are *sui generis,* possessed of qualities that no other people can be expected to share. We may call this Japan's "exceptionalism."

Community and consensus powerfully disincline the Japanese to engage in political dispute, which presupposes conflict. To the extent that there are groups with different interests conflict is inevitable. In the Japanese context, however, group conflict is mediated by the particular kind of relations obtaining among leadership strata of contending groups. Decisional interaction takes place at this leadership level, and here the rules of community and consensus obtain, albeit perhaps to a less psychologically compelling extent than within each group. Confrontation, which is the most acute form of political conflict, is eschewed; instead, there is powerful pressure toward moderation, which can be maintained only through mutual accommodation and compromise and through avoidance of issues on which such accommodation and compromise seem unfeasible at the moment. This distinctly politicophobic tendency inherent in community and consensus was powerfully reinforced by the disastrous experience of ultranationalist militarism of the prewar years, which had represented a radical form of confrontationist politics both at home and abroad. The political stability of postwar Japan is in no insignificant measure a result of the conscious avoidance of such abrasive political behavior, especially on the part of the more salient sectors and strata of society and government.

Interest Groups

As an advanced industrial and democratic state, Japan contains a wide spectrum of interest groups ranging from farmers' cooperatives to business associations, from organized labor to professional organizations. More recently, an increasing number of single-issue pressure groups concerned with ecology, welfare, women's rights, taxes, smoking, and the like has emerged. Interest groups may be divided into two broad categories: those that are institutional clients of government ministries and agencies (e.g., farmers' cooperatives vis-à-vis the Ministry of Agriculture) and those that are not. A group belonging to the first category has an inside track, so to speak, and accordingly its political activity is discreet and directed to relevant ministry offices, administrators, as well as to members of the relevant policy committee of the ruling party. More often than not, there is a triangular personal relationship among senior ministry officials, influential members of the ruling party's committee, and leaders of the interest group. Many top leaders of the group are former high officials of the ministry or agency concerned, as are those influential members of the party committee. Higher civil servants, with the exception of the few who become deputy ministers and administrative vice-ministers, by custom retire at or around age fifty, and many of them seek a second career as top officers of the very interests they once regulated and supervised. Some others seek elective offices, usually as Liberal Democratic party (LDP) candidates. This human bond facilitates mutually advantageous interaction among group, party, and bureaucracy. There is little need for public lobbying activities.

A group belonging to the second category is without such inside track or personal connections with the party or the bureaucracy. As a consequence, it engages in open political and informational activities such as marches, demonstrations, rallies, pamphleteering, petitions to ministries and parliament, and electoral campaigns. Whether these activities bring benefits to the group concerned seems to depend on the extent to which the group can generate popular sympathy and support.

Since our space is limited, we shall take a closer look at only the best-known group in each of the two categories suggested: big business and organized labor.

Big business in Japan is organizationally represented by four associations: the Federation of Economic Organizations (*Keidanren*), the Japan Federation of Employers Associations (*Nikkeiren*), the Japan Committee for Economic Development (*Keizai Doyukai*), and the Japan Chamber of Commerce and Industry (*Nissho*). They are collectively referred to as *zaikai* (literally, the high financial circle). *Zaikai* operates discreetly and unobtrusively. Many senior *zaikai* leaders are former high government officials, hence they share the career civil service human nexus with the incumbent senior bureaucrats, as well as with influential members of the ruling party who are their former civil service colleagues. They can therefore informally make relevant inputs into government policymaking. There is a very hazy line of demarcation between their personal and social relations, on the one hand, and their professional and political relations with bureaucracy and party, on the other. The informal pattern of interaction among *zaikai,* party, and bureaucracy is deeply institutionalized; leaders of these three institutions meet at regular intervals over dinner, tea, or drinks in quiet restaurants and tea houses unencumbered by the probing eyes of the press and the public. The degree of influence *zaikai* exerts on policymaking can only be guessed. It is frequently reported in Japan that a brief telephone call from *zaikai* leadership causes last-minute changes in legislative proposals and administrative directives. A veteran French "Japan hand" once remarked that *zaikai* leaders are the government behind the government.

Zaikai as a group has a penchant for discretion and seeks to avoid unnecessary abrasion with the public or its opponents, such as leftist parties and organized labor. While *zaikai* could mobilize any number of employees and workers of its member firms (corporations, their subsidiaries and subcontractors) for election campaign support for the conservative ruling party (LDP), it instead chooses to support the party through massive but largely secretive infusions of political funds into its campaign and other activities. Over 70 percent of the party's funds comes from *zaikai* sources. According to journalistic speculations that have never been refuted by *zaikai* or the party, this umbrella special-interest group in 1991 contributed in the neighborhood of $1 billion to the party, a rather tidy sum by any standard. In any event, *zaikai* stays out of the political spotlight, for its principal objective is policy input into the government decision process, which can best be done through discreet informal contact and equally discreet and informal political contribution to the ruling party.

The largest labor organization in Japan is *Rengo* (the Japan Federation of Trade Unions), which covers some 80 percent of all unionized workers. It is a grouping of traditionally mutually mistrustful public-sector and private-sector organized labor groups and its internal unity and discipline remain problematic. Traditionally, public-sector unions that were avowedly Marxist supported the Japan Socialist party (JSP), while private-sector labor (which was moderate in ideological and political orientation due mainly to its more "communitarian" relations with management in each firm) provided a small but indispensable electoral and organizational sustenance for the Democratic Socialist party (DSP). (This, of course, is not to say that all union members vote for these socialist parties.) Both public-sector and private-sector unions have been generally successful in promoting the economic interests of their members, for different reasons: public-sector unions because they consist largely of tertiary economic sector workers whose strike or work stoppage could produce an immediate impact and repercussions of grave magnitude for government and society and because their wages and fringe benefits ultimately come from public revenues; and private-sector unions because they are mostly employees of large modern corporate firms that have been the engine of Japan's economic success and that have, according to cultural dictates, treated their workers as members of the corporate families.

When it comes to pursuing political objectives, however, Japan's organized labor has been far less successful. Part of the reason for their lack of political success (i.e., in promoting these "progressive" or "socialist" parties) is that the Japanese culture, as alluded to earlier, is not hospitable to confrontational posture in politics. In an important sense, ideology divides society into good guys and bad guys (e.g., into capitalist oppressors and oppressed proletarians), and this is not palatable to the communitarian, consensus-oriented mutual-aid society that is Japan. Another cause for the general political failure of organized labor in Japan is that the unions themselves are still fragmented, despite the surface harmony recently achieved by the "solidarity" of those groups into a large national federation. Much like the opposition in the Diet, labor has been more noted for its internal ideological and sectional bickering than for its collective challenge to the government or the party in power. In an important sense, labor fragmentation and subsequent political ineffectiveness have paralleled those of parliamentary opposition.

Organized labor, like many permanently powerless groups in Japan and elsewhere, indulges itself in what is called "expressive politics," activities designed not so much to make practical political input into the nation's decision-making process as to express frustration with and opposition to it. *Rengo* indeed has proclaimed its ambition to induce fragmented opposition parties (*sans* communist) to reorganize and solidify themselves into an united and effective opposition force. Such, however, remains a mere dream, inasmuch as labor itself is yet to achieve internal coherence and unity. As a consequence, organized labor as a political interest group remains stagnant, unable to exert the kind of influence it was organized to exert.

Political Parties

The history of Japan's political parties is as brief as its constitutional history. True, there were so-called parties and political associations during the early Meiji period before the promulgation of the 1889 constitution, but they were all ineffectual, albeit often strident and pseudo ideological, personal followings revolving around prominent and disgruntled out-of-power oligarchs vying for the first opportunity to get back into power. Viable parties and party competition for power began only after the coming of the Meiji Constitution. Competition for power was exclusively among conservative parties, which alone enjoyed the financial and political wherewithal; the leftist parties that eventually emerged with incipient democratization (such as Socialist, peasant-based Populist, Communist) were intermittently suppressed and lacked both financial and organizational bases, as well as popular support, owing to the inherent Japanese disinclination toward social division and adversarial confrontation.

Competition among conservatives was not so much over policy as power itself, for they represented essentially the same spectrum of interests, attitudes, and orientations, regardless of differences in public rhetoric and electoral posturing. With the coming of ultranationalist militarism in the 1930s, these parties, after a brief effort to maintain their political autonomy and institutional integrity, capitulated to the increasing power and intimidation of the potent coalition of militarists and their like-minded higher bureaucrats and merged into an umbrella national political association that helped promote war aims. As a consequence, most of the leaders of these parties were purged from politics and government during the American Occupation after 1945.

The nation's defeat and the subsequent introduction of democracy prompted a proliferation of parties, representing a wide political spectrum from timidly democratic conservative to communist. The requirement of a majority in the new parliamentary system eventually induced coalescences by the mid-1950s of numerous parties into a unified conservative (LDP) and a single socialist party, leaving the communists at the periphery of the political arena. In subsequent years, opposition to the unified and dominant LDP became fragmented, enabling the latter to enjoy seemingly permanent supremacy in Japanese politics. At the beginning of 1993 the party division of parliamentary seats was as shown in table 5.1.

TABLE 5.1
PARLIAMENTARY SEATS BY PARTY, 1993

	House of Representatives (seats)	House of Councilors (seats)
Liberal Democratic party	276	107
Japan Socialist party	137	74
Clean Government party	46	24
Japan Communist party	16	11
Democratic Socialist party	13	12
Other parties	5	20
Independents	6	4
Vacancy	13	0
Total	512	252

THE LIBERAL DEMOCRATIC PARTY

The ruling Liberal Democratic party (LDP) came into being in 1955 through a merger of the two conservative parties (Liberals and Democrats) that had fiercely competed for power throughout the preceding postwar years and has since ruled the nation continuously. Its seemingly permanent dominance has rested on several ascertainable factors. One is the party's nonideological and pragmatic policy orientation. As a party, the LDP is without ideology, which is consistent with the politicophobic tendency of Japanese society. Despite its "conservative" appellation, the LDP has by and large been flexible enough to accommodate the parliamentary opposition's demands and govern the nation in a manner that the people at large have found acceptable.

Indeed, the Liberal Democratic party has been the political engine of the "economic miracle." In the process of promoting the nation's growth into international economic superstardom (through its vaunted "industrial policy"), it has also succeeded (through its pragmatic "compensation politics") in noticeably reducing economic differences among groups and strata of the population. It has instituted an extensive national health program and has consistently expanded welfare programs for those who were, for a variety of reasons, left out of the rising affluence and economic prosperity. In short, the LDP has been fairly reliable in meeting popular expectations for political stability and economic well-being.

A second reason for LDP supremacy is its electoral-organizational resilience. Its parliamentary membership consists of notables who are influential and respected in their districts by virtue of birth, status, accomplishment, or all three, whom local residents call *sensei* (a term of great respect and affection, literally meaning "teacher" or "master"). Each of these MPs maintains an extensive network of grassroots organizations called *koenkai* (supporters' associations), formed to provide electoral support in the district. They are personal organizations, not the party's, although in most cases their members are registered as party members. Each *koenkai* is made up of friends, associates, allies, and their friends. Their loyalty to the MP is personal, not political or ideological, and the *koenkai* constitutes a human nexus of which the MP is the head. The purpose of *koenkai* members is to keep reelecting the MP, whose policy or that of the party is of little concern to them. The *koenkai* phenomenon is particularly strong in rural and semiurban districts where there remains a much stronger sense of community than in urban and metropolitan districts. Understandably, LDP electoral strength is more pronounced in the former than in the latter.

A third cause of LDP strength is its wherewithal. As the perennial ruling party, it has government revenues and patronage at its disposal, which it can manipulate to benefit specific groups or areas as rewards for their past support or inducements for future support. In addition, the party enjoys munificent financial backing from big business, which wants it to remain in power for obvious reasons. Laws governing political contributions are relatively lax, and there are many legitimate as well as illicit ways in which extraordinary sums can be transferred from *zaikai* and other well-heeled special interests to the party, its factions, and individual MPs. These funds are used by the party and its MPs to run well-oiled campaign activities as well as a gamut of other party functions, and by individual MPs to keep their respective *koenkai* happy and beholden to them. The MP sponsors cultural and athletic activities for *koenkai* members and their families; sends them gifts on festive occasions; makes donations to charities, shrines, temples, and cultural and educational activities; and through local lieutenants, throws parties and receptions for supporters and invites them to Tokyo for sightseeing tours.

Although its largely nonideological and pragmatic policy orientation, its extensive grassroots organizations in the form of MPs' *koenkai,* and finance and patronage, among other things, have enabled the LDP to retain its dominance in Japanese politics, the party is not without serious problems. Owing to space limitation, we briefly touch on a couple of these impediments seriously affecting the ruling party's capacity to govern. By far the most critical of them is fierce intraparty factionalism. The LDP factionalism is personal and patronage centered, not ideological. A faction is an intraparty *koenkai*, whose objective is to increase its leader's influence in the party and thus help him achieve the party presidency and (since the party is in power) the premiership and, in the process, to obtain Cabinet, party, and parliamentary posts (patronage) for its members. This factionalism or faction politics discourages policy debate for two reasons: Policy dispute would divide each faction, and factional politics dictates that today's enemy may be tomorrow's ally.

Party leadership selection on the basis of factionalism is very corruptive, for it invariably encourages the crassest kinds of political wheeling and dealing among competing factions (five major ones at this time), often involving almost unbelievable sums of largely illicit funds (popularly termed "black money") changing hands among factions and between faction leaders and their followers. This is one of the reasons for the large amounts of money shifting annually from *zaikai* to the party, as alluded to earlier, and the practice inevitably threatens the party's institutional integrity and organizational autonomy and aggravates popular cynicism about the party and its credibility.

The winner in this kind of competitive bidding for (or auction of) factional support in leadership selection is the faction leader who has put together a cohesive coalition of factions or, as is frequently the case, has somehow persuaded his rival faction leaders that it is now his turn (in terms of seniority or interfactional musical chairs) to be the party leader and premier. This process of leadership selection, however, leads, ironically but inevitably, only to a sort of pyrrhic victory for the winner. The party presidency-premiership, because of the manner in which the incumbent is selected, is built on a stack of IOUs, and this critically inhibits the winner in the conduct of office. One *zaikai* leader once remarked: "It does not make any difference who becomes prime minister. It's all the same."

A second serious problem plaguing the ruling LDP is a logical as well as empirical correlate of the one just discussed, and that is its vulnerability to political corruption, which in fact has become increasingly pronounced. The requirements of vast sums of political funds thus far alluded to both for electoral and factional purposes predispose these various factions, their leaders, as well as individual MPs, to illicit financial temptations. Such temptations come in the forms of outright bribery, influence buying, corporate "favors" by way of insider stock market information and sale of new stocks and shares at discount prior to their public sale. Most public institutions and organizations have some mechanisms of internal policing and rectification, or what the Japanese call "self-cleansing function," but the LDP clearly is devoid of such mechanism. Not only all factions, but virtually all faction leaders and senior members of the party have been variously guilty of these corrupt practices, even though rather few of their misdeeds usually come to public attention. Some faction leaders and senior politicians have been seriously affected by the revelation of their corruption, but all too many of them, because of the laxity of law (made by the LDP-dominated legislature) and the "mutual-aid society" mentality (each faction, and, when the chips are down in terms of extraparty relations, the party itself being a "family" or "human nexus") that is sensitized in times of internal crisis, escape the political demise they obviously deserve and are returned by their legislative districts (controlled by their respective *koenkai* whose loyalty to them is entirely personal) in the next election. (Typically, for each such LDP politician, one of his loyal personal secretaries or aides takes the blame, and not infrequently, commits suicide to protect the patron.) Such reelection by their loyal and grateful constituents is claimed by these LDP politicians as an act of ablution and they merrily return to their positions of power within the party. There have indeed been precious few party presidents-premiers who were not tainted by such corruption (discovered before, during, or after their tenure in office).

Factionalism and those corruptive tendencies singly and in combination constitute an extremely malignant institutional affliction that, unless somehow excised, could seriously erode the party's ability to govern the nation in the future, effectively and with sufficient popular support. Power tends to corrupt, as Lord Acton long ago observed, and Japan's ruling party, whose power was never seriously challenged from its founding in 1955 until 1993, seems to have succumbed to the ultimate corruption of power.

THE JAPAN SOCIALIST PARTY

After the collapse of the Soviet Union and East European socialist regimes, the Japan Socialist party changed its English name to the Japan Social Democratic party, though the Japanese public and media continue to refer to it as the Japan Socialist party. This change, though principally cosmetic in direct motivation, may signal a search for a new direction for the party in the Japanese political map.

In the latter half of the 1950s, the Socialists entertained the hope (and the conservatives feared) that as the nation became more urbanized through economic growth, the party's electoral strength would grow, and they would be able to capture power. The hope was not at all unfounded, for European socialist parties grew in strength with economic growth and concomitant urbanization and, for example, unseated conservative parties in Britain and Germany. The Japan Socialist party (JSP), however, has failed to follow the path of its West European brethren because of its insistence on remaining the party of the revolutionary proletariat. The Japanese, as noted, are by and large nonideological. Moreover, with rapid economic growth and prosperity, members of the "proletariat" came increasingly to identify themselves as middle class (by 1970, over 90 percent of the Japanese viewed themselves as such). In contrast to its European counterparts, which deradicalized themselves as their nations became more urban and prosperous so as to broaden their bases of support into the middle and even upper-middle classes, the JSP persisted in its inflexible confrontational posture and dogmatic revolutionary polemic that were blatantly irrelevant to the political, economic, and social conditions of the nation as perceived by its people. As a result, popular support for the JSP has consistently declined even among the very groups that are the party's ideological clients, such as industrial labor, the young, and the educated, without any compensating growth in support elsewhere. As things stand at present, the party has no prospect of capturing power as its Western counterparts have done.

The JSP is not really a single party; at one level, it is two parties: the parliamentary JSP and the constituency JSP. At another level, it is many parties. We take one level at a time. In one sense, the parliamentary JSP is actually quite moderate, for it consists of MPs who have been baptized in electoral politics and tempered by imperatives of practical legislative tasks. It makes no insignificant contribution to national legislation through informal negotiations with the ruling LDP to get its views accommodated, thus often improving the quality of final legislative products. Many of its members have close personal relations with LDP influentials. If it had control over the entire JSP, so called, as it once did, the political fortune of the party might not be nearly as depressing as it is.

The constituency JSP, consisting of the mass membership and prefectural party organizations, takes a different stance in the political arena, a stance that is more ideological, confrontational, and expressive. This, of course, is not entirely surprising, for where one stands depends on where one sits, and activists among mass members and party organizations are not constrained by the imperatives of practical legislative tasks and pragmatic electoral considerations because they are amateur volunteers for whom "principles" are vastly more important than electoral or policy outcomes. This difference between any parliamentary party and its constituency party or mass organizations (or between professional politicians and their ideological constituents) is more or less universal, but the problem for the parliamentary JSP is that the constituency JSP, by virtue of party rules, controls the party's national convention, which selects party leadership and platform. (This is the predicament that the ruling LDP has assiduously avoided.) The JSP's inflexible confrontational posture and dogmatic revolutionary polemic that in the past doomed the party to political impotence was precisely the function of this anomalous relationship between the parliamentary JSP and the constituency JSP.

At another level, the JSP has become many parties because it is fragmented much more today than it was in the 1960s and the 1970s when it was split into two ideological camps—moderate reformist and radical left. Ironically, this fragmentation is a function of the party's increasingly acute recognition that it has to change its fundamental posture if it is to be a really effective opposition party, not to mention a viable alternative to the ruling LDP. This recognition, shared not only by JSP MPs but by a growing proportion of mass party membership, has precipitated a crisscrossing internal policy debate that today reveals the extent of divergence of views within the presumably solidaristic "proletarian" party. There are at least eight clearly ascertainable "policy groupings" within the party today, six of them cautiously moderate and struggling to free the party from the past leftist stranglehold. Ideological or policy factionalism of the JSP, in more senses than one, is a far more difficult problem to deal with than the ruling party's personnel factionalism precisely because it does not lend itself to simple compromise, as would the patronage factionalism. Nevertheless, the fact that the party has begun this process of reassessment and redirection may well suggest that it is now in the process of institutional and political transition. Several factors seem to hasten this transition. One is inevitable generational metabolism, a shift in leadership and activist rank-and-file strata from the essentially prewar generation to an increasingly postwar generation. This shift is particularly noticeable in the formal party leadership that came into being in the latter part of the 1980s, leadership that, in its pronouncement and search for popular support, thus far at least appears less captive of doctrinaire and radical constituencies and more pragmatic and more attuned to popular sentiments and expectations than its predecessors.

A second factor is the deradicalization of organized labor, especially former public-sector unions associated with the Marxist General Council of Trade Unions (*Sohyo* in Japanese abbreviation) that was the major portion of the constituency JSP. Under the umbrella of *Rengo* (see earlier), the former *Sohyo* has become much less militant, again suggesting in part a generational change in its leadership as well as membership. A third factor is a growing recognition that the only way to mount a feasible challenge against the LDP is through either a coalition of opposition parties or a reorganization of these parties into a single party and that, in order for the JSP either to be part of it or to take a leadership role in it, it must change its policy and image from the dogmatic leftist to the pragmatic and the popular. The evolution of the JSP in this direction would not be an easy task, given the intractability of the factional fragmentation that now characterizes the party in search of a new identity.

OTHER OPPOSITION PARTIES

The Clean Government party (CGP) and the Democratic Socialist party (DSP) are middle-of-the-road parties, although in principle both are committed to moderate socialism. They are so close in policy direction to the more liberal sectors of the LDP that there is intermittent speculation about an imminent prospect of their merging with liberal LDP MPs to form a new centrist majority party.

The CGP is unique among the Japanese parties in that it is the only mass-based party; every other party began as a party of notables at the national level and developed whatever popular following it has only as a consequence. The mass movement out of whose womb the CGP sprang is the Value Creation Society (*Sokagakkai*), a militant religio-nationalist organization whose origin dates back to the prewar period. During the 1950s and well into the 1960s, Society membership expanded rapidly among those segments of the population that had come to feel a moral anomie caused by rapid social, political, and cultural change and others who felt left out of the rising economic growth and prosperity. Less educated than most and often marginal in status as a consequence, Society members were politically and culturally conservative but populist in economic orientation. The CGP first emerged as the Society's political department in the mid-1950s and, after achieving some success in local electoral politics, entered national politics a decade later as a formal political party. Thanks to the mass organizational base it has through the Society (over 15 million members), the CGP, even though it has since severed its formal ties with the parent movement in order to broaden its popular appeal, has been assured of a certain level of electoral support, winning during the past ten years from twenty-nine to sixty-four seats in the all-powerful House of Representatives.

The Democratic Socialist party was formed in 1959 by the more moderate members of the JSP and was consciously patterned after West European social democratic parties, rejecting doctrinaire Marxism and the revolutionary rhetoric of the JSP. The distinction between it and the LDP in policy has become increasingly obscure because of the ruling party's successful cooptation of its more progressive policy proposals. The DSP derives much of its organizational and electoral strength from its close alliance with unions that once constituted the Japan Confederation of Labor (*Domei*), which were moderate in political orientation and in their relations with management. Indeed, *Domei* unionists predominate in the party's mass membership, and their unions provide much of the party's political funds, campaign logistics, and electoral support. Many DSP MPs are themselves former *Domei* leaders. The party appeals to pragmatic liberals who are tired of the faction-ridden LDP and has maintained from a dozen to over thirty seats in the House of Representatives more or less consistently. Like the CGP, it could become part of a new centrist party in case of a party realignment.

The Japan Communist party (JCP) has become a more or less stable fixture in national politics. Until the mid-1960s, it had been violently divided into pro-Soviet and pro-Chinese factions and had suffered from its traditional image of a conspiratorial subversive party with allegiance to an alien power or powers. During the 1960s, the party purged both factions and under new leadership began painstakingly to cultivate a new image of an open, democratic, "Japanese" political party, eschewing revolutionary jargon and polemic. It now professes allegiance to the constitution and favors the nationalization of only one industry—energy—and focuses its activities on grassroots issues such as environment, health and human services, and bureaucratic neglect of citizen grievances. As a result, its popularity grew significantly and since the early 1970s it has maintained a parliamentary strength approximating that of the DSP. Nevertheless, whether and to what extent it may be able to expand its base of popular support remains unclear. On the one hand, the collapse of the Soviet Union and the end of the Cold War have freed the party from the remaining popular suspicion of its "foreign" allegiance and connection and rendered its claim of being a "Japanese" party more authentic. Also, the postwar generations of Japanese (who now constitute an increasing majority of the population) are ideologically less concerned than their elders. On the other hand, the party, unlike all other established parties, has no organized constituencies and therefore must rely almost solely on its well-disciplined mass membership (around 400,000) and its grassroots activities, as well as on many protest votes against the tedious LDP dominance. It is also critical for the party that "communism" as an ideology has, as the result of its failure in the Eastern bloc, China, Vietnam, and Cuba, lost its traditional intellectual and ideological appeal among those dissatisfied with the status quo. Moreover, the JCP is likely to be left out of any party realignment precisely because it still claims to be communist.

The semipermanent and tedious supremacy of the LDP and the exasperating infirmity of the major opposition parties intermittently give rise to new political groupings. The viability of these phenomena, however, seem circumscribed. The late 1970s saw the emergence of the New Liberal Club (NLC) and the Social Democratic League (SDL), the former a handful of young reformists seceding from the gerontocratic and complacent LDP, and the latter its leftist counterpart consisting of some of the more pragmatic members of the doctrinaire JSP. Within ten years, the NLC, unable to carve out a distinct homestead on the political spectrum, disbanded, all but one of its MPs returning to the LDP. The SDL lingers, but it is akin to the NLC in its inability to establish an electorally compelling identity of its own, and thus its fate appears sealed. Since the 1984 introduction of a proportional representation system for some 40 percent of the upper-house seats, there have appeared a number of microparties (e.g., the Progressive party, the Taxpayers party, the Sports Peace party, the New Japan party—all subsumed under "other parties" in table 5.1 [p. 158]), but they are all expressive, mainly single-issue groups, with no prospects of influencing parliamentary politics.

Japan's party system has not been a competitive one, and this lack of competitiveness has created problems that may subtly affect the quality of democracy. The ruling LDP, its position secure, tended to be complacent and could be suspected of exerting itself less diligently than if it were constantly facing an effective opposition challenge. The opposition has been so fragmented that until the 1993 general election there appeared to be no immediate prospect of unseating the LDP. Despite its seeming invincibility, however, the LDP then lost control of the all-powerful House of Representatives because of the defection of a few dozen of its MPs. (LDP seats dropped from 275 to 233 in the 511-seat lower house. Still, the LDP remained by far the largest party, the second largest being the Japan Socialist party with 70 seats.) Those former LDP MPs formed three small parties and organized a coalition government with all but one (Communist) opposition party. This seven-party coalition government appeared unlikely to be able to govern with critical energy and unity for any length of time, however, because it was hastily put together only for the purpose of discomfiting the perennially ruling LDP. Because of its consequent inability to govern, it seemed that it would probably be forced to call a new election soon.

In the meantime, pressures for a political realignment would only intensify. Most, if not all, of the LDP defectors were expected to return to the party (which might change its name for public relations purposes). The most probable outcome, given the influence of big business and other potent forces, all desirous of political stability and economic recovery, would be the restoration of the LDP (with or without a new name but considerably chastened) to power. Whether such an outcome would in the long run be beneficial to the nation is another matter. Nevertheless, as this sudden upheaval suggests, the 1990s may prove to be crucial for postwar Japan's political and party history.

Governmental Institutions

A parliamentary democracy, Japan's political system consists of institutions and procedures familiar to Westerners. The monarchy is but the symbol of national unity. The highest organ of state power is the Diet (parliament), elected by and representing the people. The executive branch, headed by the prime minister and Cabinet, oversees a professional civil service and is answerable to the Diet. The judiciary, presided over by the Supreme Court, is independent and has the power of judicial review. In its general contour and structure the Japanese political system differs little from any other parliamentary system. There are some notable variations, however, in the operation and behavior of the various components of the system that reflect the nation's culture and tradition.

PRIME MINISTER AND CABINET

The prime minister is elected by the Diet from among its members, by custom from among the members of the House of Representatives. Since Diet seats are held by parties, the prime minister is the leader of the majority party and has the power to appoint and dismiss Cabinet ministers, provided that a majority of them are members of the Diet (in practice, of the majority party). Each minister heads a ministry or one or more of the specialized agencies. The Cabinet may contain a deputy prime minister. Since the prime minister's party controls a majority of the Diet seats, he is also in a position to decide, or at least significantly influence, the parliamentary agenda and conduct and the appointments of the presiding officer of each house as well as those of parliamentary committees. In a variety of ways, the Japanese chief executive's power appears extensive.

The actual power of the prime minister is quite circumscribed. Remember that the majority party leader is selected on a stack of IOUs to rival factions. The formation of the Cabinet is therefore affected in that the IOUs are paid off in patronage. The various factions receive Cabinet posts (and sub-Cabinet, party, and parliamentary posts as well), which must be carefully apportioned so as to obviate desertions. Such senior portfolios as foreign affairs, finance, international trade and industry usually go to the leaders of coalition factions or their top lieutenants. Other posts are distributed among those factions, including the prime minister's, according to their respective numerical strengths and the intrafactional seniority of MPs concerned. Cabinet formation is therefore a careful balancing act, designed not so much to promote the competence and effectiveness of government as to guard the chief executive against actual or potential intraparty opposition. Thus policy expertise, administrative competence, and political compatibility are secondary criteria in choosing Cabinet members.

Interfactional balance shifts almost constantly, albeit subtly. Moreover, leaders of factions, which are patronage groupings, in order to retain their positions, must satisfy their followers' desire for Cabinet posts in order of seniority. Thus, the Cabinet is reshuffled with great frequency, producing the so-called one-year ministers syndrome, some posts being held but for a few months. The particular criteria for appointment and the brevity of tenure cannot but reduce many, perhaps most, ministers to figureheads, and discourage seriousness on their part in the development of policy expertise and administrative competence required for ministerial responsibilities. This is indeed a very serious problem for the Japanese government.

THE DIET

The bicameral parliament consists of the House of Representatives and the House of Councilors. The former (the lower house) is all-powerful; in case of disagreement, it prevails. At this time, the LDP does not have a majority of upper-house seats, having suffered an unexpected and most likely temporary electoral setback in the 1990 upper-house election owing to a rapid succession of scandals involving its senior leaders. This fact only discomfits the party in the upper house, but does not affect its power inasmuch as it has effective control over the lower house. The only exception to the power of the lower house occurs with amendments to the constitution, which require a concurring vote of two-thirds of the members of each house. The upper house, however, has a longer and more secure tenure than the lower house. The 252 Councilors have definite six-year terms, with half of them being elected every three years; the 512 representatives have four-year terms, which may be briefer should the prime minister dissolve their house and call for a new election. The Diet, as the highest organ of the state power, has the power of the purse; it can unseat the prime minister and the Cabinet by passing a no-confidence resolution, can impeach any member of the judiciary, and can investigate the conduct of any segment of the executive branch. Each house has a range of subject-matter standing committees and special committees to deliberate legislative proposals and investigate the manner in which they are implemented.

As the nation has become more modern (industrial and hence complex), however, the effective governing power has increasingly gravitated toward the executive branch and away from the legislative. The sheer size of the latter's membership and its division among competing parties make it increasingly difficult for the Japanese legislature to deal with the continuously expanding volume of problems with coherence and dispatch. Those problems have become increasingly complex, some even intractable, requiring great technical sophistication. Most of the MPs are amateurs elected not for their policy expertise, technical competence, or political acumen but for their popularity in their districts. Moreover, much of their time is taken up in constituency business, party affairs, and particularly in the case of LDP MPs, in factional maneuvering, wheeling and dealing. MPs are quite knowledgeable about issues that directly relate to their constituency interests, and many veteran MPs (especially in the LDP) have developed high degrees of policy expertise in one or more specific issues of national importance, such as taxation, environment, education. By and large, however, the effective power of policy initiation, deliberation, and formulation still resides in the executive branch. Even the Diet's power of the purse has become merely formal; the budget submitted by the Cabinet (prepared by the bureaucracy and endorsed by the ruling party) for Diet approval is so mind-bogglingly complex that its parliamentary debate becomes little more than a ritual.

The culture of consensual democracy also affects the Diet's relationship to the executive branch even more than the fact that the Cabinet is in the Diet and strongly inclines parliamentary debate to be more ritualistic than substantive. There is little by way of an adversarial atmosphere between the legislative and executive branches. Every major legislative proposal is prepared by the executive branch and goes through informal negotiation among all parties concerned (i.e., the relevant agency or ministry, the finance ministry if it requires major expenditure or new revenue, the LDP committee or committees concerned, opposition parties). In other words, by the time it is presented to the Diet for deliberation and vote, it comes as the product of all possible compromises and accommodations. Opposition parties may still vote against it (the opposition must act like an opposition at least sometimes), but frequently it is just a matter of form.

THE BUREAUCRACY

The government bureaucracy—the civil service—is an enormously powerful institution in any modern society. Its power is the function of two major factors, among others: the imperviousness of bureaucrats to public opinion owing to their tenure, and their centralized control of information and expertise relevant to the management of problems the government faces. Both the legislature and the Cabinet depend on the bureaucracy for intelligence and skill in performing their respective functions. Moreover, the higher civil service is accorded enormous historical prestige. Government service as the most prestigious and honored career one could aspire to is rooted in East Asian tradition. In Japan this tradition was greatly strengthened during the period of rapid modernization in the late nineteenth and early twentieth centuries. The first public university system, consisting of Imperial universities, was established for the explicit purpose of educating future leaders of the nation, especially future public servants. The best and the brightest graduates of those Imperial universities, especially Tokyo Imperial, were recruited into the government through rigorous examinations, and they were viewed by the multitude as models of intellectual excellence, moral probity, political impartiality, and selfless devotion to the public interest.

As a consequence, the Japanese higher civil service was imbued with a vigorous esprit de corps and assumed the role of guardian of the commonweal. This highly elitist bureaucratic self-perception still persists. An overwhelming majority of Japanese higher civil servants consider themselves superior to either the Cabinet or the Diet as guardians of the public interest. (Only a minority of their British and German brethren, for example, have a similar self-perception.) This view is in fact shared by politicians and citizens alike. A distinct majority of MPs concede that the higher civil service, not the Diet or the Cabinet, ensures satisfactory public policy. (Only tiny minorities of British and German MPs hold such a view of their civil services.) And the Japanese people at large regard the bureaucracy as more attentive to their common interest and well-being than the Diet, the party, or the Cabinet. In short, the higher civil service is still endowed with an aura of intrinsic authority and natural competence, and this reflects itself in its relationship with the party and the party Cabinet.

One indication of the power of the higher civil service is the domination of party and Cabinet by former higher civil servants. Senior bureaucrats, as noted, retire relatively early in life, and the prestige they enjoy among the population encourages many of them to seek a second career in elective politics. Within the total LDP parliamentary membership, they are a minority, but they occupy positions of power and influence greater than that of their more numerous nonbureaucrat colleagues. Ten of seventeen conservative postwar prime ministers were former bureaucrats, and they have occupied the office nearly 80 percent of the time. A majority of ministers of most Cabinets have been ex-bureaucrats.

Another and more critical way in which the power and influence of the bureaucracy on the Cabinet is manifest has to do with policymaking. Since factionalism makes policy controversy dangerous (for any critical policy issue tends to be exploited for factional purposes, e.g., to weaken and even unseat the incumbent prime minister), the ruling party is not fertile soil for new policies and new policy directions. It can function as the ruling party on issues on which there already exists a wide consensus, but when a new problem or a difficult issue arises, factionalism seriously inhibits consensus formation. The Cabinet suffers from the same problem because it is a creature of the shifting factional alignment. Thus, in Japan's party government a critical policy vacuum on any actual or potentially controversial problem or issue is often filled by the bureaucracy.

Sometimes the bureaucracy tends to postpone a difficult decision as long as possible, but the civil service as an institution is a much more cohesive human nexus than the party because its incumbents share common school ties and career experiences, as well as a common elitist esprit de corps. Its internal competition is an objective clientele conflict, not a passion-generating competition for power or spoils. Thus a new policy consensus is much less difficult within the civil service than within the ruling party or its Cabinet. The latter can begin to operate as a decision-making institution only when the civil service, having formed a consensus of its own, makes a relevant input to it. Since the input comes from the impartial bureaucracy and not from a faction or a faction-tied MP or MPs, the intraparty consensus-building process now begins to function outside the context of factional competition. To a significant extent, it may be argued, the primary function of the ruling party and its Cabinet is to legitimize decisions made by the bureaucracy.

THE JUDICIARY

The court of law does not occupy a prominent place in the popular consciousness in Japan, for the Japanese are not commonly litigious. Because of the social forces we discussed earlier, the Japanese are not infatuated with formal rules, laws, and regulations in managing their affairs; they value unwritten codes of behavior instead. Invocation of formal laws or rules is likely to be viewed as an admission of failure on the part of the party or parties invoking them to solve their problems informally, voluntarily, and discreetly in a spirit of civility and community. As a consequence, relatively few interpersonal and social problems are politicized or litigated, and when there is a conflict (and there are many conflicts and disagreements even in Japan), the natural inclination of the parties concerned is to seek informal mediation and settlement. Even problems taken to the court (unless they are criminal cases) are more often than not settled out of court, which the judge himself encourages, to avoid the acrimony of public confrontation that would lead to bitterness and animosity between the parties concerned. As a result, there are not many lawyers in Japan, and the legal profession is not widely sought after by college students. Still, as a highly complex democratic state, Japan has an increasingly wide range of political, social, and economic issues that do not lend themselves to traditional resolution or settlement and that therefore have to be formally adjudicated.

Under the prewar constitution, the judiciary was an arm of the executive branch of government, directed by the ministry of justice. There was no recourse for grievances against acts of the government, and no power of judicial review. The postwar constitution not only established an independent judiciary free from interference by other branches of government but vested in it the power of judicial review. The only aspect of the judiciary on which the executive branch of government impinges is judicial appointment. The Cabinet nominates the chief justice of the Supreme Court (who then is formally appointed by the emperor) and appoints the other members of the same court, as well as judges of inferior courts from lists submitted by the Supreme Court. Once appointed, these jurists effectively enjoy tenure until age seventy when, by custom, they resign. Supreme Court justices need to seek popular approval of their tenure in a decennial referendum, but in practice this is a matter of formality.

The way in which the power of judicial review has been exercised is interesting. A case involving the constitutionality of a law or an executive policy is initially handled by a relevant district court, but the ruling may be appealed to the Supreme Court. District courts have tended, in more controversial cases, toward a literal interpretation of the constitution. The Supreme Court, in contrast, has usually reversed those lower-court rulings in a manner that clearly suggested the presumption of constitutionality of the acts of government pertaining to public order or national security (what has since come to be known as a "political question"), that is, ruling in favor of the government rather than the rights and liberties enumerated in the constitution. These cases were contentious precisely because they involved issues that fell in the legal twilight zone where rights and liberties of the people merge with the imperatives of the state to maintain internal order and external security. Nevertheless, the difference in constitutional interpretation between the two levels of the judiciary would seem primarily to be the function of the generational difference between Supreme Court justices and lower-court judges. Supreme Court justices are older, reared and even educated in an authoritarian period when the interest of the state always superseded the rights of the individual. Lower-court judges are generally much younger, products of democratic postwar education and experience that stressed the rights of the individual and the citizen against government power. This does not necessarily mean that the Supreme Court will, over time, become more liberal.

The System in Action

Nations that are both industrial and democratic share a range of common problems—inflation, unemployment, deficit spending, education, welfare, pollution, labor relations—on whose handling governmental stability and party fortune depend. Japan has all these problems. At the same time, each nation, by virtue of its particular cultural, historical, sociopolitical, and environmental conditions, has problems that are unique. One such problem in Japan is national defense. In most modern states, the defense capability of a nation to maintain its security and safeguard its territorial integrity is not a matter of partisan disagreement. Parties disagree over whether the nation's defense is adequate, whether this weapons system or that particular strategic option is appropriate; but there is no disagreement about the need for a strong defense capability. Not so in Japan. The manner in which this issue has been treated in the postwar period provides a good example of how Japan's political system works, for it has involved all the aspects of Japanese politics we have thus far discussed.

Article 9 (the so-called no-war clause) of the postwar constitution renounces "war as a sovereign right of the nation and the threat or use of force as means of settling international disputes" and declares that "land, sea, and air forces, as well as other war potential, will never be maintained." If taken literally, this is an astonishing declaration, with no parallel elsewhere. Precipitated by the aftermath of the traumatic defeat in war, the article immediately rendered Japan unique among nations. This pacifist "spirit of the constitution," in the eyes of a people who pride themselves on their uniqueness, indeed exclusivity, became a veritable badge of national distinction.

Pious protestations of virtue are one thing; concessions to realities another. This is true of any nation, but Japan is rather extraordinary in the way in which those protestations of virtue have been stretched to the point of what many concerned observers regard as absurdity. On the practical level, as threatening events began to emerge in the world, most of the Japanese were persuaded that the no-war clause does not prohibit the possession of means of self-defense. Consequently, shortly after the nation regained its independence early in the 1950s, the Self-Defense Forces (SDF) were established. The constitutionality of the SDF was affirmed by the Supreme Court in subsequent years, and it came eventually to be accepted by nearly 90 percent of the people. But the same people, even today, are reluctant to make the SDF really strong enough to defend the nation in case of a serious contingency. And the government, in the absence of sufficient popular consensus, is understandably hesitant to strengthen the SDF. The SDF remains, as a consequence, a "para-police force." The Japanese view of the SDF, in short, has remained extremely ambivalent.

A number of mutually reinforcing factors underlie this extraordinary ambivalence. One is what we have already referred to variously as Japanese exceptionalism, their tendency to view their nation as *sui generis*. In terms of foreign and defense policy it expresses itself in an almost religious adherence to pacifism born of the atomic crucible of Hiroshima and Nagasaki and embodied in the postwar "Peace Constitution." No other nation in the world is as fervently "peace-loving" as Japan; no other people on earth are as committed to "peaceful diplomacy" as the means of settling international disputes as the Japanese; and no other state, therefore, is as wary of its military establishment as the Japanese. Indeed, the Japanese, officials and citizens alike, are fond of referring to themselves as *tokushu kokka* (the exceptional state). Only they can be so sincerely committed to pacifism, as only they can genuinely savor the subtle culinary delights of *sashimi* and *sushi*. In a way it is only natural that the Japanese should be reluctant to forsake this uniqueness, this exclusive pride of theirs.

A second factor is the extrarational view the Japanese have historically held of nature as fundamentally benign to them. In this view nature has always favored them, with temperate climate, fertile albeit limited soil, mild and picturesque topography, tranquility and safety from the savagery of invasion and exploitation. And nature has been particularly kind to the Japanese in perilous moments: The only time their nation was threatened with foreign invasion, by Kublai Khan's Mongol Empire, nature foiled the massive alien forces with its "divine wind"—*kamikaze*—(a typhoon); the Western colonial threat of the nineteenth century was warded off because nature enabled Japan to succeed in rapidly modernizing itself; nature favored Japan in the Sino-Japanese (1894–95) and Russo-Japanese (1904–5) wars, despite her vast inferiority in power vis-à-vis the massive Chinese and Russian empires. "Let nature take its course," admonishes a Japanese saying, then all will be well in the end. In this view, the disaster and defeat in World War II was caused by Japan's uncharacteristically impatient attempt to intervene in the course of nature. And Japan has been able to live in peace since 1945 precisely because it has refrained from intervening in the course of nature (through, in this instance, an active defense policy and military preparation).

A third significant factor underlying the Japanese ambivalence about the SDF is less psychological and more mundane, and that is economic interests, especially of *zaikai,* which might otherwise be viewed as favoring a strong military force. *Zaikai* (and, for that matter, all civilian economic sectors) prospered in the postwar period in, or because of, the absence of heavy military spending. Behind the shield of American military power, Japan could engage in the single-minded pursuit of economic growth and prosperity (hence *zaikai* prosperity and aggrandizement) without the necessity of diverting its resources to military preparation. The pacifist and exceptionalist treatment of the issue of national defense was eminently compatible with the interest of *zaikai,* particularly since few Japanese corporations (and no major ones) had to depend on defense procurement for revenues and growth. Industries even marginally involved in defense contracts did form an association (called the *Keidanren* Defense Production Committee) to promote a strong military, but their activities had little discernible impact on the issue in the absence of a sufficient consensus in their favor with *zaikai* at large.

Within the government bureaucracy as well, avoidance of the issue of national defense long ago came to be regarded as expedient, and this is a fourth factor. Defense expenditures during the early years of the SDF were kept small, a fact necessitated by the economic circumstances of the nation. Early in the 1960s, defense spending averaged less than 1 percent of the GNP. This early budgetary practice soon became popular with various government sectors, especially the increasingly powerful "economic ministries" such as Finance, International Trade and Industry, Agriculture, Construction, Transportation—all institutionally tied to growth-oriented client groups. As these sectors became more and more powerful and more deeply entrenched with growth and expansion of the national economy, the 1 percent limit for defense spending came to be treated as virtually sacrosanct. The Defense Agency, in contrast, was vastly handicapped in interbureaucratic budget politics, for it was new and small, without full ministry status and without a powerful constituency.

A fifth factor is the dominant party itself. Throughout its history since

1955, the LDP's political fortune also rested on continuing economic growth and expansion, which would best be promoted by minimizing defense spending. The party had a number of MPs, including some very influential personages, who were deeply concerned about what they viewed as the dangerously low level of SDF capability. Their concern, however, was constantly overridden by fears of political dispute with the opposition parties and of public controversy, which would invariably be exploited by intraparty factions competing for party leadership. To a considerable extent, the issue of national defense was a political taboo, to be avoided as long as possible.

As is apparent, these factors underlying the Japanese ambivalence about the SDF have justified one another, thus reinforcing one another, even though their respective motives or sources were discordant. What they collectively did, in any event, was to induce the debate on national defense to be couched in a highly moralistic pacifist language, which would not even permit the identification of actual threats or potential adversaries. Instead, this language stressed the incontestable virtue of international concord and the incontrovertible superiority of peaceful diplomacy over a strong military capability. The SDF was under constant suspicion of becoming a potentially aggressive instrument instead of scrupulously remaining "exclusively defensive." Indeed, candid and critical debate of the issue became a political taboo. And the culture of consensual democracy avoided it as long as the nation was assured of protection by the United States under the Japan-U.S. security pact originally created in 1952 and revised in 1960 at the height of the Cold War. During the late 1970s and early 1980s, there was increased East-West tension as the result of the Soviet invasion of Afghanistan, the instability in the Middle East, and the Soviet military expansion in Northeast Asia, but the Japanese government as well as the people did not share cold-warrior America's threat perception (due in part to the existential optimism of "let nature take its course") and resisted Washington's pressure on them to increase their defense capability.

The Cold War, which initially compelled Japan, under U.S. pressure, to establish the SDF in the mid-1950s, ended with the decline and fall of the Soviet Union and its East European empire. Many Japanese, like many Americans, may well have anticipated "peace dividends" as a consequence, but the post–Cold War era quickly came to be characterized by an increasing range and intensity of regional conflicts eliciting rising concern among the international community, especially the advanced industrialized world and the United Nations. In the meantime, Japan had emerged as an economic giant second only to the United States and, as such, also the second-largest financial contributor to the United Nations. Now, the United States or any other nation no longer complains that Japan is not doing enough for its own defense and instead is still getting a free ride on the U.S. nuclear security umbrella. The growing international criticism against Japan today, including that from the United States, is that Japan is not carrying its share of responsibility of the management and resolution of critical regional conflicts threatening international peace and security. This criticism, which had been latent throughout UN peacekeeping operations in the past two decades, really exploded during the Persian Gulf crisis of 1990–91. Japan refused to meet the UN Security Council resolution calling for member nations to contribute troops to Operations Desert Shield and Desert Storm, and under international pressure, Japan reluctantly made only a financial contribution (albeit quite substantial) to the coalition operation under UN auspices against Iraqi aggression and occupation of Kuwait. Japan's insistence not to be militarily involved in the regional conflict was justified by its claim of being "the exceptional state" with its "Peace Constitution," which renounces "war as a sovereign right of the nation and the threat or use of forces as means of settling international disputes." This self-imposed "constraint," however, is in conflict with Japan's membership in the United Nations, where all member nations are governed by the organization's Charter, which prescribes membership rights as well as obligations.

The fact that their nation is now an economic superpower—a fact of which they are not above being proud—is beginning to cause an increasing number of the Japanese to feel uncomfortable about their nation's continuing to hide behind the self-appointed (and ultimately self-serving) virtue of being the "exceptional state" endowed with the moral superiority of the "Peace Constitution" that no other nation can share, and to refuse to share the burden of international (especially UN) peacemaking and peacekeeping operations other than to write checks for part of their expenses. The Gulf crisis and the consequent crescendo of international criticism for its refusal to make direct contributions to the UN-mandated "coalition" efforts and the emergence of regional crises in Southeast Asia, East Africa, and former Yugoslavia, among other places of the world, have since then compelled the Japanese government to engage, albeit reluctantly, in an official deliberation whether and to what extent it should modify its traditional policy of avoiding involvement in UN collective security efforts under the pretext of Article 9 of its postwar constitution. The parliamentary debate that lasted from October 1991 to June 1992 nevertheless evinced the deep-seated Japanese obsession with remaining the uniquely pacifist, hence exceptional state. The legislative outcome on the issue, therefore, was extremely ambivalent as well as ambiguous. The so-called PKO Cooperation Act (PKO = peacekeeping operations) the Diet passed in June 1992 permits participation of SDF elements in UN peacekeeping operations but with provisos that effectively restrict these SDF (i.e., military) personnel to fundamentally nonmilitary activities only (on which 71 percent of the population insists). These "rear" activities are basically engineering, civilian supply, medical, administrative, and other activities of a humanitarian nature to be carried out in areas where effective cease-fire obtains and the opposing forces have agreed to the presence of peacekeeping forces. Actual supervision/monitoring of such cease-fire and its logistical correlates (e.g., disarming combatants, evacuation of opposing troops and their weapons and equipment, SDF deployment in demilitarized zones for the prevention of resumption of conflict, weapons inspection, involvement in prisoner exchanges, among other things) either are not permitted or require prior parliamentary approval (which, given the nature and process of decision making in Japan, would amount to "not permitted" in actual contingencies). In late 1993 some six hundred Japanese (SDF) troops were in Cambodia under UNTAC (UN Transitional Authority in Cambodia), but, for all practical purposes, they might as well be civilian volunteers. But even this extent of basically nonmilitary "cooperation" with UN peacekeeping operations is adamantly opposed by a significant proportion of the Japanese population, who fear it may be the harbinger of Japan's future military interventionist policy, particularly since their country is the second-largest economic power in the world. (It is true that, while the United States and other Western nations want Japan to take an increasingly active role for the promotion and maintenance of peace and security in the world, many Asian states that suffered from Japan's aggression before 1945 are understandably wary of Japan's playing such a role.)

The issue of Japan's SDF and its role as briefly discussed here really highlights the nature and process of decision making in Japan. As we have noted more than once, Japan's consensual decisional process begins to deal with a difficult issue only when it has become impossible or palpably dangerous not to do so, or when there is a powerful input to it from without. The end of the Cold War, which, at least in one sense, vindicated Japan's passive optimism of "let nature take its course," has led not to stable peace but to the emergence of new regional conflicts (e.g., Eastern Europe, former Soviet republics) and the aggravation of old ones (e.g., sub-Sahara Africa, Middle East) that are at more levels than one far more intractable and potentially more dangerous than the old Soviet-American military rivalry. The uneasy realization of this developing international phenomenon on the part of the Japanese was suddenly brought under sharper focus by the Persian

Gulf crisis, together with an increasing international pressure on Japan to assume its share of international responsibility commensurate with its economic power. In more senses than one, therefore, the process of forming a relevant new consensus on the issue of national defense and security responsibility has, it can be argued, been activated. Given the character of leadership in Japanese culture, consensus formation takes time, especially on the nation's military capability and role, an issue fraught with conflicting motives and sentiments, such as a popular craving for national exceptionalism, the memory of a traumatic experience of defeat and devastation, a calculus of economic expediency, a politicophobic desire to avoid international disputes, the deepening fear about the nation's critical and highly vulnerable lifelines, a growing uneasiness about an increasingly palpable disjunction between the nation's enormously enhanced capability and its continuing avoidance of international responsibility, among others.

The process of this consensus formation is further compounded by the vastly changed domestic socioeconomic circumstances. To cite but a few examples: The rate of growth of the Japanese economy, which once was the envy of the world, has sharply declined with the bursting of the "bubble economy"; the highly redistributive domestic policies established during the period of rapid and sustained economic growth of the 1960s and early 1970s and continued since has produced chronic government deficits, dangerously expanding the size of the cumulative national debts; the nation's infrastructure in the meantime has come to be heavily burdened; the nation's aging population and consequent demographic changes already occurring generate a prospect of harder times and a host of new problems in the future; and the public is becoming increasingly restless as a consequence. All these factors tend to affect the process of a new consensus formation regarding Japan's defense capability and its international role at the very time when politically and psychologically the nation may be said to be inclined to seek it. In the past, the dilemma confronting the security-minded Japanese was that while the nation was economically capable, it was not so, psychologically and politically. The dilemma for the Japanese government today, committed as it seems after the passage of the PKO Cooperation Act (albeit highly diluted in its content and thrust) to gradually assuming an international security role under the United Nations commensurate with its national power, is that while political and psychological inhibitions against a more relevant consensus have been lessened, a range of new economic constraints has emerged against it.

Given those conflicting motives, sentiments, and socioeconomic circumstances converging on the issue of the SDF and its international security role, it is difficult to foretell precisely what shape the emerging new consensus will eventually take. Indeed, there is no guarantee that a critically relevant consensus will emerge. As an advanced industrial (or postindustrial) society, Japan, like other such societies of the West, is undergoing what many analysts regard as a new and fundamental transitional period in which conventional political wisdom—scholarly as well as common sense—serve less and less reliably as means of prediction. Issues that were once simple (e.g., inflation *or* unemployment) have become vastly complex, many of them indeed seemingly intractable (e.g., inflation *and* unemployment), for which no group of experts has a really workable solution that would command wide acceptance. Military forces and their role may be one of those issues in Japan because it involves so many conflicting and mutually incompatible interests, psychological, political, cultural, social, and economic. In an important sense it has, as an issue, become far more complex than when it was pigeonholed in the closet of taboos. The resolution of this issue—the formation of relevant consensus on it—will test Japanese culture, society, government, political system, and political will as a nation.

No political system operates uniformly and invariably over time or throughout its many dimensions, for no system is totally static in the criteria and parameters of its operation nor definitive in the pattern of behavior of its various components. Every system is evolving, however indiscernibly. The Japanese political system is no exception. What we have seen in this chapter, therefore, is nothing more than what a student of comparative politics should know at the first instance of exposure to the only advanced industrial democracy outside the Western world.

SUGGESTIONS FOR ADDITIONAL READING

ALLINSON, GARY D., and YASUNORI SONE, eds. *Political Dynamics in Contemporary Japan.* Ithaca: Cornell University Press, 1992.

BUCKLEY, ROGER. *Japan Today.* 2d ed. Cambridge, England: Cambridge University Press, 1993.

BURKS, ARDATH W. *Japan: Profile of a Postindustrial Power.* 2d ed. Boulder, Colo.: Westview Press, 1984.

CAMPBELL, JOHN C. *How Policies Change: The Japanese Government and the Aging Society.* Princeton: Princeton University Press, 1992.

CHRISTOPHER, ROBERT C. *The Japanese Mind: The Goliath Explained.* New York: Simon and Schuster, 1983.

CURTIS, GERALD L. *The Japanese Way of Politics*. New York: Columbia University Press, 1988.

HAYES, LOUIS D. *Introduction to Japanese Politics*. New York: Paragon House, 1992.

McCORMACK, GAVAN, and YOSHIO SUGIMOTO, eds. *Democracy in Contemporary Japan*. Armonk, N.Y.: Sharpe, 1986.

NAKANE, CHIE. *Japanese Society*. Berkeley: University of California Press, 1970.

RAMSEYER, J. MARK, and FRANCES McCALL ROSENBLUTH. *Japan's Political Marketplace*. Cambridge, Mass.: Harvard University Press, 1993.

REED, STEVEN R. *Making Common Sense of Japan*. Pittsburgh: University of Pittsburgh Press, 1993.

REISCHAUER, EDWIN O. *The Japanese Today*. Cambridge, Mass.: Harvard University Press, 1988.

STOCKWIN, J.A.A., ALAN RIX, AURELIA GEORGE, JAMES HORNE, DAIICHI ITO, and MARTIN COLLICK. *Dynamic and Immobilist Politics in Japan*. Honolulu: University of Hawaii Press, 1993.

TAYLOR, JARED. *Shadows of the Rising Sun*. New York: Morrow, 1983.

6. Politics in East Europe: The Communist Political Systems

As a student interested in discovering the nature of political systems by comparing, you often confront the question, How do we choose the political systems for our studies? The hundreds of countries, dozens of global regions, and thousands of nations of people each offer meaningful and particular (sometimes exotic) features that could stimulate and sustain our interest and effort. You have already discovered that studying political systems can draw you deeper and deeper into the fascinating and intricate web that each political system is. Comparing is the stabilizer, the point of reference, the framework of conceptual landmarks that can guide and make sense of your studies.

In the realm of comparative politics through most of the twentieth century, one political system stood in sharp contrast to the others. Four generations of American and global leaders learned, in their student years, about political systems that had developed in the mainstream of the Western political tradition or that had colonial experiences exposing them to the same tradition. These were compared not only among themselves but always with the so-called communist systems. Communist systems claimed a distinct ideological heritage, a contrasting goal culture (i.e., what societies say they want to achieve), a poignantly different institutional structure, and a pattern of political behaviors (mass and elite) unlike the other types. Most of the noncommunist systems claimed and/or perceived themselves as variants on essentially Western and European styles of politics and economics. In a purely intellectual sense, this is also true of systems that claim a Marxist heritage, but clearly the Soviet-style communist system chose to cast itself as the "alternative." In ever more stark terms, the communist system crystallized as the political, economic, and military enemy of the developed Western states—the antagonist in a thirty-year-long superpower struggle, from 1957 to 1987, from Sputnik to Gorbachev's concessions.

Students of yesteryear, figuratively and literally, were drawn to study communist politics because of the fascination with studying the sinister, the implied patriotism of "knowing the enemy," the intrigue of a system built on fundamentally different value premises, the feeling of superiority that came with the belief that Americans would not let a government do such things to them, and the intrinsic value in comparing the mechanisms and alternatives for the management of a society. With changes that caused the disintegration and collapse of Soviet Communism between 1989 and 1991, all the ideological conflict and most of the political antagonism stemming from systemic contrasts vanished! The first four motivations for study vanished as well. The fifth was marginalized. It might be said that in the past, generation on generation of university students were doing the right thing for the wrong reason. Professors, of course, were happy to have the interest.

The fundamental characteristics of the political and economic systems in East Europe changed in the 1990s, and with those changes the classic rationale for studying the seventeen established communist systems eroded. The communist system was no more; the "enemy" was vanquished; the need for study was obviated. If the story were to end there, this could have been the shortest chapter in your collegiate experience. But two important considerations activate a new purpose for the systematic study of East Europe. First, the systemic features of the Soviet Communist system and their meaning for our understanding of politics should not be lost simply because of that system's demise. In a comparative framework, it is no less interesting in social scientific terms to examine how it organized itself, adapted, managed, became ill, and died. Business studies have long recognized the value of studying failed enterprises, and whether analyzed in political or economic terms, the USSR and the eight other East European communist systems were *the* largest enterprises the world has ever known.

Second, and intellectually more vital, is the need for students to take a close, comparative look at transitional systems. Can these countries implement the West's ideological prescriptions for their political and economic systems? We need to understand the implications whether the answer is yes or no. These countries are experiencing a metamorphosis. We know what they looked like; we have no sure idea what they will turn into. We do know that they have objectives that are known and they have leaderships whose task it is to guide the changes. But there is serious doubt about the degree to which this metamorphosis is manageable. More critically, since no living system has ever been through this particular process, it is an exciting and illuminating political experiment whatever the outcome.

Students who have worked their way through the text to this point have become dependent on a common framework that has been developed for all the previous chapters. The chapters that follow try to examine and understand a number of political systems that are in stages of dramatic change. They are transitional in the most basic ways—politics, economics, culture, education. Perhaps the one constant for all these places is that the parts of the political system are not clearly established or routinized. In essence, this means that looking at these systems in the same terms as those dealt with earlier in this text would result in an inaccurate picture of where these systems are today in their development. The dilemma is how to write about new and transitional systems using a set of guidelines more appropriate for established systems—ones with established track records.

In the two chapters that follow you will find a discussion of (1) the key political parts of the systems (political institutions, political groups), (2) the ideas that motivate people in the system (social forces), (3) the attempt to create a design for the system (constitutional development, variations on the model), and (4) the actual behavior of leaders and followers (the "system in action"). But these are not organized in the same sequence as they have been in earlier chapters.

The classic Soviet model (1917–91) serves in this chapter as the starting point. From it, we examine the development of variations in East Europe, a sharp variant in Gorbachev's Soviet Union itself, and finally variations of the most basic sort in the development of postcommunist systems across the landscape that was the communist world. Change is the central theme of the chapters that follow, and students should be aware that in these settings, the picture can be fuzzier.

In this chapter and the next, you will find the text's topics organized under the following headings:

LEGACY OF THE SOVIET SYSTEM
EAST EUROPEAN EXPERIENCES
POLISH COMMUNISM
HUNGARIAN COMMUNISM
YUGOSLAV COMMUNISM
GORBACHEV ERA

THE 1990S: POSTCOMMUNIST CHALLENGES
NEW VALUES
NEW MACHINERY
NEW LEADERSHIP
ECONOMIC VIABILITY
SYNTHESIS

Social Forces
Political Groups
Variations on the Model
Constitutional Development
Political Institutions
System in Action

To survive over time, a political system needs at least three things. We use this short and simplified list to guide our look at East European politics past and present. Systems need

1. A generic *value system* shared by the bulk of the masses: ideas and expectations that enable the leaders to communicate with and anticipate the behavior of the publics they are attempting to lead.
2. *Political machinery:* structure or mechanisms institutionalized to the point that they are recognized and can produce outcomes that the leadership has targeted.
3. *Leadership:* a cadre of persons able to pursue goals by making rational policy choices accounting for costs, payoffs, and consequences.

These themes are woven throughout the two chapters that follow. At least in terms of the "transitional" political systems in East Europe, there is very serious doubt about whether these minimal requisites are met. In reality, systems must go well beyond this basic list to become healthy and prosperous.

Legacy of the Soviet System

The tsarist era in Russian politics is an intriguing and intricate period of history, displaying both the strengths and weaknesses of traditional societies. Russia was a vast, unevenly organized political system. As a political system, it had feudal qualities that minimized the sense among the masses that they were in any meaningful way connected to the system's leadership. To the extent that people in tsarist Russia knew that they were a part of a governing system, it was one that extracted from them. It erratically and sometimes brutally took from them their commodities, harvests, and taxes. It also pressed them into service, often by way of local landlords, and sent them afield to labor or fight for objectives they did not comprehend. The system was characterized by a wide gulf between the rulers and the ruled not only in terms of practical, material well-being (income and property) but also in terms of education, culture, and self-awareness.

Politics in the traditional setting for centuries leading up to the explosive ideas of the so-called Age of Liberalism meant to ordinary folk that power would be exercised over them. Leaders whose authority was unquestioned would make decisions binding on people, with no quarter for questions about legitimacy or public interests. One perception dominated the political landscape: that an elite would "naturally" guide the society, serving primarily its own interest. In a sense, this may have been a crude precursor of the "trickle down" theory—what's good for the ruling royal family must ultimately be good for the people. The notion that government should serve or enhance the lives of its citizens (broadly defined) was simply not a part of the political environment. In concept, the state provided "protection" and "order." Ironically, the energy to deliver these intrinsically violent services came from segments of the masses themselves —pressed into service in the name of the state. By today's standards, government was small, distant, and unpredictable. It was also harsh, intolerant, and preoccupied with its own objectives—sometimes obsessively.

The political system of tsarist Russia was a combination of indigenous autocratic patterns and a European system of government that promulgated arrogant, elite styles in domestic politics and exclusive, clublike behavior in foreign relations. Boundaries were a function of the elite's manipulative power, not any notion of national identity or the integrity of political units. Territory and the human resources within were mere "game pieces" in the protracted multiplayer chess match that was European diplomacy. Locked in the heart of the Eurasian land mass, Russia found it difficult and foreboding to seek colonies across the seas and on distant continents. By default, it spread to adjacent territories, conquering and incorporating lands and people with crude and traditional techniques. The Russian colonial effort stimulated no new thinking—no intellectual or social scientific "stretching" that could have set Russia more legitimately on the stage with other eager colonial powers of the sixteenth, seventeenth, eighteenth, and nineteenth centuries.

A lack of innovation marked the precommunist ages in Russia. Plodding routine in politics, economics, and education left Russia envious of the West and compelled to emulate its art, architecture, and science as a substitute for its own achievements. The special claim to distinctiveness was often simply a function of making whatever bigger. In this precommunist history was built the legacy of illusionmaking, leadership insensitivity, and mass inertia subsequently developed to new heights under the communist regimes.

Analysts often have focused on these continuing patterns of politics, with good reason. But it is crucial to understand that there is nothing inevitable about the continuation of these patterns. In fact, the failure of politics and especially the failure of the promise of innovative politics from the Bolshevik regime and its successors permitted these patterns to hold. Every liberal regime in the West today evolved from a more authoritarian regime. Communist leaders were consistently unable to change the political rhythm without jeopardizing the very existence of the political system they sought to promote. We revisit this theme a bit further on in this chapter.

Soviet Communism begins with the ineptness of the pre-Soviet "provisional government" and the zeal and eagerness of the small, clandestine, impatient, and imprudent Bolshevik party in late 1917. The tsar, Nicholas II, had abdicated his throne in the spring of 1917, giving way to a conglomerate of parties and would-be leaders who formed a government only to discover that Russia was both poorly organized and deeply entangled in a number of crises. A good history course or some outside reading can help you follow the twisting path of events that led to Lenin's leadership of a relatively small collection of dedicated revolutionaries and a larger circle of alienated followers who were able to seize power in the course of ten days in the fall of 1917. The established government displayed little resolve and no stealth in responding to the armed challenge from the Bolsheviks.

The Bolshevik party led by Lenin (whose real name was Vladimir Ulyanov) achieved power and faced the daunting task of constructing a political system for which they had only the most vague design. Marxism, built on the theoretical, abstract, and not altogether consistent writings of Karl Marx (a German philosopher and European vagabond), was the rhetorical framework for Lenin and the Bolsheviks. But practical omissions and inadequacies forced Lenin to "flesh out" and, in reality, to create a massive literature to augment Marxism, addressing *how* these ideas could have an impact on a real place and real people. Volumes have been written on the inadequacy and inappropriateness of Marxism. The essential point here is that Marxism-Leninism was an ideology only vaguely drawn from Marxism. But it did find in Marxism an intellectual rationalization for the revolution and the system's initial themes following the revolution. To the extent that Lenin provided any systemic architecture for the new political and economic systems, he did so under the pressure of acute needs for political institutions and economic policies.

He faced challenges from an ongoing world war, a confused and uncertain mass public, and an indigenous elite so threatened by the new ideology that it either emigrated or coalesced to confront the new regime in a civil war aided and abetted by European and American governments displeased with the new political rhetoric. Ultimately the Lenin government was also challenged by its own inexperience in wielding political power. This last point is too often neglected. It may have critical comparative significance for Russian politics today. The point is that those characters who succeeded in tearing down the old system (though their success was improbable) were not adept at framing a new system. Destroying the established system required certain skills and energies. Constructing a new one required different skills and energies. It is fair to say that most such abilities were lacking in the new

Bolshevik leadership. Lenin had conspiratorial skills, charisma, and a flare for enlisting the activist masses in the collective assault on the old regime. He had little or no acumen for compromise, negotiation, or institutional development. His strident leadership of the clandestine revolutionary movement was not compatible with the notion that safeguards and constraints against government abuse of power are necessary in political systems—a sensitivity he could have gleaned from Marx's writings.

Lenin's run at leading and shaping the new regime under its new label, Union of Soviet Socialist Republics, was full of contradictions that Lenin himself explained in terms of the need for social systems to take two steps forward and one step back—a rationalization for the fits and starts in early Soviet policy. His agricultural and industrial policies were sketchy and seldom implemented with any consistency. Policies and government officials reflected the strident qualities of the leader with little recognition that the problems were complex and not easily solved. Lenin died in 1924, having left a system not well defined either in political or economic terms. The rhetoric had managed to convince many in the West that the Leninist regime was antagonistic and without genuine commitment to the "people principles" that had served as the *raison d'être* for both Marx and Lenin. From the beginning, there was little doubt that a fundamental shift was taking place that would shape a new value system for the masses, frame a new set of political institutions and relationships, and draw its leadership from a new sector of society. We should reflect on these goals when we re-assess from the terminal point of the communist experience (1991) and evaluate what the consequences were.

After a three-year struggle for power following Lenin's death, Stalin secured power, firmly controlling both the Communist party and the state structure (government). Stalin, a revolutionary code name translated "man of steel," for twenty-six years lived up to his name by creating a hard, inflexible, and stalwart regime dominated by him and a cult of personality he carefully crafted. The characteristics of his regime became the working definition of "communism" for most of the world—friend and foe alike. Intellectually and theoretically speaking, the system Stalin built was consistent neither with Marx nor Lenin. Our misperception of the linkage of Stalinism to its antecedents stems directly from the fact that Stalin used the achievements and heritage of both men to package, not guide, his politics and policies. This claim served as the basis of his authority, and he prohibited challenges to it. The system he created bastardized beyond recognition the principles of his predecessors. He constructed a political system with the highest possible levels of concentrated political power. His personal leadership of the two central components of the political structure—the Communist party and the government ("state structure") endowed him with the authority to make any and all decisions he deemed useful. Beyond this, his willingness to use unmeasured and unrestrained force to reinforce his domestic policies and to intimidate any dissent became characteristic. He can be said to have had and used dictatorial power. Lenin had warned that Stalin was "too crude to rule" and that he understood too little of the purpose of the revolution. His warnings were prophetic.

Stalin's hand in the construction of the political and economic systems resulted in a political system like none other that the twentieth century had seen. Its basic outlines persisted up to the Gorbachev era (1985–91), though no leader after Stalin was able to manipulate the political system with the same singular, intimidating control. The fundamental scheme of the system was to align five vertical bureaucracies (see figure 6.1) and focus control in a very few people in each by linking the parts of the system only at the top levels via these few leaders filling dual roles. The Western literature labeled this characteristic "interlocking directorates." Each of the bureaucracies had its own rationale and, over time, developed its own distinct "interests." While the five vertical bureaucracies persisted as the backbone structure of the system until its demise, the relative strength and levels of activity differed under different regimes, at different moments in time, and when different issues were before the leadership.

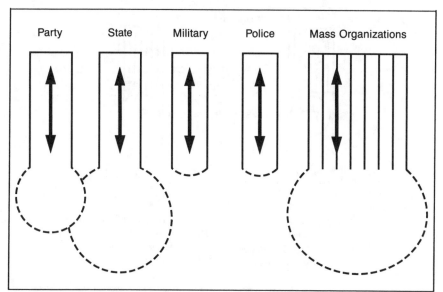

Figure 6.1. Vertical Bureaucracies of the Classic Communist System

The key to understanding this scheme is an awareness of what the vertical structure of the system does to the way the system functions. Essentially, most political systems, when schematically drawn, reveal both vertical and horizontal linkages. That is to say, parts of the system—agencies, offices, bureaucracies, or whatever—interact with offices both "above" and "below" them, as well as interacting with a number of offices and people who are on the same plane, with the same levels of responsibility. At a university, this "normal" structure might mean that the political science department links itself with the dean/college administration (political level above the department), with the undergraduate students (level below the department), and with other departments that have roughly the same role and power in the system. When most political systems are sketched they appear in general terms to be broad-based triangles with "connectors" suggesting both vertical and horizontal communication and interaction.

The Soviet system that became the prototype for other East European Communist systems avoided the kinds of linkages between elements of a bureaucracy that shared a common level of responsibility (i.e., horizontal communication) and between whole bureaucracies. What resulted was a series of bureaucracies characterized by communication up and down, rather than between bureaucracies (see figure 6.2). Take another look at figure 6.1 and think through what this could mean for policymaking.

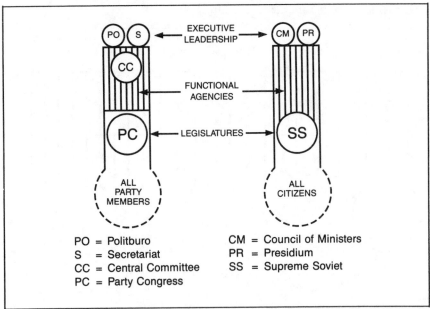

Figure 6.2. Parallel Organization of Party and State Bureaucracies

The vertical structure is not unknown in our society. Our military is organized around this principle, where it is given another name: chain of command. The corporal knows that the system functions for him only if he is acutely aware of the link he has to his superior (the sergeant) and to those over whom he has authority (the privates). He can talk to other corporals, but that serves no purpose in the vertical structure that is the military. Functionally, he gets things done, makes requests, asks questions, and gives/gets orders to/from those above and below him.

In the Soviet political system policymaking was critically affected by this structure. For reasons similar to the U.S. military, a vertical structure in the USSR enabled downward signals to be passed with efficiency and clarity. Perhaps the first responsibility of these bureaucracies was indeed to administer policies and decisions, which meant communicating, applying, and enforcing. In the course of policymaking the system also required input (facts, data, and perspective) from the bureaucracies: upward communication. To this end, the systems were relatively streamlined, though any one link in the vertical chain could block such messages. When, in the course of policy deliberation, the leadership needed input, the Soviet system gave them a number of signals each of which was unadulterated or uncontaminated by lower-level (horizontal) consultation between parts of the five bureaucracies.

While this could be an advantage in rare cases, it resulted in narrow perspectives and penetrating insecurity by all the bureaucracies. All of them feared that their recommendations, once passed up to the top leadership, would stand in stark contrast to the input of the other bureaucracies. This raised the ante in the competition and suspicion among bureaucracies and often left the top leadership with such sharply different recommendations for policy that they balked at making any policy at all. In more typical systems, discussion at low and middle levels would create opportunities for modification, compromise, negotiation, or, failing those, at least well-articulated differences that could be more adeptly handled by a policymaking elite. In Stalin's time this systemic flaw was of minimal consequence. He made decisions in a rarefied environment and without significant input. After Stalin, leaders discovered the difficulties of policymaking that stem directly from the structural design of the political system.

The overall policymaking consequence of this design was that in broad, comparative terms, the communist systems developed a pattern of making decisions not to decide! Confronted by sharply contrasting input from the different bureaucracies, they hesitated, tabled, or sent signals to the bureaucracies that they needed another set of signals. As important was the situation in which they pressed themselves to make a policy choice and then, because they were unsure from the outset, later became queasy and reversed or diluted the original policy commitment. Notable exceptions withstanding, little in the policy history of the USSR after Stalin suggests that leaders had the confidence to make key policy decisions and then stick with them —to "stay the course."

Control of the process was maintained through the mechanism known as interlocking directorates (see figure 6.3). The Communist party retained control by its power to generate or at least to approve the appointment of key officials at the top of each of the bureaucracies. A special elite in the Communist party bureaucracy ("Secretariat") performed this gatekeeper function, which in Russian was called *nomenklatura*. By ensuring that like-minded people filled the top spots and held allegiance to the Communist party (or at minimum did not challenge its preeminent position), a predictable pattern of political support resulted: team players with a vested interest in the system the way it was. Top officials of all the bureaucracies regularly crossed over to fulfill roles in the party bureaucracy at either the top or next lower level.

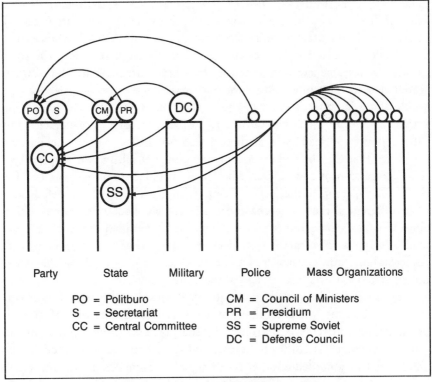

Figure 6.3. Interlocking Directorates

Figure 6.3 represents the "interlocking" characteristics of the system and identifies the key decision-making groups at the very top of the bureaucracies. Notice the remarkable parallelism between the party and the state.

The special nature of the relationship that evolved between the party and the state needs close scrutiny. In terms of real political functions, the party maintained its role because it was provided with the exclusive, monopolistic responsibility for "guiding" the society. Practically and legally, it was the only political party; this meant it was the only organization that could seek political power and government authority. Only the Communist party could place its people (or those it found acceptable) in key positions. The texture and genuine meaning of the term "guide" is critical to our understanding. Guiding meant that only the party could set goals for the society, broad themes for policy, and parameters for the policy process. Coupled with *nomenklatura*, the party was assured the central role in the political system. It was structured to look like and function like the government, except that its decisions were not official policies of the state. Its influence was dominant, but it was vulnerable in two respects.

The state (government) had a complementary role with two critical assets. Only the state could actually make and administer policies. In most of the decades of Soviet Communism, the state chose not to resist the "guidance" of the party but progressively signs developed that the state saw a need to press independent policy positions. In perspective, the differences between the party and the state have been attributed to the level and kind of expertise the bureaucrats in each brought to their jobs. The legions of government bureaucrats were better educated (at least in a technical sense) in the realms in which they were working. They were more likely to be promoted based on job performance and were younger (though not young by Western standards). Key "state" leaders were in their fifties and sixties. In contrast, party bureaucrats had less technical education but more ideological schooling. Political correctness and conduct were more central to party bureaucrats' advancement. They were older than their counterparts in the state structure—often beyond their most productive years. Top party officials were commonly in their seventies and eighties.

Western literature called this the "Red-Expert" friction. The "red" refers to the political-ideological posture (of the party), which increasingly juxtaposed the "expert" posture built on the more scientific-technical knowledge of the government (state). While easily exaggerated and oversimplified, the perspectives revealed real differences despite party bureaucrats having some expertise and state bureaucrats having their own ideological credentials.

The state was the official policymaker and could draw on more and younger, fresher expertise. The party and the state in the post-Stalin era had a delicate, out-of-focus, mutually dependent relationship. They were not adversaries or even open competitors, as many institutions are in Western political systems. But they were also not on the same wavelength when it came to the debate about methods by which to pursue the party-guided goals. This friction over the nature of policy or the application of policies was most evident in economic and foreign policy.

The Stalin era established many propensities that left post-Stalin Soviet leaders in a quandary:

- Political reality and political rhetoric had no relationship.
- The political machinery and the relationship among its parts had not been tested (or refined) given Stalin's personal control.
- There was no way to gauge public sentiment about politics.
- Centralization of control and resources resulted in highly visible "achievements" but no genuine way to measure or evaluate them.
- Socialization by way of the pervasive control of the media and of all social organizations veiled public attitudes.

While these things were evident, each in its own way presented fundamental problems for the political management of Malenkov, Khrushchev, Brezhnev (with Kosygin), Andropov, and Chernenko, who from 1953 to 1985 in turn held the top party post in the Soviet system. Distilled to their basic essence, each issue raised the question of whether the rewards of reform and adaptation were sufficient to risk the destabilization of the political pattern that had persisted and maintained the established Communist party elite. And what happens to a political system that over time resists all efforts to change it? Could the political base have been broadened? Could educational innovation have been introduced? Could economic energies have been released by decentralization or privatization? Could the society have pursued its original ideological objectives? Could socialism have been what it claimed to be? Would any change have unraveled the fabric of what was Soviet Communism?

A penetrating apprehension about change, dramatic or modest, characterized the epoch from 1964 to 1985. Only Khrushchev "rolled the dice" and put at risk the "legitimacy" based on Stalin's political style. At the Twentieth Party Congress in 1956, he abruptly and unexpectedly announced changes in domestic and foreign policy, which collectively spelled "de-Stalinization." The thrust was to change policies on an experimental basis. Economic, educational, and personnel policies were featured in domestic politics, but the overall institutional design was not changed. Thirty years later, it became clear that a generation of young persons with leadership aspirations had been excited and challenged by the reforms or political discussion of reforms that many called a "thaw" in the icy intimidation of the Stalinist control system and in the increasingly frigid relationships of the Cold War. With Khrushchev's demise, they submerged their perspectives and conformed through the 1960s, 1970s, and 1980s, until rereleased by Mikhail Gorbachev—himself one of the "children of Arbat," who had been influenced by the winds of change in Khrushchev's time. Boris Yeltsin also points to the Khrushchev period as the influence that stimulated his reform agenda, though similarly delayed for decades. Most of Khrushchev's efforts at change were undermined by one or more of the following factors. Soviets, not accustomed to candor and high energy from a leader, perceived Khrushchev to be flamboyant, courageous, and shrewd. Nonetheless, he was beset by circumstances that ultimately enabled those threatened by the changes to ambush him politically in October 1964. Khrushchev's efforts to stimulate the agricultural sector and to jump-start a rigid and routinized educational system were his most concentrated policy assaults on the classic system. Both failed, and along with the discredit associated with the Cuban missile crisis, Khrushchev's support in the party hierarchy collapsed.

The factors resisting change became dominant in the seventeen years of the Brezhnev era that followed. First, policies of change had been ill conceived. Prohibitions on independent sources of analysis and the absence of intellectual disciplines that were policy relevant—such as economics, sociology, political science, and management science—rendered reforms incomplete and unsophisticated. Second, the leadership recognition of the limited input and expertise coupled with the severe inexperience of the inner circle of the leadership resulted in poor levels of confidence in policy decisions. Third, bureaucratic inertia stemming from its size, inadequacy, and lack of professionalism could and did block efforts toward change. The homeostatic qualities of the Soviet bureaucracies were unmatched by other political systems in the Cold War era. The Soviet bureaucracies were bigger, stickier, and more spongy. Resistance was found in the deliberation stage, at the point of decision, and, most clearly, at the policy implementation stage. A simple fear that change could threaten position, privilege, and the system that bureaucrats had successfully manipulated to their own advantage generated clear and resounding resistance. Fourth and finally, the timid and partial quality of the reforms (meant to make them more palatable) caused them to be stifled by the larger resistant milieu.

Leonid Brezhnev succeeded Khrushchev as party General Secretary and Alexei Kosygin headed the state structure (chairman of the Council of Ministers). Their leadership—gray, nondescript, and plodding—was a lot more comfortable for the establishment. It attacked the pressures and dissatisfactions of masses and elites by producing illusions. Gorbachev, in his book *Perestroika,* called this the "propaganda of success." The regime's talents and energies were directed at a policy strategy that had high potential yield without threatening the established institutional order or the control of the party. The strategy of producing images of success rather than success itself had the beauty of buoying Soviet self-esteem and justifying individual hardship in exchange for purported societal achievements. It also produced an unexpected result when the West absorbed these images with more alacrity and gusto than the Soviets did. With uncharacteristic carelessness and inattention to evidence, Americans emotionally devoured the "superman," "super system" portrait the USSR manufactured of itself. In the face of this public relations success, the Brezhnev leadership redoubled its efforts, eliminating the apparent need for the Soviet leadership even to consider institutional reform. During Brezhnev's regime, relatively modest experiments in economics and politics were created, generally succeeded, and were nonetheless abandoned.

In the larger picture, the political system could not count on the same level of public passivity, single-minded elite discipline, or coercive intimidation as it had in Stalin's time. These elements continued to exist, but Khrushchev had eroded their meaning irreversibly. The Brezhnev style, absent personal charisma or stimulating, hopeful policies, had to find another basis for maintaining a minimum level of legitimacy. It did this by utilizing the structure of mass organizations (see figure 6.1) as distributive mechanisms. Simply, the public's voluntary affiliation with a wide range of affinity-based membership groups became the way in which people lined up for extra goods and services provided by the centralized Soviet system. By joining large-scale organizations authorized by the party or state and with membership qualifications built around professional, occupational, age, gender, sport, recreational, trade union, or other characteristics, the nonparty public (approximately 92 percent of the 280 million Soviets) connected with the "system." In this way, nominally system-supportive persons in mass organizations received benefits from the establishment. Some benefits seemed mundane, some consequential, but all represented a responsiveness to some aspirations of each group's membership. By attempting to enlist support and establish legitimacy "by performance"—in essence, by nurturing the perception that the system was doing more *for* people than *to* them—the bland and plodding system could be perceived in positive terms, especially given that the system manipulated all information about itself.

The vertical system was as effective in selectively distributing goods and services as it was delivering commands down through the bureaucracies. In this way, limited goods could motivate supportive behaviors and even eagerness to join multiple mass organizations each with its own indoctrination potential. By enlisting those Soviets who filled the bloated bureaucracies, those who absorbed the illusions and became patriotic, and those who were satisfied with the modest guarantees and benefits of the social system distributed through mass organizations, the Soviet leadership and the Communist party were able to retain their power.

Yuri Andropov (1981–83) and Konstantin Chernenko (1983–85) succeeded Brezhnev, but given their ages and bureaucratic disposition, neither the structure of the system nor the policies changed. The Brezhnev style —persistent mediocrity and hypersensitivity to challenge and change— dominated. Andropov sponsored Gorbachev's entry to the all-union (i.e., Soviet systemwide) leadership circle in Moscow, but by way of the traditional and established criteria and path.

East European Experiences

The countries that share the East European landscape also share many experiences rooted in the Slavic heritage, even though some are not ethnically Slavic countries. Examples of non-Slavs include Estonia, Hungary, Macedonia, Albania, and what was the German Democratic Republic (East Germany). The early twentieth century saw some national aspirations trampled, while others attached themselves to burgeoning empires. World War II galvanized the pain and devastation for virtually all East European systems. While they started the war on different sides, at the close of the war Poland, Czechoslovakia, Hungary, Romania, Bulgaria, and parts of Germany and Austria were occupied by the battered and emotionally driven Soviet army. The Baltic states of Lithuania, Latvia, and Estonia had been officially absorbed into the USSR, and Yugoslavia and Albania were not occupied. They were controlled by "independent," indigenous Communist parties that had fought Nazi occupation. In systems where Soviet forces became the guarantors of order, Stalin maneuvered and engineered the establishment of political systems patterned on the Soviet model. The actual plot and timing were different in each case, but by 1948 the result was uniform: Communist party control, though under varying local labels.

Stalin was a harsh and unyielding patron. He exacted a high price in both economic and political terms. East European Communist parties and Soviet-endorsed leaders accepted and rationalized economically costly poli-

cies whose purpose was to rebuild the USSR and coercive policies to eliminate competitive politics. Ironically, the Soviet treatment of East European
states after World War II differed little between those that had been Nazi allies and those that had been Nazi enemies. The Soviet objective was to establish client states in East Europe. A network of foreign policy techniques
tightened the Soviet grip over each separate Soviet bloc country.

In the decades following the Stalin era, the nature of the relationship
between the USSR and its East European allies became more complex and
delicate. With Khrushchev's de-Stalinization also came signals to East Europe that "separate roads to socialism" were acceptable to the Soviet
Union's leadership. This triggered many interesting encounters as East Europeans tried to decipher the limits of this apparent new latitude. The result
was an effort across East Europe to fashion variations and adaptations from
the basic Soviet model. Tinkering was evident in both the institutional structure of the political and economic systems and in the substantive policies initiated. But in a very broad sense, a pattern of limits emerged. These limits
were not made explicit by the Soviets but had to be deduced from the long
and collective experience of efforts by East European systems to probe for
the outlines of Soviet foreign policy.

A technique built on the ambiguity of rules was the foundation for
both the Soviet domestic legal/control system and the effort to manage its
relationship with its client states in East Europe. Explained simply, when
an authority wants to control behavior, two options are available. One can
make explicit, detailed, and comprehensive rules or one can make generic
and vague rules filled with implicit signals and penalties. If one opts for the
explicit strategy, the danger is that it is impossible to be explicit about all
eventualities. Gaps emerge in these explicit instructions and restrictions. If
one attempts to be precise about all those things that are prohibited, the latitude to do all other things is implied. Western-style systems with their symbolic emphasis on "freedom" reinforce the notion that unless there is a formal, lucid prohibition, one is entitled to do it. This accounts for the
superlitigating, megalegal political system that has developed in the United
States.

In contrast, an authority can exercise control by issuing ambiguous directives that might create enough insecurity in the minds of those governed
to activate caution and inhibition in their behavior. Government by its rhetoric and behavior sets the public to pondering just what is meant by the
purposefully unclear rules. A prudent subject is likely to reason conserva-
tively, especially when the punishment is equally unclear. The communist legal systems utilized the latter approach. Those accustomed to Western-style

clarity often judged the Soviet system to be oppressive and corrupt. This kind of Soviet domestic rule making was demonstrated by the laws against "anti-Soviet behavior" and "hooliganism." By the very nature of the ambiguity, an American would judge the Soviet system to have violated the "rights" to which all people are said to be entitled. An objective analyst might point out that the "right" violated is the right to do anything that is not otherwise legally prohibited. The communist legal system was seldom examined from the perspective of efficiency or in comparison with the ills and problems of the U.S.-style legal system. The purpose here is not to coax value judgments about these systems but to illuminate how the communist system functioned. Before you conclude that the ambiguous rules system is somehow a distinctly communist (and sinister) technique, you should be reminded that you have often experienced control of this sort. Every time your parents told you to "be careful," "be responsible," or "don't do anything I wouldn't do," they were employing this technique. Faced with this sort of generic, ambiguous rule, you are expected to put the broadest interpretation on the order and respond by limiting your behavior. If that does not inhibit you, there is an equally ambiguous (usually ominous) sense about what the penalty might be if you violate the rule.

This technique was such a staple for the control of the domestic political system in Soviet-style systems that it was also the choice of the Soviets for controlling East European client states. Instead of setting out a comprehensive and precise inventory of prohibitions, the Soviets made known to their Communist party peers and state leaders in East Europe that a set of rules existed but that they were generally guided by a sense of what "fraternal socialist systems" would do for and with one another. Given the unequal relationship, this effectively meant that East European states and their leaders had to walk very carefully as they searched for ways by which they could adapt, adjust, or modify the Soviet model. Only with the passage of time and experience of when the Soviets did indeed act to impose control (Berlin 1948, Hungary 1956, Czechoslovakia 1968, and Afghanistan 1979) did the pattern and essence of the rules become clear. The rules apparently prescribed that

1. Change had to be country specific; change in one East European country had no implications for the others. All change had to be packaged in these terms by the leadership and could not be exported.

2. Change could proceed in any given country on the domestic side *or* the foreign policy side, but not both. The scope of the changes did not seem to be a key as long as the state adhered to the Soviet model

in one realm or the other. Those experimenting with domestic policy were stridently pro-Soviet in foreign policy, or vice versa.

3. Soviets would not take action by force (military intervention) unless they were confident that they could "neutralize" the problem in a matter of days or weeks (based on their "intelligence" estimates) and would not engage in these sorts of actions in two venues (countries) at the same time.

4. Change needed to proceed only with the support of both the party and the state in the system in question. Soviet relations with these countries was built with parallel linkages: state to state and party to party, creating a natural inhibitor to changes that might be counter to Soviet interests.

By the time of Stalin's death (1953), the Soviet influence in any East European political system was limited only by the degree to which the Soviets were inclined to press their interests. Control was not absolute, but East European leaders clearly imagined no policy options outside the realm of Soviet objectives. At least three of the five bureaucracies in each East European system—the party, the military, and the police/intelligence—were under the supervision or direct scrutiny of their Soviet patron, counterpart organizations. At this stage, the institutional structure of Yugoslavia and Albania, though not dictated by the Soviet leadership, paralleled the Soviet example and mimicked its harsh code of conduct. The Soviets had provided tutelage to the prewar, clandestine Communist parties in these countries, and Stalin's imprint was evident. The discipline, experience, and external support provided to these resistance movements during the war increased their chances of survival and success, but more significantly created obligations and commitments that played a dominant role in immediate post–World War II Yugoslavia and Albania.

As time passed, East European communist countries, in spite of pressures to conform, established their own identities again. Their inherently individual qualities, their very different agendas, and their measures of success managing their relationship with the USSR provided a clear basis on which to contrast these systems.

Polish Communism

Poland's "communism" was bastardized by the formidable degree to which the Catholic church continued to play a central role in public life and to function as a vehicle for socialization and communication in the society. Legis-latively, a number of political parties persisted, though each was required to commit itself to the central agenda of the Polish United Workers' party (Com-munist party). Each was able to retain its identity and to promote a few partic-ular issues it established in response to its special constituency. An example was the Polish Peasant party, which articulated the priorities of the rural agri-cultural population and very genuinely affected agricultural policy especially in the 1950s. Poles are fond of saying that through all the travails of commu-nism, things were always done in a "uniquely Polish style." In fact, that was clearly the case. The line between "social forces," "political parties," and "interest groups" was purposefully blurred by the Polish leadership in order to retain as much of the Polish political culture as possible.

The Polish population was and is remarkably homogeneous and main-tained a strong sense of nationalism. But Polish politics has seldom reflected tolerance. Small but significant minorities have often faced discrimination and persecution. Nationalism, which stirs Poles to close ranks against out-siders has historically caused ugly episodes that victimized minorities. Jews were but one example.

Imposition of a Soviet political model (whatever its ideological texture might have been) was bound to hold little appeal. The communist leadership that came to power in 1956 on the heels of Khrushchev's "separate roads" policy was outwardly and outspokenly committed to Polish reforms. The Gomułka years began in a relatively popular reform mode, which progres-sively shrunk from reform over the course of its years in power. The pres-sure to change (risk-laden) was not as strong as the desire to stay in power. The bureaucracies acting on their own self-interest crystallized around Władysław Gomułka, progressively isolating him from his original reform agenda. He was finally removed from office in 1970 under the indictment that his regime was intransigent and uncommitted to making the system work. The next leader, Edward Gierek, entered the picture to reenergize re-form but also yielded to the pressures and entrenched elites resisting change. Stanisław Kania replaced Gierek in 1980. His crisis came in 1981 with the challenge from a working-class movement with broad church support: *Soli-darnosc* (Solidarity). Its agenda (simplified of course) included a strong push for uniquely Polish remedies and a stronger commitment for socialism to be what it claimed it was. It demanded more popular input and a government more dedicated to economic development. It did not challenge the socialist rhetoric but instead demanded that it be true to the ideals of socialism, in-cluding democracy.

In the face of this domestic challenge and with the Soviet perspective on it looming fuzzily just over the horizon, the Polish party's insecurity gripped its leadership. General Wojciech Jaruzelski (party leader and relatively popular general) declared martial law and activated the control agencies in ways not previously used in Communist Poland's political experience. He attempted to impose the discipline and monopolistic structures of the classic Soviet system. The *Solidarnosc* challenge could have been handled in ways more typical for communist systems, but the leadership's insecurity, explained earlier in this chapter, spawned overreaction and policy overkill. Ultimately, this solidified and broadened popular support for *Solidarnosc* and, more critically, caused the *Solidarnosc* movement to embrace many more anticommunist elements.

The Polish public found it easy to rally behind *Solidarnosc* because of the broad consensus on what they were against. *Solidarnosc* never had the luxury of a consensus about what the Polish people were searching for. Soon, the government's efforts to discipline or eliminate *Solidarnosc* failed, and negotiations began between *Solidarnosc* and the government. These were called the "round table discussions," which resulted in the abdication of the Communist party through a number of compromises that eliminated its institutional guarantee of an exclusive role. The Catholic church functioned as the memory of the Polish people, stepping in when, in its view, the society needed clear signals, identity, or organization. Changes in the mechanics of the electoral system triggered ever-widening systemic change in Poland. *Solidarnosc* tried to transform itself from a broad social movement built around its rejection of the Polish United Workers' party's stewardship of the country to a political party with a clear and forward-looking political framework and agenda. As a party, it faced the kind of splintering and dissension that one would expect given that its leadership and its membership shared no vision of what ought to be.

Through all of this, the Polish system was wrestling with the most fundamental and critical domestic policy issues, but it did not tinker at all with its commitment to pro-Soviet and Soviet-guided foreign policies. This is the phenomenon identified earlier as "Rule 2." It remained a strident member of the Warsaw Pact and Comecon—the two organizations that coordinated foreign, military, and economic policies among the communist states.

The Polish case also illustrates an interesting and complex leadership behavior pattern. In East Europe, leaders who came to power as "reformers" became progressively more conservative in their behaviors and policies, while leaders who came to power as arch-conservatives (often perceived as Soviet pawns) progressively became more committed to reforms. The Hungarian leadership is a case of the latter pattern.

Hungarian Communism

Hungary had been a Nazi ally in World War II. But the political milieu in prewar Hungary was complex. Hungary in many ways was stereotypical of a fascist society. Its twentieth-century history reveals a recurrent failure of politics. An inability to create a consensual politics built on compromise reveals itself in the regular collapse of parliamentary politics and the radical polarization of politics. The post–World War I episode where Bela Kun, leading the extreme left, was able briefly to establish a communist system was just such a case of sharply polarized politics. In the wake of this "success" of the extreme left, the radical right induced the anxious elements in the center to support an extreme right-wing government bolstered by the church, the military, and the old aristocracy. With this "reactionary" swing to the far right, Hungary was easily induced into the Axis coalition. It could be argued from cultural and historical perspectives that Hungary was an untidy fit in the sweeping Slavic landscape of East Europe. It was a predominantly Catholic country that perceived itself to be homogeneous and, on balance, had a record that reflected intolerance and had little apparent appreciation for the value of moderate politics.

The post–World War II communist regime established by 1947 was harsh and violent. So-called Moscow Communists replaced indigenous leaders of the Hungarian Socialist Workers' party. Its new leader, Matyas Rakosi, coined the term "salami tactics" to describe the strategy by which the party would undermine and defeat its opposition in parliamentary elections. Hungarians were very uncomfortable with the system imposed from Moscow. By 1956 the Hungarians were eager to hear the "separate roads" message from Khrushchev and responded with plans to restructure both the domestic Socialist system and Hungary's foreign relations (i.e., violation of Rule 2). Moscow's tutelage in foreign policy had severed Hungary's relationship with western Europe and the United States. The so-called Hungarian Revolution of 1956 began as much less than that. It was a reform thrust toward moderation and less rigid ideological politics led by Imre Nagy. In brief, the Soviets first tolerated and then reversed their position, crushing the reform effort with violence and thoroughgoing political control. Nagy and the reformers (and, conveniently, others who were irksome to the Soviets) were dispatched with prison sentences and execution. In death, Nagy became a significant symbol (first in hushed tones and later openly) of the struggle of Hungarians to establish their own identity in European affairs.

Following the events of 1956, Hungary was apparently redisciplined by the Soviets, who selected Janos Kadar to lead the Hungarian system. With minimal domestic popularity, Kadar delicately crafted policies that served and pleased his Soviet patrons. But with the passing of time and the apparent security that came with having the confidence of his Soviet sponsors, Kadar created a record of subtly resisting Soviet interests and creating opportunities for economic developments that moved Hungary well away from the strict Soviet model. By retaining the flagship principles of Soviet Communism—political control by the party and centralization of the economy—Hungary was able to adapt political and economic mechanisms to achieve Hungarian objectives. Political dialogue was encouraged within the party (Hungarian Socialist Workers' Party). By 1967, elections had multiple candidates competing for local government offices. By the 1970s, efficiency and a critical combination of autonomy and rationality were nurtured in the state farms, which enhanced production and eventually flushed the small Hungarian market with commodities.

As in Poland, many legislative groups continued to exist, but the violence of the events of 1956 pressed on them even greater timidity. Only with the collapse of the communist system in Hungary were deeply rooted political parties able to reconstitute themselves and represent interests of what had been political forces in the precommunist years. Janos Kadar remained in power until May 1988. His popularity grew as he helped form governments (from his position in the party) that were flexible and that focused on the Hungarian standard of living as a priority. Kadar's credibility grew as Hungarians were able to make comparisons between the performance of their communist leadership and that of other communist countries around them. By the 1980s, countries that had been the envy of Hungarians—Czechoslovakia, Yugoslavia, and Austria—had lost their luster in the crude comparisons that everyday citizens were prone to make. The regime made clear efforts at "consensus building," especially through the media. It offered up the political prescription that "whoever is not against us, is with us."

Kadar's economic policy was labeled "goulash communism." It appeared to make policy pragmatically and commit itself to the notion that Hungarians should judge their system in terms of what it was doing for them. Unlike many of its contemporaries, the Hungarian leadership was ready to live with the relentless pressures that this created. A commitment was made to consumerism, which the Hungarian system sustained by going deeply into debt. Hungary remained a "controlled" society but one that did not impose "control" because the Soviet model called for it. The party and the state subjected themselves to their own internal "audit" of political techniques, and to the extent that the power elite could not rationalize central control, policy flexibility often followed. This was a successful strategy because the Hungarians were not flamboyant about the systemic changes they were making.

The Hungarian pattern of reform or adaptation away from the Soviet model was different from the Polish pattern. "Rule 1" required that reform had to appear unique. The Polish approach in the 1980s (and in spasms earlier) was confrontational; the Hungarian approach was subtle and incremental. As a strategy, Hungarians often trivialized their own accomplishments, especially within earshot of the Soviets and their East European compatriots. The Czechs and Bulgars were more inclined to the Hungarian strategy; the Romanians were similar in this respect to the Poles.

Yugoslav Communism

Yugoslavia and Albania escaped direct control by the Soviets after World War II and subsequently were in a position to select the pieces of the economic and political system that the Soviets were exporting. The Yugoslav (Joseph Broz Tito) and Albanian (Enver Hoxha) leaders had established themselves by way of their leadership of resistance movements against the Nazis. Neither was especially astute about creating a new system. Both initially absorbed the rudiments of the Soviet model, but the comparison stops there. Albania became a recluse nation-state. It isolated itself from virtually all other states in the world, indicted other communist systems for ideological betrayal and corruption, and constructed a neo-Stalinist regime. It played little role in the Cold War except to irritate and disrupt Soviet leadership of the communist world by outrageous ideological indictments. Albania was unpredictable and outspoken. In tangible terms, it had no credibility or leverage in international affairs.

Yugoslavia parted company with the Soviets as well but headed in the opposite direction. It "liberalized" its approach to communism after years of ideological orthodoxy and defected from the communist bloc without joining the West. In foreign policy, it articulated a position that scorned both East and West by pleading the case of all those nations that were caught in or perceived themselves to have been made less significant by the Cold War. Tito, along with Nehru of India and Nasser of Egypt, gave form and meaning to what was called the "nonaligned movement." Unpleasant as it was for the West to hear itself criticized, it was more dismaying to the United States to discover that the simple "zero-sum" perceptions that the Cold War imposed were no longer operative.

Tito (also a code name) held an authoritarian position in socialist Yugoslavia. His status in the party and the military and as head of state im-

posed no bounds on his political power. That power was utilized to (1) eliminate other political parties, (2) coerce factions and ethnic groups to accept
their integration into Yugoslavia, (3) impose a standardized language, (4)
strengthen countrywide military organization, (5) make the system's ideology unique to Yugoslavia by commissioning original treatises, and (6) fabri-
cate a mass organization—the Socialist Alliance—that would function in
system-supporting ways. His most noteworthy achievement came after two
decades in power when he set in motion a reform of mammoth proportions.
It sought to redesign socialism fundamentally by decentralizing authority in
both the government and the workplace. It effectively created thousands of
"workers' councils," "management boards," and "committees," which participated meaningfully in the organization and administration of entities
from schools to economic enterprises to local governments to professional
organizations. It was a real test of the notion that what people want most is
an opportunity to participate in decisions that are close to them—that affect
them directly. It can be argued that the overwhelming bulk of Yugoslavs living in Yugoslavia in the 1970s and 1980s participated or had the opportunity to participate in localized policy decisions. The reforms also designed
an original legislative format with five "functionally designed" chambers
each of which had a role to play in legislation that directly affected the sector of the society that each chamber represented. It was radical, experimental, and largely unsuccessful.

Yugoslavs enjoyed more options than their East European counterparts.
They had more employment options and mobility. They were entitled by
law to a passport—providing them with the ability to travel as tourists or to
seek employment outside Yugoslavia. The role of the police in the system
was more subdued and targeted, in contrast to the intimidating role in classic communist systems. The media were more diverse and prone to wrestle
with issues that were on the minds of the citizenry. Given that Yugoslavia
had a mutually respectful relationship with the West, there was ample evidence of Western commodities, culture, and economic and political thinking.

The Yugoslav system under Tito (ending in 1980) used both "carrot
and stick" to form a "Yugoslav" identity. It tried to dilute centuries of ethnic fears and arrogance by creating broad-scale participation and promoting
tolerant attitudes toward other groups without attacking the cultural identity of any group. The strong political sponsorship of these efforts coupled
with improved levels of well-being early in the 1960s and 1970s seemed to
produce results. Gradually, socialization and intermarriage produced slowly
rising numbers who identified as "Yugoslavs," though always with a cul-

tural heritage of Slovene, Serb, Montenegrin, or whatever. In this sense the identification that was forming was similar to American patterns. Americans generally feel like Americans and behave like Americans, but when asked what their nationality is, they respond with an answer to a different question. That question is, What is your national heritage? Americans then respond, Italian, Polish, Chinese, or whatever.

The Yugoslav system had some intrinsic advantages over its East European counterparts. It was clearly less isolated from the West. It had a coastline that attracted tourism, which yielded as much as $2 billion per year. It established its own arms industry, which generated foreign earnings in excess of $1 billion annually. And it could serve international businesses as an ideologically neutral vehicle by which they could have access to trade and commercial relations with both communist and Third World markets that might be partially closed otherwise.

The Gorbachev Era

In 1985 the weak and failing Konstantin Chernenko died. His political patron, Leonid Brezhnev, had died four years earlier. Yuri Andropov had replaced Brezhnev and had died. Perceiving itself bankrupt of new leadership, the Soviet inner circle (Politburo and Secretariat) turned to Chernenko to replace Andropov. Chernenko was actually older than Brezhnev and frail by any account. When Chernenko died, the inability of the system to find leadership of the sort it was comfortable with was apparent, and it grudgingly selected a younger man: Mikhail Gorbachev. Gorbachev had had a respectable party career. The intensity of his ideological commitment was unclear, but he guided agricultural experiments in the Stavropol region that generated enough success to bring him to the attention of the all-union leadership. Gorbachev was more than the "younger" leader who could wield power for more than a couple of years. He was the first leader of the party to have a university degree. He was the first leader to have been stirred in his formative years by the Khrushchev reform dialogue. He was the first Soviet leader to see the world as a real set of parameters with which the USSR had to deal, rather than a world-to-be-shaped by the Soviets. He clung to the socialist value system but acknowledged that without fundamental stimulation, the Soviet system was experiencing decline. He and many of his closest supporters believed that the system was sick and could get sicker. It needed strong medicine, and it needed it soon. He begins his book *Perestroika* with the notion: "This society is ripe for change. It has long been yearning for it."

The change resistors in the system had not gone away. In fact, they had dug in. Politically, Gorbachev would need a strong executive position in the state to succeed in shepherding change. By 1987, he figuratively stood atop the party and state structure, straddling the two. His apparent plan was to concentrate much more power in the state structure by redesigning both the executive and legislative structures. He favored the development of a presidential system to replace the weak parliamentary system already in place. That he often referred to the American system as an example could suggest that it was at least in part his model. He proposed the creation of a new, power-laden *presidency* to replace the old, symbolic position and to place it above the Council of Ministers, which had previously provided the State's administrative leadership. The powers of the new office were to be quite concentrated, and the president was to appoint a presidential Cabinet of advisers responsible directly to him. The term was to be five years, and for the first time a formal presidential residence was established.

The legislature was also to be redesigned. In the Soviet system, the legislature was weak for many reasons. Three of the reasons that Gorbachev and others recognized were that (1) the assemblies were too large and unwieldy—more than fifteen hundred legislators meeting in two chambers twice a year; (2) no "standing" committees existed that could, over time, enable legislators to develop expertise that could be used to judge or alter policies presented to the legislature by the executive leadership (Council of Ministers); and (3) the legislators never initiated legislation. All three organizational "problems" were addressed. Through a very complicated set of intermediate stages, which we neglect here for simplicity's sake, the chambers were reformed. In the end, a much smaller legislative body (Supreme Soviet) was created, which functioned afternoons and evenings four or five days a week. Its debates were televised nightly, and the interest of the public was unprecedented. More than 200 million people were said to have watched regularly. Gorbachev wanted this body to have 100 members but in the end, compromise produced a 500-plus member chamber. These legislators had standing committees and understood that they could and should initiate and amend legislation. The original legislature continued to exist—a compromise to the interests of the large numbers of elites routinely elected to this relatively meaningless body. It came to be known as the Congress of People's Deputies (see figure 6.4). Parliamentary characteristics were retained in that one needed to be elected to the Congress of People's Deputies before one was eligible to be elected to the new smaller and meaningful Supreme Soviet. The Council of Ministers continued to be a "cabinet" selected from the Supreme Soviet, as in most parliamentary systems.

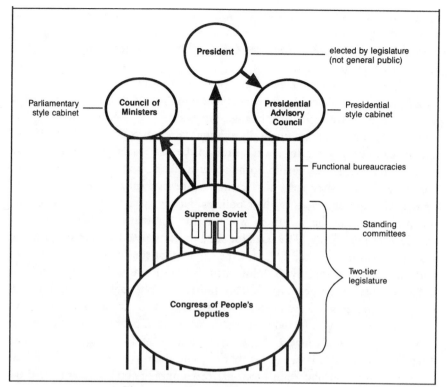

Figure 6.4. Last Soviet Government

The structure of the system was an awkward hybrid with new concentrated executive power and a presidentially appointed Cabinet (presidential council of advisers) functioning alongside a complex two-tiered parliament with its own Cabinet (Council of Ministers). To complicate matters, Gorbachev was reluctant to opt for the popular election of the president, favoring instead that the president be elected by the Supreme Soviet, which would also retain the power to reject presidential nominations for the Council of Ministers. It is clear that Gorbachev was prepared to see the old political structure undermined to the point that the state would become preeminent. This may have been because he had lost faith in the party's capacity to change or because he found dealing with both bureaucracies too laborious. If Gorbachev had been straddling the two key bureaucracies, by 1987 he had decided to shift his weight to the leg supported by the state. Certainly among the factors for the structural reforms was his awareness that the unique Soviet structure was perplexing and negatively perceived by other governments. Gorbachev often referred to the advantage that other governments would better understand and work with the Soviet political system if it were designed in a more "conventional" fashion. These structural changes were enhanced by, and themselves enhanced, the broader themes for policy that Gorbachev promoted.

Glasnost and perestroika were the centerpieces of a new Soviet approach to politics. Each needs to be understood for what it was and what it was not. Both were themes for change. Gorbachev and his supporters understood that they were fundamentally changing the fabric of the Soviet system. The original change strategy was to ration the proposals for change and by so doing enable the leadership both to gauge and to manage the impact that would result. But they were also keenly aware that they could not fully anticipate the consequences of their policies. Given the system's characteristic inexperience with change, there was no way for them to chart their own course with confidence. The risks for the longevity of the leadership, for the superpower status of the USSR, for the capacity of the economy to function, and for the manageability of public attitudes were unspecified and uncalculated. Gorbachev forged ahead. This leadership phenomenon, found in a number of systems in East Europe in this general time frame, should be recognized and respected for what it was: raw political courage. It was not political wisdom. A distinction between "courage" and "wisdom" is offered later. Walesa, Havel, Poszgoy, Gorbachev, and later Yeltsin all embarked on paths that were so uncertain that only raw courage could explain their actions. The Gorbachev years (especially from 1987 to the bitter end in 1991) were years of courage tempered by his best efforts to reduce the risk by constant political maneuvering and appeals for public patience and support.

Glasnost was often translated as "openness," but in its original intended design it was to be of limited scope. Gorbachev had recognized that the centralized control of information and the media had resulted in an absurd isolation of the Soviet public. This isolation spawned narrow-gauge attitudes, skepticism in some and naive optimism and expectations in others. These qualities made the political management of a society with profound problems more difficult because, in essence, it prevented the public from becoming part of the solution. Gorbachev reasoned that he needed the broad public to see the problems he saw so that they could be enlisted in the adjustments and sacrifices that would certainly be a part of any solutions. To accomplish this end, glasnost was supposed to be a program in which the centrally controlled organs of the media would commit themselves to a candid, critical, and more comprehensive reporting of events and issues in Soviet affairs. This included a commitment by party and state to provide some insight and some explanations for why they were doing what they were doing. To be clear, the established media were to behave differently, but *glasnost* did not intend for new media or unmanageable dialogue to be created. *Glasnost* represented Gorbachev's greatest risk and his most significant departure from the classic Soviet system. It set in motion communications and expectations that could not be managed. Journalists of all sorts seized the opportunity to display talents and opinions bottled up by the old system. Interestingly these ranged across the ideological spectrum from extreme left to radical right. Editors who had functioned in the old system as censors and inhibitors revealed their inadequacies as editors. Frictions intensified. Editors were changed in some cases, but in many others journalists left their old jobs and started new media outlets or revitalized others. The *Moscow News* was a noteworthy example. It transformed itself from a multilanguage tourist "throwaway" devoid of any issue-oriented content to an explosively controversial and politically essential source of information for any political actor or political "want-to-be" in Gorbachev's USSR. The attractiveness of the "transformation" strategy was that presses, news print, offices, and staff were already a part of the established supply system. New newspapers, weeklies, magazines, and contacts with Western media did result, but by far the greatest consequence is traceable to the new energy of the journalists in what had been the establishment media. *Izvestia,* the government-supported newspaper, quickly became a more vibrant and sought-after paper than its party counterpart, *Pravda.* The party and state monopoly control of communication vanished. It had been critical to the manipulation of public attitudes and the illusion of confidence borne by leadership circles at all levels of the system. Clearly, *glasnost* was not designed to be the information free-for-all that it became.

    Perestroika was a generic label that signaled the "commitment to structural change." It is translated "restructuring," but the plan in 1987 was to pace and contain the changes. The thrust was to restructure the economy by addressing the degree of centralization. The objectives were to "rationalize" decision making, build in incentives, stimulate efficiency and growth, and make evaluating and monitoring the economy more useful and accurate. Political (*demokratizatsia*), legal (*zavodnost*), and educational reforms were to follow. The theme of change in Gorbachev's conception was also to impact on Soviet foreign policy ("New Thinking") and the restructuring of the international milieu at least to the extent that the superpowers could affect it.

    With considerable fanfare, economic institutions that had become lethargic, even frozen, were targeted for change. Privatization in agriculture became possible. Greater autonomy was created for enterprises (companies), enabling them to adjust lines of production and engage themselves in foreign commercial relations and trade. The efficacy of the central planning mechanism was purposefully undermined. It had been a stabilizing, if also stifling, feature of the Soviet economy since 1928. Investment, distribution, ownership, and price/wage policy schemes were actively debated as thrusts away from the suprabureaucratized Soviet reality.

Politically, Gorbachev stamped the reforms with his own charismatic and open style. He embodied the conviction that leaders and the public needed to be more clearly connected. He made himself more accessible both by way of the media and by public appearances. This Gorbachev style, while significant in the way it contrasted with previous Soviet leaders in the eyes of Soviets, also was acceptable to and understandable by Western politicians and publics. It opened communication, established credibility, and nurtured a "comfort" level in relations between the USSR and the West that had not been a part of previous decades. His behavior as the first president (in its new conception) created norms for and expectations of that office domestically and internationally. He tried to justify his approach by connecting it to a Leninist heritage and to his own idealism, which he believed Soviets shared. He believed that a central core of socialist values and commitments could serve as the foundation of a newly designed system with greater democracy, dialogue, and dynamism. Gorbachev appealed for a legal system of the Western style that abandoned the "ambiguous rules" design for social and political control (see page 229 in the next chapter). An accountable and active legislature, a politically neutral judiciary, and a visible executive with a commitment to innovation shared places in Gorbachev's *perestroika*. On balance, Gorbachev took the ultimate risk with his political reforms. He suggested that the Soviet public should measure and judge its leadership (and the system at large) by its performance.

As it happened, political and economic restructuring took place simultaneously. This appears to have heightened elite insecurity, thereby softening the support for Gorbachev's reforms, especially at the middle and lower administrative levels. As experience took shape with the reforms, larger and larger numbers of Soviets found themselves uncertain and confused regarding the wisdom of the change strategy. The attempted military coup of August 1991 was not a result of this popular uncertainty. The "coup plotters" hoped to engineer their seizure of power with the passive acceptance of the masses. They were counting on the presumption by the public that politics continued to be something done to people by some elite. They miscalculated the degree to which at least a significant number of persons in the urban centers of the Soviet Union had internalized the idea that politics was something that could and should be assessed in terms of what it was doing *for* people as well. Gorbachev was on thin ice because he had not, through his policies, produced evident results (i.e., tangible positive performance), but there can be little doubt in retrospect that he did alter the way the public thought about politics. For better or worse, they were going to gauge politics by a simple self-interest that asks, "Are things better for me now?" If, as it seems, this idea had taken hold, a return to the outlines of a communist system—a system in which it was not legitimate to ask such performance questions of the leadership—was unpopular to the point of motivating them actively to resist the coup.

The August 1991 coup and its aftermath, with Gorbachev, Yeltsin, and other leaders of the Soviet republics aggressively establishing political "turf," dissolved the glue that had held the Soviet Union together. Gorbachev's earlier programs had planned for the USSR to be held together by a more sophisticated rationality and pragmatism. In fact, narrow-minded politicians conditioned by fear of change and uncertainty about public attitudes, some of which reflected intense and festering nationalisms, combined to thwart the Gorbachev strategy. By 25 December 1991, the political viability of the Soviet Union had been undermined irrevocably. Draped in the illusion of a continuing framework ("Commonwealth of Independent States"), the former republics became independent political systems.

7. Postcommunist East Europe: The Politics of Transition

The 1990s: Postcommunist Challenges

To detail the challenges that present themselves to postcommunist political systems would require volumes. The notion that once the limitations and inhibitions of communism were jettisoned, East Europe would be able to duplicate the standard of living, the security, and the political stability common in Western systems has lingered, resulting in ever-spiraling frustration. One way to examine this massive inventory of problems is to organize our analysis around the three requisites presented at the beginning of the previous chapter: *mass value system, political machinery,* and *leadership*. We have reviewed the contorted histories of communist systems in East Europe and discovered that, in general, the old system had two of the three requisites. Over time, each communist system did generate a rather amorphous value system, which accepted that government had a large role to play in guaranteeing basic needs to its public. Socialism also advocated a goal of economic equality, or "economic democracy," which in practical terms meant a leveling of the society in economic terms. These values coupled with the government's control of prices and distribution created a belief that some goods should be guaranteed by government to the masses.

As earlier portions of the previous chapter also underline, the Soviet communist system had an elaborate political machinery. It was designed and refined over time to perform its primary function, which was to maintain the party's power. If the machine's effectiveness were judged *only* in these terms, it functioned very well until Gorbachev began tinkering with the machine itself. Clearly, in comparative terms, the political machinery of the communist system was as extensive, bureaucratized, and penetrating as any. Setting aside for the moment what you might think of a system designed to keep itself in power, there can be little doubt that both a broad value system and a developed political machine existed in twentieth-century communist systems.

It is far less clear that the system generated a minimum level of leadership that could direct and manage the society. The recruitment system, the inadequate educational system (in terms of policy-relevant studies), the propensity to quash issue-oriented debate, the minimal relationship between rulers and ruled, and the very vertical nature of the political system added together to ensure mediocre leadership. The leadership in East Europe was generally detached, noninnovative, and passive. It failed to acknowledge that political systems, like all living systems, must adapt to inevitably changing circumstances and environments. It ultimately revealed itself to be disinclined and incapable of calculating the costs, payoffs, and consequences of major policy decisions. Simply, the pattern of politics produced leadership that was the functional equivalent of the weakest link in the political system. As described earlier, it was inept and narrow-gauge in its thinking. It committed more energy to illusion making than to problem solving.

Gorbachev was the first Soviet leader to wrestle with the breadth and depth of the society's problems. The seventy-year-long leadership norms were altered by Gorbachev. But, for a segment of the public, a disturbing and unusual question arose. Was the system better off with a leadership that knew that problems lay ahead and had the courage or folly to select a course to attempt to deal with those problems? To our ears, the answer is obvious, but to those whose focus was the moment at hand, security, or both, the question was a perplexing one. The political landscape in the Gorbachev era was dominated by uncertainty and unsolidified change. The United States, impartially standing on the sidelines, was "cheerleading" for change—change to "democracy," "freedom," "market economics," and "capitalism." We promoted these "causes" because they were good for us. That they were simplistic and unrealistic for the people of East Europe was not a consideration. Further, our efforts contributed significantly to the creation of unreasonable expectations in the minds of both Americans and East Europeans.

The new systems from Lithuania to Albania, Tadjikistan to Moldava share a number of concrete and complex problems. By early 1994 there were twenty-five political systems where five years before there had been nine. It is reasonable to anticipate that these twenty-five will continue to dismember themselves, creating still smaller and nationalistic countries. The comparative analyst must always remain keenly aware of the rationale for the comparisons he or she makes. The difference between the optimist and the pessimist examining East Europe is, at least in part, a function of the comparison one chooses to make. If one opts to look at communist versus postcommunist systems in East Europe, a positive sense could emerge from the realization that the old system was nonadaptive; had poor leadership; and had educational, economic, and political structures that stifled initiative and results. Certainly, one could argue (and many do) that off-loading this burdensome and unproductive system was a good thing. At least a greater potential exists for the "new" system (if it develops the qualities of a coherent system) to be better able to solve its problems.

A less common view, and one that can be argued is more valuable and productive, is to look at the educational, economic, and political systems that exist today and compare them to the systems that will reasonably be needed to face the future. The debilitating features of the old system will continue to constrain the new systems unless these countries seize the opportunity to design a system that is appropriate and effective in twenty-first-century terms.

The comparative dilemma is between comparing the present with the past or the present with the future. The first yields a positive picture; the second, a profoundly negative one. Political scientists and most students (with their lives ahead of them and their vision fixed on the future) should consider the second comparative strategy. Much of what follows is built from this second kind of comparative focus. In essence, are East European states developing political systems that will enable them to face and meet the challenges of the decades ahead?

New Values

The value system, though imperfectly formed in the old communist system, did have some broadly supported and clearly established ideas associated with it. As a value system, its specific detail was not very closely linked to Marxism. The ideas and expectations that did carry over from the earlier socialist political society were that government would (1) maintain stable prices for basic commodities; (2) ensure everyday security, which meant government should make daily life predictable—employment, housing, medical care, and so on; and (3) plan society by organizing its future. The communist system, objectively speaking (and without the contamination of poor and heretical leadership), could be understood as a system that prioritized itself around economic, rather than political, values. It articulated its goals in terms of the economic leveling of the society, rather than political leveling.

In the American system, a commitment is made to political leveling but not to economic leveling. Communism (in the real world) was about explicit political inequality just as much as American society is explicitly about economic inequality. Objectivity in place, Americans can acknowledge that both societies have a rather legitimate though sharply contrasting claim to the term "democracy." Americans give that term a purely political meaning, thus preventing another society from claiming it on economic grounds. If the term means doing things for people in response to their needs, the rationale for a narrowly political definition is in jeopardy. The East-West conflict was often characterized as a "battle for the minds and hearts"—an ideological struggle. It may well be that the intellectual debate about whether economic democracy is more important to people in a society than is political democracy has not been resolved. A protracted debate does rage about whether one goal is intrinsically superior to the other. It can reasonably be argued that the demise of the communist system was more genuinely a result of its unwillingness to commit itself to "intellectual democracy" than to any affirmative commitment it did make. Given its design, communism prohibited the competition of ideas. It did not create leveling in educational and intellectual circles, where ideas could compete and the intellectual capabilities of the system could flourish. Gorbachev wrote: "Scientific, theoretical and other discussions, which are indispensable for the development of thought and for creative endeavor, were emasculated. The presentation of a 'problem-free' reality backfired. The political economy of socialism is stuck with outdated concepts and is no longer in tune with the dialectics of life."

Equality, competition, and leveling are all related concepts that can provide insight into societies in terms of their *politics* (parties, candidates, etc.), their *economics* (material well-being, jobs, incomes, etc.), or their *ideas*. In the East-West competition, only the West was committed to the competition of ideas, which ultimately enabled it to prevail.

With the collapse of communism, a euphoria took hold that was articulated as confidence that "genuine democracy" would naturally evolve and bring with it prosperity and other economic achievements. It became clear instantly that many in East Europe, encouraged by many others in the West, were prepared to assume the therapeutic effects of capitalism and participatory democracy. Soon, a harsh reality penetrated these new systems and dramatically unsettled those societies. The newly forming value systems were met with apprehension and confusion. The people in these systems discovered that their old values, which were directed at order and economic security, were not a part of a capitalist market economy, nor was order a quality of the new political system they saw forming. In fact, the market system was no "system" at all. It had no rules, no protections, no established behaviors. It advocated the complete decentralization of authority in the economy without regard for whether key items would be produced or be affordable. It should not be surprising that societies that had little opportunity to inform themselves about Western-style systems would have fuzzy ideas about the consequences of the changes taking place. The sum of this uncertainty resulted in a kind of "value shock" that reintroduced a pessimism into the contemporary systems and may well make effectively governing these societies exponentially more difficult. A Gallup poll in spring 1993 revealed that 44 percent of Russians believe that "the free market system is not right for Russia."

More uncertainty, confusion, and inconsistency are evident among the people of East Europe as we look at the first methodologically sound efforts to gauge public opinion. In late 1992 and early 1993, a major joint research project sponsored by the European Union investigated public opinion of critical issues related to "democracy" in eighteen new East European countries. 18,500 East Europeans were surveyed by the Gallup organization. Some of the results are represented in figures 7.1 and 7.2. Carefully examine these data. They raise central questions about how clearly East Europeans understand their own situations. For example, figure 7.1 suggests that the Albanian people are the most optimistic. Albania is experiencing 500+ percent annual inflation, and the already dismal national income declined in 1992 by 25 percent. Poland and Hungary are found near the bottom of the list in spite of their *relatively* healthy economic and stable political systems. Similar confusion reigns as 77 percent of Albanians say their system is "on the right track" but nonetheless 53 percent say they are considering emigrating. In sharp contrast, in Hungary 20 percent respond that the system is "on the right track" but only 4 percent even consider emigrating. Figure 7.2 (page 220) raises as many questions. Of the top five countries on the "contented" scale, all but the Czech Republic (itself a controversial case) are very weak and declining states with little factual basis for their public's responses. It should also be noted that the data at the *high end* of this survey still suggests only *less than half* the public are "contented."

In this "larger picture" look at postcommunist systems, we need to underline that the mass publics in virtually all of these systems, but most particularly those that had more disciplined systems (USSR, Romania, Albania), had no experience with what in the West are perceived as "natural" political realities, practices, and routines. Compromise, negotiation, "winning and losing" (i.e., disappointment in politics), coalition building, and confidence building are fundamental to the ability of a Western-style system to function. People have to know about and appreciate these things, and these ideas must become part of their basic political thinking and expectations. Without

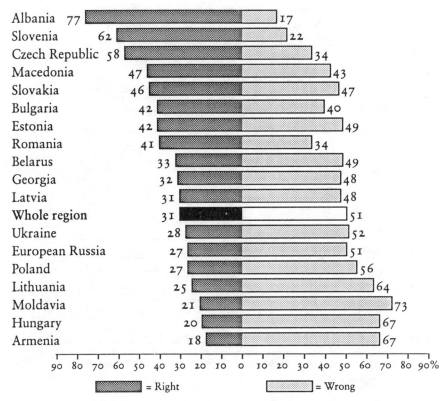

Figure 7.1. Public Assessment of Direction of Change:
"The system is on the right/wrong track."

SOURCE: Gallup Eurobarometer Project, 1993, as published in (Budapest) *Hungarian Observer* 6 (no. 4), April 1993.

values of this sort as the foundation, it is unlikely that East European systems will be able to construct the political machinery they are anticipating.

In this same vein, freedom has become a rather common and casually imposed label for what the political system is supposed to look like. Much of the popular literature (here and there) has argued that this is "what it is all about"—*freedom*. This implies for the uninitiated East European masses that the constraints imposed by the political system and those of an inhibiting legal system are things of the past. Actually, "freedom" in both the U.S. and East Europe is conceptually an illusion. Political systems by definition involve making decisions (policies, laws, etc.) that are binding on people. The overwhelming volumes of "laws" are, for the most part, prohibitions

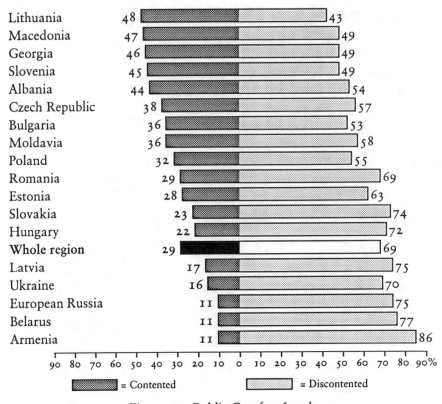

Figure 7.2. Public Comfort Level:
"How contented are you with the new system?"

SOURCE: Gallup Eurobarometer Project, 1993, as published in (Budapest) *Hungarian Observer* 6 (no. 4), April 1993.

on what you can do in society. Systems with more laws may indeed make the rules more clear, but they are making more rules. By emphasizing freedom as the key difference between the old and new systems in East Europe, we endorse an illusion. Freedom for many becomes an intellectual sedative that veils political realities and coaxes the analyst not to look more closely at empirical realities.

When Americans tout freedom, what they tend to mean is that they accept the authority of the political system to control them. They are giving the system legitimacy and naively thinking that because they "trust" or "respect" the government, the regulations and controls that emanate from it are not regulations or controls! Ironically, East European governments enjoy no such levels of legitimacy, which means that East European masses are less likely to view policies and laws in this special, twisted American way. "Freedom" entices East Europeans to believe that government will not restrict and control them. Ironically, their lingering value system, carried over from the past, accepts a large role for government, especially in social and economic policy areas. These should be recognized as fundamentally conflicting ideas. By emphasizing freedom as the central quality of the new Western-style systems in East Europe, we have served everyone poorly. This concept does little to help East Europeans understand better the complexities of the new system that will govern them.

If freedom is a poor guide to what makes a Western system function, what is at the core? What value is basic and essential for the construction of a new value system that can support the kind of polity and economy East Europeans seek? The answer is simple and perplexing all at the same time. Values supporting tolerance are the key ingredients. On reflection, it may be that historians will write that the characteristic that set the American political system apart from others in the late twentieth century was its commitment to tolerance. From a political perspective, it can be argued that tolerance is essential for debate and dialogue about issues, is essential for party and candidate competition, is essential for dealing with defeats in politics, and is essential in casting a constructive relationship between the ruling group and the opposition. From an economic perspective, it can be argued that tolerance is basic to the competitive market system and that, without it, American-style capitalism would be impossible. Corporations may wince at the notion that they think tolerating the competition is a good thing but in broad terms would concede that having and living with competition is a positive thing for the system at large and even for themselves in the long run. Most obviously, tolerance is critical to any intellectual or educational system that hopes to understand challengingly complex subjects. Only in this way can such an intellectual system nurture and harvest the ideas and energies of its citizenry.

The central questions arise: Do values supporting tolerance exist in the minds of East Europeans, and are there institutions nurturing these values? Tragically, the answer to both is *no*. The precommunist histories were devoid of this element. Some could argue persuasively that short-lived examples did exist in Poland and Czechoslovakia. A hostile environment may account for these examples' short lives. Painting the systems in broad strokes, no such public values existed before communism. Communism, itself, shrunk from making a commitment to tolerance. Much of the West's public perception of communism focuses on that system's intolerance.

But are there social institutions that are working to develop the necessary values of tolerance? In other societies that have pursued this goal, the classic "agents of socialization"—elements of society that help shape the public's thinking and attitudes—work toward establishing or reinforcing this goal. East European institutions today do not seem to be so committed. The family structure in East Europe is either very traditional and hierarchical or is disintegrating. It does not seem to be stable enough or inclined to establish tolerance as a core idea and behavior. The schools are still hierarchical, rigid and authoritarian, stifling or at least not exemplifying tolerance. Religious organizations, that can be heard resoundingly to promote tolerance of their religion, are nonetheless not prepared to advocate the tolerance of all religions. Economic managers advocate the dismantling of state monopolies but maneuver constantly to establish private monopolies. In politics, new competitive party systems have been established. But they have revealed themselves to be intolerantly prone to eliminating their most radical opposing groups. The Yeltsin government has declared two such groups illegal. In Poland and the Czech Republic laws restrict the political, economic, and private activities of former communists. The record then reveals that grassroots ideas of tolerance are not forming because they have no fertile soil to grow in. Still worse, the Establishment (political, economic, social, and religious) is sending clear signals that are in substance and style intolerant.

It is fair to say that East European systems are searching for a path to the future—searching for an ideological map that can lead to a better future. But the overriding perspective that guides this effort is tied to the past. The search for new values and ideas has not turned to the future or even to other political systems in the present but has instinctively turned to each nation's past as if it were an untapped resource. Because communism in many ways turned away from the past (at least rhetorically), and communism is gone, many have concluded that turning to the past is the right thing to do. Reinforcing this notion is nationalism. In the effort to find a new noncommunist identity, virtually all the systems have resurrected the handiest old identity without concern for how constructive or destructive a force it might be. Nationalism solidifies people who are a part of the dominant group. It gives them identity and at the same time invites them to feel superior to or to fear those of other national identities (inside or outside their countries). Given East European history, such fears and arrogance are powerful feelings. Every national group in East Europe has had episodes in its history when it was abused at the hands of a rival nationality and others when it did the abusing. These latter epochs are often touted as "moments in the sun" for the nation—when "justice and reason" prevailed and the good guys were on top. Lithuanians once controlled Poland, Poland once controlled Ukraine, Ukraine once controlled Russia, Hungary once controlled Croatia, Croatia once controlled Bosnia, tiny Albania once controlled the Balkans, and so the historical web is woven.

To the extent that any one value dominates the attitudinal landscape of East Europe, it is clearly nationalism. Nationalism asks people to think with their hearts rather than with their heads. It encourages them to "feel" about politics rather than "think" about politics. Tragically, this means that it can and is used by politicians in East Europe to explain away failure, easily find scapegoats, create artificial confidence/arrogance, and shatter tolerance. Armed with nationalism, political "leaders" can shield themselves from the hard-nosed scrutiny of pragmatists who ask about policy effectiveness and real political performance. In contrast, nationalists can guarantee that they can trigger spiraling intensity of feeling, which in East Europe frequently erupts in violence and inhumanity.

The disintegration of Yugoslavia is an inescapable example. Nationalism as a value set is devoid of tolerance and cooperative behavior. It compels people to "face backward." It demands a highly selective historical analysis that not only prescribes where the nation has been but also prescribes where the nation should be going—that is, to recapture the epoch when this particular group prevailed. The spasmodic and twisted histories of virtually all national groups in East Europe give this a perverse significance. The most ethnically diverse political systems from the communist era (USSR, Yugoslavia) have been the first and most violent cases. Yet even the more homogeneous systems (Hungary, Bulgaria, Poland, Slovakia, and the Czech Republic) are worthy of the indictment that they are facing backward. Nationalism functions like a cancer in East Europe. It was a threat to the communist systems but is no less a threat to the postcommunist political systems.

Critically, nationalism and intolerance prevent these political systems from facing forward. Evidently, each country needs to attempt to focus on the problems of today and tomorrow. All need to marshal all their expertise to identify the range of policy alternatives available to them. The political systems then need to be able to select a course with enough confidence to stay with the selected policy to give it a chance to succeed. These leadership challenges are examined a bit further on in this chapter. The news is worse, since other political and economic systems are sprinting into the future while East Europe is backing into the future.

Another subtle value-oriented problem exists for these transitional states. A change from what political scientists often call "system affect" to "output affect" adds an immense pressure to the leadership's capacity to manage these societies. System affect is the notion that people in a society have (for varied reasons) come to believe in the "system" as a system. This can develop, over a long history, through a leader's charisma, from ideological prescriptions or from a commitment to processes. In any event, people believe in the system and when they are unhappy about something that is taking place, they hold particular leaders or themselves accountable (especially in a democracy). They believe that the "system" is sound, albeit its leadership or mechanisms require adjustment. The key advantage for systems that have such system affect is that as they encounter rough spots or decline, they seem able to weather them given the momentum of support implied by system affect. In an output affect environment, however, the public has much less commitment in general terms and withholds its support for the system until or unless its output (i.e., performance) warrants support. This is a much "thinner" and more tenuous base of attitudinal support. This results in sharper and more system-threatening challenges when, inevitably, the system's performance dips. In simplest possible terms, this is the distinction between a system that has public support built on faith versus one that has public support built primarily on performance. In 1992, East European systems posted the following percentages in decline in GDP (gross domestic product = the total value of goods and services produced): Poland, 0 percent (i.e., no added decline); Hungary, 7 percent; Czechoslovakia (before break-up), 8 percent; Romania, 17 percent; and Bulgaria, 20 percent. With "performances" like this, the impact of output affect on the stability of the system should be clear.

Given the absence of a new ideology built on understandable principles, the East European countries are all in transition, for better or for worse, from polities with system affect to ones with output affect. The reality of this transition is that as each political system with its new leadership and untested institutions stumbles and performance is disappointing to the masses, the challenge to the "system" will be compounded by waning public support. Add in the reality that political participation is broadening at the same moment that economic crisis is presenting itself, and output affect will produce dramatic pressure for more systemic change and protracted political instability.

At the very heart of the changes is a trend in which the political masses in East Europe are reorienting their thinking toward increasingly seeing themselves as the shapers of politics, rather than the consequences of politics—those that can do in politics, rather than those that have it done to them. While this parallels our thinking about politics, it is both idealistic and fraught with practical problems for politics in this transitional era.

This section on political values must responsibly conclude with a caution. The people of East Europe will certainly suffer from postreform trauma as they discover that participatory democracy and market-based capitalism in fact provide no guarantees and few short-term results. These new systems provide just one promise: that the pursuit of genuine solutions is possible in a system constructed around tolerance. This will provide little solace for many. Significant numbers of East Europeans will withdraw their support. This political storm can be weathered, but the outcome is not inevitable. Nationalism will be the best barometer. If it rises, the current direction of the transition is in serious jeopardy. If the leadership displays the courage and effectiveness to replace nationalism with tangible goals for these systems, the prognosis is better.

New Machinery

The institutional arrangement in the old communist systems was both unique (see chapter 6) and not true to the constitutional designs on which it claimed authority. The actual political structure of the classic Soviet system was designed to keep the *party* in power, quell change, and prevent the public from approaching the Establishment. The old machinery was constructed to maintain power in the hands of a specific elite. As instruments of power, the institutions of the old system functioned effectively, or effectively enough to resist change for many decades. In retrospect, we know that the beginning of the end was Gorbachev's effort to tinker with the political machinery in the hope of making it capable of producing what he hoped would be measured change. Once tinkered with, it proved unable to perform either its original system maintenance function or its new system adaptation function. Basically, it was "neither fish nor fowl," and frustration with it was apparent from both old *apparatchiki* and reformers. The old machine had been more delicately tuned to its old task than we had realized. Its performance diminished as new elements entered politics, and its anachronistic features became more apparent as old elements behaved as if they still held exclusive power.

Two strategies for postcommunist institutional redesign emerged. The two share a common commitment to eliminating the former party's exclusive role. One strategy favored by many of the systems in East Europe (prominently Poland and Hungary) subscribed to the notion that the old (not operative) constitutional system that prescribed a parliamentary, multiparty political system was a reasonable and understandable base on which to build a new system. These systems retained those major components and their constitutionally designed relationships. In contrast, the countries growing out of the old Soviet Union placed far less faith in even the conceptual design of the old constitutional system and chose instead to "start from scratch." This strategy often argues that a uniquely _____ (fill in the blank; i.e., Ukrainian, Russian, Armenian, etc.) system must be designed that meets the unique and specific needs of that nation. This strategy is fed by thrusts of nationalism that reject the adaptation of models from any other political venue.

In either case, the decision was not made by the public. It was an elite decision. The issues were as fundamental as any could be in a political system: What will be the relationship between the executive and the legislature; how centralized or decentralized will the distribution of power be? While those opting for the "established" constitutional systems would seem a bit better off, the generalization that East European societies are without system architecture is nonetheless largely accurate. Even in postcommunist Poland, which began with an enlightened liberal constitution fabricated in the 1950s, the relationship between the president and the parliamentary legislature is contentious to the point of system paralysis. The "architecture" that is absent here is critical for many reasons. Without it, authority is not clearly placed or balanced in a political system. Without it, leaders do not have clearly delineated responsibilities or clearly defined constraints. Without it, the working relationship among parts of the government cannot be predicted. And without it, the public has little chance to interact with government bureaucracies because there is no map of the paths (processes) or obstacles (bureaucracies) for them to follow.

Throughout East Europe in 1989 and 1990, mass social movements became political movements that in most cases achieved power and then became political parties. At that point, parties had to articulate a policy agenda (establish what they were for rather than what they had been against), and splintering began. Though some large parties do exist in East Europe, sustained primarily by financial and other support from West European political parties, the typical political party in East Europe is what the Poles call a "couch party." The colloquial name is given because such a party could put its entire membership on a single couch. The "solidarity" of the movement phase of political participation has now faded. In most of East Europe, it has given way to dramatically lower voter turnout in recent elections.

The haunting inexperience with coalition formation, cooperation and confidence building, loyal opposition, and compromise compound the problems that stem from a lack of structure. When a structure does exist, the absence of behaviors that support or adhere to the structural design prevents any routines from developing. The output affect phenomenon discussed earlier also works against institutionalization.

One overarching transition in structural terms is the change from a vertical management structure (old system) to a new horizontal structure. This represents a major renovation in thinking and behavior in politics. Horizontal structures provide for (1) more functional differentiation—specific tasks assigned to specific bureaucracies; (2) more communication between elements with comparable responsibilities and power; and (3) more points of access for those outside the government. These institutional advantages may be offset in East Europe by the short-term (and perhaps long-term) reality that government and the costs of government may be perceived to be growing. The promise of the new system is that government will shrink and "get out of the lives of its citizens." The reality of the new system is that it will violate that promise whatever its form.

Two important structural features of any political system are selected here to underline the difficulties of the transitional period in East European politics. The first is the extractive and distributive mechanisms. It is easy to see how extracting resources from people (taxes, ideas, labor, etc.) and distributing goods and services to people are essential mechanisms for the process of governing. Both are critical problems in the new East European systems. In the communist system, the extractive function was performed in largely invisible ways by the supracentralized management of the economy. Though a taxation system existed, it performed a secondary role in the process of financing government. The primary vehicle for financially lubricating government was the manipulation of prices and wages in the old system. By monopolistically controlling these things, as well as the banking function, the system was always able to marshal the necessary funds to operate. The nature of this system did generate a general discontent, but it had the advantage of reaching into people's pockets for revenues without their noticing it. It was a relatively invisible method of extracting resources from the public.

With the postcommunist systems, and, in principle, their rejection of price and wage controls and the pluralization of business and banking, governments can no longer use the old technique. Instead, they have turned with only modest awareness of the fall-out to more conventional taxing schemes. Such taxes are visible and painful in a struggling economy, and often prove counterproductive in terms of other policies, including the nurturing of private businesses. Perhaps most dramatically, the cost of governing is coming into alarming focus for many of these countries. The numbers take shape well beyond what any of them had imagined. Politically timid leaders operating in institutionally unclear systems are unable to make the policy decisions to impose taxes and firmly stand by those decisions. They do not know who to tax, what to tax, or at what level to tax. These issues are especially volatile for the many small systems like Latvia, Lithuania, Estonia, Moldavia, Slovakia, Slovenia, Armenia, and Georgia, but they have an impact on the larger ones with equal levels of political discomfort. It is fair to say that the mass public in East Europe perceives such efforts by the new governments to be obtrusive and unreasonable, resulting in immense pressure on the new governments, each of which purports to be popular, elected, and democratic.

The distributive mechanisms leave new governments in a similarly unworkable dilemma. The old system distributed some goods and services to everyone (everyone not singled out as a dissident) and distributed the rest by way of the vertical organizations known as "mass organizations." To benefit, you had to join, pay very modest dues, and get the benefits associated with whatever that organization was designed to do—learn to fly, meet famous writers and poets, take camping trips, engage in youth activities, et cetera. This appeared to place the onus on the individual and connected the public to the system's distribution network. It was not a perfect system and it did frustrate some, but for the overwhelming bulk of people, it made the system understandable and accessible. With the dismantling of these quasi-official organizations and their special privileges, the government has gotten out of the business of providing many of the goods and services previously distributed. In theory, such opportunities are now available to everyone by way of the private sector. In reality, in many realms the private sector has not responded, and where it has, the costs prevent most from participating or benefiting. Theater tickets, skiing lessons, vacations, and many other services are not affordable. With budget constraints tightening, not loosening, the ability of governments to provide benefits of even the essential variety, let alone the more life enhancing, has virtually vanished.

Is life better today than it was yesterday? If that commonplace question is raised in East Europe, the predictable answer in these transitional times is no—at least in the minds of most people. Public attitudes in the various East European countries vary in proportion, but a significant number give this disturbing answer. A Gallup survey in the spring of 1993 indicated that 59 percent of Russians responded that "life was better under communism." One important reason is that the system has not designed the new architecture for the political and economic lives of its citizens in ways that can be understood and appreciated by them. These problems are less acute in such systems as Hungary and Poland, where greater effort is made to package reforms, but they are acute to the point of system collapse in Georgia, Lithuania, Ukraine, Slovakia, and the like. In social systems where guarantees of basic lifestyle were characteristic, the new systems seem to be taking more and giving less. This is a pressure that the new governments must address proactively or face mounting alienation.

The second major mechanism with which all people have direct experience is the legal system. Earlier, in chapter 6, some discussion focused on the technique by which political systems can control their publics by using ambiguous rather than specific rules. Communist systems used the technique prolifically. The key advantage was that people inhibited their own behavior, making it unnecessary for the government actively to control them. Certainly the most obvious benefits of this system for managing (controlling or manipulating if you prefer) people were not apparent to the public but certainly must have been clear to those governing. It was efficient and effective. Most of the new systems and all of those with which we are more familiar in East Europe have committed themselves to change to a system in which laws are specific, understandable, and applied in a nonarbitrary way. In essence, they are developing a system based on Western principles and experience. Surprisingly, this will mean for most East Europeans that they will have more, not fewer, encounters with the police and the government as the people probe the limits of this new and specific set of rules. More, not fewer, police will be needed to deal with the pressure from the public to find the new limits, especially in terms of economic behavior. More court cases, attorneys, regulations, and visibility for legal considerations will certainly be the result of the new legal systems. If one can assume that most encounters with the legal system are perceived negatively, then we should also anticipate some negative feedback from these new legal systems in East Europe.

These two sets of mechanisms (extractive/distributive and legal) demonstrate the need for both sophisticated design of the new systems and the management of public expectations. The new systems and their particular design features can be crushed under the weight of public resentment and reaction. An even stronger case can be made that without a grand design, a grand strategy, that is put before the public in some effective way (perhaps a referendum), there is little reason to expect that people will show restraint whenever electoral opportunities present themselves. They will articulate their frustration with their ballots. The absence of referendums and presidential-style fixed terms may highlight the need for structures that can accomplish certain essential stabilizing goals. The fluidity of parliamentary terms and elections is not an asset in East Europe's situation today.

The political system must also be held accountable for the failure to provide some economic architecture to these systems. More than half the new countries are still without commercial codes and comprehensive economic policies. Legislatures are largely to blame, but the executive leadership seems unable to provide even the outlines of a strategy for the structure of the economic systems. Privatization, with the fanfare removed, is either woefully behind schedule or in many settings a failure. In most systems of East Europe the percentage of economic firms (agricultural and industrial) that have become privatized is in the single digits. The programs are in general so ill conceived that when a firm is privatized, it normally finds that the process has left it without any working capital and assuredly without the investment capital necessary to breathe life back into what are often comatose firms. East Europe is trying to establish capitalism without capital!

The lack of systemic architecture is also reflected in the absence of features in the political system that could work toward developing the public's awareness of and confidence in political institutions. New curricular materials for schools, media campaigns, public forums, and public interest or "watch-dog" organizations are just a few illustrations of mechanisms that could have been designed into the system but were not. The design of any political system must include both the structure of authority and mechanisms that will enable the system to establish public confidence in it—that is, to build legitimacy. There are many perspectives in political science on how this is most effectively done. In the special context of the transitional East European systems, one obvious answer is to ensure that an infrastructure is created for education that can actively support policymaking at all levels of the society. The communist system by design neglected the social sciences, journalism, and "developmental" technology. It restricted the comparative study of politics, economics, sociology, and management. In this way, it left its successor systems with a shortfall in expertise that makes "solving" problems (especially when nationalist impulses insist on indigenous "solutions") next to impossible. If there was evidence that the educational systems in East Europe were renovating themselves to position education on the cutting edge of the transition, one could be more sanguine. No such evidence exists in the policy sciences, and only formal, structural changes have emerged in three or four countries involving the "management sciences" curriculum.

In the course of thinking or rethinking the shape of new political and economic systems for East Europe, a number of critical considerations have been overlooked. As suggested, the trend is to look to the past for a remedy for the future. Bolstered by nationalism, a distasteful experience with communism, and a soft foundation of expertise on which to base decisions, the design function has been seriously corrupted, to the point that East Europeans can be indicted for "reinventing the wheel." They are neglecting important signals emanating from Western Europe. The political/economic systems in West Europe—most of which are the envy of their East European counterparts—have dedicated their leadership and intellectual resources to the task of assessing the challenges of the twenty-first century. What they "see" is an economic world with hyperchallenging markets, global interdependence, and a breakneck pace of technological change. In order to meet these challenges and play a meaningful role, the relatively strong West European countries have set about the arduous task of redesigning their political and economic structures (and their collective identity) to enable them to cope with the future.

With the possible exceptions of Russia and Ukraine, the systems of East Europe are small and getting smaller. Even Russia and Ukraine are threatened by disintegration. The "independence" spurred by nationalisms has created and seems bound to continue to create ever-smaller political and economic states. This is a central structural issue. If the units that are evolving are indeed too small and weak to be viable, some effort must be made to create structures that improve the chances of systemic survival or, ideally, systems that can be healthy over time.

One such effort by a number of states in East Europe is the discussion about forming the Central European Initiative (CEI). It appears to be an early framework to discuss regional integration between Poland, the Czech Republic, Slovakia, Hungary, Austria, Slovenia, Croatia, and Ukraine. Prospects are not encouraging, but the effort does suggest that some leaders have become aware of the impending disadvantages of singular, independent, and relatively weak states competing or even surviving in the global economy and international political arena.

If political machinery is a requisite for a system to survive (and prosper), the unsettling reality seems to be that the old communist system had machinery; the new systems do not. The pressure to form the machinery is acute, yet little has developed. The short-run remedy is obvious: Borrow structures—political, economic, legal, educational—from functioning systems that are in some meaningful way comparable and use their routines and credibility to develop a relatively stable pattern of politics. With this strategy, legislatures and national leaderships could then go about the task of tinkering, fine tuning, or making adjustments to idiosyncratic sensitivities or priorities. The alternative, driven by arrogance or naïveté (the notion that each nation is altogether politically unique), is for inexperienced legislatures and executive branch officials to build incrementally a unique and untested social system. If that sounds a bit reminiscent of the communist experiment, it should.

New Leadership

The communist system failed to produce leaders who could assess and guide the system through its problems and toward its goals. Leadership has been characterized as the weakest link in the communist political system. It is broadly assumed that with the transitional political climate established, new, talented, and sophisticated persons will come forward to lead from a platform of popular legitimacy. On closer scrutiny, it is an unfounded assumption and an unreal expectation.

Those who did step forward in the years and months before the collapse of communism, often to lead movements that claimed broad consensus, were of two types. In the USSR and Yugoslavia, they were politicians convinced that change was essential. They enjoyed modest popular support and prevailed in their political hierarchies because the leadership was split. These had all been professional politicians in the communist system. Examples are Gorbachev, Yeltsin, Kravchuk, Shevardnadze, Milosovic, and Tudjman, along with many others. The second variety were those in the old socialist bloc countries. They were not insiders pressing for change but voices for the "politics of principle." They were reluctant heroes of the various broad social movements that articulated the movements' views in progressively sharper political terms. They included an electrician, a playwright, and a librarian. Both kinds of leaders shared a common critique of the classic communist system, though the East Europeans were more unequivocal in their criticism. These movements were against the mismanagement of the economy, arbitrary politics, and the subjugation of their cultures.

Lech Walesa (Poland), Vaclav Havel (former Czechoslovakia/now Czech Republic), and Joszef Antall (Hungary) carried no political "baggage." They were patently without responsibility for what the system had done in the past. In fact, they were among the masses who had been the targets of politics. They were not distinguishable by their knowledge of politics or of the noncommunist world. They were credible by default and untainted by the narrow party politics of the past. They were also not experienced in politics nor versed in the study of policymaking nor conceptually sophisticated about how political systems are structured or behave. They understood the basics about the aberrant case of communist politics with which they had been living. They were courageous in a very special sense of that term.

When a man stands on the edge of a pit and has no idea of how deep it is, what the bottom is made of, or what will happen to him if he jumps in—and he still jumps in, he has courage. If he knows how deep it is, what the bottom is made of, what bones he will break when he jumps, how long it will take to heal, and so on—and he jumps in, he has wisdom. In East European politics, this distinction is meaningful. In the first case, no calculation is possible, and yet leaders have "taken the leap." They displayed raw political courage. Alternatively, political systems might hope for a leadership that could make calculations about the consequences of their actions and act accordingly—that is, act wisely. The point here is not that timidity is best or that leadership can always act wisely based on information and experience, but rather that raw political courage must be recognized for what it is and acknowledged to have serious shortcomings. Most everyone (save for the old communist establishments) applauded the political courage of leaders like Walesa, Havel, Yeltsin, and Gorbachev, but it is important not to attribute political wisdom to their actions. They did not know what would happen to them or the masses they were leading when they did what they did.

The absence of political wisdom as described here is not the fault of the leaders themselves. It is a direct reflection of the shortcomings of the educational and political systems that prevailed in East Europe for generations. Gorbachev, from the pressurized position of leadership he held, observed: "Philosophy and sociology, too, are lagging behind the requirements of practice." The expertise, experience, and perspective are absent to the point that there is no foundation on which leaders can assess policies, predict consequences, or remain confident.

The challenges of effective governing given East Europe's situation are so formidable that leadership and masses alike need a genuine sophistication and patience. Both commodities are in short supply. The political results are (1) unstable and profoundly frustrated leaders; (2) policy that, at best, appears in fits and starts; (3) naïve and manipulable masses; and (4) a mutual and poignant frustration between rulers and the ruled.

The leadership perceives itself in an inescapable bind: whether to address problems with incremental or radical styles of policymaking. The dilemma faces every leadership of every political system that ever was, but it is a choice with more immediacy and meaning in transitional societies. If radical policymaking is the choice, the inability of the system and its leaders to calculate the consequences could bring very threatening results. This decision in such places is also accompanied by a sharp centralization of power, which is, and most certainly is perceived to be, counter to the direction of postcommunist reforms. Every postcommunist leader, even Gorbachev, has argued for this "temporary" centralization strategy.

Alternatively, incremental policymaking minimizes the negative consequences at the risk of accomplishing nothing and conceding to the bureaucratic lethargy of the old system. Collectively, East European legislatures prefer incrementalism and, for this reason, find themselves in direct conflict with the executive leadership.

The focus of any concern about the quality of leadership in a system is the executive. Given the emphasis in these new political systems on broadening the representative institutions, however, close scrutiny of their legislators and their legislative leadership is also warranted. Political systems experiencing revolutionary political change are resource poor when it comes to legislative leadership. The communist legislatures were inactive and inconsequential. Persons with that sort of "legislative" experience are useless today; some East European systems have summarily discredited them. Without those with even minimal legislative or policy experience, however, legislatures tend to be filled with genuine "common man" types, local bosses, intellectuals, and those close to the creation of political parties. While an interesting mix, there is little professionalism, few rules to guide the uninitiated legislator, and no breadth of view. Legislators grope for their role, for a legislative agenda, and for a base of popular support. As a general rule, they act based on narrow, parochial interests. Legislative experts would ask, What's new or different about that? Perhaps nothing, but in a political system that is barely forming itself and that insists on designing a uniquely nationalist system from scratch, these qualities doom the legislative effort to failure.

When history judges this transitional period, it will observe that the leadership that followed the communist period was weak, directionless, and without the fundamental skills to be effective. A political system can survive (perhaps marginally) if the society has a broad value system and political machinery with institutions and routines that the masses and the elites understand. Without these, and without strong leadership, a negative prognosis for these systems is inescapable. They cannot be healthy today, and they will certainly struggle to stay alive tomorrow.

The transitional East European political systems do not demonstrate that they meet the "necessary" criteria identified early in this chapter. One might well conclude that from a totally value-neutral perspective (not a meaningful notion in the real world), these systems are more in jeopardy today than they were in the past. This conclusion should be understood as a proposition about these systems' viability tomorrow.

Economic Viability

The viability of any state at any point in time is a function of many factors. Analysts regularly argue about how these should weave their way into a formula. East Europe in a tragic way neutralizes this debate, since all the variables point in the same direction. The optimist would have us view East Europe as starting from zero—a clean slate, no bad habits, carryover problems, or inescapable realities. The Eurobarometer study cited earlier in this chapter found that in 1993, 59 percent of Russians responded that their economic well-being had deteriorated from 1992; 53 percent of Hungarians answered similarly. Across East Europe, less than one-fifth of the people believed that they were "better off." Reality in place, countries in East Europe are limited by their geographic, physical, and human resource bases, which are thin at best. Most are geographically small and suffer from an absence of mineral resources, especially the exotic ones sought after by modern industry. Agriculture is limited from the lack of vast fertile territory. More critically, East Europe suffers from problems with its human resources. While in some traditional occupations East Europeans have a reputation for worker skills, a broad examination reveals one key carryover reality that diminishes productivity in very real ways. This is the old socialist work ethic that has negatively shaped the East Europeans' impression of work and its place in their lives. Generations of motivationless work in totally secure, heavily redundant work environments in which labor relations were meaningless results in a pattern that can be restructured only with significant time and painful personal adjustments.

In terms of its structural and physical development, industry in East Europe is, in the main, outmoded and inefficiently positioned. The old system located factories in places that were "politically" rational rather than economically rational. Without competition, the central planners of the various communist systems saw little need to reinvest in, retool, or modernize factories. No effort or monies were devoted to the salability (i.e., packaging, quality, or marketing) of goods.

The economic infrastructure was neglected in many ways, resulting in fundamental problems in transportation, communications, energy, pollution control, financial accounting, and banking. No modern system was established to monitor, diversify, or manage the activities of the socialist firms in East Europe. To respond to these shortcomings in postcommunist systems requires time, expertise, and finances that are simply not there. The new systems claim to be committed to establishing capitalist market systems with no indigenous capital! It will surprise many experts if that magic can be worked.

More subtle, experience with the communist system (ranging from two to four generations depending on country) has left people in these places without one other key ingredient for their participation in the new capitalist systems. The public's aversion to risk has thwarted a number of reform programs. Virtually all the current governments have underestimated the degree to which people have become risk averse. This is not so surprising if you remember that one of the carryover value sets is security—the desire to be able to anticipate and rely on tomorrow. This reflects itself in a dampening of the entrepreneurial spirit and has meant that the overwhelming majority of new businesses are small, labor minimal, unproductive, and mobile, requiring little or no investment. Such efforts in the service sector or in retail do little to bolster the system's overall economic strength.

Production co-dependency is another problem. The centrally planned systems often made political decisions to separate factories producing component parts required to produce a finished product. In so doing, they distributed jobs and growth throughout their countries, often resulting in increased public support. This pattern was not only evident in large and small multiethnic countries like the Soviet Union, Yugoslavia, Czechoslovakia, and Romania, which are today experiencing disintegration, but was also a part of the development strategy brought to East Central Europe by the Soviet-controlled Council of Mutual Economic Assistance (East European Common Market). The argument was made and policy reflected the notion that duplication was unnecessary among East European communist countries and that by tying them with mutual dependencies, they would become more efficient. So not only were parts of a country dependent on components from other parts of that country, but very often they were also dependent on components from neighboring countries. With the splintering of many countries and the nationalist regimes controlling decisions in many others, this co-dependency has resulted in the collapse of essential supplies of components for the production process. Some estimates place the number of industries affected above 80 percent. Czechoslovakia split into two countries on 1 January 1993. By 15 March 1993 trade between the two new countries had declined to half of what it had been between the same two regions when they were part of a single country. The problems are especially acute across all of East Europe in heavy and consumer manufacturing, transportation, and energy supply.

Money is always a problem in political systems, but in East Europe the impact is more dramatic. These countries have "soft currencies," which means that their money is not recognized to be worth anything in the international marketplace. Basically, Polish, Bulgarian, or Ukrainian money is not exchangeable for other currencies unless that exchange takes place in the country in question and then only under severe restrictions. A soft currency cannot be used by a company or a person from a country to purchase anything outside that country. All East European countries would prefer to have "hard" or convertible currencies, but the established Western capitalist countries have denied them that privilege—first for political reasons (because they were communists) and subsequently for a host of complex reasons. Without involving our analysis with the intricate details, the result is an inability of these countries to conduct business with the rest of the world on an essentially "normal" basis.

The history of this region reveals a constant struggle over borders, neighbors, and assets that must inevitably raise the issue of long-term viability. Can a political and economic system be created that has the essential size and capacities to exist and thrive on its own? The task of answering the question requires the analyst, here or there, to face forward—to face the future and examine this critical question in those terms. The case has been made earlier in this chapter that the natural and politically expedient tendency in East Europe is to look backward. This nurtures thinking with one's heart rather than one's head. Emotions and feelings drive the new systems' politics. In one of the most impressive ironies of this century, the year 1992 saw two diametrically opposed trends developing adjacent to one another in Europe. This theme has surfaced at two other points in this chapter. On the one hand, West European states, drawing on open and dynamic political and educational dialogue, have each made a long, hard, and forward-looking appraisal of their individual futures—their prospects for coping and sustaining their systemic health in the twenty-first century. They have concluded that, in spite of their formidable accomplishments now, they would be at a significant disadvantage "going it alone" in the extremely fast-paced and ruthlessly competitive economy of the next century. They have chosen to turn away from their nationalist and tumultuous histories, face forward, and create a political and economic unit that can deal effectively with the challenges of the future. They have formed the EU (European Union) and in so doing formed a "megastate." This megastate creates a large market for itself, introduces new efficiencies in both politics and economics, and rationalizes and standardizes regulations and policies that make governing easier and cheaper.

On the other hand, East Europe, perhaps because political and university-level dialogue was absent for generations, has not found itself able to focus on the challenges that lie ahead. Facing backward, it compartmentalizes its problems, looks for uniquely nationalist solutions, and frequently balks at radical policymaking. Nationalism and failed leadership have driven parts of countries to believe that their problems would go away if they could organize themselves into a homogeneous nation. As this happens, countries become smaller and smaller. More than a dozen East European states have populations smaller than metropolitan Chicago. Rather than construct a political strategy to cooperate and sacrifice, East European people are moving toward elaborate splitting and splintering. The result is a proliferation of state systems that are, with the possible exception of Russia and Ukraine, so small they are economically not viable or militarily defensible. These states are now "microstates." It is likely that they have reduced themselves to units that cannot survive in the accelerating competitive environment that will characterize the next century. To all the economic costs and consequences of separateness must be added the overpowering burden of costs associated with governing domestically and in international affairs. It certainly seems to be the case that none of the new microstates can even afford to send diplomatic representation to the countries of the world that have diplomatically recognized them. The mix of political attitudes that combines strident nationalism with the noxious memory of Soviet-imposed integration precludes consideration of policies to create macrostate efficiencies.

The burden of these changes and unanticipated costs has resulted in what East Europeans have taken to calling the "pauperization of the majority" in each country. The historical impulses cited in East Europe are easy to understand. The consequences of these feelings as they guide politics will also be easy to predict. The revolutionary transformation of East Europe triggers an analogy that is very unsettling. It suggests that it is reasonable to see a parallel between the behavior of East European countries and the behavior of an adolescent child living in an abusive home. The Soviet period was certainly perceived by other East Europeans in these terms. The "natural" response on the part of the teenager or the East European system was to flee the abuse and seek "freedom." In essence, they have done that without hesitating to assess where they were going to go. As in the case of the young runaway, the harsh reality of the streets (the global economy) in concrete ways prevents these countries from finding prosperity or "freedom." The pace and complexity of the global marketplace prevent new East European states from becoming self-sufficient or even from earning "hard" currency for survival. The adolescent runaway on the streets predictably finds poverty, exploitation, and untenable choices. East Europe's new states will find similar constraints imposed by the global economy. The "freedom" either finds is a harrowing reality—a mere shadow of the expectations each had for their future.

Those who see such imminent problems lying just ahead and who understand that, like the teenager, most systems have little that they can market in an effort to support themselves reveal another illusion soon to be shattered. They seem to believe as a matter of faith that the ultimate developmental "magic" is to be found in technology transfer and high-tech production. The lack of realism is startling. Not only does this sort of production require high infusions of investment capital but as soon as (or if) a competitive product of this sort finds its way to the world market, that production will be targeted by the world's major high-tech producers and multinationals for competitive assault. Without refined marketing expertise, R & D experience, and investment support to keep pace, any initial East European success will be swept away.

This survey of economic problems leads directly to a tentative conclusion that, given the size and circumstances of East European states, none is viable as a "stand-alone" entity in the twenty-first century. The conclusion seems more certain when one factors in the inventory of explicitly political problems these societies also face. In fact, the greatest shortcoming may be that the political system is not poised to address these imposing and intimidating economic problems. If this were a patient, a prudent medical doctor would recommend a hospice.

Synthesis: Past, Present, and Future

This moment in East European political development is an especially troublesome one. It is made more unsettling because so many Americans and East Europeans want desperately to believe in the futures of these new systems. The claim is made here that these political systems are facing backward and are backing into the future. This is a poor strategy and severely limits their ability to compete and survive in the next century. The past is a bedeviling guide to a bright future. The present is barely manageable because these systems are saddled with carryover problems from the past and have little way of marshaling human resources and experience to design political and economic structures. Without a master societal architecture in which people can believe and to which leaders can turn for guidance, coping and muddling become the objectives.

Students of comparative politics will watch carefully to see if values, political machinery, and leadership emerge from this political drift. In the interest of the survival of new East European political systems, the questions raised here must be answered in the next few years.

SUGGESTIONS FOR ADDITIONAL READING

BATT, JUDY. *East Central Europe from Reform to Transformation*. New York: Council on Foreign Relations Press, 1991.

BREMMER, IAN, and RAY TARAS, eds. *Nations and Politics in the Soviet Successor States*. New York: Cambridge University Press, 1993.

BUKOWSKI, CHARLES, and MARK CICHOCK, eds. *Prospects for Change in Socialist Systems: Challenges and Responses*. New York: Praeger, 1987.

DILLER, DANIEL. *Russia and the Independent States*. Washington, D.C.: CQ Press, 1993.

DRAKULIC, SLAVENKA. *How We Survived Communism and Even Laughed*. New York: HarperCollins, 1993.

GORBACHEV, MIKHAIL. *Perestroika*. New York: Harper & Row, 1987.

ISLAM, SHAFIGUL, and MICHAEL MANDELBAUM, eds. *Making Markets: Economic Transformation in Eastern Europe and the Post-Soviet States*. New York: Council on Foreign Relations Press, 1993.

LAPIDUS, GAIL, VICTOR ZASLAVSKY, and PHILIP GOLDMAN, eds. *From Union to Commonwealth: Nationalism and Separatism in the Soviet Republics*. New York: Cambridge University Press, 1992.

McFAUL, MICHAEL. *Post-Communist Politics: Democratic Prospects in Russia and Eastern Europe*. Washington, D.C.: CSIS Books, 1993.

MOTYL, ALEXANDER. *Dilemmas of Independence: Ukraine after Totalitarianism*. New York: Council on Foreign Relations Press, 1993.

PEREIRA, LUIZ C., JOSÉ M. MARAVALL, and ADAM PRZEWORSKI. *Economic Reforms in New Democracies*. New York: Cambridge University Press, 1993.

SAIVETZ, CAROL, and ANTHONY JONES, eds. *In Search of Pluralism: Soviet and Post-Soviet Politics*. Boulder, Colo.: Westview Press, 1994.

SMITH, HEDRICK. *The New Russians*. New York: Avon Books, 1991.

STOKES, GALE. *The Walls Came Tumbling Down*. New York: Oxford University Press, 1993.

WHITE, STEPHEN, JOHN GARDNER, GEORGE SCHÖPFLIN, and TONY SAICH. *Communist and Post-Communist Political Systems*. 3d ed. New York: St. Martin's Press, 1990.

WHITE, STEPHEN, ALEX PRAVDA, and ZVI GITELMAN, eds. *Developments in Soviet and Post-Soviet Politics*. Durham, N.C.: Duke University Press, 1992.

WHITE, STEPHEN, JUDY BATT, and PAUL G. LEWIS, eds. *Developments in East European Politics*. Durham, N.C.: Duke University Press, 1993.

8. Political Systems of the Third World

The first four chapters of this book surveyed several political systems in what some have called the First World. These North American and Western European polities were among the first to undergo the political and economic changes associated with the Renaissance, the Enlightenment, and the Industrial Revolution. From feudalism through monarchy and mercantilism emerged a number of national societies whose political systems came to be called "democratic" and whose economic systems came to be known as "capitalist." Widespread political beliefs in each of them came to emphasize some version of "popular sovereignty" or "rule by the people," and of national independence or "self-determination." Their governments included elected civilian chief executives and/or legislatures, and their customs and laws provided some measure of civil rights and liberties. Their economies were based on private (individual or corporate) ownership of land, businesses, and factories and on beliefs about markets and competition as mechanisms for setting wages and prices and as arbiters of economic success or failure. The changes that brought these politicoeconomic systems into being were accompanied by a great deal of civil strife, violence, and international warfare.

We have seen in chapter 5 how Japan, a latecomer to the industrial world, succeeded in dramatically transforming itself after World War II into both an industrial power and a political democracy. Today, as a consequence, Japan has joined this First World and become the first non-Western nation successfully to make the transition to a fully developed market economy and a consolidated democracy.

We have also seen, in chapters 6 and 7, how a very different transition has taken place in what used to be called the Second World of communist nations—which came into being with the Bolshevik phase of the Russian Revolution of 1917 and collapsed in 1989–90. There, a very different kind of transition is currently going on, for which we cannot determine the outcomes. But for a very long time after World War II, a number of "old" and "new" nations were added to the list of communist political systems, before they too began to experiment anew with market economies and more open forms of governance.

In the latter instances, for a very long time, factories, businesses, and land did not function under private ownership but were instead considered the property of the state. All economic activity was coordinated during these years by central planning organs of government. Government thus became the primary instrument for speeding economic development, especially by industrializing the economy. In each of these countries, one party, the Communist, claiming to represent workers and peasants, monopolized political and economic power. Other parties were either eliminated or, in some instances, were tolerated only if they were very small and did not challenge the ruling party's ideology and control of the politicoeconomic system. Thus did this Second World embark on its own path to economic and political transformation, seeking to "catch up" economically with the First World —only to discover by the end of the century that its attempt to transform the economy and society by alternative means had failed.

During the same period, and continuing into the present, an even larger number of countries came to be referred to as the Third World.* Many of these countries think of themselves as "new nations." Mainly erstwhile colonies of First World nations and located in the Middle East, Africa, and Asia, this third category also includes older countries, primarily in Latin America. Although they vary considerably among themselves in size, resources, culture, and historical background, these countries have been called Third World because they embody a "third wave" in modernization initiatives, especially in their aspirations and efforts to develop economically. Consequently they represent yet another set of concerns in world politics. During the Cold War between the Western and Soviet-bloc countries, Third World countries continued to interject concerns and interests of a very different nature from those found in the United States and the Soviet Union. Today, while the transitions going on in the successor states of the former

---

* Irving Louis Horowitz, *Three Worlds of Political Development* (New York: Oxford University Press, 1966). Other frequently used designations are "developing nations," "emerging nations," and "LDCs" (less developed countries). According to Horowitz, the phrase "third world" was first used by Frantz Fanon, an Algerian, in *The Wretched of the Earth* (New York: Grove Press, 1965).

Soviet Union and in East Europe continue to reflect a distinct body of concerns, North-South tensions have persisted unabated.

While the term Third World really is no longer appropriate, given the collapse of the Second World, these "developing countries" continue to seek their own routes to attain the levels of living and economic productivity identified with the industrial world. While the developing countries possess raw materials and natural resources, some of which are needed by the industries of the more developed world, the industrial countries continue to be the only sources of capital and technologies so desperately needed for their development. In addition, the industrial countries remain interested in existing and potential markets for both capital investment and manufactured goods in the developing countries. Moreover, because the developing countries often found in the competition between the First and Second Worlds a way to minimize their external dependency, today these tensions are manifest in their quandary as to the best way to emulate the development of the industrial countries without falling into new forms of dependency on them.

The labels of this three-part classification are far from satisfactory. Portugal, for example, nominally a First World nation because of the nature of its economy, imperialist history, and more recent democratic government, is poorer than the rest of Western Europe and much in need of further economic development. The People's Republic of China, the Democratic People's Republic of Korea, and the Socialist Republic of Vietnam are likewise very poor, but because of their ruling parties, official ideologies, and international alliances, they were long considered part of the Second World. Today, while they are experimenting with various market reforms, they continue to stand alone as countries ruled by Communist parties. Further complicating these images of the international community is the fact that the metropolitan regions of a number of the Latin American, Middle Eastern, and Asia countries are comparable in many ways with First World urban areas. Japan, in particular, calls attention to the limitations of all these attempts at classification. As noted earlier, it is today an integral part of the First World in that its political history has been noncommunist; it possesses a consolidated democracy; and its high level of economic development has become the envy of the older industrial countries. Yet in its long history as an independent country and in its culture, it differs considerably from Western nations.

Moreover, while within each of these three different groups of countries there is recognition of important shared interests in international relations, none of them—and least of all the developing countries in Asia, Africa, the Middle East, and Latin America—acts as a unit in relation to the other two.

True, the NATO Alliance links together many of the Western nations. Also, during the heyday of the Soviet Union, the Warsaw Pact included most of the East European communist nations. And, over one hundred developing country government leaders meet periodically in conferences of "nonaligned" nations. But NATO does not include Austria, Finland, Ireland, Sweden, and Switzerland in Western Europe, while it does include Turkey in the Middle East. Furthermore, France has long placed significant limitations on its participation in this Western alliance. In addition, the NATO system is in the midst of redefinition in view of the collapse of the Soviet Union and the abolition of the Warsaw Pact. Yet, even before the enormous changes in these various alliances that followed the dissolution of the Soviet Union, the communist world was split by differences between the USSR and Yugoslavia, on the one hand, and the USSR and the People's Republic of China, on the other. Under Tito, Yugoslavia was one of the leaders of the nonaligned nations, only to find that once the Cold War came to an end and without an heir to Tito (who died in 1980), it too became subject to dissolution. Likewise, the developing countries defy any easy categorization. During the Cold War, some, such as South Korea and Panama, Cuba and Afghanistan, clearly "aligned" themselves with the United States or the USSR. Others, although "nonaligned" (notably India), have considered themselves socialist; still others reject labels associated with the Cold War era and have proclaimed their own third way, arguing that such choices are necessary to avoid the excesses and defects identified with the earlier competition between the communist and noncommunist countries.

Why should we be concerned with these ill-defined categories in general and the various designations used for the developing countries? They come to the attention of most of us, at least momentarily, when the news media report natural or other disasters in them, or abrupt (to us) changes in leadership, and crises, often violent, in their governments and politics. In recognizing the presence of so many such countries—well over a hundred—how can we possibly hope to make any sense of the fleeting news images of military takeovers, assassinations, urban riots, and guerrilla warfare? Surely we cannot be expected, even as informed and conscientious citizens, to know enough of individual countries to understand the causes and meanings of the religious fighting in India, the war between Iraq and Iran, the assassination of Anwar Sadat in Egypt, or the new fighting in the Balkans and the Transcaucasus (in the former Soviet Union).

Besides, there are so many baffling differences in culture; in political, economic, and social systems; and in what we each consider to be relevant to our own concerns. Small wonder, then, that many people—even among the presumably "educated"—tend to treat most such events, and the news reporting them, as peripheral, as not important enough to warrant sustained attention, much less serious "background" study.

Sometimes, however, dramatic events, such as the capture and holding for more than a year of U.S. diplomatic hostages in Iran or U.S. involvement in the fighting in Central America and later in Kuwait, not only can grip our attention but also can have a direct and keenly felt impact on our daily lives and our political processes. Yet it is no exaggeration to say that prior ignorance aggravates the importance of such episodes in faraway lands—ignorance not only on the part of the vast public but also on the part of many of those at the highest levels of government, both civil and military. Lack of adequate knowledge and the resulting use of inappropriate assumptions in the analysis of events and trends outside the range of our experience have led to tragic chains of miscalculations and policy decisions. The events that were termed "Irangate" or those that have led to an escalation of the bitter civil war in Bosnia are classic examples of woeful ignorance in high places. Better knowledge and understanding can help control more effectively the circumstances that produce such events and minimize their impact on larger issues of a regional and worldwide nature.

There are additional reasons for trying to learn more about the politics and governments in the developing countries. Three-fourths of the world's population are Asian, African, or Latin American; their net population growth rates are well above those in European, North American, and other industrialized parts of the world. Large proportions of the world's supply of various natural resources essential to the survival of industrial societies come from this third set of countries, those we designate here as "developing" in the absence of a more appropriate term. Petroleum is one of which we have become acutely conscious. But there are others, such as bauxite and aluminum, chromium, cobalt, and zinc.

To the extent that we ignore what is happening in the developing countries, to the extent that we "screen out" these nations and people from our attention, we contribute to conditions in which our government (and other important representatives of the industrial countries, such as large multinational corporations) can more easily make the kinds of mistakes that increase the tensions, hostilities, and restiveness already apparent in relations among these three sets of countries—the industrial countries, the postcommunist regimes in the successor states of the USSR and in East Europe, and the developing countries. Such ignorance can have calamitous consequences.

Just as important in the long run, although less obvious, is one essential kind of knowledge we can acquire by directing our attention to the developing world. Political change, interacting with economic and social change, is under way there at a very rapid rate. Cultural distance—as well as geographic—makes it possible for us to observe the complexities of such change much more objectively than we can in our own society. The more we understand political change in the varying conditions of the developing countries, the better we can understand it at home, since the common denominator everywhere is the human species, with its potentials as well as its limitations. The knowledge we gain through comparison can be crucial to our hope of bringing politics and government within the range of our aspirations for our own society.

We cannot go into much detail or depth about individual countries here. But we can try to specify some of the salient general considerations that can provide a context and framework for understanding the political systems of many developing countries. With this in mind, it should at least be possible to ask the most relevant questions when, for whatever reason, we want to be able to interpret and assess political events in the developing world when they are reported in the mass media.

Great Variety–Common Economic Problems

Given their geographic distribution around the world and their individual histories, it is hardly surprising that there is extraordinary variety among the developing countries. They range in population from a few tens of thousands (Dominica, Seychelles) to hundreds of millions (India). Ethnic groups speaking all the major languages and between 2500 and 5000 other languages (depending on how "language" is defined) can be found, usually several and sometimes many per country. All imaginable races and racial mixtures, all the major religions, and many more religions than most of us have even heard of, some based on combinations of elements of others, some ancient and some new, flourish in profusion. Differing languages, racial characteristics, and religious identifications are often related in complex ways to class, caste, and social status and are often important factors in political conflict. But some examples of relatively harmonious coexistence among such diverse groups can be found, as new and old nationalisms seek some form of political unity and recognition.

Other aspects of cultural variety among the developing countries are also important for understanding their politics. In some there is a long and rich heritage of sophisticated artistic expression, including literature, music, sculpture, and architecture. Much of this, just as in the history of Western art, expresses or is inspired by religious themes. In others, art mainly takes the form of handicrafts, body decoration, storytelling, and folk music and dance. In both instances, some political activists and leaders find a wealth of symbols to draw on to mobilize popular sentiments for political purposes. This may be related to movements of awakening national consciousness or of opposition to foreign (Western) technology and lifestyles, which are depicted as threats to traditional values, or to both. In India, Mahatma Gandhi chose the spinning wheel to symbolize both his opposition to foreign colonial rule and his desire to resist the erosion of village institutions by industrial technology. At the same time, he and his followers promoted far-reaching social reforms in the name of justice, such as the abolition of caste oppression of "untouchables."

Some traditional cultures emphasize a division of labor in which women do the agricultural work as well as the housework, in addition to bearing and raising children. Men are responsible for hunting, animal husbandry, fishing, village or tribal politics and religious ritual, and fighting to defend the village or tribe or to acquire booty, including wives. In other cultures both men and women share the agricultural and other heavy work and divide other tasks and activities according to different patterns. Values associated with some cultural patterns, such as handicraft production and trade as well as agriculture, are more receptive to technological change than are other values rooted in differing cultures. These factors are of obvious relevance to governmental programs of economic development, which are under way almost universally in the developing world.

Among all the kaleidoscopic diversity within and between these countries, we can nevertheless point out a few similarities that are crucial for any approach to understanding their politics. A fundamental problem that conditions much of life in developing countries is poverty. To envisage entire societies as poor may not be easy for those who have never lived in such a society or who have never experienced real poverty. Yet we must try, for poverty and its consequences pervade so much of the life of most developing countries that, unless we can begin to comprehend it, we will find it next to impossible to see clearly their governments and politics.

Imagine, first, that your chances are small to live much beyond the age of forty or fifty. Imagine that you have had no more than three or four years of schooling—or none at all. This you may not see as a deprivation, for the same is true for all your family and friends. And perhaps, given the life ahead of you, you may not even be able to conceive of any use for formal education; certainly it will not make you rich, for everyone knows that the few who have any wealth got it because they were lucky enough to be born into families that already had it. What would your life be like if you had never read a book? Imagine also that your mother or father is very ill and that there is no medicine, no doctor, no hospital. While the illness lasts, you and your brothers and sisters may have to reduce the amount of your already insufficient food to contribute to the nourishment of the sick parent, and you will have to do his or her work in addition to your own. Imagine that one or two of your brothers or sisters died as infants—and that such is the normal experience in all the families you know. Imagine having had to work in the fields since the age of six. Imagine not being able to think about doing much else for the rest of your life.

These examples are but an effort to gain a few glimpses into the lives of the great majority of the people in most developing countries. They are intended to give human meaning to otherwise cold statistics such as the following: A quarter of the world's population lives in economically developed countries where they enjoy the fruit of more than three-quarters of the world's total output. Nearly half of the human race live in poorly developed countries where they must try to survive with only 5 percent of the goods produced. Furthermore, this huge chasm is widening. Per capita income in the United States grew (in constant 1980 dollars) from $7000 in 1955 to $11,500 in 1980. During that same period, it grew in India from $170 to $260. By 1990 the income gap in these two countries was even greater: $21,790 in the United States to $350 in India (in 1990 dollars).

World poverty is even worse than per capita income figures suggest. Per capita income is calculated simply by dividing a country's income by its population; it tells us nothing about the distribution of income within the country. Several developing countries—chiefly oil producers—have high per capita income figures ($20,140 for the United Arab Emirates, compared with $22,240 in the United States in 1991 dollars), but national riches have done little to improve the quality of life for the bulk of the population. Typically, in developing countries there is a small elite of wealthy or privileged people. Its size in relation to the total population, although very small, varies; but their homes, automobiles, clothing, clubs, banks, and the restaurants and other retail businesses they support stand in stark contrast to the masses of the poor in the cities. The contrast is all the greater with rural peasants, who typically make up the largest proportion of the total population. In the cities, one can also see middle-class people. Many are civil servants—functionaries of the government. Others work in or own small shops or are professional people: lawyers, doctors, engineers, and so on. But such middle classes as exist are proportionally much smaller than the comparable classes in the United States, Canada, or Western Europe.

The poverty of much of the world's people is worsened by growing indebtedness in the developing countries. Many less developed countries are unable to sell enough products to other countries to pay for the goods they must import to survive. They must borrow from developed countries—in many cases from large American, European, or Japanese banks—to pay for these imports. The huge budget deficit of the American national government produced extraordinarily high interest rates during the 1980s. Many (about 40 percent) of the loans to developing nations carry variable, rather than fixed, rates of interests. Thus when interest rates rise either in the United States or Germany, they greatly increase debts already larger than many of these countries can ever hope to pay off. The interest payments *alone* on Argentina's foreign debt a decade ago were 70 percent of all that it earned in a given year by the sale of exports, and they remain around 50 percent for both Mexico and Brazil. A mere increase of 1 percent in the U.S. interest rate adds well over $4 billion to the debt of developing countries. As a consequence, developing countries have run up a total debt of over $800 billion, and a large number of them continue to lag behind in the payments on their loans.

The bulk of the big debtor countries are in Latin America, and much of their debt is owed to U.S. banks. While much has been done to restructure this debt, and Argentina and Mexico have embarked on ambitious privatization programs to redress these imbalances, Brazil remains the world's largest debtor nation, with approximately $116 billion (1993), and public-sector debt continues to climb in Africa. Thus, for all the progress made in some countries in market reforms, there is always the danger that a Brazil or a Peru will not be able to meet its payments. Default on their loans would provoke a major crisis for U.S. and European banks. Even apart from such an event, the economic implications are serious for the United States and other industrial countries. For excessive debt burdens—be they private or public in nature—can impose further restrictions on world trade and constrain export markets.

Fluctuations in interest rates in the major industrial countries also introduce distortions into world trade and affect individual national currencies. Not so many years ago, the U.S. dollar was strong; today it is weak vis-à-vis the Japanese yen and the German mark. When a currency is strong, it creates opportunities for citizens of that country when they travel abroad or wish to acquire luxury items. But it greatly increases the cost of these countries' products that developing countries need to buy, thus adding to their debt and their difficulties in obtaining necessary goods and services. It also has an impact on the industrial countries themselves. For, as export markets decline, companies are forced to cut back their production and lay off workers, thus creating unemployment and recession in the domestic economy.

During the 1980s, as these economic relations among countries grew in complexity, we all became much more vulnerable to external conditions over which we had less and less direct control. Whereas historically the U.S. domestic economy was relatively independent of the world economy, and it was easier to see direct correlations between actions of the U.S. government and what occurred at home and abroad, new forms of global interdependency and the development of a world economy have constrained the ability of the U.S. government to make major adjustments alone. An example would be the ending of high interest rates in the United States and the shift from a strong to a weak dollar. While this situation had the effect of making American goods and services cheaper abroad and hence more desirable in some countries, it did not automatically produce the stimulus hoped. Part of this situation is a consequence of the emergence of three very different economic centers—one in North America dominated largely by the United States, another in Asia centered in Japan, and a third in an expanded Europe focused around the European Union. Thus, whereas the reduction in the debt burden of many of the Latin American economies, coupled with privatization initiatives and economic restructuring, has stimulated Western Hemisphere trade, the competitiveness of the Japanese economy has made Japan an even stronger world economic center and changes in the U.S.-Japanese trade imbalance have been minimal. Independent of these developments, after a decade of economic productivity and expansion within the European Union, the high cost of incorporating East Germany into a reunited German Federal Republic, coupled with a similar inability to compete with Japanese goods and services, has triggered a recession in Europe, which in turn has had an impact on the United States.

As a consequence, older images of a world divided into industrial nations, such as the United States, dominating trade and finance, and a much larger number of developing countries dependent on them for trade, finance, and assistance no longer have the same explanatory power. In this regard perhaps further reference to the Latin American scene can clarify what has been occurring on a worldwide basis: notable differentiation among individual countries in terms of their response to the development of a world economy and increased global interdependency. Whereas Chile, Mexico, and Argentina have begun to experience dramatic turnarounds in comparison with their dismal performance a decade earlier, offsetting their accomplishments are instances such as Brazil, Venezuela, and Peru, where inflation, indebtedness, and poor economic growth rates continue to constitute major constraints.

At the same time, enormous shifts have been occurring in U.S. trade patterns. For example, in 1980, for the first time, U.S. trade with twenty-one Asian Pacific basin countries surpassed that with Europe. And by 1983 U.S. trade with the Pacific rim was a quarter larger than it was with Europe. Even more incredible, much of what the United States sells to these Asian countries is farm products and natural resources, and most of what it imports is manufactured products. In other words, trade patterns between the United States and these Asian states reflect a very different set of economic relationships from those occurring between the United States and its Western Hemisphere trading partners—all of which raise the question of who is dependent on whom.

Nothing illustrates better than changing patterns in debt and trade how interrelated the world economy has become. The United States simply cannot isolate itself behind a barrier of tariffs, quotas, and other constraints on international trade and hope for economic health. Much of the world's poverty is located outside U.S. boundaries, but Americans can ignore it only at their peril. Having indicated the economic problems common to much of the developing world and why and how they have become American concerns, we turn to consideration of the political problems of the developing world to see how these further complicate efforts to deal with economic weaknesses. (Other factors, e.g. religious, tribal, and ethnic loyalties, also have an impact on economics and politics at home and abroad.)

Common Third World Political Problems

In looking for general explanations of patterns of politics in developing countries, we need to go beyond the immediate historical causes, such as the interrelated events that resulted from the overthrow of the shah of Iran and the replacement of his government by one dominated by Islamic religious leaders. To understand such events, we must interpret them in a framework of ideas about trends and causes that are applicable to other instances of political change. To the extent that our general explanations are applicable to more than one such instance, we can save much time and effort in understanding each individual case. We often do this anyway, consciously or not; for example, we project our beliefs about human nature, or morality and immorality, into our explanations. The problem facing the analyst is to find concepts that can be used without allowing personal preferences to prejudge the means and outcomes under consideration.

Here we use the concepts "traditional society" and "modernization" to organize our explanations. In doing so, we must avoid the implication that one concept is good or bad, and the other is therefore bad or good. This is difficult, for we do assume that modern society (of which the United States is an example) is more consistent than traditional society with such things as science, industrial technology, and rational bases of law, much of which we consider good. We need to keep in mind that change related to these has been and still is accompanied by violent conflict, exploitation, and misery and that incorporating modern ideas and ways into society by no means guarantees an end to such scourges.

The economy of traditional societies tends to be poor and predominantly agricultural. The bulk of the population is rural, typically living in many small villages. There is little mobility, social or geographic. Families tend to be large, and family obligations (e.g., taking care of the aged and the ill, defending family honor, and treating relatives more favorably than others) are stressed. Very few people are literate, and those few are often priests or officials—members of a privileged class. Infant mortality is high, and life spans are generally short. Custom, tradition, and ritual govern most aspects of life.

Towns and cities may exist as centers of religious worship, government, and trade. But their size is limited by the agricultural production of surrounding areas, or of other areas with which trade is carried on, for such urban centers depend on the availability of an agricultural surplus for their survival. A tiny minority of relatively wealthy landowning families often constitutes a ruling class, access to which is closed to most of the population. Trade, commerce, and military conquest may permit growth of such cities to considerable size, and in some the arts may flourish.

Government maintains the social order in relative internal peace by supporting the prevalent religion, often leading the performance of important rituals; by settling disputes; by punishing transgressors; and by maintaining armed forces. It sometimes constructs temples, monuments, roads, dikes, canals, and other kinds of what we would call public works. For all these things, as well as to provide a privileged and comfortable if not luxurious way of life for rulers and officials, it collects taxes or tribute. When needed, it drafts labor for construction work and manpower for military service. Often, religious, economic, and political beliefs and institutions are blended and combined, or at least are not clearly separated.

Such societies may eventually support civilizations, as in ancient Egypt or Babylonia, or the Olmecs in what is now Mexico. Classical Greece and Rome are examples closer to us in culture as sources of Western civilization.

But most of us are aware mainly of the lives and achievements of the elite of such civilizations, rather than of the much more numerous rural populations supporting the elite. Traditional society need not be restricted to earlier "civilizations." More generally, the concept can, with allowance for variations of degree, be usefully applied to most preindustrial societies, including those whose basic organization is tribal.

The beliefs common in traditional society tend to foster acceptance of the status quo. To identify a problem is, for many people in modern societies, to set in motion a search for its causes. There is an almost automatic assumption that there must be one or more causes that "explain" the situation we define as a problem. Once found, the causes may turn out to be (or can be made) susceptible to human intervention. By dealing with the causes, we can hope to eliminate, reduce, or otherwise change the problem so as to make it more tolerable. At least we may discover a way of getting around the problem or avoiding contacts with it. This applies as much to economic and social problems as to those of the "natural" physical world. All this is but common sense, we would say if asked.

It was not always so in what are today modern societies. And it is not always merely "common sense" in many other societies today. For the overwhelmingly greater part of human existence, traditional views of life explained as being ordained by "nature" or divine power many kinds of events and conditions that we regard as avoidable, changeable, or fixable by human actions. Conservative traditional beliefs counseled resignation to natural disasters such as devastating storms, floods, droughts, and earthquakes. The social order, no matter how grotesquely unjust, harmful, or inefficient, was also a part of "nature," divinely sanctioned, or both. The path of wisdom was therefore to accept them. If we look about, we can see surviving influences and remnants of such beliefs in contemporary society. Many, for example, conceive of economic competition in a capitalist system of private ownership—quite apart from its virtues of technological innovation and productivity—as somehow more "natural" than other economic systems. Such a view overlooks the human-made changes and innovations that created property law, market systems, the legal invention of the corporation, and the like.

What we call "modernization" began with technological innovations in Western Europe only a few centuries ago, in association with the Renaissance, the Enlightenment, and the Industrial Revolution. Mining, manufacturing, construction, travel, and trade began to transform societies as economic production and productivity increased far beyond the limits imposed by traditional technologies. Such changes rested on and went hand in hand with the increase of scientific knowledge. Much of the old order was swept away, often to the accompaniment of wars and revolutions. What remained of it had to adapt and accommodate itself to new and continually changing patterns of living and thinking.

We can single out three components of this fateful transformation. Ancient beliefs and attitudes gave way to new ways of viewing the world, nature, and the role and destiny of humankind. A "new psychology" began to spread in England and on the Continent. Many things, it was learned, could be brought under human control and rearranged to a much greater degree than traditional beliefs had conceived. A better life on earth could be achieved by knowledge and action. If traditional culture included such ideas, they were relegated to the realms of magic and the supernatural.

A second component of modernization is the physical or material. Application of new knowledge, which gradually was organized into the sciences, led to more and more complex and powerful technologies. Machines increased economic production. Disease control lowered mortality rates and prolonged life. Construction and travel were revolutionized. New sources of energy and new methods of converting it to human uses vastly increased human control of the natural environment—and the potential for human freedom. New material standards and styles of living became possible. These had the effect of greatly increasing the range of choices open to individuals and societies. This led to the third component: the social and political. New forms of human organization became possible. Among them were huge factories, far-flung business firms, cities of millions of people, and governments of vast complexity and power. New forms of social controls as well as new forces of social disruption appeared. Both greater democratization of government and greater concentrations of governmental power were made possible.

While these changes in Western thought, technology, and society were under way, their consequences began to be projected around the globe. European exploration, trade, religious missions, and military and political expeditions established and expanded colonial empires. A few Western nation-states extended their influence, control, and exploitation to traditional societies on distant continents. But inevitably, the revolutionary ideas and technologies of the imperial powers sowed the seeds of destruction, not only of non-Western traditional societies, but of the colonial empires themselves.

Nevertheless—and here we can begin to understand some of the problems of the developing countries today—the various processes of modernization do not proceed at the same rates and certainly not in harmonious patterns. They produce dislocations, disorganization, and conflict in all aspects of political, economic, and social life. These processes have themselves contributed powerfully to the extent of human poverty and misery. A leading example is modern medicine and public health technologies. These have brought many diseases under control and have reduced infant mortality. The result is more people, living longer lives, who make even greater demands on already overburdened economies.

Also, modern means of transportation and communication have disseminated ideas and images from the more modernized societies to the less modernized part of the world. This has fed and intensified the aspirations and expectations of hundreds of millions of people whose traditional institutions are increasingly unable to satisfy their needs and hopes. But the spread of images of modern life was begun well before the economic, technological, and political means were available that might allow for the realization of such aspirations. As aspirations for a better life are reduced by population growth to a basic struggle for mere survival, and as traditional beliefs and order-maintaining social structures are weakened, little imagination is needed to foresee mounting political pressures and problems. Thus we can see that it is not poverty as such that causes the political problems of the present world, but poverty in conditions of weakened traditional beliefs and structures, that is, of weakened social-control mechanisms, where awareness of possibilities of a better life is widespread.

Let us look more closely at four clusters of political problems confronting many developing countries: ambivalence and frustration related to modernization, internal cleavages based on subnational loyalties, political instability, and prominence of the military in politics. As traditional beliefs about the bases of legitimate government, such as divinely sanctioned hereditary monarchy, have eroded, more modern beliefs, such as the consent and representation of the governed, have not been widely accepted beyond the educated few. In many countries, elites with Western-style educations reveal ambivalent attitudes, seeking to conserve valued elements and aspects of traditional culture while adopting much of modern knowledge, technology, and ways of living. In some instances, such as Pakistan and Saudi Arabia, many of the educated few seek a viable way of retaining and strengthening the religious basis of governmental authority. This may be accompanied by both resentment of the West and reluctance to give up positions of influence and privilege as economic and social change spreads through society. Or some of the elite may share the frustration and sense of injustice of the less advantaged at the inability to break the grip of poverty on the country. Whatever the individual reaction to the experience of socialization by two different cultures, traditional and Western, problems of self-identity and ambivalence toward goals often prove difficult to handle. Their effects on behavior render the latter more difficult to understand by observers who have not had such experience. It is in some ways analogous to the experience of racial minorities in a society such as the United States, except that in the developing world it is the favored elites who have experienced this "double socialization."

Another constellation of problems aggravated by modernization processes in many developing countries has to do with cleavages based on ethnic, regional, and class differences. The problem discussed earlier is one manifestation of this kind of cleavage, in which socioeconomic class differences are reinforced by a foreign-style language, the lack of which may effectively bar many from possible channels of upward social mobility such as governmental employment at levels other than the lowest and most menial and has often caused suspicions about the true loyalties of members of the elite. But on a larger scale, loyalties to groups such as tribes or to those speaking different languages, particularly when such groups are identified with particular regions, may result in extremely difficult problems of integration and assimilation into a "nation-state."

For the "new" nations, especially in Africa, boundaries are a legacy of colonialism, drawn by colonial powers. Such boundaries were often the results of conflict and treaties among colonial powers; thus they sometimes grouped traditionally hostile people within a colony while splitting previously unified people and their lands on both sides of a colonial boundary. Postindependence political leaders have had to get diverse people to accept a common and newly created national identity so that a government of all can acquire enough legitimacy to function. This has never been easy, and in some instances brutal civil wars have been fought, as in Nigeria. Such situations have provided regional leverage for foreign involvement, as in Zaire (the Congo) just after independence. Given its many different languages and internal ethnic antagonisms, which erupt into violence not infrequently, one of India's principal accomplishments has been sheer survival without breaking into pieces along ethnic lines. It is significant that the common language of governmental administration has continued to be English. The imposition of the official language, Hindi, is still resisted in non-Hindi-speaking states.

Given the presence to some degree of divisive factors such as these, many developing countries lack sufficiently widespread acceptance of basic rules to govern political conflict. Political leaders often cannot assume that their opponents will refrain from violence and are therefore ready to use it themselves. Significantly, this has become true of older developing nations as well as newer ones, as the unsettling forces of modernization have spread.

Latin American politics, perhaps more clearly than African, are often riven by conflicts along socioeconomic class lines, as in Argentina, Brazil, Bolivia, Chile, Nicaragua, and El Salvador in recent years. In such conflicts the military forces of the government are often the decisive factor. Nicaragua is a recent exception—as was Cuba over two decades ago. In these two the government's armies were not able to resist guerrilla forces.

A major part of the explanation in Cuba and Nicaragua was corruption and repression on the part of the government and the military, which destroyed the government's legitimacy in the eyes of much of the population, especially rural peasants and many of the middle- as well as lower-class urban people. On the other hand, one of the frequently used justifications for military forces turning on their civilian masters, overthrowing their government, and setting up a military dictatorship is the corruption and incompetence of civilian government.

To summarize, we can often find a few important, underlying, explanatory factors in the seemingly unpredictable processes of political conflict and change in developing countries. One of these is poverty, which has often become more acute and more politically explosive as a consequence of partial modernization of traditional societies. Such partial modernization has weakened or undermined traditional institutions and values and has disseminated images of and aspirations for a better life to millions. But the means for realizing such aims are insufficient or absent. Elites, partly modernized, are ambivalent toward the modernization process, not only because they are socialized into the Western as well as the domestic culture, but also because the changes that process produces may threaten their privileged positions. Internal cleavages hinder the development of national consciousness in many countries. Without sufficiently institutionalized rules for the nonviolent resolution of political conflict, the military forces are often involved in the maintenance of order by repression of rebellions. The outcome is often military dictatorship, which is one of the most common forms of government in the developing world.

We now can survey several specific political institutions and processes that have emerged in the developing world as its nations have attempted to deal with the economic and political problems we have discussed.

Political Institutions and Processes

In relatively stable political systems it is possible to identify fairly well defined institutions of government. Through the activities of officials who hold office in them, legitimate and authoritative decisions are made or ratified:

laws, decrees, and so forth, which establish government policies and spell out rules that affect the people subject to that government. Specific governmental institutions are authorized to enforce or carry out the decisions made. Other political processes, involving individuals, parties, interest groups, and nongovernmental institutions, go on in relation to the governmental decision-making processes, seeking to influence them. The general reason for seeking such influence is that the outcomes of governmental decisions affect the distribution of burdens and benefits throughout society: who pays how much in taxes; whose activities are regulated and in what ways; who receives what services, subsidies, authorizations, exemptions, and so on. Although the threat of coercion by police or military forces is never absent in enforcing such decisions, rules, and policies, it is normally used only in maintaining public order and apprehending and punishing criminals.

The organization, processes, and functions of these governmental institutions can be examined on the assumption that one is dealing with matters directly relevant to the question of how that society is governed. This is so even if one discovers that other individuals, groups, institutions, or classes or people, not a part of the formal governmental institutions, and contrary to official doctrine and public symbolism, exercise great influence, even to the point of controlling the decisions made by the government.

But in many developing countries, the situation of some governmental institutions is not as clear-cut as just described. In some, change may be occurring so rapidly, or may have occurred so recently, that both participants and observers may be uncertain as to who is doing what, or who is supposed to be doing what. Some government organizations may be at a standstill, doing little or nothing, or engaging in activities that result in things not expected, to judge by their titles or their place in the structure. Other organizations and activities may exist only on paper. Officials may be giving attention and deference to persons or organizations whose place and role in the political process are far from obvious, even if detectable. In short, both image and reality may be not only unclear but also inconsistent with each other, or related in such complex or indirect ways that even participants may be uncertain about some of them.

The consequences of this is that formal governmental structures, often designed according to models taken from the industrial countries, may not be the best place to start looking for evidence as to how developing countries are governed. One may find offices such as president or prime minister or organizations labeled "legislature," "senate," "assembly," or "high court of justice." But until we discover just what the officials in these offices and organizations do, and with what consequences, it is not safe to assume that the functions associated with such names in governments of modernized countries are those actually carried out.

This is not to suggest that in the industrial countries there is an exact one-to-one fit between the formal structure and image of government and the actual structure of power and influence. Inevitably discrepancies exist. For example, it is commonly recognized in the U.S. government that the office of the presidency exerts much more influence over lawmaking than a reading of the Constitution might suggest. But the office itself and its relations with Congress and the courts are sufficiently institutionalized that a fairly elaborate and intricate set of understandings and expectations exists for any incumbent. This is often not the case in offices of the chief executive of the government in developing countries.

Here we need to be more specific about the concept of "institution" and the process of "institutionalization." When we say that certain organized activities are institutionalized, we mean that they have become habitual and normal and that they endure because they are *valued* by participants and by others affected by or related to them in beneficial ways. A criminal justice system composed of police, courts, and jails becomes institutionalized because both the people employed by them and the public at large value them. This support is enough to outweigh the lack of support by those who are punished by the system. Similarly, other organizations set up to perform governmental functions by exercising legitimate power ("authority") can become infused with value and can endure as long as they are so valued. To say that an institution is valued means more than that it is wanted or desired. It means that those valuing it share some degree of consensus that it *should* or *ought* to exist, as a matter of what is "right" or "proper."

Three further points must be noted about institutions. It takes *time* for a structure of activities to be institutionalized to the degree that it will be supported and maintained beyond the time that particular individuals who happen to be popular occupy and perform roles in them. Second, to endure, institutions have to change so as to *adapt* to changes in their *environment*. At the same time, and third, they do not merely react passively to such changes. They usually seem, and are able, to *influence* or *control* significant parts of their environment so as to ensure their survival.

From these comments we can gain some understanding of why some governmental organizations in developing countries seem not to be doing what one would expect, or why they seem to lack permanence and strength. Let us take the example of a body set up as a legislature. Leaders of many newly independent nations came to power, over the last forty-five years or so, promising to set up democratic governments. Many tried this by drafting

and promulgating written constitutions modeled on those of more modernized countries of the industrial world. To be democratic, it was assumed, a
government should have, among other things, an elected legislature. Thus
the new constitution provided for one. But two problems had to be faced.
One was that many in the population had little or no understanding of elections or legislative bodies. Their conception of government may have been
limited to experience with colonial officials or to traditional chieftains or
kings often supported (and manipulated) by colonial officials. This problem
was not fatal; it was possible for the new government to mount a campaign
of public information and propaganda and to have its supporters get large
numbers of the population to turn out to vote.

The other problem was more serious. Before and at the time of independence, there may have been other contenders—rivals—for leadership.
Some or all of them might be regarded by leaders currently in control, not
merely as rivals, but as traitors to the national cause. Could one actually
risk being defeated in an election by such people? Of course not. They could
not even be allowed on the ballot. Or if, for whatever reason, they could not
be excluded that way, there were other ways to assume that one's opponents
would not win. (Along with other modern ideas, political leaders in developing countries have also learned something of the fine art of rigging elections.)

The trouble with such methods of electing legislative bodies was that
people—even uneducated rural peasants—were not so ignorant as to fail to
see through the charade. If they did not see through it immediately, the
rivals and their supporters made every effort to ensure that they did see
through it. Thus the legislative body eventually elected did not stand much
chance of becoming a working, effective institution. Even supporters of the
leaders who organized such elections were hardly unaware of how they had
won, and so they could not give unadulterated respect to this new symbol of
democracy. Most of the time they adjusted to the reality that their legislative
activity had to occur within limits acceptable to those wielding effective executive powers—often those assuming the title of president, sometimes military leaders. Meanwhile, the opponents, seeing their path to legitimate
power blocked in such a way, were sometimes persuaded that their only
chance was to foment revolt aimed at overturning the new government. Not
a very good start for a government whose leaders may have been sincere in
their desire to institute democracy.

Not all new nations, or older nations undergoing modernization, followed paths similar to that just outlined. India, Colombia, Costa Rica,
Chile, and Venezuela are examples of developing countries that appear to

have made successful beginnings toward the institutionalization of elected governments and moderately democratic politics. Several of them have experienced crises and setbacks, however, as well as severe economic problems. Typically in developing countries, often even in the more successful ones, the role of an elected legislative body is primarily symbolic. Its presence may express an aspiration for popular representation in lawmaking and in checking possible excesses of executive power. Additionally, and often primarily, a docile and compliant legislature is useful as a means of legitimating decisions made by chief executives, regardless of the intentions of the latter with regard to the eventual democratization of the political system.

The importance and power of chief executives in governments around the world reveal that such prominence is not uniquely a developing-country phenomenon. What is more characteristic of developing-country politics is that such powerful political leaders come into office by military *coups d'état,* and many leave office the same way. Some of the reasons for and circumstances surrounding such military intervention have already been suggested. Here we need to inquire into variations in this pattern.

First, however, we should note that there are about a dozen hereditary monarchies or royalist governments in the developing world, in which the military are influential but subordinate to the rulers. These include such nations as Jordan, Saudi Arabia, Morocco, and Nepal. In Thailand the monarchy has been retained, but the military control the government. Such governments, generally conservative, seek to keep the disruptive forces of modernization under control through authoritarian government, some adaptation, and the guidance of economic development so as to preserve the existing socioeconomic structure.

In another twenty or so developing countries, ranging from Mongolia, North Korea, and Vietnam in Asia, through such African countries as Angola, Guinea, and Mozambique, and Libya and South Yemen in North Africa and the Middle East, to Cuba in the Western Hemisphere, Marxist regimes led by or closely supported by military forces took power after *coups d'état* or guerrilla wars. Leaders of most of these governments sought to organize single parties to mobilize and control popular support. And, before the collapse of the Soviet Union and its satellite regimes in East Europe, they relied on military and economic aid from the USSR and governments allied with it. Even at the high point of support from these governments, however, military forces proved to be more important than the official parties, and the model of state socialism failed to resolve their historic problems of underdevelopment. This was especially true in Africa. Like the successor states to the Soviet Union and the new governments in East Europe, this

group of countries is in the midst of significant economic and political transitions, with some countries—such as Mozambique—farther advanced in
the process of economic restructuring while others—namely Cuba—are desperately attempting to preserve state socialism.

In other parts of the developing world—ranging from South Korea,
Taiwan, Bangladesh, and Indonesia in Asia, through Iraq and Yemen in the
Middle East, to Somalia, Sudan, and Zaire in Africa and Peru, Bolivia, and
Guatemala in Latin America—equally important transitions are under way,
away from authoritarian regimes in which the military played a significant if
not a dominant role. Again, individual country cases vary greatly, especially
in how they have handled questions of economic policy. South Korea and
Taiwan, for example, have behind them impressive economic records. In
contrast, Peru and Bolivia—despite very different experiences with economic restructuring—remain very poor societies. In all of them, disillusion-
ment with military intervention in politics is high, but in none of them can
one say that the recourse to authoritarian rule has been superseded.

Latin American experience is of particular interest here. During the
1960s and 1970s the military seized power throughout the region. In the
Southern Cone of South America the breakdown of democratic regimes
took place in a setting where constitutional government with reasonably fair
and competitive elections, and effective civilian chief executives and legislative bodies, seemed to be well along toward institutionalization—although
each of these countries faced severe economic difficulties. Notable among
these were Brazil, Chile, and Uruguay. In Brazil and Chile, elections had
produced governments and policies that, to conservative and not so democratically disposed officers with the support of major segments of the upper
and middle classes, appeared dangerously radical and leftist. Specifically, the
position and interests of landowning, business, and financial elites were
threatened. The military officers seized power in *coups d'état* and instituted
purges that included the use of uncharacteristically brutal torture of suspected leftist opponents. Many suspected opponents were killed or simply
disappeared.

In Uruguay, the military intervened in a situation of a deteriorating
economy, aggravated by the inability of the civilian government to suppress
an urban guerrilla movement. Yet this was a country that for decades had
been proud both of its relatively high living standards, ones that placed it in
the upper tier of the developing world (in the category the World Bank calls
the "upper-middle-income countries"), and its accomplishments as a stable
democracy that approximated the welfare states of northern Europe. The
country's severe economic difficulties, coupled with a stalemated democracy

in which the civilian political leadership was unable to respond to these deteriorating economic and social conditions, ultimately brought the military into politics. The military replaced the civilian president, established a repressive authoritarian regime, and stamped out the guerrillas and terrorists. Eventually, the military proved no more able to resolve the country's difficulties, and by 1984 the country had begun a transition back to democracy.

While the authoritarianism of the 1970s was superseded by the movement back to democratic regimes in the 1980s, the Latin American cases serve to underline the fragility of democratic institutions. In many areas of the world, modernization has created expectations and demands that threaten the interests of well-entrenched economic elites and that in any event are difficult to satisfy through democratic processes. This creates a painful dilemma for those who see the undeniable need for fundamental economic and social change in the interest of social justice, but who are dedicated to orderly and legal processes for effecting change. The actions of military governments in these circumstances contribute to intensified hatreds that, in the absence of significant improvements in the socioeconomic conditions of large majorities in such countries, portend even more violence in the future. Even though democracy has been on the upswing throughout Latin America recently, the unanswered question in the new cycle of preference for market economies and democratic governance is whether or not these countries will be any more successful in the 1990s in transcending the cycle of periodic economic and political crises and the subsequent breakdown of democratic institutions.

The fact that chief executives so often have been military men in recent decades serves to call attention to the need to differentiate between the appearance of the person holding office as the most powerful individual in the political system, when in reality such persons are often significantly dependent on others in their entourages. In many instances, for example, the military governments in Argentina (1976–83) and Greece (1967–74), these were councils of officers, whether or not such arrangements were formalized. Moreover, the formal title of president does not provide immunity from being removed by a fellow officer or a group of them. Such has occurred both as a consequence of policy disagreements and because of the ambition of other officers. Politicizing the upper levels of the armed forces can greatly weaken the discipline of military command. To the degree that an army has become professionalized, generals often discover that the aptitudes, skills, and knowledge required for a successful military career are not the same as those required for successful political leadership. Leaders of guerrilla forces, in contrast, are more likely to understand political leadership and can more easily function as leaders of governments. Nevertheless, nothing guarantees that either kind of leader will have much understanding of the complexities of economic policy. For this they often have to turn to people in the one set of structures that are likely to be fairly well institutionalized in developing-country political systems—the civilian bureaucracies.

The bureaucracies, or administrative components of government, are employers of a fairly large proportion of the professional and technically trained people in many developing countries. Whether the product of colonial administration or of long-standing independent government, these agencies are indispensable instruments for the exercise of governmental authority. If the decisions and policies of political leaders are to be carried out, if the programs launched are to have any effect, it is the administrators who will do it.

Political leaders learn that their commands are not alone sufficient to ensure that these things will be done. They also find that they are dependent on administrators for much of the information they need for governing. Such information may be in the form of reports on the status and effects of programs. It may be in the form of technical knowledge required to plan and design such programs in the first place. The political leaders also discover that their orders and instructions are subject to much interpretation and reinterpretation as they pass downward and outward through the bureaucratic hierarchy. For all these reasons, it is often difficult for governmental leaders to accomplish what they intend. The administrative structure, in appearance nothing more than a tool for doing the government's work, is in reality a baffling network of power, resistant to change and often full of obstacles to action.

Whether political leaders seek to stimulate modernization or to channel it in desired directions, they often discover that the attitudes, knowledge, and skills required are scarce in the bureaucracy. Officials experienced in collecting revenues, issuing licenses and permits, drafting regulations, and keeping voluminous files of records may find it impossible to think of innovative ways of instituting and managing developmental programs. They may lack initiative or be unwilling to take responsibility for decision making when situations require flexibility and quick decisions.

Such shortcomings as these are frequently compounded by long-standing practices of petty bribery and the exchange of favors among administrative officials as a means of getting things done. Employment by and advancement in administrative agencies may depend on complex networks of patronage and nepotism. On a larger scale, the complexity of regulations and procedures makes it possible for some administrators, who understand them from years of experience, to delay or block action—or to conceal the embezzlement of funds or engage in smuggling of contraband materials. In other words, corruption of various degrees of magnitude may be embedded in the bureaucracy. Some political leaders may wish to profit from it themselves. Others may close their eyes to it, realizing that serious efforts to root it out will drain time and energies needed for trying to bring about desired or mandated results in governmental action.

Paradoxically, conditions such as these—and they are not unusual —present problems that are the opposite of those discussed previously with reference to modernization. Bureaucracies often suffer from an excess of institutionalization. This is often linked to traditional cultural patterns and other elements of society, such as the family. Thus bureaucracies cannot be easily reoriented, nor can they be purged and repopulated by new officials because there are not enough such new people with the necessary skills and experience.

Courts of law in developing countries, in contrast, are often more vulnerable to the political changes related to modernization. This is because, as organized structures, they are smaller in size than the complex of bureaucratic institutions. More important, the locus of judicial decision making is more visible. A judge, or a small panel of judges, presides at trials and renders decisions or hears appeals from lower courts and renders decisions. Judges may delay, but eventually they must decide. Thus, when political struggles break the molds of institutionalized government and become matters of sheer power and coercion, the very survival of judges and judicial institutions usually requires a keen awareness on their part of the goals and wishes of those wielding the greatest power. This can result in judicial decisions ranging from general bias in favor of the dominant leaders and their supporters to the outright politicization of courts. In the latter event, harassment and persecution of the regime's opponents and dissidents can be given an aura of judicial legitimacy. (The politicization of courts of law is not, however, an invention of the developing world. Models in the industrial world can be found as well in Europe in Nazi Germany and Fascist Italy or in the former Soviet Union. It is now standard practice for revolutionary regimes, once in control of government, to set up "revolutionary tribunals" to convict and often execute captured leaders and followers of the overthrown regime.)

The emphasis thus far given to some of the consequences of modernization should not be allowed to imply that political turmoil is constant in the developing world. Between crises, changes of leaders, and outbreaks of civil disorder, individual countries may experience years of relative calm. During such periods, patterns of politics and governmental action proceed normally—but "normal" is of course shaped by the kinds of factors discussed and by memories of the kinds of events mentioned. Depending on time and place, political discussions are often carried on with a semiconspiratorial air, with words chosen carefully and many indirect allusions. Or, if a foreigner joins the group, the subject may be quickly changed during such events, and its commentary is typically supportive of the regime, for the mass media often operate under government supervision. Tourists passing through may get a few insights into the workings of the political system. But if the regime is authoritarian, the tourists usually see little evidence of it.

Political parties will exist if not prohibited, and to varying degrees will go about their work of trying to mobilize and extend their support. If there is but one party, the official one, its posters carrying pictures, symbols, and slogans, are much in evidence. Many of its activities may be carried out by government employees, and the distinction between party and government may be blurred. If there are several competing parties, they are often small, with relatively little formal organization and few full-time workers. Some may be little more than loose networks of friends and relatives, inactive except at times of elections.

The country's political elite is small, and most of its members know one another personally. It includes, in addition to the top officials of the regime, high-level bureaucrats and military officers; members of wealthy business and landowning families (unless the regime happens to be Marxist), partly in, but not of, the elite; resident foreign business people; and such cultural and intellectual figures as editors, artists, and prominent professors. There may be leaders of important interest groups, such as importers and exporters, producers of and dealers in raw materials and export crops, or students. But interest groups are not as numerous as in more economically developed and modernized countries, and the number of distinct interests is relatively small. In the capital city, much of the social life may revolve around the embassies of foreign governments, which give frequent receptions and formal dinners.

Despite its relatively small size, the elite is not a homogeneous group of people with identical political views. A frequently found difference is that between pronationalist and proforeign groups. In time of crisis this can become bitter. Another line often distinguishes those with modern scientific, technical, and professional education from those with more traditional educations, such as law or the liberal arts.

Usually, the urgency and critical nature of political, economic, and social problems facing the country are not much in evidence in the daily lives and the official assemblies and ceremonies or social gatherings of the elite. It is politics and business as usual—until the next crisis begins to build or the next outbreak of open struggle or public disorder. It may be tomorrow. Or it may be next year.

Futures in the Developing World

The changes of modernization in the industrial world have had several centuries to transform traditional into predominantly modern societies. Even so, these transformations produced revolutions, civil wars, wars of independence, and great international wars, not to mention hardships forced on the rural and urban poor. Developing-country political systems are having to undergo the transition—or its beginning phases—in a much briefer period. The destabilizing and exploitative effects of early modernization create revolutionary situations in which both indigenous rebels and foreign powers can seek to shape the direction of political change.

This basic problem of acceleration is intensified by three ominous trends. The first is rapid population growth, which exceeds many societies' ability to increase food production. The prospect is for more famines and epidemics as population pressure on resources increases. These have already begun in the poorest countries in Africa.

Second, the entire globe's natural resources, needed to sustain the world's "high technology" societies, are being depleted at dizzying rates. International struggles for access to and control of such resources by the industrial powers are likely to intensify. The Persian Gulf crisis may be repeated in other regions, with reference to other natural resources. Weaker developing countries may well become increasingly dependent clients and pawns of the major world powers.

Third, this voracious consumption of resources is producing changes, some of them irreversible, in the earth's land surface and water. This includes the depletion of agricultural topsoil, the destruction of oxygen-producing foliage, the increased need for poisonous herbicides and insecticides, and the need for increasingly expensive (in energy conversion terms) fertilizers. Groundwater levels are being lowered in industrialized regions; acid rain has become a cause of international dispute; and rivers, lakes, and even oceans are showing serious consequences of continuing industrial pollution. In the earth's atmosphere, long-term temperature changes may already be under way as a result of smoke with chemical and particulate pollution, and solar radiation may become more dangerous because of such things as damage to ozone.

All of this leads to a pessimistic prognosis, particularly for the developing countries. Many of them will never "catch up" economically with the present industrialized countries. Furthermore, some developing countries may well once again come under political and/or military control of rival industrial nations. The industrial world cannot assume that it will emerge unscathed, for none of this latter group of countries can escape the consequences of resource depletion and environmental damage.

Science and technology have helped us into this dangerous impasse; we have little else to use to find a way out. But, for such ingenuity to be fruitful, we will have to develop greater wisdom in managing our collective affairs than has been apparent in the past. We will have to cope with the vast, degrading, and dangerous disparities in wealth between the rich and the poor nations. The benefits of modern life will have to be shared more equitably. And both rich and poor nations will have to learn to do much better in conserving the remaining natural resources. All this is likely to call for more sacrifice and means greater changes in lifestyle on the part of the rich and resource consuming nations on behalf of the poor.

Coping with world problems also is likely to require many people to rethink their moral priorities. Birthrates in developing countries continue at high levels, contributing a major share of the world's population growth —growth that rapidly is outrunning technology's ability to expand and distribute the food production required for survival of much of the world's population. Humanity took a million years to grow to a population of one billion. The next billion increase in size took not much more than a century—120 years. A third billion was added in only few years and a fourth in just fifteen years. In the past three decades the world's population increased by more than the total number of people alive throughout the world in 1900. A billion of this increased population of the past forty years has come in nations with per capita incomes of less than $400.

Faced with such facts, one must wonder how persistent opposition to birth-control mechanisms can be justified. How can the prevention of conception be immoral when bringing human life into the world means only to let it starve to death or live for a short time in misery? And what is the morality of official U.S. government policy that refuses to provide support for birth-control programs in developing countries unless they outlaw abortion? Moral platitudes asserted without reference to reality are likely only to call themselves into disrepute.

Finally, our many political systems and the people selected to operate them must transcend the dangerous conflicts of power and ideology in today's world. Awareness of common problems and efforts to identify and make meaningful the commonalities of contending ideologies may seem —given the millennia of conflicts among humanity—merely pious utopianism. The failure to achieve this, however, seems likely to be calamitous. For modernization has forced not only the developing world but all of us into a race with time. And the process by which we seek to reconcile our differences and solve our problems is nothing other than politics. Thus, the study of politics, in order to make the process more effective and equitable, is essential for our survival.

SUGGESTIONS FOR ADDITIONAL READING

BINDER, LEONARD, et al. *The Politics of Modernization.* Chicago: University of Chicago Press, 1971.

DIAMOND, LARRY, JUAN LINZ, and SEYMOUR MARTIN LIPSET, eds. *Democracy in Developing Countries.* 4 vols. Boulder, Colo.: Lynne Rienner Publishers, 1988.

FANON, FRANTZ. *The Wretched of the Earth.* New York: Grove Press, 1956.

FEIT, EDWARD. *The Armed Bureaucrats: Military-Administrative Regimes and Political Development.* Boston: Houghton Mifflin, 1973.

GRINDLE, MERILEE S., ed. *Politics and Policy Implementation in the Third World.* Princeton: Princeton University Press, 1980.

HOROWITZ, IRVING LOUIS. *Beyond Empire and Revolution: Militarization and Consolidation in the Third World.* New York: Oxford University Press, 1982.

HUNTINGTON, SAMUEL P. *The Third Wave: Democratization in the Late Twentieth Century.* Norman: University of Oklahoma Press, 1993.

JANOWITZ, MORRIS. *Military Institutions and Coercion in the Developing Nations.* Expanded ed. Chicago: University of Chicago Press, 1977.

KOHLI, ATUL, ed. *The State and Development in the Third World.* Princeton: Princeton University Press, 1986.

MIGDAL, JOEL S. *Strong Societies and Weak States: State-Society Relations and State Capabilities in the Third World.* Princeton: Princeton University Press, 1988.

NELSON, JOAN M., ed. *Economic Crisis and Policy Choice: The Politics of Adjustment in the Third World.* Princeton: Princeton University Press, 1990.

O'DONNELL, GUILLERMO, PHILIPPE C. SCHMITTER, and LAURENCE
WHITEHEAD, eds. *Transitions from Authoritarian Rule.* Baltimore:
Johns Hopkins University Press, 1986.

PRZEWORSKI, ADAM. *Democracy and the Market: Political and Economic Reforms in Eastern Europe and Latin America.* New York:
Cambridge University Press, 1991.

STEPAN, ALFRED. *Rethinking Military Politics: Brazil and the Southern
Cone.* Princeton: Princeton University Press, 1988.

WIARDA, HOWARD J. *New Directions in Comparative Politics.* Rev. ed.
Boulder, Colo.: Westview Press, 1991.

WORLD BANK. *World Development Report 1993: Investing in Health.*
New York: Oxford University Press, 1993.

9. The Mexican Political System

Of the developing countries, the closest and most important to the United States is Mexico. The 2000-mile common frontier extending across the southwestern United States from Texas to California is the source of this contact. It was never an effective barrier, and today the affairs of the United States and Mexico are becoming more and more intertwined. Already to the north, where the border between the United States and Canada is even longer, trade barriers have been reduced, and there is an increasing flow of population, goods, and services between the two countries. But while the Canadian-U.S. trade agreement is not without its tensions and conflicts, economic disparities are far less than is the case between them and Mexico. Given these realities, it should surprise no one that the move to broaden this agreement to include Mexico in the North American Free Trade Agreement [NAFTA] engendered enormous controversy. To the south, differences in culture and levels of living are much more noticeable, for despite all its progress, Mexico remains a poor country. Then, too, there is the inescapable fact that what was fully one-half of Mexican territory at independence has become an integral part of the United States.

The self-image that most Americans hold of themselves is not one that finds an easy place for the fact that U.S. expansion westward in the past century entailed the conquest of the northern tier of Mexico and the treatment of its Spanish-speaking population as a conquered people. Granted, such a population was sparse in the nineteenth century, and far more Spanish-speaking people today live in the southwestern United States than was the case before 1848 (the date that marks the end of the Mexican-American War and the loss of these lands to the United States). But Mexican schoolchildren cannot study the history of their country without becoming aware that the independence of Texas in 1836 and the loss of Mexico's northern territories to the United States constituted traumatic events. Today, more than a century later, the psychological implications of this legacy in which one nation was the victor and the other the vanquished have been compounded by the fact that despite the Mexican Revolution of 1910, Mexico has become more dependent on the United States than ever.

The Mexican economic crisis of the 1980s and the economic reforms since, however, have marked an important shift in U.S.-Mexican relations from dependency to interdependency. In 1986, for example, a substantial part of Mexico's debt ($98 billion at the time) was owed to the private banks of one country, the United States. And when economic restructuring of that debt began, it became as much a U.S. problem as a Mexican one. Likewise, while the fluctuation in oil and gas prices has had a different impact on each economy, the economic effects produced in each have had consequences for the other. The devaluation of the Mexican peso, coupled with inflationary pressures in the 1980s and with major economic restructuring in the 1990s, has led to severe economic dislocations and limited employment opportunities in Mexico. While discussions of the social consequences of structural adjustment and market reforms in developing countries may sound theoretical, these are not abstract issues but concrete ones when one looks at the consequences of these policies in Mexico for the U.S. labor market and trade between the two countries. For one cannot separate the increased flow of migration northward from these events, since the poor—more so now than ever before—see in employment in the United States, illegal or otherwise, an escape valve to economic hardship and the absence of employment at home. Not surprisingly, the free flow of labor within the developing North American market has been and remains an issue of great sensitivity.

However one assesses this situation, one thing is certain: The two economies have become so closely interrelated that actions on either side of the border can no longer be handled as self-contained. Moves by either the United States or Mexico in economic and social policy have come to have great impact on the other. Consequently, it has become increasingly difficult to separate internal domestic affairs—be it labor legislation, welfare benefits, education, interest rates, sales and services, or the drug traffic—from diplomatic relations between the two countries.

A major cause of this changing U.S.-Mexican relationship is economic change in Mexico. Since World War II, Mexico has been undergoing fundamental transformation, ceasing to be a rural society and becoming instead a semi-industrialized country with a rapidly growing urban population. If in 1940 two-thirds of the labor force was to be found in agriculture, by

1970 this fraction had declined to a little more than one-third. Then stagnation set in, and with the devaluation of the Mexican peso in 1982, economic crisis replaced sustained growth rates of over 6 percent. During these years, on the U.S. side of the border, the loss of Mexican purchasing power not only led to a recession in these regional economies but produced an overall decline in trade with Mexico. Then, in 1989, when the presidency was turned over to Carlos Salinas de Gortari, major structural adjustment was undertaken, with extensive privatization and the reduction of controls over the private sector (domestic and foreign). All this carried with it enormous social costs.

In this respect Mexico is a microcosm of many of the patterns characteristic of the developing world, discussed in the previous chapter. Rapid modernization; continuous change and uncertainty; and extensive social, political, and economic transformations have had major impact on the developing world over the past forty years. These same elements can be found in Mexico—in the sense that, despite the aggregate progress being made at present, conditions of life for the majority of Mexico's citizens have shown little improvement. Regardless of an external image that frequently leads to Mexico's classification as an "institutionalized elected government" and as a country with "moderately democratic politics," the realities of political life are such that, like many other developing countries, "the good life" belongs to a restricted political and economic elite whose stake in society is defended and maintained by authoritarian practices and the primacy of hierarchical relations designed to keep the masses at bay.

At the same time, Mexico has unique characteristics and is an excellent example of why facile generalizations about the developing world must be followed with specific cases explaining individual political system differences. More important, this example can be used to make a more general point regarding comparative analysis and why the U.S. case has been dealt with as an integral part of this text on "politics and government." There is a whole body of literature that deals with what is called "American exceptionalism," that is, the viewpoint that the U.S. experience is so different from that of Western Europe that it must be dealt with apart and on its own terms. There are important reasons why this is the case. But from a wider comparative perspective, this is true of all political systems: Each has its own distinctive characteristics and experiences, which set it apart from other countries. Whereas this point has been made in the past and seen as relevant theoretically but not practically, the current realities of the primacy of world markets and increased interdependency among all countries, regardless of differences in levels of economic development, require of all of us greater capacity to see how our own society fits into a larger international setting, without sacrificing our understanding of what makes it unique.

Contrasted with U.S. government, Mexican government is authoritarian. Yet, when compared with the authoritarian experiences of other countries (e.g., Chile under General Pinochet, 1973–90), it is not as oppressive nor is it a regime maintained essentially by force. Even more important, it is a political system in transition in which old-style mechanisms of political control no longer function with the same efficacy as in the past; but it still does not fall within the range of countries whose current political practices may be characterized as democratic. Military officers no longer participate in politics, however, for they clearly are subordinate to civilian authority. Elections are held regularly, and even though they frequently resemble a plebiscite designed to ratify the choices of a single dominant party (the Partido Revolucionario Institucional, or PRI), there is an elaborate and complex process of internal ratification and consultation that fulfills the function of legitimizing the selections made for major sectors of Mexican society. Also, every six years there is sufficient turnover in appointed and elected officials to ensure that no single clique will continue to dominate national politics to its own exclusive advantage beyond the six years of rule accorded to each president, since no president may serve a second term. Finally, there is sufficient differentiation between political and economic elites, and competition within and between each of these groups, to ensure that no single, coherent power structure will take control. In a very real sense, Mexican government has become the domain of the middle sectors of society.

For all these reasons, Mexico provides both a fitting note on which to end this introduction to the study of politics and government and a beginning. The categories, the concepts, the concerns are largely the same there as they are in the study of any government and its politics. But the outcomes, the practices, the motivations that lead people to become involved in political life in Mexico, as in other developing countries, differ widely from those identified for the United States and other countries classified as part of the industrial world. If through this approach we can enable the reader to see more clearly some of the similarities and differences in politics and government as we move from one society to another and back home again, then we will have accomplished a good part of what we set out to do. Now more than ever before, it is important to understand the larger political world surrounding us, the interdependencies that link our futures, and the interrelatedness of the domestic and the foreign. In this quest to comprehend the wider world, perhaps the best place to return in the comparative study of politics is nearest home, with a developing country more closely connected with the future of the United States as it enters the twenty-first century than most Americans would care to acknowledge.

Constitutional Development

The first step in understanding Mexico and how it differs from the United States is familiarity with its basic constitutional document: the Constitution of 1917. The embodiment of ideals coming out of the Revolution of 1910, the constitution is first and foremost a statement of Mexican nationalism. It clearly establishes control over the country's natural resources and promises land to the peasantry. Equally important is its defense of effective suffrage for all and no reelection of officials for executive offices; these were the slogans with which Francisco Madero initiated the revolt against the dictator Porfirio Diaz in 1910. In addition, there are provisions for advanced social legislation, demonstrating a concern for the masses that comes out of the popular social movements that swept across Mexico after the initial political revolt. This document also contains principles that have become an accepted part of U.S. constitutionalism: guarantees of political freedoms and liberties, federalism, separation of powers, and a bicameral national legislature.

In many respects, the Mexican constitution states political values and principles that have come out of Western experience in general and the United States in particular. Yet it is also different and illustrative of how constitutionalism outside Western Europe and the United States reflects fundamentally different experiences. This constitution is above all a statement of political and social ideals, not political and social accomplishments brought into existence by the revolution and guaranteed uniformly to all Mexican citizens. In this regard it reflects a different set of philosophical premises and a way of thinking about the state that is common to Iberia and Latin America. Such political traditions emphasize the importance of writing into the nation's basic charter the *desiderata* of advanced political and social thinking and leaving to future generations the responsibility for implementing these ideals through legislation. These traditions also embody two assumptions alien to U.S. experience: Government should take an active role in the nation's political, social, and economic life; and the constitutional document should spell out governmental goals as well as establish the political and administrative institutions to carry them out. As a consequence, constitutions such as the Mexican are frequently hybrid documents that seek to embody the framers' view of what is best from universal experience with national grievances and expectations developed out of the prevailing political context. In this century this has come to mean as much attention to socialist precepts (taken from Marxist experience emphasizing collective rights) as capitalist ones (coming out of Western experience designed to guarantee individual rights of life, liberty, and property).

In contrast to Anglo-American constitutionalism, Ibero-American constitutionalism emphasizes the value that when individual and collective interests come into conflict, interests of the community, as defined by the state, take precedence over individual rights and liberties. Thus, for example, when the constitutionally elected government of Lopez Portillo chose to nationalize all private Mexican banks in 1982 before turning over power to the incoming Miguel de la Madrid administration, it was acting fully within the norms and expectations of Mexican constitutionalism. Mexican nationals may well have questioned the wisdom of this action and attacked the government for the arbitrariness with which it implemented its decision, but the legality of the action could not be challenged, as it certainly would have been if such an occasion were to arise under U.S. constitutionalism. An important difference in these two variants of constitutionalism can be seen by contrasting this action with that of the U.S. Supreme Court in 1946, when it found unconstitutional President Truman's decision to intervene forcefully in a steel strike and send in federal troops. The Mexican Supreme Court has no such right to declare actions of the president illegal. At the same time, the Mexican constitution does make provision for what is known as the writ of *amparo,* whereby individuals may seek redress in the nation's courts when individual rights and liberties have been violated by arbitrary state action. (Incidentally, in the case just cited, a political solution was worked out later in another administration—that of Carlos Salinas de Gortari—under economic reforms linked to privatization of state-owned enterprise.)

One of the most salient examples of the gap between constitutional ideals and political realities in Mexican experience is to be found in the practice of federalism and the separation of powers. The Constitution of 1917 is definitely a federalist document with a strong commitment to the separation of powers. Yet the realities of Mexican political life are such that there is a high degree of centralism, to such an extent that the Mexican political system really functions as a unitary form of government under executive supremacy. State governments have little or no autonomy. Like the United States, Mexico has a bicameral legislature and a separate court system, but neither in effect serves as a constraint on presidential power. Consequently, divided government—a problem that emerges in U.S. politics when different parties are in control of the presidency and Congress—does not occur in the Mexican system. The Mexican Congress is clearly subordinated to the chief executive and merely ratifies policies and guidelines developed by the president. The "power of the purse" may well be vested in Congress, but it is the president in cooperation with the secretary of finance (and the bureaucratic officials under their authority) who determine what and how public monies will be spent.

Nevertheless, for all the economic difficulties and reforms that Mexico has undergone since 1982, one fact stands out: the stability of the system. This sets Mexico apart from the majority of developing countries and places it in a category shared by the industrial countries. There can be no doubt about the existence of a common body of rules regulating politics and succession in government. There is a fixed set of government institutions capable of processing conflict, making economic policy, and implementing social policy. Since no president may succeed himself, every six years a new governing team takes over. Accompanying these changes is considerable turnover in public office, which ensures that an incoming president will be able to manage his own programs and to carry out those policies to which he is committed.

Yet neither continuity nor peaceful change in government was always the case in Mexico. From 1810 to 1876 *caudillo* politics predominated as a rapid succession of military and political bosses entered and exited from power. By the end of the Wars for Independence (1810–21), viable central rule from Mexico City—the former viceregal capital—no longer existed, and much of the country was in disorder and decay. The legacy of extended conflict was frequent military intervention in politics; the standard means of seizing power became the military coup. With personalism reigning supreme, rival cliques vied for control of the state.

As time passed, these cleavages led factions to coalesce around two distinct concepts of the state. One group looked to the formation of a constitutional monarchy, the revival of aristocratic values, and the protection of the church as the solution to Mexico's national problems. Others rejected such "conservative" ideas and saw in "liberal" concepts of government the solution to Mexico's difficulties. They sought to break definitively with Hispanic traditions, to limit the power of the church and the military, to institute liberal democratic values, and thereby to build a new state and nation. These ideas received their clearest statement in the Constitution of 1857, which brought to culmination the movement led by Benito Juarez known as *La Reforma*. The conservative reaction was immediate, and a new round of civil war ensued. From 1863 to 1867, the conservatives gained the upper hand and attempted to rule with the Austrian prince Maximilian von Habsburg as the reigning monarch, but this aristocratic experiment was only to end in disaster with Maximilian's capture and execution. Subsequently, Benito Juarez and the liberals returned to power.

Not until 1876 did an independent Mexico begin to experience prolonged and stable rule by a single government. But what followed as an alternative to more than a half century of intense conflict were thirty-five years of dictatorship (1876–1910) that proved to be disastrous in their consequences for most Mexicans. Under the rule of Porfirio Diaz as supreme *caudillo,* centralized political authority was reestablished for the first time since independence. His government attracted foreign investment to develop Mexico's natural resources and gave attention to the development of railroads and highways. While these conditions favored economic growth and visible signs of progress became evident throughout the country, only a very small percentage of the population benefited from them. Severe political repression, low wages in a countryside dominated by large landed estates (*haciendas*), and bad working conditions in the mines and the newly developed mills and factories meant that by far the majority of the population remained outside the effective economy. As Porfirio Diaz aged, so did those who staffed his government, until by the turn of the century Mexico was ruled by a gerontocracy increasingly out of touch with national realities and unsympathetic to those suffering under oppressive social conditions.

Hence, when a younger generation of middle-class intellectuals and lawyers, led by Francisco Madero, challenged the regime in the elections of 1910, all the conditions were present for fundamental change. What began as a political revolt of a small group of disaffected citizens soon became a massive upheaval, without direction or well-defined goals. Above all else the peasantry wanted land, and in the social movements that swept across the countryside the old order disappeared rapidly. With it went the *hacienda* system. For the next two decades one revolutionary coalition followed another, with none being able to rule the country effectively. Out of this prolonged conflict, a new array of political forces eventually emerged under the leadership of Plutarco Elías Calles.

In 1929 leaders of the various groups identified with the revolution joined together to form an official party of unity. In its first version it was known as the Partido Nacional Revolucionario (PNR) and was heavily influenced by Calles from behind the scenes. Later, Lázaro Cárdenas reorganized the party during his presidency (1934–40) as the Partido de la Revolución Mexicana (PRM). From this reorganization in 1938 dates the division of the party along functional lines: peasant, labor, and middle sector. Included within this organization was a fourth sector representing the military, but when Miguel Alemán (president from 1946 to 1952) reorganized the party yet again in 1946 as the Partido Revolucionario Institucional (PRI), the military was dropped as a formal group. Ever since, the party has maintained the same internal organization and has so thoroughly dominated the political scene that there has been no effective challenge to its hegemony. Most notable in this process of building and institutionalizing a single, dominant, mass-based party have been the displacement of the military as a major political force and the sustained capacity of the party to attract and absorb newer and younger generations of political leaders as the revolutionary era has passed into history.

This record of successful resolution of political crises and maintenance of institutional stability under a single major party since 1929 stands in marked contrast to the political and economic uncertainties that characterized Mexico earlier and that have proven to be endemic to so much of the developing world. In considering Mexico's institutional development, this political evolution deserves much more attention than whether or not the norms embodied in the constitution have been fulfilled.

In this political lineup, four power groups frequently present elsewhere in Latin America are missing: the landed elite, the church, the military, and business interests. The first two have been eliminated, for all effective purposes. The landed elite disappeared as a consequence of the agrarian revolution that accompanied mass upheaval, and the church found its political role so radically changed by the course of events and the failure to constitute a new right in Mexican politics that it ceased to exercise overt influence in political life. More interesting in understanding the dynamics of postrevolutionary Mexican politics is the way in which the two remaining groups were coopted by the new regime in the making.

While military *caudillos* took an active part in the revolution, from the time an institutionalized revolutionary party took form, one cannot speak of a parallel organization of the military into a single, coherent institution. While individual military officers were a vital part of the original revolutionary coalition, as civilian forces organized themselves into more formalized sectors, the military moved to the sidelines. Only after the consolidation of the PRI can one identify the emergence of an organized military institution, and by this time the question of civilian supremacy was no longer open to discussion. As a consequence, while the military is an important group in Mexican politics, especially when questions of national security and defense policy are analyzed, the principle of civilian leadership has become as well established there as in Western constitutional democracies.

Business interests, too, have become a very important component of modern Mexico as the country has undergone sustained economic development. But, given the outcomes of the revolution, business has remained a power group apart, without formal representation within the PRI. Since 1940, however, business interests have had direct albeit informal access to the mainspring of the system: the presidency of the republic. Their influence has been a constant in all major decisions affecting the nation's economy. Nevertheless, theirs is and remains a limited and controlled influence through the effective use of rewards and sanctions by those controlling the centers of power in Mexican politics.

Over time, formal legislation has been introduced to guarantee opposition parties representation in Congress, but none of these arrangements has changed the reality that there is a single dominant party from whose ranks the country's political leadership is always selected. Still, as the system has evolved, the PRI has proven to be responsive to the need for change within the country through the selection of a new president every six years. Although all PRI presidential candidates have been victorious to date, one should not overlook the extensive process of consultation that goes on within party circles during the years preceding a presidential election. Not only has this process served to sensitize potential candidates to existing political, social, and economic conditions but also it has brought forth candidates with a capacity to respond to these realities.

This combination of formal and informal political practices has produced a constitutional system that is quasi-authoritarian as well as quasi-democratic. If, on the one hand, Mexican government has little in common with the military governments dominant in South America during the late 1960s and 1970s, it is also not a fully developed democratic regime, in the sense that the parliamentary governments in Western Europe are. The appearance of a more vocal opposition, with the capacity to win gubernatorial elections in three states, in mayoral elections in many state capitals, and legislative elections for nearly half the seats in Congress, should not deflect attention from the fact that this remains a system controlled from the center through the PRI party apparatus. Nevertheless, beneath the public outcry over electoral fraud and attempts to control the electoral process, the fact remains that this is a political system that has emerged out of Mexican realities, responded to them, and established a set of procedures through which policies of the most diverse sort have been discussed, debated, and acted on. Individuals may attack the actions of a given administration and disagree radically with governmental policies. In this regard, for all the problems of corruption that have come to light in recent years, Mexican government since 1940 bears absolutely no relationship to the extremely limited social base and restricted participation characteristic of the *porfiriato* (the era of

Porfirio Diaz) that preceded the revolution and was a direct cause of the social upheavals that ensued.

Social Forces

In the building of modern Mexico the revolution marks a fundamental dividing line. Before 1910 Mexico was a society fragmented along class, ethnic, and regional lines. Rather than a single nation, it was a series of self-contained communities. The social structure consisted of a small upper sector that identified itself closely with Hispanic values, many of whose members prided themselves on their Spanish heritage. In the larger society, where by far the majority of the population was mestizo or Indian, the *gachupín* (the hispanophile) was seen as the most visible part of a generally disliked privileged minority. Whether upper or lower sector, individuals identified themselves predominantly with their region of origin and, within the individual states into which the Mexican federation was divided, with the local community above all else. In such a context Mexico was an amalgamation of *patrias chicas,* "little countries." Few people before 1910 readily identified themselves with the larger political unit we know as Mexico.

The Revolution of 1910 changed this dramatically. Social, ethnic, and regional differences continue to exist, but a larger sense of national identity has emerged within which people take real pride in identifying their Mexicanness (their *mejicanidad*). A core concept linked to this sense of nationhood is the perception of Mexico as a mestizo culture, an amalgam in which European and Indian influences have become fused into a new and distinctive national culture. Whereas before the revolution Mexico's Indian past was generally looked down on by elite groups, postrevolutionary Mexicans take pride in cultivating an awareness of the nation's Indian past. With this self-discovery and consciousness of the creativity of its popular culture has come a flowering of the arts—in painting (especially murals), dance, music, architecture, and literature.

If one is to understand modern Mexico, it is this reality that one should endeavor to appreciate. For the great strength of the PRI in the eyes of many Mexicans is its image as the receptacle of the revolution, one that is rekindled every six years. Accordingly, one may point to the fact that there has always been a sizable percentage of the electorate that has refrained from voting on the grounds that there is no effective choice. Yet no competing political organization on the right or left has ever been able to capture this identification with the revolution and Mexican nationalism that has become the special preserve of the PRI.

In this setting, poverty continues unabated in rural and urban areas without creating the conditions for mass protest. This does not mean that protest movements have not occurred, or that there is an absence of strikes and demonstrations. On the contrary, state politics in Mexico has often been turbulent. Also, urban protest movements, strikes, and demonstrations have taken place from time to time, as when violence broke out in Mexico City in 1968 at the time of the Olympic Games. But these events have remained confined to the immediate arena where protest has emerged, without becoming national in scope. Furthermore, political authorities have always responded to these occurrences with a great deal of effectiveness, either by a show of force or by accommodation or by a combination of the two.

At the national level, in plotting the course of presidential leadership since 1929, one can identify movement back and forth from one administration to the next, between progressive policies designed to respond to mass needs and conservative ones intended to maintain order, stability, and a favorable climate for economic development. For example, one can single out the administrations of Lázaro Cárdenas (1934–40), Lopez Mateos (1958–64), and Luis Echeverría (1970–76) as progressive in nature in their appeal to nationalism, improved social conditions for the masses, and flexible wage policies. Offsetting them are the administrations of Calles (1929–33), Miguel Alemán (1946–52), and Diaz Ordaz (1964–70), which were much more conservative in character and given to assertions of state authority.

Yet there are also administrations whose actions have been decidedly mixed and oriented to the political center—for example, those of Avila Camacho (1940–46), Ruiz Cortinez (1952–58), and Lopez Portillo (1976–82). Whether or not the earlier pattern of contrasting administration has been changing since the crisis of 1982 remains open, for one can argue that Miguel de la Madrid (1982–88) and Carlos Salinas de Gortari (1988–94) have preferred this alternative pattern and used it to undertake a fundamental transformation of the system. This is especially the case with Salinas, given the extensiveness of his reforms, beginning with a significant privatization initiative and extending through an opening up of Mexico to foreign investors and to an accommodation with the church.

In whatever way one interprets presidential behavior, two facts stand out. First, Mexican presidential leadership has shown a great capacity over the years to respond to changing conditions in Mexico and to guide the country into new directions when shifts in the country's national and internal context have required adjustments. Second, when one moves beyond the national level to the states, one can identify wide variation in the response of the political leadership to regional, social, and economic conditions.

In this regard Mexico remains today, as in the past, a society divided between privileged sectors (comprising at present approximately one-third of the population) and those who, because of their poverty, do not participate actively in national life politically or economically (about half). Yet this is far from a static society, for the whole postwar era is one marked by tremendous social and economic change. The most notable shifts in the distribution of Mexico's social forces have come in the expansion of the middle sectors of society. While the figures vary greatly, most counts point to a doubling of middle-income groups since the 1940s.

As Mexico has shifted from a rural to an urban-based society, a corresponding increase has occurred in population. Whereas 70 percent of the population in 1900 lived in communities under 2500, by 1970 this percentage had dropped to around 40 percent. What had been a population of 19 million in 1940 had become an estimated 92 million in 1990, as Mexico has ceased to be an economy based on agriculture and the extraction of raw materials and has become increasingly industrialized. From the 1940s through the 1970s, this economic growth was centered on an import-substitution model for economic development. And even though economic growth slowed in the 1970s, from a rate of over 6 percent per annum to around 3 percent, the oil boom both internationally and in the expansion of national production contributed to the maintenance of a positive image at home and abroad regarding Mexico's growth potential.

The economic crisis of 1982 had its most immediate impact on the urban middle sectors, on those people in Mexican society who had been the primary beneficiaries of the economic growth of the previous forty years. In political terms this rapid deterioration of economic conditions, which led to frequent devaluations and eventually a floating peso exchange rate and acute internal inflation, cut directly into two of the three major social sectors on which the PRI was based: labor and the "popular" or middle-income strata of Mexican society. During the 1980s, however, what was notable about this crisis, in comparative perspective, was the stability of the Mexican system and the way in which government went about responding to it.

In contrast to the turbulence that has accompanied major economic and political adjustments elsewhere in the developing world and in the postcommunist states, the government's ability to inaugurate major policy change through revamping its presidential teams each six years and to implement economic and social policy stands out. The nationalization of private Mexican banks and the imposition of strict exchange controls in 1982 by the Lopez Portillo government, shortly before the transfer of power to the new Miguel de la Madrid administration, permitted the government to establish immediate and direct control over the internal and external markets in areas where it was most vulnerable to fluctuation: the flight of domestic capital and Mexican private-sector indebtedness. Such action was taken in the name of Mexican nationalism, and although attacked by the domestic and foreign business communities, it generally received wide-scale popular support in Mexico. The corresponding shift to the de la Madrid administration and the inauguration of a much more conservative set of economic policies removed the incoming government from responsibility for the previous government's actions and permitted it to negotiate a new set of international accords with the International Monetary Fund (IMF) and those private U.S. banks to whom the major part of the loans was owed. When foreign banks and businesses questioned the propriety of the bank nationalizations, the new administration explained that conditions were such, both in terms of the inability of the Mexican private sector to meet its external obligations and Mexican nationalism, as to preclude the banks' return to private ownership.

Equally important is how urban labor and the middle sectors of Mexican society—those linked most closely to the PRI's urban base—have accepted economic austerity measures. Pressures were brought on the de la Madrid administration to permit wage adjustments, but what is most notable is the extent to which this administration was able to guarantee and enforce commitment to the IMF program, one that imposed severe constraints on the domestic economy and meant an immediate reduction in domestic consumption and alteration of patterns of living based on easy credit, to which union and middle-level professionals had become accustomed. Regardless of speculation in some quarters that Mexico would experience an economic crisis so severe as to destroy the social supports of the government and the PRI, Mexican governmental institutions held firm. A campaign was immediately mounted to limit the corruption that had become so blatant during the Lopez Portillo administration's final days, and a number of officials in that government were taken to court for misappropriation of public funds. Economic austerity ensued in the name of a national emergency and defense of the nation. No event in postrevolutionary Mexico has demonstrated so clearly the degree to which the present system has become institutionalized and has developed the capacity to make and implement public policy.

Interest Groups

Interest groups in Mexico are organized in a very different way from those in the United States and Western Europe. Although they are as numerous as in any Western country, interest groups are much more likely to be organized and licensed by the state. Whereas interest-group pluralism is characteristic of parliamentary and presidential democracies, and such groups enter and exit from the political process according to the issues at stake, in Mexico interest-group behavior is much more subject to the control of the state and likely to be influenced by governmental action. Such a pattern of behavior is corporatist rather than pluralist. Although not all developing countries follow this pattern, many do, and it is important to understand what the implications of these arrangements are before discussing a particular country's pattern of interest-group behavior.

Under corporatist arrangements, the state assumes primary responsibility for licensing and regulating interest-group activity. In following this form, rather than permit groups to organize spontaneously and in competition with one another, the state, operating through the mechanism of a single, dominant official party and/or government bureaucracies, sets the terms for organization and recognizes one official umbrella association in each social sector. Such forms of organization are not readily compatible with the assumptions of liberal democracy. For this reason, identification of how interests are organized in any society and how they behave becomes an important indicator of the real nature of politics. Especially in the politics of developing areas, one must always be sensitive to the possibility of divergence between official forms and actual political realities. Governments called democracies in terms of their formal constitutions may well be authoritarian in regulating interests; others termed authoritarian are at times more permissive in allowing groups of citizens to organize, demonstrate, and protest than is the case in those called democracies. In yet other situations, one encounters official organizations sanctioned and licensed by the state concurrent with interest groups organizing themselves spontaneously in society to protest state controls.

Mexico is a case in point. If, on the one hand, there is a list of officially organized interest-group associations in which membership is often required by law, there are also groups organized and involved in politics outside the purview of the state. Also, officially sanctioned interest groups are not always closely regulated by the government and frequently take on a life of their own, which makes them more representative of diverse groups in society than existing legal arrangements would suggest. Seen from this perspective, Mexican government can be characterized as a quasi-authoritarian, quasi-democratic regime. More important, as Mexico's economic transition from a state-controlled to a free-market economy moves ahead, opposition politics has increased in intensity, and one is much more likely to find citizen groups organizing themselves outside the state to protest government actions in economic and social policy.

As noted, the official party, the PRI, is made up of three major sectors or groups of interests: the peasantry, urban labor, and the middle sector of society. Each sector has formal organizational status, within which individual groups are organized on a local and regional basis; these are banded together into confederations at the national level. Accordingly, representing the interests of the peasantry within the official party is the Confederación Nacional Campesina, the CNC. Complementing it in the urban sector is the Confederación Nacional de Trabajadores Mexicanos, the CTM. The third official organization, the Confederación Nacional de Organizaciones Populares (CNOP), embraces a wide range of middle-class groups—schoolteachers, governmental employees (municipal, state, and federal), small businessmen, small landowners, and urban neighborhood associations.

None of the three confederations represents all interests within each sector. Major segments of society, such as landless agricultural workers, nonunionized labor, and more affluent upper- and middle-income groups remain outside the confines of these political organizations. Furthermore, frequently the national confederations find it difficult to speak with a single voice because of the diversity of individual regional and local interests that constitute these national organizations on issues that affect them, such as wage policies, social security benefits, price controls, and inflation. By far the most amorphous of the three confederations is the CNOP because of the wide range of interests to be represented within the middle strata of urban Mexican society. Furthermore, since these are the sectors that have been most directly affected by inflation and spiralling price increases in consumer commodities, they have come to constitute an important part of the social forces organizing themselves outside government and in opposition to continued PRI dominance of politics. In contrast, the CTM is illustrative of how divergent interests may be within the same social sector and yet function as a single umbrella organization defending the interests of a particular sector. For example, petroleum workers employed by the state-owned oil company, PEMEX, enjoy a privileged status accorded no other labor group. Also, not all labor unions necessarily fall under the CTM label; for example, the FSTE (the Federation of Unions for State Workers) is assigned to the CNOP. Others, such as unions for electrical workers and railroad workers, maintain separate and independent status.

The institutional history of each of the three major sectoral organizations is illustrative of the cooptive mechanisms common to corporatist interest-group representation. The original alliance that led to the formation of a national labor organization took place outside the official party and predates its formation. The government in 1918 assisted in the formation of the first national labor organization, which was known as the CROM, the Confederación Regional Obrera Mexicana. Even then, it played an independent role in subsequent elections—in 1924 as well as 1928. Relations with the state were not always peaceful, as was the case in the late 1920s when Luis Morones, its leader, mounted a campaign to become president. In 1936, during the Cárdenas presidency, CROM was reorganized as the CTM, and Vicente Lombardo Toledano became its president. In 1938 Cárdenas incorporated the organization into the official party, as a means of solidifying closer relations between the government and organized labor.

Consideration of organized labor in Mexico over time, even in the encapsulated form just stated, serves to illustrate that one cannot assume that the close relationship between the state and these semiofficial sectoral organizations necessarily means manipulation and automatic acceptance of the dictates of an incumbent administration. From time to time, strikes have been called by individual unions independently of the government's preferences. For example, the 1983 economic austerity policies of the de la Madrid administration did not automatically generate quiescent labor support for the government.

Another example would be the rural sector. The CNC has been essentially an organization representing that portion of the peasantry that benefited most from land distribution, either through receiving small parcels of land or rights to work the land under communal arrangements. While an estimated 2 million families have received land over the years, many rural inhabitants remain outside the system and have periodically protested the failure of the government to meet its promises of land for them. In the mid-1960s this led some of the peasants to form an independent peasant confederation, the CCI. While the CCI eventually joined the CNC, independent organization of interest groups outside the confines of state regulation is not unknown and has occurred when the national government failed to respond to mass demands in one social sector or another. For the CNC, the close relationship between the CNC and the government through the PRI has been especially tense since the Salinas administration took office. As Salinas has extended privatization and economic reform to embrace the countryside, the peasantry has found itself increasingly at odds with the government and pressed the CNC to take a stance more independent of the government policies designed to enhance private, commercial agriculture, and in defense of the rural poor's right to own the land they work, under either individual or collective arrangements supported by the state.

Other important groups of state-regulated interest associations are those organized for the business community, although they lie outside the confines of the official party. Three in particular warrant mentioning: the Confederación de Cámaras de Comercio de México (CONACO), the Confederación de Cámaras de Industrias (CONCAMIN), and the Cámara Nacional de Industrias de Transformación (CANACINTRA). While CONACO and CONCAMIN date back to the early years of the revolution—to 1917 and 1918, respectively—and have long received state support, they have been autonomous in action and critical of government policies from time to time. This is especially true of the association of industrial producers, CONCAMIN, and that for manufacturing interests, CANACINTRA. Regulation of business interests and the presence of these state-sponsored organizations should not lead one to conclude automatically that they are subservient to the state. On the contrary, the Mexican private sector, while smaller than that of many countries, constitutes a very independent and different set of interests from other groups in Mexican society, enjoying more direct and official representation. Just as there are also instances of independent rural and urban labor organizations, the same is true of business interests. Illustrative of the latter would be COPARMEX (an employers organization), the Mexican Bankers Association, the Mexican Association of Insurance Institutions, and the Mexican Council of Businessmen.

Thus the lines between government and interest-group association are often blurred and cannot always be separated. There is clearly a dynamic present in which Mexican interest groups neither dominate government and influence policy directly nor are they entirely state controlled and regulated. There is also a certain degree of pluralism in which more than one interest group has come to the fore representing social forces from the same sector. More important is a realization that not all groups in Mexican society are organized. This is especially true of the lower sector, where the majority of Mexicans are located. Outside the effective economy and marginal to the developments of modern Mexico, these people have a precarious existence. For most Mexicans, neither protest nor representation of their interests is commonplace.

Finally, while no mention has been made of the church, the military, and private commercial agricultural interests (the latter of which is much more substantial than is apparent on first examination), all three groups make their interests known informally, effectively, and independently. Nei-

ther the church nor the military is officially recognized as a power con-
tender, but no one who is knowledgeable about the Mexican scene will deny
that both constitute powerful, autonomous institutional interests. Although
less formalized, commercial agricultural interests (which cultivate fresh produce for the U.S. market and thereby bring in important foreign currency
earnings) must be recognized as an equally influential group. Their significance becomes particularly clear when the Mexican government makes
strong representation to the U.S. government about U.S. agriculture interests
that lobby for restrictive legislation limiting Mexican produce, which com-
petes with U.S. production.

In a similar fashion, while many "Mexicanists" for years underestimated the importance of the military, today the revival of rural violence in
isolated areas, especially in the south, and preoccupation with the spillover
into Mexican territory of the guerrilla movement in Guatemala, has made
much more apparent the presence of the military as a power group and the
importance of military interests, especially when joined with internal security concerns. In a similar fashion there are numerous church-related groups,
some linked closely with the institutional church and others more directly
affiliated with independently minded lay groups. As interest-group activity
by church-related associations has increased, albeit informally and discreetly, it has coincided with a waning of the strong anticlerical stance of the
state originally identified so closely with the revolution.

Political Parties

As should be apparent by now, Mexico is dominated by a single official
party, the PRI. Other parties exist, but none has the capacity to challenge
PRI dominance of the Mexican political system. Only one opposition party,
the Partido de Acción Nacional (PAN), has been able to defeat the PRI at
the state level and has been permitted to take office. The PAN is the party of
the right and has received strong support from the Mexican private sector
and church-related groups. Generally speaking, PAN campaigns on a platform arguing for a stronger role of the private sector in the Mexican economy and against the political corruption that has become endemic to the
PRI. It is in the north, the southeast (Yucatán), and the center (to the west
of Mexico City in the agricultural region known as the Bajío) that PAN has
developed its strongest support. PAN is quite visible as an alternative party
along the northern frontier, especially in the states of Nuevo León (with its
industrial capital of Monterrey), Chihuahua, and Baja California, where an
independent-minded business community has emerged. In contrast, in the

Yucatán peninsula PAN draws it supports from conservative social forces in a region where the impact of the revolution was minimal. In the Bajío the strength of the PAN resides in its appeal to conservative Catholic forces, those elements that supported so strongly the *cristero* revolt in the mid-1920s and vehemently opposed the revolution's anticlericalism.

The other opposition parties all fall to the left of the PRI (except for the very small right-wing PDM). They draw their support primarily from left-wing intellectuals and other social forces identifying themselves with the more radical side of the revolution. Some make use of Marxist rhetoric, and all argue that they, rather than the PRI, give more adequate representation to Mexican revolutionary ideals as the PRI has moved to the center and away from its revolutionary commitments to the masses.

Since the 1988 elections, the major left political organization has been the Partido de la Revolución Democrática (PRD). An amalgamation of disparate elements, it has attempted to pull together groups on the left into a united front. These older organizations would be the Partido Popular Socialista (PPS); the Partido Comunista Mexicano (PCM); the Partido Socialista Trabajador (PST); the Partido Mexicano de los Trabajadores (PMT); and the Partido Auténtico de la Revolución Mejicana (PARM). In the 1982 election the PCM called on all left parties to form a united front, the PSUM—the Mexican United Socialist party. Several smaller parties and factions were willing to do so, but the PPS, the PST, and the PMT opted to retain their independent organizations. In the 1988 elections, Cuauhtémoc Cárdenas was more successful in bringing together the opposition in the center and to the left of the PRI under the banner of the Frente Democrática Liberal (FDN). It is out of the FDN that the PRD has emerged. While Cárdenas was able to gain an impressive showing with 31.06 percent of the vote and the other opposition candidate, Manuel Clouthier, of the PAN received 16.81 percent, their votes combined still did not produce a plurality, and the PRI reported a victory with 50.36 percent of the vote.

To date, while the size of the opposition vote has increased and opposition parties continue to report important gains (despite PRI-initiated attempts linked to fraud and manipulation of results), none of these parties has had the capacity to displace the PRI from the centers of power. While the PPS and PSUM were able to pick up support in peripheral areas disaffected with the PRI, such as the Tehuantepec isthmus in Oaxaca, and conservative opposition forces continue to grow in the north, none of these had success in building a coalition of sufficient size and force to challenge PRI hegemony. The PPS, which was founded by the labor leader Vicente Lombardo Toledano in 1948, attempted to change this, but as the party moved into the 1980s and 1990s, it was unable to retain what little support it had. The PST and the PARM looked to disaffected PRI elements—the former identified with the 1968 political movement that led to the demonstrations in Mexico City, and the latter, with retired army generals in the 1950s. Likewise, while Cuauhtémoc Cárdenas was able to build up sizable support by appealing to the PRI's traditional mass base in 1987 and 1988, he has shown little capacity for building an independent political movement that can sustain itself as a mass-based political organization. Yet, despite the failure of the opposition to displace the PRI from power, what is significant is the way in which opposition to the PRI has increased since 1988.

Generally speaking, however, parties on the center and left have been unable to provide a viable option. Only the PAN has been able to develop and maintain a viable political organization across the years. Yet the PAN remains clearly a minority party with little hope of ever winning a national election. Nevertheless, it has repeatedly served the useful function of calling attention to excesses in state PRI organizations where political cronyism and corruption have become particularly acute.

When the PRI is contrasted with these alternative parties, it becomes very clear that it alone has the political organization, extending down to grassroots level, to be able to mobilize the electorate consistently for national, state, and local elections. It is a gigantic political machine designed to select political leaders at various levels and has become an enormously effective organization providing both rotation in public office and continuity in political leadership. It is above all the primary institution through which new generations of political leaders are recruited, trained for political careers, and advanced to important positions. Its primary function is to deliver the vote, and as is true of all political machines (and not unlike those that have functioned in U.S. metropolitan areas), political largess becomes a way of rewarding both those who turn out the vote and those who are willing to serve in public office in jobs where the financial remuneration is minimal. This cycle is repeated every six years for national leadership, the most important of which is clearly presidential, and in alternate years at state and local levels, where the key positions are governorships and municipal presidencies within the nation's major cities. Given this political apparatus, one should not conclude that the victory of opposition political forces recently in the northern states and along the periphery has challenged in the least PRI hegemony and control of national politics.

Seen from this perspective, the PRI and the government are an interlocking network of political cliques known as *camarillas* and political clienteles dependent on those holding office in state and party organs. Those pursuing political careers are essentially middle-sector individuals, who today come increasingly from urban areas and have university educations. In the early years, when the official party was in formation and government was still conflictual, there was a much higher incidence of political figures drawn from rural areas, identified with the peasantry, and military men, heading armed bands. As violence receded and the party became institutionalized, civilians replaced military men and those with more advanced and specialized education superseded those with less education.

In the 1950s and 1960s these changes resulted in the preeminence of an institutionalized and bureaucratized party and its interfacing with organs of state power. Mexicanists in these years drew a distinction between *técnicos* and *políticos*. *Políticos* were essentially professional politicians who had risen through the ranks of the party on the basis of service and through identification either with the peasant and labor sectors or with those mass organizations crucial to producing PRI majorities at election time. No less political were the designated *técnicos,* who as lawyers, engineers, economists, and agronomists had acquired specialized university educations that gave them skills essential to managing public positions tied to the country's economic development. While there were instances of those who followed predominantly political or technical careers as the Mexican economy became more complex and the importance of political and managerial roles increased, these divisions have become blurred. As a consequence, in examining political elites today, university education—especially at the national university in Mexico City, UNAM—and career patterns involving both party service and successful public officeholding in specialized government programs are the norm.

In describing the PRI it is important to emphasize the flexibility that the party has maintained over the years and its capacity for self-renewal. Viewed in these terms, what sets aside the post-1940 political elite from the pre-1910 elite is not class origin. For comparative studies have shown that both groups were essentially urban middle class and were equally committed to economic modernization of the country. Once corrections are entered for the fact that a much larger percentage of the population resides today in urban areas than was the case around the turn of the century, the primary difference lies in the openness of access to elite positions, after 1940, for those who were upwardly mobile and possessed leadership potential. An important component of elite circularity in present-day Mexico and continued renewal of leadership elements has been the commitment to rotation in office at the presidential level every six years. Turnover at the top for the most powerful individual in the system, the president of the republic, and the constitutional prohibition against reelection, has kept a single cohesive power structure from developing. An additional check within the system against having a closed power structure staffed essentially by the same individuals over an extended time period, as occurred during the *porfiriato,* is institutional separation between the country's political and economic elites.

Given these dynamics, some observers of the Mexican scene have gone so far as to emphasize that the price of political patronage and system stability in a regime dominated by machine politics is political corruption. Those subscribing to this theory emphasize how political kickbacks, the use of public monies for private gains, and bribery (*mordidas*) are necessary evils. This line of reasoning argues that the extent of the corruption is the dividing line between what is permissible and what is unacceptable, not its presence or absence, and is the appropriate criterion by which to judge the functioning of the system. Seen from this vantage point, it was the extensiveness of the corruption and its public character during the Lopez Portillo administration plus the amount of money taken from the government by prominent individuals in the regime that discredited this administration. However one looks at these practices, what is certain is that payment for goods and services in the Mexican system frequently entails the exchange of money outside official channels. Furthermore, individuals in public office frequently amass resources on the side for their personal benefit later, after their terms of office come to an end, for major public office may well never again be available to them under the rotation system currently in use.

In assessing the performance of the PRI and the dynamics of Mexico's dominant one-party system, one should realize that the prospects of the system evolving into a competitive two-party or multiparty system are not good. The integration between the government and the official party is close enough to preclude the possibility of an alternative party taking power. By the same token, a coup within the regime by a group of military officers is equally unfeasible, given the long-standing practice of civilian control of the military through the PRI apparatus and the presidency of the republic. The most important political outcome in postrevolutionary Mexico has been an all-embracing single official party with the capacity to provide political leadership over time while renewing itself periodically and responding to political, social, and economic pressures for change in the larger society. If all this is kept in perspective, it should not be the least surprising that PRI leaders have been able to undertake major economic reforms since 1988 and to tolerate an increasingly active opposition without seeing its hegemony over national politics threatened in the least.

Governmental Institutions

Like the United States, Mexico has a presidential form of government; such is also true for the rest of Latin America, except for Cuba (which continues to follow a system of government similar to those dominant in East Europe before 1989). Unlike the United States, however, one institution reigns supreme: the presidency of the republic. Very clearly, the Mexican Congress is a secondary institution and subordinated to the wishes of the president. The consequence of this institutional development has been a political system that functions quite differently from the U.S. model from which it was originally derived.

Executive-centered power combined with a high degree of centralism has produced a system of government best characterized in policy terms as a bureaucratic polity. In such a context the real issues is politics, and the more important questions of public policy are not resolved in open public debate and through discussion of these matters in legislative session. Instead, the policy arenas are bureaucratic, either the executive offices of the president or the *salas* of government ministries. Only after the interested parties reach an accord within these private corridors does public discussion occur, either through the announcement of an executive decree or the introduction of the appropriate legislation in Congress. Consequently, while legislation is discussed in Congress and the budget must be passed by the legislature, such discussion is largely symbolic and has the function of rendering public support for government decisions already arrived at.

The contrast between these informal and formal mechanisms for handling public policy in Mexico is best captured by examining the budgetary process. Preparation of the budget is initiated within the bureaucratic arena with each public organization drawing up an estimate of its individual needs for the next fiscal year. These estimates are pulled together into budget documents by sector, according to the major administrative units. In Mexico these are *secretarías* and *departamentos,* which are the equivalent of ministries in other governmental systems. In addition to these organs of the central administration, numerous commissions, public enterprises, agencies, and other public entities enjoy considerable autonomy; these parastatal organizations number in the thousands.

Because of the size and complexity of the governmental bureaucracy, beginning during the Lopez Portillo administration a separate staff unit called Programming and Budget (*Programación y Presupuesto*) was set up, independent of the Finance Department, to rationalize the whole process, only to be abolished in the Salinas de Gortari administration because of the conflict engendered with Finance and the creation of new problems in the coordination of fiscal and monetary policy. For two administrations (Lopez Portillo's and de la Madrid's), the preliminary budget document was pulled together in this office; today this is done in Finance. It is then discussed within the presidency of the republic by those closest to the president. While this internal process of consultation varies from administration to administration, during the Lopez Portillo years there were two staff units attached to the Office of the President: *Estudios Económicos* and *Coordenación de Estudios Administrativos*. The former was involved directly with questions of economic policy, and the latter was charged with responsibility for improving control and coordination within the nation's administrative system.

Once approved by the president, the budget document goes to Congress for formal discussion and action. But the process does not stop there. Because the official document consistently underestimates governmental expenditures, supplementary funds and reserves are set aside by the executive and allocated on the basis of individual program requests and needs as the budget year proceeds. Such procedures have several benefits. They permit the Office of the President and Finance to maintain greater control over actual expenditures, and they permit greater flexibility in funding programs according to actual needs. One of the problems that consistently emerges in poor countries is the difficulty of forecasting governmental expenditures accurately. Two problems arise: the lack of sufficient information on which to base forecasts, and economic uncertainty because of difficulties in predicting public revenues and/or estimating expenditures in an inflationary context. Generally speaking, the whole postwar period in Latin America has been characterized by inflationary pressures. While Mexico was less susceptible to acute inflation during its era of sustained economic growth, during the 1980s it too suffered from acute inflation, peaking at 157 percent in 1987 before it was brought under control in the Salinas administration (where it ran around 12 percent per year). In such a context, where major economic adjustments have had to be made, budgetary flexibility along these lines becomes absolutely essential.

These budgetary procedures and the problems they are designed to confront point to a governmental bureaucracy that functions in a way very different from that of the United States. In this regard Mexico can be used to illustrate a pattern of government common to much of the developing world. While there are the usual governmental services provided by the administrative agencies of any government, what is particularly characteristic of Mexican bureaucracy and that of many developing countries is the central role government plays in creating the conditions for economic growth and developing social policies that will respond to and anticipate mass needs. Because the private sector has historically been weak in these countries, commitment to economic development has usually required active intervention by the state. Salinas's commitment to privatization and the extent to which the Mexican government has engaged in reducing the size of the public sector should not, however, lead one to conclude that Mexico has embarked on a radically new set of policies. While these economic reforms are significant and important in preparing Mexico for the North American Free Trade Agreement (NAFTA), the centrality of the Mexican state in determining economic and social policy has not been altered in the least.

This active role in developing basic industries and expanding manufacturing has led to the emergence of a host of governmental agencies, state-owned banks and financial institutions, and public enterprises. In explaining this pattern of development, especially in Mexico, it is important to add that state action in these areas has not taken place to the exclusion of domestic private capital or foreign private investment; instead, it is handled on a cooperative basis. Especially under the Salinas administration, government economic policy has actively promoted the strengthening of the domestic private sector and creating appropriate conditions for attracting foreign private capital. In Mexico a major outcome of the revolution was economic nationalism and the determination to see that in the future the nation's economy would never again become dominated by foreign interests to the extent that had become characteristic of the *porfiriato*. Since 1940, the Mexican government has continued to maintain a policy designed to attract foreign investment, but in a context whereby the Mexican state regulates, controls, and directs where such investment will take place. And, it should be added, this sustained policy of providing guarantees and opportunities for the foreign investor has attracted a great deal of U.S. capital over the years. Especially active and successful in creating opportunities and developing a business climate attractive to the investor, domestic or foreign, as well as beneficial to the government's objective of producing real economic growth, has been the institution known as Nacional Financiera.

As a consequence, Mexico today has a very large and diverse public sector in which economic agencies and organizations constitute a major component. For purposes of illustration, a listing of the government's major financial institutions, in addition to Nacional Financiera, will suffice: the Bank of Mexico, the National Agricultural Credit Bank, the National Urban Mortgage and Public Works Bank, the National Ejidal Credit Bank, National Warehouses, the National Foreign Trade Bank, the National Workers and Industrial Development Bank, and the National Bank for Cooperative Development. In addition to those financial organizations, one should add a host of public enterprises involved directly in productive activities. While the Salinas administration has privatized many of these enterprises, organizations such as PEMEX (which has a monopoly on the exploration and production of oil), the Federal Electrical Commission (which has developed the nation's electric power industry and supply network), and CONASUPO (which is responsible for subsidizing basic food commodities and maintaining a national system of stores where these goods are sold at below-market prices) remain under state control.

As in the United States, public bureaucracy in Mexico is not limited to agencies of the federal government. Complementing the federal bureaucracy are numerous state and local government organizations. While it was pointed out earlier that Mexico is in reality a unitary republic and not a federal system when it comes to questions of political power, federalism does function in the administrative sphere. Like the United States, Mexico has a two-tiered administrative system (federal and state) and within each state government, a separate system of municipal organizations. Even though the states historically have been starved for funds and many have become dependencies of the federal government, where there is a vital regional autonomy, one finds substantial amounts of program autonomy and administrative action through autonomous state and local organizations.

Accordingly, in every state one finds a parallel set of state bureaucratic organizations replicating federal entities, as is the practice in the United States. Four in particular stand out as significant in the functioning of Mexican government: state departments of education, since they have responsibility for primary education; state roads and public works departments, which must maintain all public roads outside the federal highway system as well as all public buildings not included within the patrimony of the national government; state finance departments, charged with responsibility for collecting those taxes that belong exclusively to state government; and state departments for public security (state *Direcciones de Gobernación* which parallel the federal agency responsible for public security at the national level and which have oversight authority over local governments and jurisdiction over questions of local conflict).

As Mexican government has increased in complexity and bottlenecks have developed because of excessive centralization of decision making and financial resources in Mexico City, there has been increased reliance on state governments to attend to state needs. But even before this became the practice in the larger and more important states, state government has long constituted a distinct policy arena in Mexico, one that has frequently been over-looked as of significance because of the emphasis on the concentration of power at the center. During the 1920s and the 1930s regional *caciques* (po-litical bosses) dominated state governorships, and this pattern continued in many states until the 1970s and 1980s. As the national government grew in size and complexity and the economy developed, important changes took place also in state government. Paralleling developments in the Mexican presidency, the offices of state governors likewise have grown in size and im-portance. Today regional alliances center on the individuals occupying these offices and provide crucial linkages between center and periphery in a vari-ety of roles: as political brokers for the states they represent, as government officials responsible for the maintenance of law and order, as representatives of the national government within the periphery, and as leaders of state PRI organizations. While these roles have changed somewhat in the states more recently captured by the opposition, governors constitute important public officials and serve as focal points in subnational politics and as spokesmen for regional interests at variance with those of the federal government.

Until the Lopez Portillo administration (1976–82), the primacy of poli-tics in state government meant that coordinated administrative action on a territorial basis was the exception rather than the rule. By the late 1970s, however, politics as usual was no longer sufficient to meet the country's de-velopmental needs. In response to the need for greater coordination and control of economic and social policy at the subnational level, *técnicos* in the Office of the President (*Secretaría de la Presidencia*) undertook adminis-trative reforms designed to increase the administrative responsibilities of state governors; they shifted to the state governors' jurisdiction responsibil-ity for coordinating on a territorial basis the actions of various administra-tive agencies. To give meaning to these endeavors, grants-in-aid were intro-duced through which funds could be transferred to state governments from the federal government, and the governors could be given primary responsi-bility for coordinating such activities. Accordingly, two new programs were introduced: *Convenios Unicos de Coordinación* (CUC, Program-Specific Coordination Agreements) and *Programas de Inversiones Públicas para el Desarrollo Rural* (PIDER, Public Investment Programs for Rural Develop-ment). Whereas the latter programs were designed to pull together public agencies with overlapping activities affecting rural communities and to stim-ulate integrated rural development schemes, the former were more con-cerned with public works and programs involving physical construction. Complementing these activities was the creation of state committees under the chairmanship of the governors known as *Comités Promotores del Desa-*

rrollo Socio-Económico (COPRODE, State Action Committees for Socio-Economic Development).

These specific programs have since come to an end, but these developments and practices once again illustrate why it is important to see government and politics in operation in developing countries in terms of continual changes and adjustments in formal and informal patterns of power. When Mexican governmental institutions are viewed from this perspective, it becomes clear that federalism is not entirely without meaning, although in no way does it approximate the U.S. case. Just as the regime was characterized earlier as both quasi-authoritarian and quasi-democratic, one must conclude that institutionally it is both quasi-unitary and quasi-federal. Mexico today has two distinct tiers, or levels of government, with separately elected and separately appointed public officials. The sheer size of Mexican government both in area and in the number of bureaucratic organizations precludes its day-to-day operation in unitary terms. If on first inspection one is likely to conclude that the Mexican system operates administratively like that of France (a unitary state), then it must quickly be added that what makes Mexican practice different from unitary systems is the separate selection, appointment, and distinct spheres of action belonging to federal and state officials.

At the same time, there is far more reliance and greater dependency on the federal government in Mexico than there has ever been in the United States. Nevertheless, where there is a coincidence between political demarcations and regional centers of economic and political power, one can point to the existence of a set of governmental relationships that, for the absence of a more adequate term, can only be termed "federal." Such is the case with the economic and political cores of the state of Nuevo León and the city of Monterrey, as well as with Jalisco and its city of Guadalajara. Perhaps even more appropriate examples would be economically poorer states where regional ties and identifications are very strong: the states of Guanajuato and Michoacán, where, in addition to their state capitals, there are networks of medium-size cities that are viable economic entities in their own right. Equally important would be states on the periphery, such as Oaxaca and Yucatán.

In comparison to these executive-centered political and administrative institutions, Mexico's legislatures and courts are of much less significance. Formally speaking, there are separate sets of such institutions at the state and federal levels. But, given their peripheral character, they are of even less importance at the state level. It should be pointed out, however, that whereas the Mexico Congress is bicameral, the state legislatures are unicameral. Also, given the preeminence of executive-centered institutions, a series of administrative courts and state-controlled arbitration commissions has jurisdiction over cases that involve governmental action.

Because of the marginal role of legislative institutions in the Mexican political process, it has been possible for governments to take steps to increase the representation of opposition parties without threatening the system. Thus the 1977 reform law could be used to demonstrate liberalization of the regime, with its provisions for permitting the legal registration of Communist party members and guaranteeing seats for the opposition in the Chamber of Deputies. Under this law the number of deputies was increased to 400, with 100 places reserved for opposition parties. This same law also made it easier for opposition parties to gain legal status. Under these regulations, all a party now has to do to retain legal status is poll 1.5 percent of the vote in national elections or register under its name a minimum of 65,000 members.

Even more marginal to the political process, but equally in evidence in federal and state constitutions, are local governments. In principle strong legal status is given to local government, to provisions for free and autonomous municipalities. But local governments have few functions other than to administer the day-to-day affairs of the community. Replicating patterns at state and national levels, mayors (*presidentes municipales*) are the most important local officials. Their major role is to serve as political brokers for their communities in extracting external resources from extracommunity political and administrative organs. Prevailing practice provides for a *síndico*, who is designated to look after local financial affairs and substitutes for the mayor in his absence; a *secretario*, who looks after legal affairs and attends to routine administrative activities; and several *vereadores* (councilmen), who generally divide among themselves responsibility for overseeing the municipality's various administrative offices.

The System in Action

According to most accounts, contemporary Mexico has one of the most inequitable income distributions in the world. Simultaneously, it has a national ideology identified with the revolution that gives wide support to concern for the social conditions of the rural and urban masses. To date, the PRI's virtual monopoly of the rhetoric and symbolism of the revolution and its identification with Mexican nationalism have given it that essential margin of public support that has enabled its most recent governments to agree to and implement severe economic reform measures designed to limit further public spending, stimulate new economic growth, attract new foreign investment, and hold wages and salaries down in spite of severe inflationary pressures. Also, despite reported instances of political corruption and individuals amassing personal fortunes during their tenure in public office, the official party has demonstrated considerable capacity for renewal and response to popular pressures for change.

All in all, while one can speculate about alternative scenarios leading to regime breakdown and the mounting of alternative governments, to date there has been no real alternative to continued rule by the PRI and to the fact that the official party has continued to absorb and accommodate the nation's political elites from one generation to the next. The nation's economic and social problems are immense, yet within the present setting one can always discover a certain degree of realism that there are no short-term and easy solutions available and that there is no real and viable alternative to the economic austerity measures currently being implemented. Furthermore, most prognoses credit the incumbent administration with the capacity to maintain general support for its economic policies of austerity, economic restructuring, and returning the country to a positive economic growth rate. In short, so well institutionalized has the present regime become that, for all Mexico's current difficulties, continuity within the midst of moderate reforms and a reorientation of economic and social policy seem the most likely courses of action for the future.

SUGGESTIONS FOR ADDITIONAL READING

BAILEY, JOHN J. *Governing Mexico: The Statecraft of Crisis Management.* New York: St. Martin's Press, 1988.

CAMP, RODERIC AI. *Generals in the Palacio: The Military in Modern Mexico.* New York: Oxford University Press, 1992.

_____. *Politics in Mexico.* New York: Oxford University Press, 1993.

FAGEN, RICHARD, and WILLIAM S. TOUHY. *Politics and Privilege in a Mexican Community.* Stanford: Stanford University Press, 1972.

GRINDLE, MERILEE S. *Bureaucrats, Politicians, and Peasants in Mexico: A Case Study in Public Policy.* Berkeley: University of California Press, 1977.

HAMILTON, NORA. *The Limits of State Autonomy: Post-Revolutionary Mexico.* Princeton: Princeton University Press, 1982.

HANSEN, ROGER. *The Politics of Mexican Development*. Baltimore: Johns Hopkins University Press, 1977.

LEVY, DANIEL, and GABRIEL SZEKELY. *Mexico: Paradoxes of Stability and Change*. Boulder, Colo.: Westview Press, 1983.

NEWELL-GARCIA, ROBERTO, and LUIS RUBIO. *Mexico's Dilemma: The Political Origins of Economic Crisis*. Boulder, Colo.: Westview Press, 1984.

PHILIP, GEORGE. *The Presidency in Mexican Politics*. New York: St. Martin's Press, 1992.

PURCELL, SUSAN KAUFMAN. *The Mexican Profit-Sharing Decision: Politics in an Authoritarian Regime*. Berkeley: University of California Press, 1975.

REYNA, JOSE LUIS, and RICHARD S. WEINERT, eds. *Authoritarianism in Mexico*. Philadelphia: Institute for the Study of Human Issues, 1977.

SMITH, PETER H. *Labyrinths of Power: Political Recruitment in Twentieth-Century Mexico*. Princeton: Princeton University Press, 1979.

WEINTRAUB, SIDNEY. *A Marriage of Convenience: Relations between Mexico and the United States*. New York: Oxford University Press, 1990.

WILKIE, JAMES W. *The Mexican Revolution: Federal Expenditure and Social Change since 1910*. 2d ed. Berkeley: University of California Press, 1970.

Index

Nationalism: East Europe, 222–24; Mexico, 275, 281, 284, 296; Poland, 201
National Republican party (U.S.), 27
National Socialist German Workers (Nazi) party, 86
NATO Alliance, 244
Nature, Japanese view of, 174–75
Neustadt, Richard, 1, 40
New Jersey Plan, 6–7
New Liberal Club of Japan (NLC), 166
Nicholas II (tsar, Russia), 187
Nixon, Richard M., 42, 44, 46
Nomenklatura, 192
North American Free Trade Agreement (NAFTA), 271, 296

Operation Desert Storm, 43, 177
Ordaz, Diaz, 282

Packwood, Robert, 56
Panetta, Leon, 46
Parliaments: Britain, 48–49, 52, 98, 130; EU, 141, 142–43; European systems of, 80–121; France, 49; Germany, 52; Japan, 158, 159, 162, 167, 168–70
Partido Auténtico de la Revolución Mejicana (PARM), 290
Partido Comunista Mexicano (PCM), 290
Partido de Acción Nacional (PAN), 289–90, 291
Partido de la Revolución Democrática (PRD), 290
Partido de la Revolución Mexicana (PRM), 278
Partido Mexicano de los Trabajadores (PMT), 290
Partido Nacional Revolucionario (PNR), 278
Partido Popular Socialista (PPS), 290
Partido Revolucionario Institucional (PRI), 274, 279–80, 281, 286, 289, 290, 291, 292, 293, 301
Partido Socialista Trabajador (PST), 290
PDM (Mexico), 290
PEMEX, 286, 297
Perestroika (Gorbachev), 196
Perestroika, 207, 211–12
Perot, Ross, 29, 34–35, 36
PIDER (Mexico), 298
PKO Cooperation Act, 178
Plessy v. *Ferguson,* 27
Poland, communism in, 200–202
Polish Peasant party, 201
Polish United Workers' party, 201, 212
Political action committees (PACs), 22, 35, 43–44

Political culture: and American dream, 14–16; Germany, 132
Political institutions, Third World, 237–67
Political parties: Britain, 108–9; East Europe, 226; European, 104–21; France, 109–16; Germany, 116–20; Japan, 157–66; Mexico, 289–93, 300; Third World, 266–67; U.S., 24–26
Political systems: Britain, 122, 123; communist, 189–97; East Europe, 182–213; Europe's, 140–44; France, 122, 124; Germany, 122, 123; Japan, 173, 180; Mexico, 271–301; new machinery for, 185, 214, 225–32; Third World, 241–70; U.S., 1–80, 122
Population: Mexico, 283; Third World, 268
Poverty, 15, 247–49, 282
Powell, Colin, 46
Powers: fusion of, 122; separation of, 122. *See also* Separation of powers system
Presidency: dynamics of, 1–38; France, 2, 124–25, 127–28; Germany, 123; as head of state, 123; Mexico, 282–83, 294; sources of power of, 40–42; Soviet, 208–9; U.S., 39–48, 259
Primary elections, 33, 108
Prime minister: Britain, 2, 108, 125, 126–27; Japan, 167–68
Proportional representation (PR), 115, 120–21
PSUM (Mexico), 290
Public interest groups, 19–20
Public policy, implementation of: Britain, 133–35; France, 136–37; Germany, 137

Race, 10–11; as social force, 93–96
Radicals (France), 113
Rally for the Republic (RPR, France), 114–15
Reagan, Ronald, 35, 36, 42, 43, 44, 46
Regents of the University of California v. *Bakke,* 71
Regionalism, European, 96–97
Reich, Robert, 46
Religion: Britain, 92–93; France, 93; Germany, 92–93
Rengo (Japan), 156, 164
Republican party (Germany), 120
Republican party (PR, France), 113
Republican party (U.S.), 28, 29–31
Reynolds v. *Sims,* 70
Roosevelt, Franklin D., 27, 41, 44
Roosevelt, Theodore, 29, 41